W.C.

Published by the Getty Research Institute for the History of Art and the Humanities

~~sorship~~ ~~and~~ ~~lencing~~

Censorship and Silencing:
Practices of Cultural Regulation

Edited by Robert C. Post

Issues & Debates

The Getty Research Institute Publications and Exhibitions Program

Issues & Debates
Julia Bloomfield, Thomas F. Reese, Michael S. Roth, and Salvatore Settis, *Editors*

Censorship and Silencing: Practices of Cultural Regulation
Edited by Robert C. Post
Rebecca Frazier, *Manuscript Editor*

This volume, the fourth in the series Issues & Debates, evolved from a symposium titled "Censorship and Silencing: Practices of Cultural Regulation," which was held at the Getty Research Institute for the History of Art and the Humanities, 15–16 December 1995, in collaboration with the American Academy of Arts and Sciences and the Humanities Research Institute of the University of California.

Published by The Getty Research Institute
for the History of Art and the Humanities
Los Angeles, CA 90049-1688

Printed in the United States of America

03 02 01 00 99 7 6 5 4 3 2

Frontispiece: Toppled statue of Stalin, Hungary, 1956. Courtesy Regnery Publishing, Inc.

Library of Congress Cataloging-in-Publication Data
Censorship and silencing: practices of cultural regulation / edited by Robert C. Post.
p. cm. — (Issues & debates)
Symposium titled . . . held at the Getty Research Institute for the History of Art and the Humanities, 15–16 December 1995.
Includes bibliographical references and index.
ISBN 0-89236-484-X (paper)
1. Censorship — United States. 2. Freedom of speech — United States. 3. State rights.
I. Post, Robert, 1947– . II. Getty Research Institute for the History of Art and the Humanities. III. Series.
KF4775.C46 1998
342.73′0853 — dc21 97-25546
CIP

Contents

Preface

This volume is the outcome of a remarkable collaboration between the American Academy of Arts and Sciences (AAAS), the Getty Research Institute for the History of Art and the Humanities, and the Humanities Research Institute of the University of California (UCHRI).

Beginning in 1993, the Executive Council of the Western Center of the AAAS, the Getty Research Institute, and UCHRI envisioned the possibility of an ambitious California-wide program to explore the subject of "Censorship and Silencing: Practices of Cultural Regulation." Nationally controversial and intellectually challenging, the question of censorship touched the work of artists, scholars, and political activists. By pooling their resources, AAAS, the Getty Research Institute and UCHRI sought to create a novel and influential institutional structure to address this important topic.

The program had two phases. Phase I consisted of a series of loosely coordinated but largely decentralized conferences, in which local institutions were invited to explore a wide variety of issues pertaining to the topic. Some half-dozen conferences were held between November 1994 and May 1995; they are listed in Appendix A. Phase II consisted of a two-day seminar at the Getty Research Institute, composed of selected contributors to the local conferences as well as additional invitees. The seminar was designed to produce this volume. UCHRI provided leadership in administering and supporting Phase I of the program; the Getty Research Institute served this role in Phase II. Robert Post was responsible for the overall intellectual co-ordination of the program, with the financial support of AAAS.

Acknowledgments

This volume would not have been possible without the generous support of the Executive Council of the Western Center of the American Academy of Arts and Sciences (AAAS), the Getty Research Institute for the History of Art and the Humanities, and the Humanities Research Institute of the University of California (UCHRI).

The idea of a collaborative program on censorship was initially conceived in 1992 by Professor David B. Kaplan of UCLA (AAAS), Tom Reese (Deputy Director of the Getty Research Institute), and Mark Rose (Director of UCHRI). These three deserve great credit for designing the innovative institutional structure and purposes of the program.

Patricia A. O'Brien succeeded Mark Rose as Director of UCHRI in 1994, and she continued to provide superb logistical and financial support, particularly during Phase I of the program. She was assisted by a fine UCHRI staff consisting of Mia Larson, Debra Massey, Deanna Nunez, and Linda Arias. M. Gerald Bradford and later Joyce E. Keath of the Western Center of the AAAS offered moral encouragement throughout the long years of this project. And the Getty Research Institute provided outstanding fiscal and administrative assistance, particularly in Phase II of the program, and most especially in the preparation of this volume. In addition to Tom Reese, I am especially grateful to Julia Bloomfield, David Jensen, Moira Kenney, Lynne Kostman, and Lynn O'Leary-Archer. This volume would not have been possible without the elegant and discriminating editing of Rebecca Frazier at the Getty Research Institute.

I would especially like to thank the participants at the seminar held at the Getty Research Institute in December 1995. The sharp and lively dialogue, stretched across the surprisingly deep chasms of disciplinary difference, was profoundly exciting and instructive, and I know that it helped to refine and improve the contributions to this volume.

—Robert C. Post

Censorship and Silencing

Robert C. Post

Censorship used to be a very dull subject. Aligned along predictable and venerable divisions separating liberals from conservatives, oriented toward ancient and well-rehearsed chestnuts such as obscenity and national security, the topic promised little of analytic interest.

In recent years, however, the landscape of censorship has altered dramatically.[1] Now feminists in Indianapolis join with fundamentalist Christians to seek the regulation of pornography.[2] Critical race theorists join with Jesse Helms to regulate hate speech.[3] Advocates of abortion rights seek to restrict political demonstrations while conservative pro-life groups defend the freedom to picket.[4]

Many contemporary liberals scoff at traditional First Amendment jurisprudence, viewing it as a "breeding ground of libertarian sentiment,"[5] and they demand instead a "New Deal" for speech that would empower the state to regulate campaign financing and the broadcast media.[6] Constitutional restraints on government intervention are said primarily to protect the status quo, with its entrenched hierarchies of power and wealth.[7] Conversely, many conservatives have displayed a resurgent and largely libertarian appreciation for the value of freedom of expression, invoking it to check proscriptions of pornography and hate speech, as well as to block campaign finance reform.[8]

This represents a remarkable disintegration of traditional political alignments. The historical causes of this transformation are no doubt multifarious and complex. Certainly one important factor, rendered vivid by the demise of the Cold War, has been the pervasive perception, most fully theorized for this generation in the work of Michel Foucault, that the state holds no monopoly of power.[9] While histories of censorship used to chronicle official legal suppression of speech,[10] Foucault's work invited us to "escape from the limited field of juridical sovereignty and State institutions, and instead base our analysis of power on the study of techniques and tactics of domination."[11] In the last two decades we have begun to perceive power as dispersed, as circulating, as spinning out from the enactment of discursive and disciplinary practices.

A profound effect of this vision has been the tendency to focus on "power as such," with a consequent equation of state force with private domination.[12] In the words of Catharine MacKinnon, "The operative definition of censorship accordingly shifts from government silencing what powerless people say, to powerful people violating powerless people into silence and hiding behind state power to do it."[13] The call for juridical force to check oppressive discursive practices has thus come to be seen not as invoking the state "as a censor, but rather as a parliamentarian, requiring some to shut up so others can speak."[14]

Liberated from traditional inhibitions against official suppression of speech, the left has mobilized to pursue a rich variety of political agendas, ranging from restraining the speech of the wealthy to avoid submerging the voices of the poor, to restricting pornography to avert the silencing of women. From a political point of view, the most striking aspect of these agendas is their trust of government action. Henry Louis Gates has remarked how difficult it is to imagine these agendas being "expressed by ... activist counterparts in the sixties, who defined themselves through their adversarial relation to authority and its institutions.... Today, the aim is not to resist power, but to enlist power."[15]

Political efforts to enlist state power, like those of Catharine MacKinnon, have typically sought to mobilize support by portraying censorship as a form of oppression. But within the academy there has emerged a remarkably innovative new scholarship that has taken a more rigorous and uncompromising view of the matter. Focusing with a sharp Foucaultian lens on the constitutive micromechanisms of power, on the minute intersections of resistance and domination through which power is exercised, this new scholarship follows Foucaultian premises to their fundamental and radical implications.

If censorship is a technique by which discursive practices are maintained, and if social life largely consists of such practices, it follows that censorship is the norm rather than the exception. Censorship materializes everywhere. It is for this reason that Pierre Bourdieu can refer to the "censorship constituted by the very structure of the field in which the discourse is produced and circulates."[16] For Bourdieu the necessity for a practice of censorship manifested by "explicit prohibitions, imposed and sanctioned by institutionalized authority, diminishes" precisely to the extent that "the structure of the field itself" is capable of governing "expression by" controlling "both access to expression and the form of expression."[17]

To the extent that the new scholarship conceives censorship as "pervasive and insistent in all disciplines that mediate language," the force of censorship as a normative concept must proportionately diminish.[18] Thus it is rightly said that "[t]o be for or against censorship as such is to assume a freedom no one has. Censorship is."[19] Censorship establishes the practices that define us as social subjects. Hence censorship transmutes from an external, repressive force to "a positive exercise of power" that constitutes practices as it defines their boundaries.[20]

Foucault had himself always seen power as productive, as constructing knowledge and social practices. He had consequently rejected any simple opposition between power and person, concluding instead that power "makes individuals subjects."[21] In the new scholarship, censorship is analogously characterized as productive, "not as one or more discrete acts of repressive

Detail from the front cover of the annual report issued in 1898 by the New York Society for the Suppression of Vice. Courtesy Library of Congress.

control over free expression, but as a 'normal' and 'constitutive' part, indeed, a very condition, of free expression."[22] The striking and anomalous consequence of this characterization is precisely to cut against attempts to use the charge of censorship as grounds for political mobilization.

These are exciting and important intellectual developments. For all their undeniable power, however, they seem to miss something of importance featured in more traditional accounts. The new scholarly orientation toward censorship seems blind, for example, to the "high drama of repression and suppression" retold by Zamir Niazi in his effort to "preserve . . . for posterity" the courage of Pakistani writers resisting the oppression of a tyrannical regime.[23] Nor does it seem able to appreciate the "heroic names" celebrated by Seamus Heaney in his "modern martyrology, a record of courage and sacrifice" presented in his study of the sacrificed poets of Eastern Europe.[24]

By focusing so intensely on the quotidian operations of power, the new scholarship of censorship ultimately centers attention, like Foucault himself, on the "agonism" in which "the recalcitrance of the will and the intransigence of freedom" form a "permanent provocation" to "the power relationship," which itself establishes a necessary and inescapable "structure" for "the possible field of action."[25] Agonism signifies that while we are always both bound and enabled by existing power relationships, we are also always potentially at odds with those relationships. Agonism, however, does not distinguish Joyce struggling to publish *Ulysses* from, say, the "struggle" of the client of a poverty lawyer to overcome the "violence of silencing" imposed by "the order of discourse" of the usual "lawyer-client relation."[26] Agonism is precisely universal. It is precisely omnipresent.

The enormous expansion of understanding facilitated by the Foucaultian perspective on censorship (and, to be old-fashioned about it, the immense increase in the possibilities of sympathetic apprehension it enables), is thus purchased at the price of a certain abstraction. Foucault's work itself exhibited a vertiginous oscillation between extreme abstraction and minute detail; the space between, where most people live most of their lives, was persistently and scrupulously effaced. The new scholarship of censorship can be similarly characterized. It tends to veer between the concrete mechanisms of silencing and the abstraction of struggle. The result seems to flatten distinctions among kinds of power, implicitly equating suppression of speech caused by state legal action with that caused by the market, or by the dominance of a particular discourse, or by the institution of criticism itself. It tends also to flatten variations among kinds of struggles, de-emphasizing the difference between, say, the agonism of poets and that of legal aid clients.

The challenge is thus how to preserve the analytic force of the new scholarship without sacrificing the values and concerns of more traditional accounts. Recognizing always the pervasive, inescapable, and productive silencing of expression, can we say anything distinctive about the particular province of what used to define the study of censorship: the "direct control" of expression by the state?[27]

Assembling a group of extraordinarily talented scholars, this volume interrogates that issue from divergent disciplinary perspectives, ranging from political science to philosophy, from law to cultural theory, from literary criticism to anthropology. Our strategy is to re-examine state censorship with the insights of the new scholarship firmly in mind. In Part I we inquire into the specific dynamics of explicit legal control of speech through criminal and civil sanctions. In Part II we investigate other forms of state regulation of speech, ranging from subsidies to property rights. And in Part III we examine justifications for state interventions to regulate private power that constrains expression.

Part I begins with an essay by Richard Burt, one of the foremost proponents of the new scholarship. Carefully focusing on court suppression of the English playwright Thomas Middleton, Burt invites us to suspend our usual conception of censorship as a process of "removal and replacement," and instead to visualize censorship as a matter of "dispersal and displacement." Burt's ambition is to undermine any simple opposition "between the censored and uncensored," thus calling into question traditional theories of free speech that rely on postulated polarities between repressed and authentic versions of an author's work.[28]

Middleton was subject to a court officer, the Master of the Revels, whose judgments were highly personal and discretionary. Although such individual discretion to censor still exists with respect to speech within state organizations,[29] direct official control over public discourse (like the theater) is today almost entirely dependent upon the application of judicially interpreted legal principles.[30] Quite apart from the well-rehearsed debate as to whether the ideals of free speech ought to exempt public discourse from direct official control, we may therefore also ask whether legal proceedings are themselves a suitable instrument for the regulation of speech.[31] These questions do not depend upon any implicit opposition between censored and uncensored versions of a text; they instead concentrate on the internal requirements of a modern legal system.

Both Ruth Gavison's and Lawrence Douglas's contributions to this volume discuss the many and subtle ways in which these requirements affect the law's ability to fulfill our purposes when we seek to use the law to regulate expression. Although many in Israel have called for the suppression of speech that incites to political violence, Gavison probes the law's capacity to serve this function, and in particular she demonstrates how such factors as the law's internal need for public justification causes it to be over- and under-inclusive and otherwise generally ineffective in fulfilling this task. Douglas observes how the ambition to enshrine a certain view of the Holocaust by criminalizing speech that denies it has been undermined by the law's own internal requirements of advocacy and agnosticism.

Of course there are many different purposes for which the law can be used to control speech, and some may prove more amenable to legal realization than others. The last two essays in Part I examine further justifications for legal intervention. Debora Shuger offers an historical exegesis of how early modern English proscriptions of slander and libel not only served the purpose of minimizing incitements to political violence but also instantiated a particular vision of Christian community. If the first of these goals would presumably be subject to the caveats outlined by Gavison, the second would not, and to this day the so-called dignitary torts aspire to enforce analogous forms of community self-definition.[32] That aspiration, however, is queried by E. S. Burt, who uses French judicial decisions first condemning and then rehabilitating poems from Baudelaire's *Fleurs du mal* to explore efforts to employ the law to suppress obscenity within literature. Burt's point is that the law can extract particular versions of communal norms from literary texts only by blinding itself to the "negative knowledge of a disintegrating memory" carried in the very language of such texts, a knowledge that is independent of any "poet's agency."[33] This knowledge, this literariness, evades all censorious efforts to affix texts with determinate meanings.

Part II of the volume turns from the issue of direct legal control of expression and examines the use of state power to maintain and privilege particular discursive practices. Every time the state educates a student, or establishes acquisition criteria for a public library, or chooses to subsidize one form of speech rather than another, the state uses government resources to establish a discursive field. It supports some speech and marginalizes other speech. In popular debate, these actions have come to be characterized as a form of censorship. Those who oppose the imposition of "decency" restrictions on NEA grants, for example, charge that they "censor artists' speech,"[34] while those who defend the restrictions write "In Praise of Censorship."[35] A recent report from People for the American Way documents "300 incidents of attempted censorship," defining these incidents as efforts "to remove from a classroom, library or curriculum, books or other materials or programs for ideological or sectarian reasons."[36]

This usage of the concept of censorship is odd, because no matter what speech the state does or does not fund, no matter what material it assigns or does not assign within a classroom, no matter what books it acquires or does not acquire for a library, the state will be acting for reasons that can properly be termed "ideological." This suggests the practical truth of the theoretical insight that all discursive practices establish themselves through the marginalization and suppression of competing practices. If we wish to condemn this as "censorship," then censorship is indeed everywhere and inescapable. Yet in popular rhetoric the term "censorship" continues to be used as if it denotes a particular kind of especially egregious and voluntary state action, one that could, like direct civil and criminal sanctions, be avoided.

This is the paradox addressed by Frederick Schauer in the first essay in Part II. Schauer's point is that if the term *censorship* is applied to the empirical processes by which our "expressive possibilities" are constituted and consequently restricted, then "the very concept of censorship is problematic." Schauer also suggests, however, that the persistent use of the concept within popular debates implies that the term does not in fact refer to these empirical processes, but that it serves instead as a label applied post hoc to conclusions about "the allocation of content-determining authority."[37] These conclusions do not depend so much upon the mere fact that expression is suppressed, as they do upon political and purposive considerations like "institutional competence," "separation of powers," or the maintenance of professional autonomy. They depend, for example, upon whether we wish politicians or artists to determine the allocation of NEA grants.

Schauer's argument implies that the new scholarship of censorship may conflate the descriptive fact of silencing with the ascriptive judgment of censorship.[38] To recognize this conflation, however, is merely to invite deeply perplexing inquiries about how exactly an ascriptive and normative judgment of censorship should be applied to state action that does not impose direct civil or criminal sanctions. The remaining three essays in Part II explore the difficulties of this problem.

David Wasserman canvasses the rich complexities involved in assessing restrictions on government subsidies for scientific research into genetic predispositions to impulsive, violent, or antisocial behavior. Wasserman demonstrates how judgments of censorship must in the end turn on sensitive assessments of institutional and professional competencies, political purposes, and so forth. Sanford Levinson examines this same set of issues as applied to state efforts to educate the public to particular visions of history. Whereas Douglas probes efforts to enshrine a specific version of the Holocaust through direct criminal sanctions, Levinson discusses the state's tutelary attempts to achieve the same end through the erection of public historical monuments. Levinson spins the reader in a dizzy circle, teasing out a humbling array of disparate considerations that might inform ascriptive judgments of censorship.

One of the subtlest, most pervasive, most unobtrusive, yet most powerful methods by which the state establishes discursive fields is through the creation and allocation of property rights. Property rights undergird what the new scholarship of censorship has termed "market censorship."[39] But however much we may acknowledge that "the market is itself a structure of constraint," it is difficult to imagine a modern society entirely without property rights, so that once again the descriptive and ascriptive concepts of censorship must be disentangled.[40] In the last essay in Part II George Marcus ventures into this difficult terrain, examining contemporary claims to cultural property by aboriginal peoples in the United States, Canada, and Australia. Such claims distribute power and hence have fundamental political consequences; they reflect cultural identities that challenge deep assumptions of "autonomous individualism" otherwise embodied within intellectual property law; they interfere with the free circulation of ideas and expression; yet ought they to be characterized as censorship? Marcus worries the issue, but, like Wasserman and Levinson, ultimately reserves judgment.

Part III of the volume returns to the insight that nonstate power pervasively constrains expression, and that sometimes these constraints operate in ways that could be ascriptively characterized as censorship. In such circumstances it might be justifiable to invoke state power to remove these constraints, even at the price of direct government regulation of speech. This reasoning underlies contemporary calls for restrictions on pornography and hate speech, for state controls over public access to media broadcasting outlets, and so forth.

Judith Butler begins Part III with a theoretical account of the ways in which "the speaking subject is produced through constraints on speech that precede the subject itself." Because these constraints establish "the domain of speakability" and "the conditions of intelligibility," they are inevitable, indispensable, and unspeakable. Butler speculates that for this reason they may be misdescribed by the language of "censorship," and she herself proposes to use the term *foreclosure*. She wishes to designate a "primary form of repression, one that is not performed by a subject, but, rather, whose operation makes possible the formation of the subject." Butler contrasts such foreclosure with the censorship performed by a sovereign actor, whether that actor be the state or the speaker of hate speech. Censorship performed by a sovereign actor, which is explicit, discrete, and from outside the subject, is necessarily incomplete, because of the continued independence of the subject and of the inability "to circumscribe effectively the social domain of speakable discourse."[41]

The social power to censor, albeit limited, can nevertheless prove considerable. The essays of Rae Langton and Leslie Green explore the characterization and consequences of that power in the particular instance of pornography. At the outset Langton rejects accounts of censorship that universalize it, that place it "everywhere." Censorship as a normative concept must refer to something discrete and remediable. Using J. L. Austin's speech act theory, Langton argues that pornography functions as a form of "illocutionary disablement" that prevents women from having the full power to speak in certain kinds of ways. It is thus a form of censorship, and if "the free speech of men silences the free speech of women—then there is a choice about which speech is to be protected."[42]

In Austinian terms, the illocution of an utterance refers to the action constituted by the utterance. To say "I agree" in the appropriate context is to have the illocutionary force of, and to perform the action of, making a contract. The success of the illocutionary force of an utterance depends upon "felicity conditions" that permit the "uptake" of the utterance. This implies, however, that the illocutionary force of every utterance is pervasively and inescapably constrained both by felicity conditions and by the social forces that enable the fulfillment of these conditions. These conditions and forces are historical and contingent. For this reason Green argues that illocutionary force is precisely "censored" everywhere, so that one cannot speak of a freedom of speech that encompasses freedom from constraints on the illocutionary force of one's speech. No one can complain of being silenced merely on the ground that uptake is not secured. If pornography is to be regulated, suggests Green, it should be on other grounds, as for example on the basis of norms of equality which, like the norms of charity evoked by Shuger, reflect a particular vision of communal identity.[43]

Wendy Brown concludes Part III with an extended meditation on the theme of silencing. Brown is concerned to unravel the usual equation that reads voice as registering authenticity and power, and that reads silence as reflecting repression and domination. Brown identifies the subtle dangers associated with what she calls "compulsory discursivity," which conscripts subjects into the regulatory norms of the very discursive practices that enable speech. From this perspective, silence can function as a "resistance to regulatory discourse," as a quiet and sheltered place in which freedom can be practiced. Brown treads a fine line, carefully distinguishing "between the pleasures and freedoms of silence on the one hand and habituation to being silenced on the other."[44] Brown's point is that, having once tasted the Foucaultian apple, we can neither view expression as the simple opposite of censorship, nor silence as the simple antithesis of freedom.

We have come, therefore, full circle. We have learned to see regulation in the very formation of our speech; we have learned how thoroughly we are subject to natural causal constraints. Nevertheless, to the extent we continue as agents to act and to judge, we require criteria by which to discriminate among restrictions on speech: to accept some and to reject others. Because we have learned that such judgments cannot rest merely on the fact that expression is constrained, we must reformulate them to depend instead upon purposive considerations, upon ideals of juridical enforcement or of institutional competence or of freedom or of equality. The concept of censorship can guide our judgments only if it is reabsorbed into this normative language. But the concept comes to us now stripped of its prior innocence by the acid of Foucaultian sophistication. That loss has momentous political consequences, as we have learned in the last two decades. The challenge addressed by the essays in this volume is how these consequences may be mastered and subordinated to an informed political will.

Notes

1. For a good discussion, see Kathleen M. Sullivan, "Free Speech Wars," *Southern Methodist University Law Review* 48 (1994): 203; Kathleen M. Sullivan, "Resurrecting Free Speech," *Fordham Law Review* 63 (1995): 971.

2. For an account, see Donald Alexander Downs, *The New Politics of Pornography* (Chicago: Univ. of Chicago Press, 1989).

3. Compare Mari J. Matsuda et al., *Words that Wound: Critical Race Theory, Assaultive Speech, and the First Amendment* (Boulder: Westview Press, 1993), with *Congressional Record,* 101st Cong., 1st Sess., 1989, 135: 16276 (proposed statute by Jesse

Helms prohibiting NEA funding for, inter alia, "material which denigrates, debases, or reviles a person, group, or class of citizens on the basis of race, creed, sex, handicap, age, or national origin"). For the story of the Helms Amendment, see John H. Garvey, "Black and White Images," *Law and Contemporary Problems* 56 (1993): 189, 191–97.

4. See, for example, *Madsen v. Women's Health Ctr., Inc.,* 114 S. Ct. 2516 (1994).

5. Owen M. Fiss, *Liberalism Divided: Freedom of Speech and the Many Uses of State Power* (Boulder: Westview Press, 1996), 34.

6. Cass R. Sunstein, *Democracy and the Problem of Free Speech* (New York: Free Press, 1993), 16. For historical antecedents, see Zechariah Chafee, Jr., *Government and Mass Communications* (Hamden, Conn.: Archon Books, 1965; originally published 1947), 26–29, 680–719.

7. See, for example, Frederick Schauer, "The Political Incidence of the Free Speech Principle," *Colorado Law Review* 64 (1993): 935.

8. For a recent decision on pornography, see *American Booksellers Ass'n v. Hudnut,* 771 F.2d 323 (7th Cir. 1985), aff'd per curiam, 475 U.S. 1001 (1986). For hate speech, see *R.A.V. v. St. Paul,* 112 S. Ct. 2538 (1992); Eugene Volokh, "Comment: Freedom of Speech and Workplace Harassment," *UCLA Law Review* 39 (1992): 1791. For campaign finance reform, see *Austin v. Michigan State Chamber of Commerce,* 494 U.S. 652, 679 (1990) (Scalia, J., dissenting).

9. It is instructive to compare the reception accorded to Foucault with that given to the work of Herbert Marcuse, who in 1965 made this same point (in a quasi-Marxist register) to justify a call for state intervention and censorship. See Herbert Marcuse, "Repressive Tolerance," in Robert Paul Wolff, Barrington Moore, Jr., and Herbert Marcuse, *A Critique of Pure Tolerance* (Boston: Beacon Press, 1965). Whereas Foucault's work has been enormously influential, Marcuse's was largely dismissed as advocating a fringe position.

10. See, for example, Paul S. Boyer, *Purity in Print: The Vice-Society Movement and Book Censorship in America* (New York: Scribner, 1968); Guy Phelps, *Film Censorship* (London: Gollancz, 1975); The New York Public Library, *Censorship: 500 Years of Conflict* (New York: Oxford Univ. Press, 1984); "A Chronology of Censorship in America," *The Congressional Digest* 9 (1930): 35; Sidney S. Grant and S. E. Angoff, "Massachusetts and Censorship," *Boston University Law Review* 10 (1930): 36, 145.

11. Michel Foucault, *Power/Knowledge: Selected Interviews and Other Writings,* ed. and trans. Colin Gordon (New York: Pantheon Books, 1980), 102.

12. Steven L. Winter, "The 'Power' Thing," *Virginia Law Review* 82 (1996): 721, 728.

13. Catharine A. MacKinnon, *Only Words* (Cambridge, Mass.: Harvard Univ. Press, 1993), 10.

14. Fiss (see note 5), 85.

15. Henry Louis Gates, Jr., "War of Words: Critical Race Theory and the First Amendment," in Henry Louis Gates et al., *Speaking of Race, Speaking of Sex: Hate Speech, Civil Rights, and Civil Liberties* (New York: New York Univ. Press, 1994), 42. "You don't go to the teacher to complain about the school bully," Gates writes, "unless you know that the teacher is on your side" (ibid.).

16. Pierre Bourdieu, "Censorship and the Imposition of Form," in idem, *Language and Symbolic Power,* ed. John B. Thompson, trans. Gino Raymond and Matthew Adamson (Cambridge, Mass.: Harvard Univ. Press, 1991), 137.

17. Ibid., 138.

18. Michael Holquist, "Corrupt Originals: The Paradox of Censorship," *PMLA* 109 (1994): 14, 17.

19. Ibid., 16.

20. See, for example, Richard Burt, "Introduction: The 'New' Censorship," in Richard Burt, ed., *The Administration of Aesthetics: Censorship, Political Criticism, and the Public Sphere* (Minneapolis: Univ. of Minnesota Press, 1994), xvii.

21. Michel Foucault, "The Subject and Power," in Hubert L. Dreyfus and Paul Rabinow, eds., *Michel Foucault: Beyond Structuralism and Hermeneutics,* 2nd ed. (Chicago: Univ. of Chicago Press, 1983), 212.

22. Francis G. Couvares, "Introduction," in idem, *Movie Censorship and American Culture* (Washington, D.C.: Smithsonian Institution Press, 1996), 10. See Sue Curry Jansen, *Censorship: The Knot That Binds Power and Knowledge* (New York: Oxford Univ. Press, 1988), 7–8; Francis Barker, *The Tremulous Private Body: Essays on Subjection* (New York: Methuen, 1984), 51–52.

23. Zamir Niazi, *The Web of Censorship* (New York: Oxford Univ. Press, 1994), xv, xviii.

24. Seamus Heaney, *The Government of the Tongue: The 1986 T. S. Eliot Memorial Lectures and Other Critical Writings* (New York: Faber, 1988), 38–39. See J. M Coetzee, *Giving Offense: Essays on Censorship* (Chicago: Univ. Chicago Press, 1996).

25. Foucault, "The Subject and Power" (see note 21), 221–22.

26. Anthony V. Alfieri, "Reconstructive Poverty Law Practice: Learning Lessons of Client Narrative," *Yale Law Journal* 100 (1991): 2107, 2126, 2139, 2142. For the Foucaultian influence in this conceptualization, see "The Subject and Power" (see note 21), 2120 n. 43.

27. Annabel Patterson, "Censorship," in Martin Coyle et al., eds., *Encyclopedia of Literature and Criticism* (Detroit: Gale Research Inc., 1991), 901. Or, if not by the state exactly, then, as Patterson also puts it, "by men with sovereign power" (ibid.).

28. Burt also intends to undermine any simple opposition between governmental and non-governmental constraints on speech, proposing instead a concept of censorship that can "be located virtually anywhere: not only in the marketplace and in governmental agencies ... but also in the institution of criticism itself." See Richard Burt, "(Un)Censoring in Detail: The Fetish of Censorship in the Early Modern Past and Postmodern Present," page 32 in this volume.

29. For a discussion, see Robert C. Post, "Between Management and Governance: The History and Theory of the Public Forum," *UCLA Law Review* 34 (1987): 1713; Robert C. Post, "The Management of Speech: Discretion and Rights," *Supreme Court Review* (1984): 169.

30. *Freedman v. Maryland,* 380 U.S. 51 (1965). For a discussion of the scope of public discourse, see Robert C. Post, "The Constitutional Concept of Public Discourse: Outrageous Opinion, Democratic Deliberation, and *Hustler Magazine v. Falwell,*" *Harvard Law Review* 103 (1990): 601; Robert C. Post, "Between Democracy

and Community: The Legal Constitution of Social Form," *NOMOS* 35, "Democratic Community" (1993): 163–90. For a discussion of indirect state control over public discourse, see Robert C. Post, "Subsidized Speech," *Yale Law Journal* 106 (1996): 151.

31. There is a vast literature on this subject, which is not duplicated in this volume. A good place to begin is Frederick Schauer, *Free Speech: A Philosophical Enquiry* (New York: Cambridge Univ. Press, 1982); Thomas I. Emerson, *The System of Freedom of Expression* (New York: Vintage, 1970).

32. See Robert C. Post, *Constitutional Domains* (Cambridge, Mass.: Harvard Univ. Press, 1995), 1–4, 51–88, 127–140, 179–96.

33. See E. S. Burt, "'An Immoderate Taste for Truth': Censoring History in Baudelaire's 'Les bijoux,'" page 133 in this volume.

34. Donald W. Hawthorne, "Subversive Subsidization: How NEA Art Funding Abridges Private Speech," *Kansas Law Review* 40 (1992): 437.

35. Stanley C. Brubaker, "In Praise of Censorship," *The Public Interest*, no. 114 (Winter 1994): 48–64.

36. People for the American Way, *Attacks on the Freedom to Learn* (People for the American Way, 1996), 10–11.

37. See Frederick Schauer, "The Ontology of Censorship," pages 149, 163 in this volume.

38. On an analogous conflation of descriptive and ascriptive accounts of autonomy, see Robert C. Post, "Meiklejohn's Mistake: Individual Autonomy and the Reform of Public Discourse," *Colorado Law Review* 64 (1993): 1109, 1128–33.

39. Jansen (see note 22), 167, also 16–17.

40. Fiss (see note 5), 143.

41. See Judith Butler, "Ruled Out: Vocabularies of the Censor," pages 255, 253, 251 in this volume

42. See Rae Langton, "Subordination, Silence, and Pornography's Authority," page 276 in this volume.

43. For a discussion of the communitarian structure of such egalitarian norms, see Robert C. Post, "Racist Speech, Democracy, and the First Amendment," *William and Mary Law Review* 32 (1990): 267.

44. See Wendy Brown, "Freedom's Silences," pages 318, 324 in this volume.

Censorship: The Repressive State

Lucas Cranach,
Book Burning in the Presence of a Nobleman,
sixteenth century.
Courtesy Bettmann Archive.

(Un)Censoring in Detail: The Fetish of Censorship in the Early Modern Past and the Postmodern Present

Richard Burt

How censorship operated in the early modern English theater has become the subject of intense debate: some critics have argued that censorship was a systematic and fully conscious contractual arrangement, others have maintained that it was capricious and arbitrary; some have seen the theater as a prime site of censorship, others have considered it as exceptional in relation to the censorship of other media; and some have concluded that theater censorship was severely repressive, whereas others have argued that it was enlightened, tolerant, and virtually non-existent.[1]

Despite the breadth of this debate, a fundamental question has gone unasked: What is censorship? When debating the relative repressiveness or leniency of theater censorship, for example, critics have largely ignored the way that the similarity between censorship and noncensorship puts the definition of censorship into question. They assume instead that censorship operates in terms of *removal* and *replacement;* that is, the censor demands cuts from the text, and the author or an editor seeks to circumvent the censor by replacing the cut material. Censorship is implicitly defined as a strictly repressive activity centered in the court and implicitly opposed to the antithetical practice of uncensoring.

By contrast, I offer a more complex and nuanced model of censorship involving *dispersal* and *displacement.* Early modern stage censorship, I will show, was dispersed among a variety of regulatory agents and practices; it was productive as well as prohibitive; it involved cultural legitimation as well as delegitimation. Censorship was more than one thing, occurred at more than one place and at more than one time. More crucially, texts were displaced from one channel or medium to another (for example, from print to manuscript or performance to print), not obliterated wholesale.[2] Even an apparently destructive act like a book burning could be understood as a symbolic rite of purification rather than an attempt to block completely access to forbidden books.[3] I offer less a way of clarifying some of the contradictions of stage censorship than a call for a more deconstructive definition of censorship, one in which the spatial and temporal location and limits of censorship come into question and in which censorship and editorial revision or literary criticism—censorship and noncensorship—cannot be rigorously distinguished.

Defining censorship in terms of displacement and dispersal displaces and absorbs, so to speak, a definition of censorship as removal and replacement. It is both an alternative categorization and a more inclusive one, both an opposition and an expansion. On the one hand, a dispersal and displacement model of censorship keeps in place a sense of the graduated differences between forms of punishment and repression (between having a hand removed and having a word removed), with "soft" forms of censorship (like critical censure) at one end of a continuum and "hard" forms of censorship (like imprisonment) at the other. Yet, on the other hand, a dispersal and displacement model unsettles a traditional hierarchy of more or less repressive punishments insofar as it shows that no one form of legitimation or delegitimation necessarily has priority over others. Cultural capital may in some cases count more than economic capital. More important, displacement yokes, often paradoxically, precisely those terms that the more traditional model wishes to oppose: *repression* and *diversity; production* and *consumption; censoring* and *uncensoring;* and *public* and *private,* among others.

To reconceptulatize theater censorship, I focus on the dramatist Thomas Middleton, largely because his canon and career present us with quantitatively significant and highly detailed evidence of censorship.[4] Moreover, Middleton paradoxically documents instances of what Annabel Patterson calls "those famous puzzling cases of *noncensorship*" as much as he does of censorship.[5] A quick review of the production and reception of *A Game at Chess* makes this paradox clear. The play was first licensed for performance by the court censor, the Master of the Revels, ran nine days continuously, and was then shut down. Middleton was "on the run" for some months in a failed effort to escape the authorities and was imprisoned briefly, and the company that acted *A Game at Chess* in 1624 was briefly prevented from performing. Neither Middleton nor the company suffered any lasting harm, however: Middleton obtained his release from prison through a witty epigram to James I,[6] and, remarkably, the company went on to perform *The Spanish Viceroy,* a play on the same subject, without a license the following year (for which they received no punishment at all). Middleton continued to receive patronage from the City of London, and *A Game at Chess* was printed (albeit illegally) in 1625, a year after the banned performance. The asymmetry between the play's major political transgression and the near absence of repressive consequences suffered either by the written text, the author, or the actors, then, can as easily be called noncensorship as censorship.[7]

I have divided what follows into two parts. In the first part, I show that the case of Middleton demands we reconceptualize censorship in terms of dispersal and displacement. This means attending to a series of regulations over literary production and consumption to which his plays were subject: I take these networks of regulation to be part of the formation of what Pierre Bourdieu terms the *literary field.*[8] According to Bourdieu, the literary field emerges as a form of cultural legitimation: texts circulate as negotiable currency, as both symbolic and economic capital, insofar as they are differentiated from other versions in the same or in different media: a text in manuscript form, for example, may be valued over printed versions because a select, elite readership alone has access to it, while a performance may be valued over a printed version because the former is thought to be fuller than the censored printed text; conversely, the printed text may be valued over a performance because the former is regarded as fuller than a censored performance. *Fetishism* is a key term in my analysis of the way censorship permits or blocks access and entry to the literary field. I suggest that censoring is a version of the fetishizing critical practice Naomi Schor has termed "reading in detail": censorship involves the negotiation and construction of small differences that make the text desirable (either because it is the uncensored version or because it is the censored version).[9] Censorship may be usefully regarded as a metaphor for the fetishistic practices of cultural differentiation and legitimation by which texts are put into circulation as desirable commodities. Middleton presents us with what might be called a hyperfetishized model of textual culture. By *hyperfetishism* I mean a mainstreaming practice—bringing something from the margin to the center—that increases the possibilities for a text's access and entry to the literary field yet, at the same time, allows its entry not as an uncensored whole (or forbids its entry as a censored whole) but as a partial, always already-censored text whose value is constituted by (and which accrues from) its small differences from other versions.

In the second part, I consider some of the current implications of thinking about censorship in terms of dispersal and displacement rather than in terms of removal and replacement. I maintain that a negative conception of censorship (a concept held by critics across a wide spectrum of political affiliations) depends for its coherence on a series of repressions which make up what I call the professional unconscious of criticism. Although what counts as censorship is now often debated, as this collection itself evinces, what counts as criticism is not generally open to debate among critics themselves. The kinds of repressions this assumption entails are worth examining.

Since it may seem counterintuitive to think of censorship in terms of dispersal and displacement, let me begin by calling attention to the limitations of the removal and replacement model. This approach assumes a model of textual transmission in which censorship was clearly located in an external authority, like the Master of the Revels. In this model the process of submitting a theater manuscript (a promptbook) to the court censor for licensing would be fairly straightforward. One could trace a line from the text's beginnings to its endings; from plot to foul papers, to authorial or scribal promptbook, to a licensed promptbook (private transcripts may have been made from the foul papers or from promptbooks), to performance, to acquisition by a publisher or printer, then to a compositor (who set the type and made corrections), to the printing of the first edition, and on possibly to later editions and possibly a theatrical revival and resubmission of the promptbook for licensing.[10] In this view, censorship is a specific form of intervention and interference in an otherwise clearly transmitted set of signals from the theater company to the audience. The censor was granted a central kind of interference or imposition, significantly different from the kind of interference introduced, for example, by a printer, whose mistakes could be corrected at will. The underlying assumption is that the court censor was at the apex and center of transmission: he would read a manuscript and then assess it positively or negatively, either burning it or licensing it as submitted or on condition that it be revised. Censorship is understood, then, as a clearly defined (in the sense of limited) activity, located in time and space.

This understanding of censorship is not entirely wrong, of course. The Master of the Revels licensed a text by signing his name and giving his authorization at the end of the text. He had punitive powers and exercised them. In at least one case, he burned a manuscript he was unwilling to license; he demanded that some texts be revised; and one Master, Sir Henry Herbert, threatened authors, theater managers, and actors with "public punishment."[11] The censor's powers were increasingly centralized after 1606. Whereas early in Middleton's career there were a number of censors, including the bishops of London and dramatists like John Lyly, by the time of his last play, *A Game at Chess,* there was a single court official and his deputies. The (apparent) intervention of the bishop of London in *Sir John Van Olden Barnavelt* in 1619 is the exception that proves the rule. The Master of the Revels also put into practice the *Acte to Restraine Abuses of Players,* passed by Parliament in 1606, making it illegal "jestingly or prophanely [to] speak or use the Holy name of God or Jesus Christ, or of the Holy Ghoste or of the Trinity, which are not to be spoken but with fear and reverence."[12]

A closer look at the evidence begins to complicate the assumption that censorship had a precisely defined location and definition. Consider the manuscript of *The Second Maiden's Tragedy.* One sees a number of different markings and a number of different handwritings. Not all of the cuts are in the hand of the Master, Sir George Buc. Some are by the bookkeeper, some by the scribe. Buc has, for example, "struck out a number of oaths in the manuscript, but the specifically Catholic oath 'By th' mass' uttered by the Tyrant, has been deleted by a different hand."[13] Similarly, a wavy line alongside the passage signifies its removal, although again the color of the ink does not link the instruction directly with Buc. In her recent study of stage censorship, Janet Clare concludes that the cuts and marks imply "a degree of collaboration between the censor and the playhouse bookkeeper."[14] She maintains that the manuscript provides "clear evidence that plays were censored in the playhouse, either in anticipation of the [court] censor's objections or in response to his verbal instructions."[15] This play is not by any means an exceptional case. Middleton's *Hengist, King of Kent* evinces a similar dispersal. As R. C. Bald comments, it is unclear whether *Hengist* has been censored at all: the cuts may have been made by the actors rather than by the censor.[16] Grace Ioppolo doubts that the cuts can be attributed to censorship.[17]

To buttress Clare's point about collaboration, we could add that dramatists might function as censors in the repressive sense. In a discussion of the *Acte to Restraine Abuses of Players,* Gary Taylor points out that when a text has been expurgated, the source of that expurgation is almost always the theater.[18] One might infer from the low number of oaths in the Middleton canon, much lower than in the plays of Shakespeare, that Middleton acted as a self-censor.[19] The existence of collaboration is further confirmed by the fact that the Master of the Revels did not double-check to make sure that the acting company had made the revisions he requested. He could rely on the company to obey him, and they generally did.[20]

Thus, censorship was dispersed, not centered in the court, despite the increasing centralization of the Master of the Revels's powers. However much power the Master amassed, that power remained partly decentered by its dispersal even at court and within the office itself—there were always ecclesiastical censors, and the Revels office had deputies.[21] We can identify collaboration not only in exchanges between the Master of the Revels and the playhouse but also in factional struggles over patronage that involved the Revels office, as Richard Dutton has pointed out.[22] Furthermore, the *Acte to Restraine Abuses of Players* dispersed censorship across all areas of theatrical production and reception, and actors as well as members of the audience served as spies and informers.[23] Individuals sometimes successfully sued for libel, managing to shut down performances.[24]

My point that censorship was dispersed confirms a current consensus among critics working on early modern theater censorship that it operated in terms of complicity and collaboration between censors, authors, and critics rather than in terms of radical oppositions between dumb censors and intelligent literary writers.[25] Dutton has observed that court censorship of the theater was neither authoritarian nor totalitarian.[26] If we agree that censorship occurred through collaboration and complicity, the question remains: does it alter our understanding of censorship? The fact that censorship was dispersed, some might argue, does not (and should not) significantly alter our sense of it as a repressive practice. Instead, we have only a more rigorous, more nuanced conception of it: censorship remains externally imposed by the court censor and similar officials and internally self-imposed (as self-censorship) when undertaken by anyone else. Furthermore, censorship was still located temporally, occurring either before or after performance or publication. That is to say, we would still have a stable model of censorship, one that places it on one side of an axis moving between the opposite poles of repression and freedom, one that opposes agencies and clearly demarcated discursive spaces, one that believes dramatists could choose to collaborate or resist.

I suggest that Middleton presents us with a much deeper sense of collaboration and complicity, one that extends to all points of the agencies and practices of literary consumption and production. Consider again the manuscript of *The Second Maiden's Tragedy*. It might appear to provide incontrovertible evidence of censorship in the repressive sense of removal, since crosses and wavy lines mark passages that the court censor demanded be deleted. But things are not all that simple. Take the much discussed change from "most ladies" to "many ladies."[27] What the censor wants removed—"most"—is replaced by the scribe (or author or bookkeeper) with an alternative—"many"—that is nearly synonymous.[28] Similarly, the tyrant's line "Yor kinges poisond" is changed to the virtually synonymous "I am poisond." How either of these examples of censorship differ from revision is hard to tell. The marking of a change in the last line of the play "from might all be borne so... to your rooms or so... to your rooms" looks just like the marking used to change "Yor kinges poisond" to "I am poisond." These examples return us to the ambiguous way in which a case of censorship can look like a case of noncensorship.

Critics have recently tried to explain the difference between "most ladies" and "many ladies" in terms of a specific topical allusion to the court of James I that focused on Lady Essex, Frances Howard, who divorced her first husband on grounds of nonconsummation and who along with her second husband murdered Sir Thomas Overbury.[29] This allusion has been used to explain the censorship of a surprisingly large number of plays, including Middleton's *The Witch*. I do not want to rule it out as an explanation in this example, but I do think the manuscript shows that the censor's revision cannot be decisively differentiated from theatrical revision in terms of its verbal outcome.[30] As one editor notes, not all the marks necessarily suggest censorship: some mark theatrical revision.[31] My point is that this lack of difference suggests that the censor operated productively as a kind of editor. The change from "most ladies" to the less pointed "many" softens but, I would argue, hardly neutralizes the topical allusion, since in both cases "ladies" remains as a figure for court corruption. The censor has asked for an editorial revision that involves a fine degree of tact.[32] Editing and censorship thus overlap. I would add that the practice of using the same marks by the censor and by actors, authors, and bookkeepers in the playhouse suggests that censorship and theatrical revision were understood as parallel, complementary activities, not as opposed or different in kind.

Understanding how the censor functioned as an editor allows us to begin to understand the ways in which censorship was structurally complicit with what is often taken to be its opposite—namely, criticism.[33] The Master chose plays for performance and was therefore an extraordinarily important critic as well as a censor: what he liked and thought highly of would get performed at court. As an editor, the censor read critically in detail. We can adduce further evidence of the censor's critical abilities and interests. It is worth pointing out that Buc, himself an author and owner of an impressive library, gave *The Second Maiden's Tragedy* its title to differentiate it from Francis Beaumont and John Fletcher's (also censored) *The Maid's Tragedy*.[34] John Lyly and Ben Jonson both sought to become Master of the Revels (Jon-

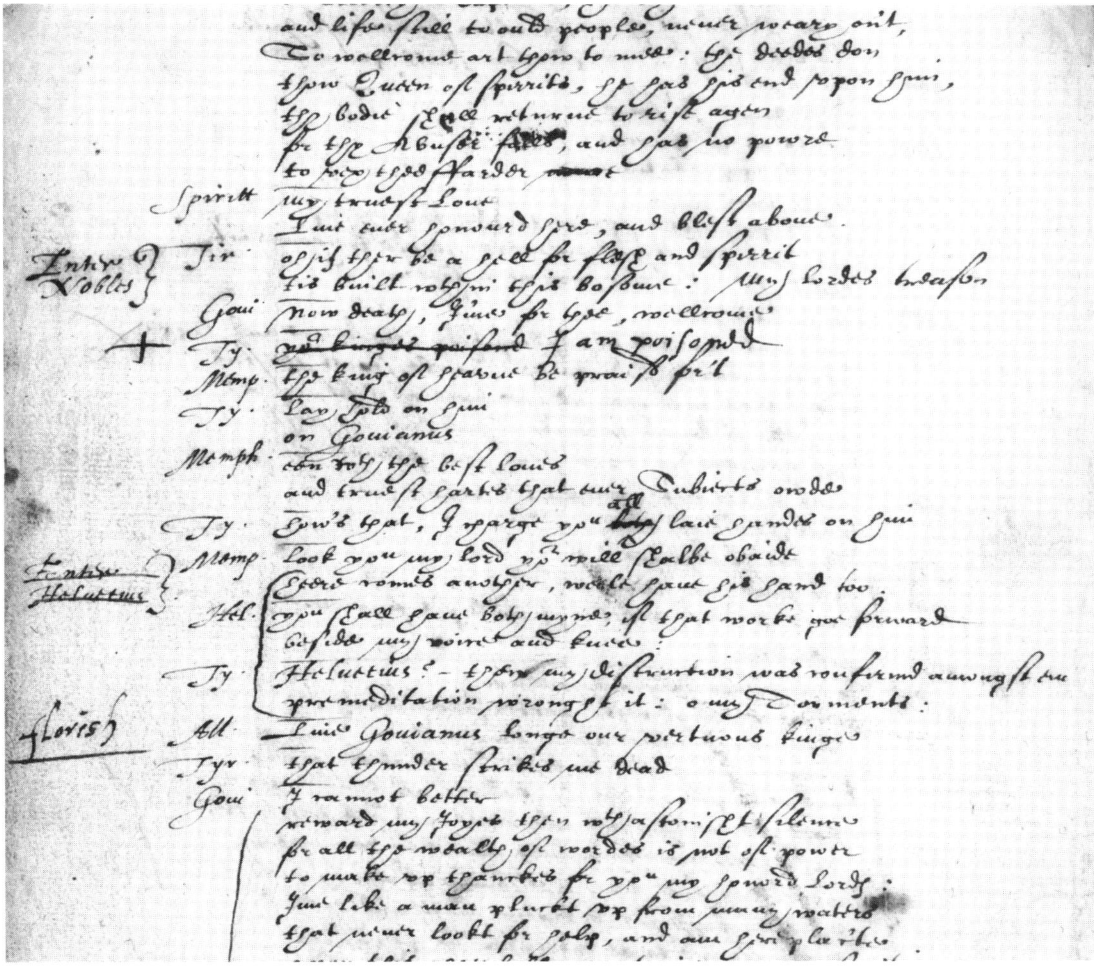

Manuscript page from *The Second Maiden's Tragedy,* showing the censor's change from "Yor kinges poisond" to "I am poisond."
Courtesy British Library.

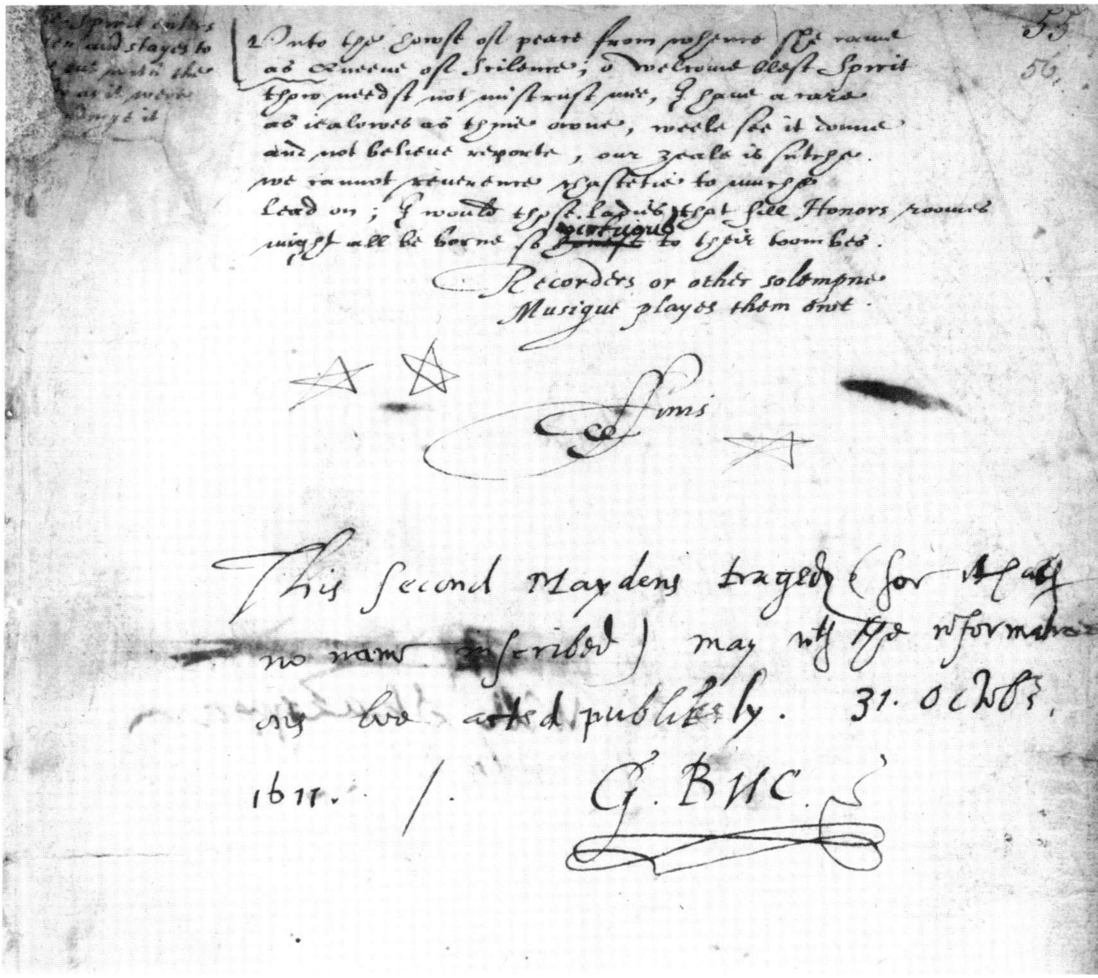

Manuscript page from *The Second Maiden's Tragedy,* with the signature of Sir George Buc, Master of the Revels. Courtesy British Library.

son obtained a reversion to it in 1624). And Sir Henry Herbert, Master of the Revels after George Buc, wrote the following in 1624 in regard to a court performance of Middleton's *More Dissemblers besides Women:* "The worst play I ever saw."[35] Censorship and criticism were complicit, then, in the sense that they were overlapping activities.

Before pursuing the implications of the structural complicity between censorship and criticism, it is worth pausing to map out the full extent of censorship's penetration by and of literary consumption and production. Censorship may be defined to encompass state censorship, market censorship, and criticism, which would join obtrusive suppression to a continuum that also includes active support or patronage, as in the support Middleton received from the city for his civic entertainments or his masques.

Consider first market censorship. It is often assumed that court censorship is radically different from market censorship—the one blocking production, the other blocking consumption—but it is not always easy to tell them apart. Middleton's tragicomedy *The Witch* illustrates this ambiguity by showing that it is difficult to differentiate a censorship practiced by the court from a censorious reception on the stage. *The Witch* exists only in a single manuscript, and the evidence of its production on stage is contained in a note by Middleton. He explains to Thomas Holmes, the person for whom the manuscript was made, that he has

> (meerly uppon a tast of yor. desire) recouverd into my hands (though not without much difficultie) This (ignorantly-ill-fated) Labour of mine. Witches are (ipso facto) by ye Law condemned, & yt onely (I thinck) hath made her lie so long in an imprisoned obscuritie.[36]

Anne Lancashire has suggested that the phrase "ignorantly-ill-fated" refers not to the play's failure on the stage, as is frequently assumed, but to its political censorship by the Master of the Revels.[37] By contrast, I would argue that the phrase is ambiguous: it may be taken literally or metaphorically since the play's lack of stage productions could have been due either to censorship by the court or to what was termed "censureship" on the public stage.[38]

We can further understand the way that censorship extends to the regulation of consumption by looking at Middleton's reception by competing dramatists. Criticism is a form of censorship insofar as it involves legitimating certain dramatic discourses and delegitimating others. Criticism operates productively in terms of establishing exclusive hierarchies and repressively as censure (the aim being a kind of postpublication censorship) in order to secure these hierarchies.[39] In the productive sense, criticism, as a form of patronage, establishes capital through elitist forms of censorship: the exclusiveness of a given performance is part of its appeal. The nonalienability of a court masque, say, helps create a sense of the court as the charismatic center of power.[40]

Criticism operated repressively as delegitimating censure. Dramatists like

Ben Jonson and George Chapman who sought to establish literary hierarchies as a way of reforming what they took to be the unacceptable diversity of the popular theaters had little regard for Middleton. In his epistle to his translation of Homer, Chapman used Middleton as an example of Londoners' bad taste, saying that they preferred Middleton's Lord Mayor's pageant, *The Triumphs of Truth*, to Homer: "Why should a poor Chroonicler of a Lord Maior's naked Truth, (that peradduenture will last his yeare) include more worth with our moderne wizerds, then *Homer* for his naked *Vlysses*, clad in eternall Fiction?"[41] Ben Jonson was even more censorious. In *Conversations with Drummond*, he remarks "that Markham (who added his English Arcadia) was not of the number of the Faithful Poets and but a base fellow that such were Day and Middleton."[42] He excoriated *A Game at Chess* in *The Staple of News* (1626):

> Lickfinger. What newes of Gundomar?
> Thomas. A second *Fistula*,
> Or an *excoriation* (at the least)
> For putting the porre *English-play*, was writ of him,
> To such a sordid use, as (is said) he did,
> Of clensing his *posterior's*.
> Lickfinger. Iustice! Iustice!
> Thomas. Since when, he lives condemn'd to his Chaire, at *Bruxels*.
> And there sits filling certaine politique hinges,
> To hang the States on, h'has heau'd off the hookes.[43]

The use of a text for toilet paper is as effective a means of taking it out of circulation as burning it. It is worth noting that Middleton too engaged in critical practices. He wrote a commendatory poem to accompany the first publication of *The Duchess of Malfi* and an epitaph on the actor Richard Burbage. Furthermore, references to plays are scattered throughout his dramatic and nondramatic works. He offered an appreciation of Joseph Hall in the prefatory matter to *Two Gates of Salvation* (1609) and praised Thomas Dekker and *Utopia* in *The Owl's Almanac* (1618).

Just as the complicity of censorship with criticism extends to all areas of literary consumption, both permissive and prohibitive, so too does it extend to all areas of literary production. A number of critics have recently called into question the notion of an original unrevised authentic draft.[44] Texts are always already-revised versions originating out of impure, heteroglossic conversations. Although some manuscripts may rightly be identified as "authorial" for editorial purposes, there is no unrevised *Urtext* originating out of a single author sitting in his private study.

Our consideration of Middleton allows us to extend this insight into authorial revision to censorship: if texts cannot be unrevised, they cannot be uncensored either. The differences among some of the manuscripts of *A Game at Chess* make it clear that just as there is no point at which one can locate an unrevised text, so there is no point at which one can locate an uncensored text. In discussing the lengths of the various manuscripts, critics have differentiated between more complete or less complete versions of the play in terms of whether passages in one version that were not in another were added after the play was licensed and, if so, whether the censor knew of them.[45] Censorship of the play only makes sense for these critics if, at some point in the production of the play, the author or the actors circumvented the censor's wishes. These critics assume that authorial and theatrical revision can be separated from censorship, and that Middleton, at the actor's instigation, revised in order to add passages that he had feared the censor might not approve. The actors might also have made a clear equation between the hated Spanish Ambassador Gondomar and the Black Knight by using Gondomar's litter (which was required to relieve discomfort from an anal fistula) and one of his suits, thereby changing the text's meaning in a way that the court censor presumably could not have anticipated. One critic has used textual evidence to explain the censorship of the play in precisely these terms: "It is almost certain that the playbook which Henry Herbert licensed was somewhat less provocative than the play seen on the stage of the Globe."[46]

Given the complicity between the playhouse and the Master of the Revels, however, there is no reason to assume that the additions amounted to an evasion of what are presumed to be the censor's politically more conservative desires. As Trevor Howard-Hill points out, "It is unlikely that the actors would commission a substantial revision unless they were already convinced they could go ahead with performances."[47] He maintains that the additions make no serious difference: "That the Black Knight represents Gondomar is transparent in the early version; the additions make the satire no more offensive than it was in the manuscript Herbert approved."[48] He adds, "It is possible that Herbert himself might have encouraged enlargement of the satirical depiction of Gondomar."[49] Indeed, the revisions may have been corrections by the Master.[50] In any case, the actors maintained that they had not performed more than had been licensed. When the Privy Council demanded "whether there were noe other parts or passages represented on the Stage then those expressly contayned in the Booke, they confidently said they added or varied from the same, nothing at all."[51]

Whereas critics have tended to assume that the manuscripts of *A Game at Chess* can be clearly positioned along a line beginning with an uncensored early draft and ending with a licensed final draft in the form of a promptbook or a first edition, I would argue that the manuscripts suggest the reverse. Rather than moving toward a final full draft either in manuscript form or printed form, Middleton and the scribes he used put different versions, some shorter and some longer, into different kinds of circulation. As Howard-Hill points out, "textual analysis reveals that Middleton had decided to make transcripts for sale even before the play had been revised for performance."[52] In one case, a presentation copy was shorter than the performance copy.

Whether any manuscript is an incomplete transcript or an early draft, whether the additions or omissions were made by the author or by the scribe acting as an editor, or whether the additions involved an evasion of the censor or were suggested by the censor may sometimes all be, in my view, undecidable questions. If there is no moment at which we can definitively establish the author's unrevised text, that is because there is no uncensored original any more than there is an unrevised original. Any search for the origin of censorship will be frustrated by an infinite regression: court censorship (defined in its repressive and productive senses) generates self-censorship in the actors and the author that may be regarded with equal validity either as being an anticipation of court censorship or as following after the suggestions and demands of the censor. The various versions of *A Game at Chess* suggest that censorship was a negotiation over what would or would not play in a number of different venues, not the establishment of a monumental, authorized, final version.

The details of Middleton's censored plays alert us to a structural complicity that is much deeper than critics have thus far allowed, a complicity not between opposed agents and spaces but between regulatory agencies at all points of literary production and consumption. I hope it is now clear that this structural complicity significantly changes our understanding of censorship from a practice that operates in terms of removal and replacement to one that operates in terms of dispersal and displacement. The dispersal of censorship decenters the court censor, who occupies one of many competing sites of authorization and license that legitimate particular revisions. He is not at the apex of power but is caught up in a contestation over who is going to censor, on the basis of what criteria, and to what extent. Censorship is as much about displacing one version with another, and displacing texts from one channel to another, as it is about blocking access or destroying transgressive material. As Thomas Cogswell notes in a discussion of censorship in the 1620s:

> Political tracts, sermons and verse, which had no hope of receiving a license, could find a wide circulation in the unofficial market for news. Lack of access to a printing press was not a crippling blow.... Few authors slipped ... direct criticism into print in 1623. Yet the government's particularly tight control of the press in this period did not forestall similar efforts; it simply forced them into channels that newsletters-writers had developed for circulating their manuscripts.[53]

Similarly, the *Acte to Restraine Abuses of Players* was directed only at profanity in performance, not in print. The crosses in the manuscript of *The Second Maiden's Tragedy,* for example, may mark passages for removal only during the text's performance.

Having established the way censorship operates in terms of dispersal and displacement, we can begin to appreciate the way censorship functions fetishistically in the literary field. Displacement is not just about more or less narrow kinds of readership and access, but involves a differential system in which texts circulate and become exchangeable by becoming cultural and economic capital. It involves the commodification of small differences meant to increase the text's value, either by limiting a text's circulation (the fact that it is not available elsewhere gives the manuscript reader, for example, an elevated status as critic, insider, and so on) or by exceeding the limits previously placed on a text's circulation—the full uncensored text, as opposed to another version of its performance. As Gary Taylor remarks in a discussion of expurgated texts,

> although profanities could not be played, they could be printed, or circulated in manuscript.... Once authors and publishers recognize a distinction between the play as performance and the play as literary commodity, the door is opened to various literary embellishments of the theatrical text, including particularly the restoration of material cut in performance.[54]

Commodities are fetishized not, as Marxists have argued, because they are reified, alienable products of labor, but because their value as economic and cultural capital is created within an intensely differentiated literary field.[55] As I am defining it, however, commodity fetishism is not just economic or even primarily economic. Cultural critics (Marxists foremost among them) assume that the market precedes the literary, that fetishism depends on the market: a commodity aesthetic, so the argument goes, is an effect of capitalism.[56] Marxists assume that a specifically literary marketplace follows upon the emergence of a generalized marketplace. I am suggesting that the opposite is the case: the commodity is an aftereffect of the literary and is modeled upon the literary form: indeed fetishism creates the market, not the reverse. The proliferation of manuscripts of *A Game at Chess* is due, as we have seen, to the perceived markets for them, some being sold and others presented as gifts; markets here are understood to include economic and cultural capital (although patrons sometimes made cash payments, the cash could be less important than the prestige attached to their patronage). I am suggesting, moreover, that all number of texts, ranging from those privately circulated as manuscripts to those publicly circulated as printed texts, and those privately performed to those performed at court, could be commodities only because they had already been fetishized. What looks like historical specificity from a Marxist perspective—the emergence of a literary marketplace in the sixteenth century—is, rather, a misrecognized instance of a critical fetishism: "history" is fetishized as that which stands outside of fetishism.

Some critics might object to my account of censorship as a fetishistic practice on several grounds. Even if texts are not wholly blocked but displaced from one medium or channel to another, they might argue, it would still be crucial to differentiate between more or less narrow channels, "softer" or "harder" forms of censorship, and greater or lesser access and availability of a text to readers and of performances to spectators. Indeed, some critics might argue that the most diverse range of texts and performances ought to be able to circulate as broadly and as freely in as big and heterogeneous a market as possible, and if discourses and their circulation were truly diverse and truly free of censorship (in its repressive sense), displacements from official to unofficial channels would not be necessary.

While I am sympathetic to what I would call the "diversity position," I also think that many of its fundamental assumptions about censorship as a strictly repressive agency are untenable. To begin with, the circulation of discourses depends on their being commodities. This paradoxically both makes access and entry possible and limits what, where, and how texts can circulate; commodity fetishism is not an antidote to regulation but is itself another (paradoxical) form of regulation. A related problem with the diversity position is the correlative assumption that there is a strong opposition between direct and indirect criticism, between official and unofficial discourses—that is, an uncensored text would be direct, immediately readable, and, in short, nonliterary (unambiguous, without irony or equivocation). Yet nonliterary texts were prosecuted on the basis of their perceived literary strategies, not because of their naked, unveiled attacks on the Crown. For example, William Prynne's index entry to *Histrio-mastrix,* "women actors, notorious whores," was taken (mistaken, Prynne maintained) as an attempt to parallel classical Roman and contemporary Caroline courts, to the massive discredit of both.[57]

Moreover, the diversity position assumes that uncensored versions of a text existed, however difficult they might be to read. The uncensored version might be an unperformed manuscript, a printed text containing material that had been censored for performance, or a performance of a text. The fetishistic proliferation in the literary field of small differences, resulting in the multiple versions of the text (censorship being one location of the construction of such differences), contradicts this assumption, however. No one medium can be said by definition to be more radical, more free, or less subject to censorship than another. More precisely, censorship functions fetishistically in allowing such a claim to be made for all media. Hence print can be regarded as fuller than manuscript because it allows for greater access; conversely, a manuscript can also be regarded as fuller precisely because it was not subject to state censorship (*Hengist, King of Kent,* for example, exists in two manuscripts that are fuller than the 1661 printed version). Similarly, theater may be regarded as harder to police than print because performance is more fluid, allowing the actors to inflect the text's meanings through gestures and props, while, conversely, print may be regarded as fuller than performance because it includes material censored for the stage.

But in none of these cases, I would argue, is one getting a completely uncensored version of a text. Middleton's plays show us, rather, that if censoring is always a matter of censoring in detail, then it follows that there is no whole uncensored original version but a proliferation of always already-revised, always already-partial, always already-censored versions. In clarifying the way that texts are always already censored, Middleton allows us to see that early modern textual culture was not only fetishized but hyperfetishized. In psychoanalytic terms, the fetish "replaces" what was never there to be removed in the first place, the mother's phallus: the fetishist misreads sexual difference, substituting an originary fullness for an originary lack. To paraphrase Octave Mannoni's account of the logic of fetishism as a knowledge and disavowal of sexual difference *("Je sais bien, mais quand même...")*,[58] we might say that the logic of censorship is as follows: "I know very well that texts are always already censored. Nevertheless, I want the uncensored version of this text."

Fetishizing censorship means affirming yet disavowing a difference between censored and uncensored texts. Through hyperfetishism, fetishistic affirmation and disavowal of textual difference is projected in different ways along multiple axes. Texts enter circulation at a variety of points, becoming commodities in terms of various kinds of small differences, not only between more or less accessible texts but also between more or less well-bound, more or less expensive, more or less well-printed editions. More significant is the fact that commodification both permits and excludes entry to the literary field on the basis of whether or not a text can succeed in the marketplace. Hyperfetishism draws our attention to the fact that censorship is not reducible to repression: mainstreaming is not always easy to distinguish from its opposite—namely, censorship in the sense of exclusion and marginalization—since a text must accommodate the constraints of the commodity form in order to circulate.

What, if any, are the implications of this analysis of censorship for our understanding of censorship in the postmodern present? Some critics, especially those on the left who think of themselves as opposed to censorship, might ask a series of related questions: Won't some normative model of censorship be employed when a particular cultural artifact comes under fire? And won't a deconstructive model of censorship merely obfuscate matters when actual concrete cultural texts are under fire? Won't censorship lead, as deconstructive criticism is generally reputed to do, to political quietism?

Rather than address these questions directly, I think it is more useful to reflect on the pressure behind them—not only the pressure the public intellectual feels to find an effective means of intervening in contemporary debates and struggles over practices of censorship but also, more broadly, the pressure he or she feels to legitimate his or her status as an intellectual in a mediatized age. What the desire for a definition of censorship often entails, I suggest, is a fetishism of political criticism. "Politics" gets its force only through a series of repressions and constitutive exclusions, only through a foreclosure of the question of what counts as legitimate criticism.

In discussions of censorship critics typically agree that censorship in the traditional sense is a bad thing and must be checked.[59] Two kinds of positions regularly emerge, however, given that censorship is no longer institutionalized in a censorship office but dispersed across a wide range of sites and agencies: in one view, censorship must be broadened to include market forces, government agencies awarding grants, museum curators, newspapers, and so on. In the other, censorship must be kept to a narrow definition so as to avoid confusing it with regulatory mechanisms that are distinct from it. In my view, this debate persists in ways that are not very productive. It does not secure the aim of those who oppose censorship, because censorship now has no fixed place; it can no longer be located in a censor. Instead, censorship, or what might be better marked as "censorship," can be located virtually anywhere: not only in the marketplace and in government agencies like the NEA. but also in the institution of criticism itself (one man's criticism is another man's censorship).[60]

While I too think that censorship as it is traditionally defined is a bad thing, I think it is more productive to examine the ways in which cultural critics and legal theorists paradoxically reinscribe the very kinds of exclusions and foreclosures they seek to overcome when they attempt to arrive at a functionally oppositional mode of evaluating censorship. In putting into question the integrity of censorship as a discursive concept, I also implicitly put into question the integrity of related concepts. Precisely because censorship is a process of displacement rather than a process with a fixed place, it cannot stand as a master concept to which concepts like fetishism and criticism would be subordinate.

At stake for the coherence of concepts such as censorship, fetishism, aestheticism, and criticism is the capacity of the intellectual to speak not only in the public sphere but also, more crucially, to the state as an expert witness. At the Getty seminar, several contributors mentioned that they or someone they knew had spoken to government officials like Lynne Cheney, past chairman of the National Endowment for the Humanities, or testified against censorship before congressional subcommittees and presidential commissions. It was clear that these critics counted performing for the state in the name of opposing its attempts to censor as among the most serious things one could do as an intellectual. Intellectual seriousness has come to mean crossing over from the classroom into the congressional hearing room.

Yet cultural critics regularly doubt criticism's capacity for serious political opposition. Consider Houston Baker's comments about critics like Henry Louis Gates, Jr., who testified in court on behalf of the rap group 2 Live Crew (whose album *As Nasty as They Wanna Be* was being prosecuted for obscenity). Baker criticizes what he calls the "start in the middle of the game" expert witnessing practiced by other critics:

> The demand felt by forty-something experts seems to be to get "hip" and provide instant replay analysis in the fashion of commentators for Monday night football. However, the instant-replay mode vis-à-vis historically situated and resonantly important forms of transnational cultural expressiveness constitutes only a self-aggrandizing act of scholarly hipsterism. It is, one might say, a totally self-interested form of popular hucksterism.[61]

According to Baker, critics like Gates are so enamored of celebrity that they rush to testify in what are less legal trials than media events, and in the process they actually put criticism aside, never pausing to reflect on whether a group like 2 Live Crew should be defended (Baker thinks not). Baker contrasts this irresponsible, media-oriented hucksterism to his own responsible in-depth knowledge of rap as a black studies scholar. I would argue that Baker's distinction between expertise and "instant replay analysis" is really a distinction between the hip and the hipper. The trumping of instant expertise by in-depth knowledge does not really serve to uphold Baker's morally serious distinction because his in-depth knowledge is an attempt (in my view a failed one, since he was not invited to testify in court) to establish himself as the one who is really in the know—that is to say, the one who is really hip.

The very contamination of serious expertise by trendy hipness (and, by extension, media celebrity) threatens to trivialize not only the critic's capacity to testify in court against censorship but to function as a serious public intellectual. Again and again, one hears from a variety of critics, those who oppose and those who defend cultural criticism, that criticism, insofar as it focuses on culture or on the media, is either insignificant or irrelevant or merely gives voice to "academic" politics. This is particularly a problem for critics who seek to oppose censorship not just through more speech, as traditional liberals do, but through a performative, transgressive mode of criticism that subverts the impact of censorship by resignifying and thereby parodying social norms. In his book *Homos,* for example, Leo Bersani scathingly criticizes the political emptiness of Judith Butler's performative notion of subversive parody:

> At its worst, the emphasis on parody in *Gender Trouble* has the effect of exaggerating the subversive potential of merely inane behavior.... Resignification cannot destroy; it merely presents to the dominant culture spectacles of politically impotent disrespect. Is this truly subversive, and, more fundamentally, what does subversion mean? Subversion, still a central term in Butler's thinking, means first of all, according to the dictionary, overthrowing a system, but in current academic political discourse it seems to mean something weaker than that, referring to behavior that undermines general principles. In any case, it is extremely doubtful that resignification, or redeployment, or hyperbolic miming, will ever overthrow anything.[62]

To avoid the trivializing of their efforts, critics like Butler, for whom all discourse is performative, implicitly retain a modified Austinian account of speech acts such that J. L. Austin's distinction between performative and constative speech acts is not actually totally dissolved.[63] If everything is a performance, it seems that certain performatives, particularly those having to do with the law, are not subject to irony: they are totally serious. Apparently not everything can be folded into subversive parody. Through this implicit modification of Austin, the critic appears to assume uncritically that two significant effects are secured. First, the split between theory and activism (which haunts so much queer theory) is apparently reconciled: one can speak to the state as a theorist and as an activist at the same time. Second, having secured the seriousness of criticism by seeing it in nonironized, nonparodic terms, one can chiasmatically reintroduce the performative: when one speaks to the state one is not bound by its sometimes censorious norms. The performative speech act would appear to operate, that is, against the foreclosure of subjectivities, against censorship.[64] Critics like Butler appear to want it both ways: on the one hand, they want to adopt a normative position—they want to speak not just in public but to the state because they have a certain academic authority; on the other hand, they want to adopt a transgressive position—they want to oppose not only specific policies but the codes and strategies of normalization.

Yet far from actually reconciling antagonisms between theory and activism or academic politics and real politics, or producing a transgressive critique of normalization, this modified Austinian account of speech acts actually exacerbates the problem it appears to resolve—namely, the triviality of criticism. One finds no concern to persuade the state: there is no attempt to learn if the government official or the congressional committee has listened to the critic, no attempt is made to determine if minds have been changed. Only the performance—the act of testimony—counts: it does not matter if one performs before other academics or before senators.[65] Insofar as performance and parody are aligned, the performative speech act is subject to a much deeper, more corrosive irony than Butler appears to allow. Hence a critic like Butler will always be vulnerable to Bersani's charge that a media centered politics of resignification will be unimportant and will always be trumped by "real" politics.

For criticism to have a normative or a transgressive function, what must be foreclosed, if not entirely repressed (and understood as such by political critics themselves), is what I call the critic's professional unconscious.[66] In my view, the professional unconscious will exceed any attempt to subsume cultural criticism immediately and totally within a political unconscious.[67] As I conceptualize it, the "raw" data that constitute the discourses of the professional unconscious include introductions to books by critics other than the book's author, introductions to special issues of academic journals, book jacket blurbs, book reviews in academic journals and mainstream newspapers and magazines, gossip, letters of recommendation, notes on contributors in essay anthologies, footnotes, prefaces, acknowledgments, printed and televised interviews, memorial issues of journals dedicated to recently dead critics, eulogies, the use of visual technologies in teaching, the use of photography in journalistic coverage of academia and on book covers, letters to the editor, and "tabloid" journals like *Lingua Franca* and *Heterodoxy*.

Any critique of the professional unconscious would miss the point were it to assume that the unconscious constitutes the "uncensored" truth of the profession. That would merely reinscribe a division between criticism and tabloid journalism, replace dismissing marginal criticism or attention to it (on grounds that it is rude, partial, distorting, irresponsible, mean-spirited, or sensationalizing) with embracing it as the "censored" (all too scandalous) truth of the profession. My point is precisely that there is no clear separation between tabloid journalism, conceived of as trivial, and legitimate criticism, conceived of as serious. The force of my analysis of censorship is to suggest that we consider the possibility of an alternative mode of "criticism" altogether, a hybrid of critical and tabloid—fanzine—discourses, a genre I term *critizine*. Critizine is bastard criticism, paradoxically fragmented and coherent, that is disseminated in both written forms and oral presentations (the talk show, the interview, and so on). It seeks not to define the proper subject of criticism so that it may effectively "intervene," but plays out the consequences that arise when criticism lacks a definitively proper subject. Although at certain points transgressive, tabloid discourses like gossip cannot be comfortably or entirely assimilated to recognizably legitimate transgressive critical discourses.[68] This is to say that transgressive criticism has its own norms too, norms that may entail the exclusion and even demonization of discourses like fanzines. Precisely because there will always be a conflict over what counts as criticism, there will always be a range of discourses that cross the boundary between legitimate and illegitimate criticism. Because it is not a unified, effective oppositional criticism, critizine brings into relief the way the status and value of criticism are always in question, most of all for critics themselves. It enjoys the symptoms of criticism, reading the local ways in which self-deconstructing oppositions between high and low culture, between the hegemonic or normative and the "transgressive" or "subversive," between the new and important and the trendy and trivial, between the censored and uncensored, and so on, both enable and disable the production of legitimate criticism.

Notes

1. See, for example, Margot Heinemann, *Puritanism and Theatre: Thomas Middleton and Opposition Drama under the Early Stuarts* (Cambridge: Cambridge Univ. Press, 1980); Annabel M. Patterson, *Censorship and Interpretation: The Conditions of Writing and Reading in Early Modern England* (Madison: Univ. Wisconsin Press, 1984); Philip J. Finkelpearl, "'The Comedian's Liberty': Jacobean Censorship Reconsidered," *English Literary Renaissance* 16, no. 1 (1986): 123–38; Kevin Sharpe, *Criticism and Compliment: The Politics of Literature in the England of Charles I* (Cambridge: Cambridge Univ. Press, 1987); A. B. Worden, "Literature and Political Censorship in Early Modern England," in A. C. Duke and C. A. Tamse, eds., *Too Mighty to Be Free: Censorship and the Press in Britain and the Netherlands* (Zutphen: De Walburg Press, 1988), 45–62; Janet Clare, *'Art Made Tongue-Tied by Authority': Elizabethan and Jacobean Dramatic Censorship* (Manchester: Manchester Univ. Press, 1990); and Richard Dutton, *Mastering the Revels: The Regulation and Censorship of English Renaissance Drama* (Iowa City: Univ. Iowa Press, 1991).

2. For a fuller account of this definition of censorship, see Richard Burt, *Licensed by Authority: Ben Jonson and the Discourses of Censorship* (Ithaca: Cornell Univ. Press, 1993); Richard Burt, "Baroque Down: The Trauma of Censorship in Psychoanalysis and Queer Film Re-visions of Shakespeare and Marlowe," in Michael Hattaway, Boika Sokolova, and Derek Roper, eds., *Shakespeare in the New Europe* (Sheffield: Sheffield Academic Press, 1994), 328–50; Richard Burt, "Introduction: The 'New' Censorship," in Richard Burt, ed., *The Administration of Aesthetics: Censorship, Political Criticism, and the Public Sphere* (Minneapolis: Univ. Minnesota Press, 1994), xi–xxix; Richard Burt, "Uncut: Castration, Censorship, and the Regulation of Middleton's Dramatic Discourse," in Gary Taylor, ed., *Thomas Middleton and Early Modern Textual Culture* (Oxford: Oxford Univ. Press, 1998); and Pierre Bourdieu, "Censorship and the Imposition of Form," in idem, *Language and Symbolic Power,* ed. John B. Thompson, trans. Gino Raymond and Matthew Adamson (Cambridge, Mass.: Harvard Univ. Press, 1991), 137–59.

For a Foucaultian account of censorship, see Francis Barker, *The Tremulous Private Body: Essays on Subjection* (New York: Methuen, 1984). For an opposing humanist account, see Patterson (see note 1); Annabel Patterson, "Censorship," in Martin Coyle et al., eds., *The Encyclopedia of Literature and Criticism* (London: Routledge, 1990), 901–14; and David Norbrook, "*Areopagitica,* Censorship, and the Early Modern Public Sphere," in Burt, *The Administration of Aesthetics* (see above), 3–33.

3. See, for example, a print in John Foxe's *Actes and monuments...* (1563) illustrating the burning of heretical books by Martin Bucer. At the center of the illustration is a pile of books being burned. In front of this pile is a procession of priests reading books accompanied by torch bearers. As in executions, the burning is a public performance: fire takes on metaphoric significance, not only as a purifying agent (destroying the corrupting influences of heretical books) but also as a source of religious illumination—the torches "light the way," as it were, toward the true Church.

4. In addition to *A Game at Chess,* which is perhaps the best known case of censorship in the Renaissance, one that continues to receive sustained attention is Middleton's *The Second Maiden's Tragedy.* Two of his other plays, *Hengist, King of Kent* and *The Witch,* may also have been censored. On *Hengist,* see *Hengist, King of Kent; or The Mayor of Queensborough,* ed. R. C. Bald (New York: Charles Scribner's Sons, 1938); and Grace Ioppolo, "Introduction to *Hengist, King of Kent,*" in Thomas Middleton, *The Collected Works of Thomas Middleton,* ed. Gary Taylor et al. (Oxford: Oxford Univ. Press, 1998). On *The Witch,* see Anne Lancashire, "*The Witch:* Stage Flop or Political Mistake?" in Kenneth Friedenreich, ed., "*Accompaninge the players": Essays Celebrating Thomas Middleton, 1580–1980* (New York: AMS Press, 1983), 161–82. The cases themselves are often extremely detailed. There are six manuscripts and three printed quartos of *A Game at Chess,* the total number of manuscripts being significantly larger than that of any other Renaissance play; the single manuscript of *The Second Maiden's Tragedy* contains evidence of censorship in the censor's own hand. Moreover, there is an unusually full record of contemporary responses to *A Game at Chess,* including a lengthy eyewitness account. For the audience response to *A Game at Chess,* see Trevor Howard-Hill's "Appendix A," in

Thomas Middleton, *A Game at Chess,* ed. Trevor H. Howard-Hill (Manchester: Manchester Univ. Press, 1993).

5. Patterson (see note 1), 17. Patterson cites *A Game at Chess* as one of her examples of noncensorship cases. Janet Clare (see note 1) and Richard Dutton (see note 1) have confirmed her point. Heinemann (see note 1) says, along similar lines: "The question remains: given the censorship, how was it possible for the play to be put on at all?" (165). For further details, see Howard-Hill's appendix to Middleton, *A Game at Chess* (see note 4), 22. For an opposing account of the play and of Middleton's career, one that stresses Middleton's progressive politics, see Gary Taylor, "The Renaissance and the End of Editing," in *Palimpsest* (Ann Arbor: Univ. Michigan Press, 1993), 121–49.

6. Those who believe that theater censorship was repressive might take as further proof of Middleton's lack of favor with the court the facts that Middleton did not write for the stage after *A Game at Chess* and that his entertainment for Charles I (paid for by the City of London) was cancelled. Given the paradoxical reception of *A Game at Chess* by the court, it is difficult to see Middleton's withdrawal from the stage as a consequence of that reception. Howard-Hill (see note 4) comments: "The official reaction to *A Game at Chess* was not harsh" (22). He notes that

> James, Charles and Buckingham "were all loth to haue it forbidden, and by report laught hartely at it" . . . and [John Woolley] later passed on the rumour "(how true it is I know not) that the Players are gone to the Courte to Act the game at Chesse before the Kinge, which cloth much trublle the spanish Amba*ssador*." (ibid.)

7. For fuller accounts of this case, see Howard-Hill (see note 4); Clare (see note 1); and Dutton (see note 1).

8. Pierre Bourdieu, *The Field of Cultural Production: Essays on Art and Literature,* ed. Randal Johnson (New York: Columbia Univ. Press, 1993). See also Pierre Bourdieu, *Distinction: A Social Critique of the Judgement of Taste,* trans. Richard Nice (Cambridge, Mass.: Harvard Univ. Press, 1984); and Bourdieu, "Censorship and the Imposition of Form" (see note 2). For a New Historicist use of Bourdieu, see Stephen Greenblatt, *Shakespearean Negotiations: The Circulation of Social Energy in Renaissance England* (Berkeley: Univ. California Press, 1988).

9. Naomi Schor, *Reading in Detail: Aesthetics and the Feminine* (New York: Methuen, 1987). For a psychoanalytic account of fetishism, see Sigmund Freud, "Fetishism," in idem, *Sexuality and the Psychology of Love,* ed. Philip Rieff (New York: Collier, 1963), 214–19. On fetishism and displacement, see Sigmund Freud, *An Outline of Psychoanalysis,* trans. James Strachey (New York: Norton, 1969); and Mark Wigley, "Theoretical Slippage," in Sarah Whiting, ed., *Fetish* (Princeton: Princeton Journal and Princeton Architectural Journal, 1992), 88–129.

10. A version of this model is constructed by Gary Taylor in his "General Introduction," in Stanley Wells and Gary Taylor, eds., *William Shakespeare: A Textual Companion* (Oxford: Clarendon Press, 1987).

11. Great Britain, Office of the Revels, *The Dramatic Records of Sir Henry Herbert, Master of the Revels, 1574–1673,* ed. Joseph Quincy Adams (New Haven: Yale Univ. Press, 1917), 23.

12. E. K. Chambers, *The Elizabethan Stage,* 4 vols. (Oxford: Clarendon Press, 1923), 4: 339.

13. Clare (see note 1), 158.

14. Ibid., 159.

15. Ibid., 157.

16. Bald (see note 4), xxx–xxxiii.

17. Ioppolo (see note 4).

18. Gary Taylor, "'Zounds' Revisited: Theatrical, Editorial, and Literary Expurgation," in Gary Taylor and John Jowett, eds., *Shakespeare Reshaped: 1606–1623* (Oxford: Oxford Univ. Press, 1993).

19. David J. Lake, *The Canon of Thomas Middleton's Plays: Internal Evidence for the Major Problems of Authorship* (Cambridge: Cambridge Univ. Press, 1975), 79.

20. Dutton (see note 1), 203.

21. Clare (see note 1); Dutton (see note 1); and Martin Butler, "Ecclesiastical Censorship of Early Stuart Drama: The Case of Jonson's *The Magnetic Lady,*" *Modern Philology* 89 (1992): 469–81.

22. Dutton (see note 1), 247–48.

23. On spying and the theater, see John Michael Archer, *Sovereignty and Intelligence: Spying and Court Culture in the English Renaissance* (Stanford: Stanford Univ. Press, 1993). The use of spies and informers formed part of a larger pattern of administrative dispersal in early Stuart culture. On this pattern, see Linda Levy Peck, *Northampton: Patronage and Policy at the Court of James I* (London: Allen & Unwin, 1982).

24. Clare (see note 1).

25. Patterson's contribution (see note 1) is perhaps strongest in this regard. She has been seconded directly by Richard Dutton (see note 1) and indirectly by Natalie Davis, "Rabelais Among the Censors: 1940's 1540s," *Representations* 32 (1990): 1–26; and Robert Darnton, "The Good Old Days," *New York Review of Books* 38, no. 9 (1991): 44–48.

26. Dutton (see note 1).

27. Thomas Middleton, *The Second Maiden's Tragedy,* ed. Anne Lancashire (Baltimore: Johns Hopkins Univ. Press, 1978), 47; Clare (see note 1), 161; Dutton (see note 1), 198.

28. Gary Taylor (see note 5) finds similar synonyms in expurgated and nonexpurgated oaths in Shakespeare editions.

29. Lancashire (see note 27), 47, 276–77; Clare (see note 1), 161; Dutton (see note 1), 198.

30. Lancashire (see note 27) uses it to explain censorship of *The Second Maiden's Tragedy* and to explain censorship of *The Witch.* The same allusion has been used to interpret *The Changeling* as well. See Christina Malcolmson, "'As Tame as the Ladies': Politics and Gender in *The Changeling,*" *English Literary Renaissance* 20, no. 2 (1990): 320–39. As will become clear in the second section of this essay, I think the underlying premises of this kind of topical identification bear scrutiny.

31. Lancashire (see note 27), 280–81.

32. One could contrast this example as a soft version of censorship to a hard

example such as the revision of "Yor kinges poisond" to "I am poisond." I would only observe that the displacement of one phrase by another complicates the degree to which both soft and hard instances may function smoothly as acceptable replacements. Consider again the substitution of women for court politics. Anne Lancashire (see note 28) notes "the odd substitution of 'woman' for 'courtier'" at 2.1.76, which she points out "removes one kind of criticism only to add the other" (277). "Woman" also figures as an object of censorship in *Hengist* at 4.2.268; see Heinemann (see note 1), 144.

33. For a fuller account of the relation between criticism and censorship, see Burt, *Licensed by Authority* (see note 2), 27–77; and Burt, "Introduction: the 'New' Censorship" (see note 2).

34. Clare (see note 1), 165.

35. Adams, in *The Dramatic Records of Sir Henry Herbert* (see note 11), 26.

36. Sara J. Steen, *Ambrosia in an Earthern Vessel: Three Centuries of Audience and Reader Response to the Works of Thomas Middleton* (New York: AMS Press, 1993), 36.

37. Lancashire (see note 27), 162–63.

38. For instances of *censureship* and for an account of the way its meaning overlapped with *censorship* and *criticism,* see Burt, *Licensed by Authority* (see note 2), 30–31, 53, 65.

39. Middleton's court patronage can be reviewed in Yoshiko Kawachi, *Calendar of English Renaissance Drama, 1558–1642* (New York: Garland Publishing, 1986).

40. On the breakdown of a distinction between the masque as inalienable and public theatrical performances of dramatic texts as alienable under the early Stuarts, see Burt, *Licensed by Authority* (see note 1), 115–49.

41. Quoted in Steen (see note 36), 30–3.

42. Ibid., 35.

43. Quoted in Howard-Hill's appendix to *A Game at Chess* (see note 4), 212.

44. See Stephen Orgel, "The Authentic Shakespeare," *Representations* 21 (1988): 1–26; Leah Marcus, "The Shakespearean Editor as Shrew-Tamer," *English Literary Renaissance* 22, no. 2 (1992): 177–200; and Taylor, "The Renaissance and the End of Editing" (see note 5).

45. Dutton (see note 1); Clare (see note 1); Howard-Hill (see note 4).

46. Clare (see note 1), 193.

47. Howard-Hill (see note 4), 18.

48. Ibid., 19.

49. Ibid., 32.

50. Ibid., 19.

51. Dutton (see note 1), 244.

52. Howard-Hill (see note 4), 4.

53. Thomas Cogswell, *The Blessed Revolution: English Politics and the Coming of War* (Cambridge: Cambridge Univ. Press, 1989), 21 and 45.

54. Taylor, "The Renaissance and the End of Editing" (see note 5), 147.

55. See Karl Marx, "The Fetishism of Commodities and the Secret Thereof," in idem, *Capital: A Critique of Political Economy,* vol. 1, ed. Frederick Engels, trans.

Samuel Moore and Edward Aveling (New York: International Publishers, 1967), 71–83; and Georg Lukacs, "Reificiation and Class Consciousness," in idem, *History and Class Consciousness: Studies in Marxist Dialectics,* trans. Rodney Livingstone (Cambridge: MIT Press, 1968), 183–222. For an explicit critique of Marxist notions of commodity fetishism, see Jean Baudrillard, "Fetishism and Ideology: The Semiological Reduction," in idem, *For a Critique of the Political Economy of the Sign,* trans. Charles Levin (St. Louis: Telos Press, 1981), 88–101. See also the essays in Emily Apter and William Pietz, eds., *Fetishism as Cultural Discourse* (Ithaca: Cornell Univ. Press, 1993).

56. Wolfgang Fritz Haug, *Critique of Commodity Aesthetics: Appearance, Sexuality, and Advertising in Capitalist Society,* trans. Robert Bock (Minneapolis: Univ. Minnesota Press, 1986).

57. William Prynne, *Histrio-mastrix* (London, 1632).

58. Octave Mannoni, *Clefs pour l'imaginaire; ou, l'autre scene* (Paris: Editions du Seuil, 1969), 174.

59. In this collection, perhaps Debora Shuger, who sees civility as a benefit of censorship, is an exception; see pages 89–110.

60. I elaborate further on the problem of defining censorship in my "Introduction: The 'New' Censorship" (see note 2), xii–xxii.

61. Houston A. Baker, Jr., *Black Studies, Rap, and the Academy* (Chicago: Univ. Chicago Press, 1993), 81.

62. Leo Bersani, *Homos* (Cambridge, Mass.: Harvard Univ. Press, 1995), 48. See also the following examples. Richard Rorty offers a critique of Andrew Ross: "I suspect that Ross and his friend, who believe themselves to be conducting cultural politics, may find that they have been engaged only in academic politics." Richard Rorty, "Intellectuals and Politics: Too Far In? Too Far Out?" *Dissent* (1991): 483–90. Stanley Fish's view of cultural criticism is that "the language of literary theory is not subversive, but irrelevant; it *cannot be heard* except as the alien murmurings of a galaxy far away." Stanley Fish, *Professional Correctness: Literary Studies and Political Change* (Oxford: Oxford Univ. Press, 1996), 91.

63. Jacques Derrida was the first to deconstruct it, and Judith Butler takes up what she considers to be the subversive implications of this deconstruction. See Jacques Derrida, "Signature, Event, Context," in idem, *Limited Inc,* ed. Gerald Graff, trans. Samuel Weber and Jeffrey Mehlman (Evanston: Northwestern Univ. Press, 1988); and Judith Butler, *Bodies That Matter: On the Discursive Limits of Sex* (New York: Routledge, 1993).

64. See Judith Butler's essay, pages 247–59 in this volume.

65. At the Getty seminar, for example, one contributor not only presented his paper but actually spoke throughout the conference as if he were at that very moment testifying before a congressional committee.

66. Richard Burt, "Getting Off the Subject: Iconoclasm, Queer Sexuality, and the Celebrity Intellectual," *Performing Arts Journal* 50/51 (1995): 137–50.

67. This is to say that psychoanalysis will be in tension with rather than fully subsumed by a political criticism that takes politics as the final horizon of any interpretation.

68. Near the end of the seminar, one contributor attempted to articulate a consensus on a variety of points that had emerged during the discussions. I objected to any attempt to do so and pointed out that we had divided up into groups during breaks and meals and that no doubt some if not of all of us had gossiped about others. I said it might be worthwhile to consider the status of our extraconference discussions rather than simply be embarrassed by them or regard them as extracritical.

Incitement and the Limits of Law

Ruth Gavison

Introduction

Freedom of expression has been a central ideal of free and pluralistic societies since the classical period. Standard justifications for it precede the modern trend toward democracy,[1] but clearly a commitment to democracy as a system of government significantly strengthens these justifications.[2] Freedom of expression takes pride of place in all Bills of Rights and international human rights documents. It is supported by the value of freedom and liberty, as well as by the additional reasons special to the freedom to express opinions, disseminate information, and publish and perform artistic creations. The general liberal presumption in favor of freedom of action applies to speech; in addition, speech is distinguished from action and is deemed deserving of special protection.

According to the liberal tradition, the primary enemy of free speech is government's attempt to perpetuate its own power through the suppression of expression it deems subversive, dangerous, or immoral. The paradigmatic form of curbing free speech is censorship—prior restraint of unwanted expression by state officials—combined with a legal liability for speech deemed illegal.[3] The content of the speech that the state wants to curb is usually public; it relates to criticism of the government, to the dissemination of ideas deemed pernicious or blasphemous, or to the corruption of public morals.[4]

The story may be cast in a simple public-private framework: the public state, via public law and its enforcement, is the enemy of the freedom of speech of private individuals and civil society. In the absence of state action, freedom and the free flow of information and ideas prevail. The state, threatened by this freedom, reacts by activating mechanisms of censorship and repression. The classic implications for action are also simple and clear: the forces of light should struggle to keep the state out of the regulation of speech.

Recently, however, the picture has become more complex. People argue that there is no real freedom of expression in civil society, even when the state does not exert its power via prohibition, regulation, or punishment. A variety of other mechanisms exist that effectively silence. These include self-restraint by speakers themselves, effective censorship by peers and superiors, a variety of market devices, social implementation of norms of unacceptability, and the systematic marginalization of groups of people who are discouraged from speaking their minds and feelings. These complex processes have nothing much to do with the law and legal constraints; nonetheless, their impact on freedom of expression may be more pervasive and deeper than the effects of legal curbs.[5]

From this descriptive claim—that threats to freedom of expression are private as much as public—comes an interesting conclusion. The remedy against public curbs of speech is a struggle for freedom of expression and the absence of legal constraints, but it may well be that an effective fight against private limitations on free speech may require public involvement in various forms, including enlisting the legal system to prevent, minimize, or mitigate the effects of private silencing. When the silencing is caused by the speech of others, this enlistment may itself permit or require public curbs on speech.

People also are returning, in new ways, to often-made arguments that freedom of expression is not necessarily all good. The marketplace of ideas does not always work, the truth does not always win, and occasionally the price of truth's victory is prohibitive and extremely wasteful. The prevalence and legitimation of unfettered speech may have caused some of the most terrible atrocities in human history, including those perpetuated by Nazi rule in Germany. Speech may, together with other social forces, reinforce and perpetuate long-term and persisting patterns of oppression and discrimination against weak and victimized groups.

If these arguments are valid, the classic liberal reluctance to limit freedom of expression may seem less justified in some cases. One conclusion is that some public limitations of speech may be permitted; a stronger conclusion might be that such public limitations of some sorts of speech are required. These revisionist claims are sometimes made as critiques of liberalism,[6] and sometimes they are presented as taking liberalism itself to its rightful conclusions.[7]

There are also arguments that more profoundly challenge the utility of invoking the public-private distinction to conceptualize legal curbs on speech. These challenges claim that the ascription of "publicness" and "privateness" to speech and its curbing mechanisms may be misguided: in both cases, the reality is a complex combination of elements that cannot be easily classified. The implication is that public-private talk in such contexts may be misleading and that we should design a new framework for discussion of such issues. In this new framework, we would have neither a presumption against the use of public legal force against speech nor for the immunity from state regulation of private activity and speech; rather, we would see all social processes—the ones we want to regulate and the ones invoked by regulation—in their full complexity.[8]

In this chapter I will argue that although it is important to see the forces that facilitate and inhibit speech as complex public and private mechanisms, and although regulation of speech (and action) should take into account this complexity and seek to use public and private means of many sorts to guide individual and social behavior, maintaining the distinction between public and private realms is important. The basic liberal attitude of suspicion toward legal means of curbing speech, invoked and enforced by the state, is strengthened rather than weakened by this more sophisticated, richer approach.

In part, the state and the law should in principle not regulate speech because of reasons of political morality. These reasons have been rehearsed extensively in the literature and I shall not repeat them.[9] I will concentrate on reasons having to do with the characteristics of law as a public institution that invokes the state monopoly of the justified use of force. My argument will focus on the internal institutional limitations of law that in many cases render it unfit for regulating speech, often precisely in the circumstances where we may be most keenly interested in effective regulation. Even if there is a strong case of political morality for curbing some speech, these limitations of law should be considered before reaching a final decision.

Clearly, if an argument of political morality in favor of curbing speech exists, society may be permitted, or required, to use nonlegal means to discourage and delegitimate the offending speech. Consequently, the argument against legal sanctions is not necessarily an argument against all attempts to limit speech. It is, rather, an argument against putting the force of the state, with its legal mechanisms and institutions, behind the efforts to curb the complex processes that are often connected with illegitimate and dangerous abuses of freedom of speech.

My argument is presented against the background of a traumatic test case: the assassination of Israeli Prime Minister Itzhak Rabin and the debate conducted in Israel, before and after the murder, about the proper limits of legal prohibitions against incitement. The case study provides a dramatic illustration of the possible role of law, as well as its systemic limits, in fighting the dangers of incitement in situations of deep and divisive controversy.

The Test Case

Prime Minister Rabin was assassinated on 4 November 1995. It is too early to know the long-term effects of this political murder; however, it clearly intensified a prolonged debate in Israel about the limits of free speech. Many saw the assassination as the culmination of a nasty process of hate, incitement, and delegitimation directed at the government, at the political process Rabin's government was leading, and at Rabin in particular. Some claimed that this atmosphere made the murder possible and that not preventing it was, among other things, a failure of the legal system. Now, more than a year later, we have some information about how attempts to enforce the law against incitement have fared and what changes have occurred in the social atmosphere.

The political background of the assassination was extremely charged, centering on the negotiations for an Israeli-Palestinian settlement, which began in 1993. In 1994 Rabin's government signed and started to implement the second stage of the Oslo agreements, under which the control of the major cities of the West Bank was to transfer to the Palestinian Authority and elections were to be held. The Oslo agreements had been approved in Israel's parliament by a very small majority. The Israeli population was intensely divided, and the settlers living on the West Bank, many of them orthodox, increased their opposition to the agreements.

Rabin was called a murderer and a traitor. He was described as cooperating with Nazis and was shown in posters wearing Arafat's headcover and an SS uniform. These posters were carried in Likud demonstrations, in which the head of the opposition, Binyamin Netanyahu, participated and spoke without clearly condemning these attacks on Rabin. Some rabbis in Israel and the United States declared that, according to Jewish law *(halakhah)*, Rabin deserved to die because he was willing to give parts of the land of Israel *(Eretz Yisrael)* to gentiles *(din mosser)* and because he was creating a threat to the life of Jews in the territories *(din rodef)*. An Israeli professor seriously looked into the possibility of indicting Rabin for treason. Each Friday a group of demonstrators stood near the Rabin residence and called out insults; they were quoted as saying that Rabin and his wife would be executed as traitors in the city square. Hooligans attacked Rabin's car. It became extremely hard for Rabin to speak in public gatherings because of the intense critical reaction he received.[10]

In addition to targeting Rabin personally, protests were also mounted against his policy and his government. Some took the form of speech. Rabbis declared that Jewish law prohibits any participation in the evacuation of settlements or even army bases. The government as a whole was called bloody and evil. Attempts to delegitimate the government were made through claims that the 1994 agreement had been approved by a majority that included non-Jewish Israeli citizens and that such policies should not be pursued without the backing of a "Jewish majority." A leading head of a yeshiva allegedly ruled that it was legitimate to throw hand grenades at Israel Defense Force (IDF) soldiers who tried to evacuate settlements. Other protests went beyond speech and took the form of illegal acts such as blocking roads and settling without permission in areas that the settlers claimed to be theirs. Small Jewish groups were accumulating arms and organizing to stop the implementation process.

Israel has a broad arsenal of legal measures that may be used against inciting speech of various sorts.[11] Prosecution under most of these provisions requires the approval of the attorney general, and his permission has always been given grudgingly, especially when Jews are implicated. In 1986, after a long internal debate played out against the background of Meir Kahane's initiatives against Arabs, Israel added a special proscription against incitement to racism. In 1994 this law was used to bring an indictment against Rabbi Iddo Elba.

Elba was indicted for racist incitement because he published a monograph declaring that, as a matter of Jewish law, Jews have a religious duty during a war to kill all members of the enemy group, including women and children. He stated that the duty applies not only to the organized Jewish community but also to individuals. Elba also stated that his monograph was for learning, not for action, but at the same time he was involved in collecting arms and conspiring to act against Arabs. At the trial in a Jerusalem district court, Elba refused to testify as to his interpretation of the text or his purpose in publishing it. His lawyer conceded, however, that part of his intention was to present the acts of Baruch Goldstein, the perpetrator of the Hebron massacre, in a good light.[12] The judge convicted Elba, deducing the required intention from the surrounding circumstances. He appealed to the Supreme Court, arguing mainly that his conviction for incitement was not consistent with previous rulings on freedom of speech. In September 1996 the Supreme Court upheld the decision by a vote of seven to two.[13]

A few days after upholding Elba's conviction, the court sustained in part the conviction of Hassan Jabbarin, an Israeli Arabic writer, for incitement and praise of violence. Jabbarin had written a literary text in which he said he had been empowered by the *intifada,* since it meant Palestinians were willing to take active steps such as stone throwing to present the Palestinian plight to the world.[14] In the Jabbarin decision the court hardly looked at the facts of the case, or at the elements of the different offenses involved, and reached its conclusion by relying heavily and explicitly on the reasoning in *Elba.*

Throughout the public debate about the negotiated Israeli-Palestinian settlement, Attorney General Michael Ben-Yair was bombarded with requests from all sides to invoke the law against what was deemed incitement and seditious libel; Israeli society is as judicialized as American society. When a group of important rabbis, some of them state employees, published a "*halakhic* judgment" calling on soldiers not to participate in the evacuation of army camps, the attorney general decided not to invoke the criminal law, noting that most attorneys general before him had been extremely cautious about using their prosecutorial discretion in issues involving speech about matters of public importance. He added that suppression of speech might be counterproductive, particularly when the suppressed speech involved political debate that had polarized Israeli society. Some praised this decision; others expressed fears that the message was too permissive: by not even investigating the conduct, the legal system communicated that these expressions were exempt from law enforcement and might even be legal and permissible.

In addition, there were confused messages about how to treat illegal *conduct* in the context of the debate. Dispersing the demonstrators involved clashes with the police, resulting in accusations of violence and unjustified violation of human rights. When the leaders of these demonstrations were detained, public pressure led to their early release. Similarly, when police and the army tried to evacuate illegal settlers, they were accused of violating the human rights of peaceful protesters.

Reaction by the courts to attempts to prosecute participants in illegal demonstrations was also erratic. Demonstrators and their supporters declared that the protests were acts of civil disobedience, falling within their democratic right to protest, and that they would paralyze the legal system if the demonstrators were prosecuted in large numbers. When the police and the attorney general asked the courts to speed up the trials to circumvent this threat, dissenters persuaded Chief Justice Aharon Barak to ask the attorney general not to interfere with the autonomy of the courts.

The Israeli media saw its task as giving full representation to all views. They hosted representatives of the groups expressing extremely critical views of Rabin and the political process. One television broadcast showed a masked youth pledging to use violence against Arabs and, if need be, against Jews as well.

In short, the assassination was preceded by intensified acts of protest, including blatant, delegitimating verbal attacks against Rabin and his policies. The legal system's response was ambivalent. On the whole, it took a passive, ultracautious approach toward the prosecution of speech and an erratic and ineffective stance toward illegal action.

The shock of the assassination led many to reassess the developments that had preceded it, including the response of the legal system to expressions that might be seen as inciting or legitimating the murder. For a short while, this issue dominated public debates. The attorney general and the minister of justice planned to add new laws that would prohibit incitement to murder and violence and the praise of such conduct, explaining that present laws were too broad for effective enforcement. There was talk about a special prosecutorial unit to deal with incitement. The attorney general reminded the media that disseminating incitement was an offense on the part of the media as well as on the part of the speaker. Some Israelis who expressed joy at Rabin's murder were detained and interrogated under a law that makes expressions in support of terrorism a criminal offense.[15]

Opinion within right-wing political and religious groups was divided. A minority were willing to accept indirect responsibility for the atmosphere of incitement and delegitimation, but most counterattacked, claiming that the left was trying to glean political capital from the tragedy by inciting public opinion against the right as a whole, without acknowledging that the murder was the act of a radical individual. Right-wing groups pledged to change their political style, but they objected to proposals for new legislation imposing more specific curbs on speech. This position was shared, more or less, by human rights groups of all persuasions.

The ambivalence toward law enforcement persisted. The high court clarified that the media were not controlled by the attorney general and that he could not direct their actions. There was a public outcry when a few rabbis were interrogated by the police to find out whether they had explicitly said that Rabin was "executable." Most of the demonstrators who had been detained either were released or received very light sentences. Three leaders of the settlers' protest movement who had been indicted for incitement argued in court that the indictment infringed their right to protest and complained that the government was using the law to persecute its political opponents.[16] Talk about changes in the law gradually subsided. People in the legal civil service explained that trials for political expression were extremely hard to conduct and win and that prosecution necessarily singled out some speech without guaranteeing that it was speech that most deserved such treatment. Security arrangements for political leaders tightened significantly.

By the summer of 1996, important parts of the second stage of the Oslo accords had been implemented by Peres's government without serious public protest.[17] Public discussions of political issues and, especially, of political leaders were extremely subdued in most political circles.[18] The caution was so great that Rabin's murder was hardly mentioned in the election campaigns that led to the rise to power of Netanyahu in May 1996. Labor party strategists felt that appearing to capitalize on the assassination might alienate members of the right whom they hoped to attract.

When redeployment in Hebron started to seem more likely, right-wing rhetoric escalated again. Rabbis repeated their public statements against evacuation. On many occasions, criticism of the government took the form of support for the motives, goals, and courage of Rabin's murderer, Yigal Amir.[19] Nonetheless, redeployment took place in January 1997 without any serious protest.[20]

Legal Regulation of Incitement

Decisions about using law to suppress incitement may be made at a number of different junctures: At each, decisions are made by different bodies and in different processes of decision making and accountability. The questions asked are different, but interrelated: Should there be laws prohibiting some types of inciting speech? What should the elements of such offenses be? Should this law grant discretion in its application? To whom? Should a speaker be prosecuted in a particular case? Should he be convicted? How serious should the punishment be?

By definition, inciting speech is speech that leads, at least potentially, to bad results, and laws that attempt to curb such speech seek to prevent or minimize these bad results.[21] In general, the case for having a law and using it is strongest when:

1. The speech in question has substantial undesirable results and weak or nonexistent desirable functions.
2. The causal relationship between the speech and the bad results is clear and strong.
3. The effectiveness of law enforcement is high.
4. The costs of law enforcement are low.
5. The costs of nonenforcement are high.
6. The availability of nonlegal measures that can effectively minimize the bad results is low.

These are complex considerations, raising factual and evaluative issues. Both law and the processes it seeks to regulate can be described in terms of a public-private continuum. Law is specifically public in many senses. It is the reflection of the fact that the state claims supreme authority and the right to be the only normative system having the power to use justified force. The results I discuss here are mostly public ones, affecting people other than the speaker and often large numbers of them. Law seeks to regulate complex social and individual processes, which together determine the causal connections between speech, beliefs, attitudes, and conduct. Most of these processes are not controlled by the state through law. Some are elements of our public culture (for example, accepted patterns of speech and behavior in public life, which may affect individual expectations and conduct) and some are intensely individual and private (for example, the way particular individuals respond to a stimulus or are moved to act on their interpretation of a reality or norm). As we shall see, the complexity of social processes is relevant to the role of law. In part, the relevance has to do with the relationships between the public nature of law and the complex private-public nature of both the conduct the law seeks to regulate and of the processes that facilitate and hinder such conduct.

A test case such as Rabin's assassination frames questions about the role of law in attempts to curb incitement in a special and specific way. It makes a great deal of difference whether we consider the six factors listed above in the abstract or in the context of a specific case. The particular context of a specific case, in which harm has already materialized, may change our assessment of these factors. As we saw, before Rabin's assassination the attorney general declined to prosecute inciting speech; after the assassination his policy changed. I believe the court's decisions in the speech cases were also affected by the assassination. By analyzing these cases, we can better see how the murder affected the decisions and whether it should have affected them in the way they did.

Identification and Evaluation of Results

The first set of elements to be considered in seeking to limit incitement is the identification of the consequences of speech, the evaluation of the worth and weight of these consequences, and the probability of their occurrence. The strongest case for legal prohibition is that of speech that creates a "clear and present" danger of a harmful result, with no mitigating features whatsoever. Shouting "Fire" in a crowded theater is a familiar hypothetical example. Encouraging an angry and hungry mob to storm a granary and kill the owner is another. In real-life situations the picture is often more complex, and the picture is further complicated when we design laws to deal with such situations. Let's look at some of these elements one by one.

Taking Rabin's assassination as the starting point focuses our attention on one event that may have resulted from the speech and activities described. Many people, including Rabin's political opponents, concede that Rabin's murder was an extremely unfortunate and undesirable event. Because the assassination was committed to undermine the political program of a democratically elected head of state, sanctity of life, the rule of law, and democracy were all put at grave risk. Assassination can threaten the stability of regimes, affect a country's international standing, and harm the well-being of those who rely on the effectiveness of law enforcement in that society.

When we look at the consequences of similar speech in similar circumstances from other junctures, or even at the situation in Israel prior to the assassination, the picture changes radically. The Rabin assassination was not the only consequence of the inciting speech. Clearly, this speech served functions other than the facilitation of the murder, and many of these functions are an essential part of democracy. We should recall that the Oslo process is far reaching and that opinion in Israel at the time of the assassination was truly and deeply divided. For many people in the opposition, free speech probably provided a way of participating in the process of national decision making. Most of the harsh words against Rabin were used to mobilize political opposition and clarify the depth of the feelings that inspired that opposition. Naturally, effective mobilization of the opposition can be extremely threatening to supporters of the government's policy, and they can easily be led to see accusations and caricatures as forms of incitement and delegitimation even as they pay lip service to democracy. It is not easy to draw the line between legitimate harsh criticism and dangerous delegitimation, and it is not clear that those connected with the government under attack should be the ones to make these judgments.

Despite the truth of these observations, one may be reluctant to conclude that the law must be helpless in the face of even the most blatant incitement. Surely there are types of speech whose bad results are obvious and imminent and whose beneficial value is small or nonexistent. Yet, when we seek to formulate a general law capturing this intuition, the quest is not an easy one. The distinction between legitimate and illegitimate speech must be independent, as much as possible, from substantive political views. Some try to draw a line between speech encouraging and legitimating legal activities and speech encouraging and legitimating illegal activities. Although this line has the advantage of being relatively clear, there is a serious debate about the limits of a citizen's obligation to obey the laws, even in a democracy. *Speaking* about disobedience, especially when it is not violent, and justifying it, per se, do not seem good targets for prosecution.[22] Thus, mere illegality does not provide the answer.

A stronger candidate for illegal speech might be speech that explicitly calls for the use of force or violence. It might show the deterrent capacity of law that such explicit speech is not present in public debates in Israel. Calling Rabin a murderer and a traitor and describing him as a *rodef* or *moser* were not such explicit calls: the conclusion that he should be murdered was not publicly stated. The *Elba* decision shows the willingness of the court to view a somewhat disguised message that legitimates violence—here against Arabs—as a case of incitement. To avoid overinclusiveness, the law must identify speech that is explicit and intended. Such a law is likely to be easy to manipulate, and the likely result will be that it is underinclusive in important ways.

The problem may be further exemplified by looking at the suggestions to prosecute those who publicly expressed joy at Rabin's murder. At first blush, this appeared to be an easier case to justify than the prohibition of statements such as "Rabin is a murderer" or "Rabin is a traitor." Whereas the latter statements may be the legitimate expressions of political frustration and dissent, stopping short of recommending specific outcomes, the blessing of a political murder has no redeeming features. On the contrary, public toleration of such blessing may seem inconsistent with the official condemnation of the murder.

Nonetheless, serious difficulties exist both at the level of draftsmanship and prosecutorial discretion. How would such a prohibition be drafted? "Expressing support for murder" might be underinclusive: it would not cover expressions of joy for other illegal acts of violence. Expressing support for a general use of force or violence would, unfortunately, be applicable to quite a bit of talk in Israel, and, clearly, it would also be overbroad:[23] would the law apply to any murder, including the murder of an arch-criminal or a political assassination that took place decades ago?[24] A decision not to prosecute someone who publicly expresses admiration for those who attempted to assassinate Hitler may seem obvious. Is the decision so obvious when Rabin is compared to Hitler? What exactly is "blessing"? Is expression of joy, or a declaration of an absence of sorrow, enough? What about support of the murderer's motives and goals without explicit public support of the deed itself? On the one hand, the expression of this attitude cannot be prosecuted; on the other hand, it may well serve as an encouragement to a person contemplating murder.

The Causal Relationship

Describing an action or an event as the "consequence" of speech presupposes that there is some causal connection between them. A central issue in any debate about the limits of free speech is the nature and the imminence of the causal connection between speech and its alleged consequences. When the connection is very close, some see speech itself as being a form of violent act.[25] The decision to punish speech that is closely and inevitably linked to undesirable consequences is rationalized by the fact that it would seem strange and counterintuitive to view the almost inevitable result of some conduct as highly undesirable, but to refrain from prohibiting that conduct. As we move away from the paradigmatic cases of direct and strong causation, we may be less willing to punish speech.

The juncture at which the decision is made is significant: judgments about causal relationships made when we contemplate a general law against incitement will be very different from those made when we consider prosecution for a specific act of incitement. In addition, judgments will tend to be different depending on whether they are made before or after a specific undesirable result occurs.[26]

After Rabin was assassinated, it was easy, and I think plausible, to say that his murder was facilitated and aided by the general atmosphere of incitement and delegitimation. Part of the trauma of Rabin's death, however, stemmed from the fact that for most people the assassination came as a total surprise, despite the climate of unrest that preceded it. Even if the atmosphere facilitated the murder, it does not follow that we would be able to identify particular acts of speech or conduct that caused it.

In actual social situations it is impossible to isolate factors and determine their contribution to effects. Such control is extremely complicated even in a scientific laboratory. We cannot easily identify and disentangle the precise causal contributions of angry or even inciting speech, of harsh political criticism, of hooliganism, of a general tendency in Israeli society to solve problems by force rather than by debate; we cannot identify the effects of feelings of betrayal and desperation on the part of the settlers, of tension between religious and state law, of the existence of groups that support and legitimate murder, or of the special psychology of Rabin's murderer that made him respond in this way. The causal efficacy of inciting speech is not independent of these factors. Not only might the speech preceding the assassination have had less intensity had other factors been absent, but such speech may have had less impact on Amir than did other factors, such as his combination of military service and religious education.[27]

Rabin's assassination demonstrates that political murder is a possible outcome in such a complex situation. This is a meaningful statement, because before the assassination many believed that a Jew would not murder another Jew under such circumstances.[28] Nonetheless, the contribution that inciting speech made to Rabin's assassination is far from clear. Background conditions are relevant, without doubt, but the ultimate decision to act was made by one particular individual. The need for caution in deciding to connect specific speech to the murder, and deciding to prosecute for that speech, grows when we remember that, for psychological as well as political reasons, many were looking for someone, or something, other than the murderer to blame for the assassination.

In sum, a feeling of guilt and frustration at not preventing Rabin's assassination may well be consistent with the inability to use the law productively to suppress speech that may have contributed to the murder.

Enforcement of the Law

Identification and evaluation of consequences and assessing the strength of the causal relationship between speech and outcome are relevant both in drafting laws and in deciding to invoke laws in particular circumstances. We should not have laws against incitement if these cannot be justified in terms of preventing undesirable results. The enforcement of such laws also generates social costs. If these costs are high, they might support a case against all legal regulation. This is a general truth about legal regulation,[29] and it applies with special force to the legal regulation of speech. This cluster of issues includes the effectiveness of enforcement, the costs of enforcement and nonenforcement, and the availability of nonlegal measures.

Costs of Enforcement

We saw that laws prohibiting speech are likely to be both overinclusive and underinclusive. Since the content of speech alone cannot decide the issue, and since legal norms cannot enumerate the context of their own application, someone must have discretion in enforcement of the laws. This may raise concerns about equality before the law. If the law is enforced against some speakers but not others, charges of political inequity may result. Singling out individuals may cause injustice, and it may also make the silenced groups feel persecuted and martyred. In addition, such laws may have serious chilling effects. While some of the discouraged speech will be the kind of speech the law wishes to deter, the robustness and power of necessary public debate may be reduced as well.

The most serious problem in this context, however, stems from the nature of law itself, and the role of its enforcing agencies. Law is an arm of the state. Laws aim, at least in part, to maintain order. To do that, the state claims supreme authority and the right to be the only normative system having the power to use justified force. This claim of exclusive authority suggests serious constraints on the law. If the state claims authority, not naked power, the law must have a basis of legitimacy: there must be existing, known, and general norms that make the conduct illegal; suspects must be given an opportunity to present their case in an open court, where they are allowed to challenge the facts and the law; and the courts must be constructed in a way that will guarantee independence from the government. For the law to operate smoothly and legitimately, individuals accused of crimes must be seen as offenders, not persecuted heroes or martyrs, by most of society. If the law or its enforcement are perceived by too many, and for too long, as being simply the vehicle of persecution and oppression, the power of the law to regulate conduct declines. Law may ultimately be seen as a partisan tool used by the "enemy," against which society is justified to rise, instead of a system within which differing perspectives can work together for the advancement of a united, cohesive society that accepts its pluralism. Moreover, this ambivalence about law may be present within the law enforcement system itself, since police and courts usually reflect, to some degree, deep ideological and political divisions within the society in which they live and work.

All these presuppositions of the work of law in society are usually present in well-ordered and stable societies. They may be weak in cleft and divided societies. Situations of great division thus create dangers to the fabric and legitimacy of law and call for special care in its enforcement. This is an important part of the lesson of the Rabin assassination and of the general background of Israeli society. Recall that the legal machinery to prosecute both speech and actual violence was available before the assassination. Despite this fact, enforcement of the law against Jews who committed violence against Arabs was extremely weak. No similar difficulties were experienced with Palestinian Arabs, however.[30] Arabs who expressed explicit or even indirect support of violence were detained or prosecuted and no leniency was shown toward those convicted of terrorism. The factors creating this inability to enforce equitably the law reflect a deep ambivalence about the morality of acting against Arabs within Jewish Israeli society. Some of the ambivalence concerning acts of violence may have become more subdued after the murder, but the ambivalence concerning speech has not weakened, either among law enforcement personnel or among the broader public.[31]

The fact that enforcement requires discretion, and that this discretion is exercised by law enforcement personnel who may share the social ambivalence about enforcement, gains special importance when we remember that the control of enforcement is, constitutionally, the responsibility of the executive. While all legal systems contain mechanisms designed to separate legal enforcement from government, the ultimate responsibility for enforcement of the laws lies, as it should, with the branch that controls the daily use of governmental power in specific cases.

The responsibility of the executive creates two special risks: first, the government may, even in good faith, use laws against incitement to promote its own political goals; second, this fear, even if unjustified, may help delegitimate the legal system and the courts, making them appear to be servants of the current regime rather than protectors of human rights and the rule of law.[32] Both dangers are very real and should be counted as heavy costs of enforcement, especially in explosive social situations.

Effectiveness of Enforcement

The considerations against the use of law to curb inciting speech might have been overridden if the prosecution of speech had proved to be an effective way of decreasing the chances of political murder. It is far from clear that a fierce enforcement of the law against speech would have prevented Rabin's assassination, and it is not at all clear that it could restrain murder or violence triggered by a future political situation.

The relative ineffectiveness of law in this area is related to the fact that the causal chains leading to the murder are complex, and it seems that the role of identifiable speech acts within these chains is rather minimal. Furthermore, the attempt to prosecute for speech may decrease the occurrence of inciting speech, but it may increase the probability of the violence the law wishes to prevent. I noted above that Elba explicitly added that his analysis of Jewish law on "killing non-Jews" was for the purpose of study, not action. People may indeed more carefully control what they say if they realize that they may be prosecuted for what they say; nevertheless, prosecution for speech in volatile political situations seems likely to arouse as much resentment and suspicion as hoped-for internalization of the limits and dangers of free speech.[33] If a person feels that the power of the state is being used to persecute him and to prevent him and others who think like him from expressing their protest, he may feel victimized. If his desperation grows, he may be moved to believe that violence is the only route open to him. Under these circumstances, he may refrain from publicly expressing joy at political murders but may be more willing to support and join groups that plan to repeat such deeds.

The effectiveness of the law in preventing violence may be further decreased by the fact that those prosecuted for inciting or blessing violence are usually tried and sentenced long after the initial speech occurs and long after the urgency that was dictated by a volatile political situation has passed. Under these circumstances it is not surprising that courts tend to acquit when they have to balance risks to life and security against free speech.

The Costs of Nonenforcement

The arguments so far seem to indicate that great caution should be used before the law is mobilized to regulate political speech uttered in the context of an intense public debate about extremely consequential policies.

Nonetheless, the case of Rabin's assassination should give us pause, as it did to law enforcers in Israel after the murder. Is the law helpless in such a terrible national trauma? Is Israel doomed to be a society that tolerates incitement only to witness the murder of a national leader? These and similar questions suggest that the legal system may be in a real bind: if law is not effective and the costs of its enforcement are heavy, one should not prosecute. Conversely, a divided society might not be able to maintain its integrity as a democracy without clearly condemning inciting speech and the kinds of actions that the speech encourages. Law is the only mechanism that can impose official punishments through fines or imprisonment: conviction is the official mechanism of imposing social stigma. It seems strange that we cannot use this mechanism to deal with the kinds of activities that contributed, however remotely, to the assassination of Rabin.

Not using the law in such circumstances has social costs of two interrelated kinds. First, nonenforcement may suggest a willingness to give up the deterring effect of enforcement as a way of promoting the desirable state of affairs in which public debate is robust but avoids incitement. Secondly, it may be seen as approbation and legitimation of inciting and delegitimating speech.

The feared loss of deterrence is a substantial cost, but it is dangerous to let the trauma of the assassination and the frustration over the public support it has received allow us to forget the long list of difficulties and costs concomitant to invoking the law. It is not at all clear that strict enforcement of laws against speech can promote robust debate while proscribing incitement, and that it could have prevented the murder. While the guilt felt by law enforcers is understandable, it is not clear that it is justified. Even if it had been, we should make sure that guilt does not dictate bad solutions just to prevent similar guilt in the future.

More troubling is the possibility that a decision not to prosecute will be seen as a declaration of permissibility and legitimacy. It is extremely important, in this context and in many others, to stress the fact that nonprosecution, or noncriminalization, is not tantamount to legitimation and approbation. In fact, this is precisely one of the points in which law must be supplemented by social norms of various sorts. This declaration calls for some humility on the part of the law which is, I believe, quite beneficial. Admission of the law's limits may be hard for some lawyers, but it is an extremely important reminder for society at large.

I have explained why using the law to curb *speech* in such circumstances is a bad solution. The law need not feel completely helpless, however. It can make a contribution, and should do so, by strictly enforcing of the law against *violent subversive action.* Support for illegal acts, especially violent acts against innocent people, is likely to be much less focused and public than support for inciting speech. Violent acts are clearly dangerous to individuals and to the rule of law—they have no redeeming value whatsoever. Nonetheless, in conditions of great division and cleavage, when even the enforcement of laws against action is likely to be difficult, it is a mistake to attempt to use the law against speech. In this regard, feelings of guilt are justified: I have documented above the lenient treatment given in Israel to the Jewish perpetrators of ideological and political violence against Arabs. It remains to be seen whether this lesson has been learned by the legal system and by Israeli society as a whole.

Alternative Measures

If laws were the only agents of expressive condemnation available and the only way to discourage inciting speech, the dilemma of the law would be sharpened. Such condemnation would not make laws more effective, but it would make it harder to claim that nonenforcement is justified and that nonenforcement does not amount to legitimation. Similarly, if laws against incitement had been the only way to fight against political murder, justification for not using them would have been hard. Fortunately, however, other mechanisms often exist that do not have law's structural limitations, and they may be more effective than (or at least as effective as) legal curbs on speech. There is in addition a host of other ways, legal as well as nonlegal, to minimize the risk of political murders. The atmosphere before Rabin's assassination indicates that such mechanisms were not used effectively in Israel. Developments after the murder suggest that these forces can be relied on to do at least some of the work of curbing incitement.

After the assassination, political parties in Israel—especially the main opposition parties, secular as well as religious, who had been ambivalent about extreme right-wing rhetoric and activities—somewhat changed their ways, realizing that public support of incitement, whether active or passive, could alienate most of the public. These parties had an electoral incentive to support law enforcement against violent actions and to condemn publicly expressions made from within their camp that seemed close to incitement. Clearly, such moves from the political forces that participated in incitement and delegitimation, if they are thought to be sincere and if they persist, will be more effective deterrents of both incitement and violence than would be enforcement of the law against speech by those who are viewed as the long arm of a hated government. Thus, a party's internal decision to exclude or marginalize members who carry unauthorized inciting posters or endorse *halakhic* legitimation of murder may be more feasible and more effective than legal prosecution of the same conduct.

Moreover, if a divided society is to avoid civil war and disintegration, all parts of the political system must cooperate in the effort to present the courts and law enforcement agencies as national mechanisms that are beyond partisan political controversies. They are more likely to do this if the activities of the courts and law enforcement agencies do not threaten them directly.[34]

The prohibition against inciting speech is not our main way of protecting political leaders. Obvious alternatives are laws against murder and assault. Stepping up security arrangements is another obvious measure. The failure of such arrangements in Rabin's case was the subject of a special commission of inquiry. Even before their report came out, however, it was quite clear that the failure consisted of much more than the fact that the prime minister was murdered despite having taken all reasonable protective measures.[35]

Additional measures that do not involve legal curbs on speech are suggested by a careful analysis of the events preceding and following the assassination. Education is clearly indicated, although results may be apparent only in the long term.[36] More interesting and controversial is the suggestion that an effort should be made to lessen the intensity of political polarization within Israeli society. Supporters of this idea suggest that this is the only effective way to discourage the demonization of political leaders. Critics argue that this would benefit the camp that used violence in that it would create a superficial and nonexistent unity that would inevitably give a veto power to those who object to the Oslo process and to similar policies that would require relinquishing Jewish control over parts of Greater Israel.

This debate may have far-reaching implications for my subject: if Israel cannot avoid or contain the deep divisions among its various camps, it may sadly have to go through a period of civil strife in which conflicting ideologies will seek victory through war. During that period, the law would be in a sense suspended, and it could re-establish itself and its authority only when a large part of the population agreed to work within the same framework of rules.

Some Conclusions

The atmosphere that preceded Rabin's assassination, and probably made it possible, resulted from complex social and political processes; inciting speech was but one factor. The main opposition parties were ambiguous in their reaction to such extreme speech, fearing to lose the electoral support of radical objectors to Rabin's policies, whose numbers were not clear. The murder appeared to undermine the stability of democracy itself and suggested that Israel was splitting apart.

This is the kind of unruly situation in which some call for more public legal intervention in the hope that laws and their enforcement will change the atmosphere and prevent further violence. Law enforcement agencies in Israel decided to step up law enforcement as a response to the trauma generated by the murder. They felt that there was a present danger of more political violence among Jews; the feeling more generally was that only strict enforcement of the laws could reintegrate Israeli society.

I have tried to show why these arguments, in this context, were not sufficient to justify the use of the law against speech. Moreover, I have tried to show that the very nature of the situation and the threats to democracy it reflected made the law the wrong tool to deal with the crisis. Prosecution and punishment are uniquely legal measures, and they are public in the strongest sense of state power. Their utility is extremely limited when the outcome the laws seeks to prevent is deeply controversial. Law enforcement, especially against speech, must therefore be wary of appearing to take sides in such controversies.

My analysis of why the law should not attempt to regulate inciting speech does not rely on classic justifications for freedom of speech or the resulting moral reasons against curbing it by laws. It instead focuses primarily on the structural and systemic features of law itself and on an analysis of the background social conditions against which the law must work.

Israel chose to combine its long-standing laws against incitement with a policy of nonenforcement. If I am right that law enforcement of political incitement laws is most problematic at times of great political division, when the tendency to use inciting language is great, should we not aim at abolishing such laws? Should law declare that it is out of this field altogether, thus "privatizing" speech, or should those who uphold the law be open to the possibility that there may be an occasion in which enforcement will be justified or even required?

I have no firm opinion on this matter, in part because generalizations are difficult. It is not necessarily the case that inciting language exists or is very dangerous only when there is a deep division within the population, nor are violence and murder the only undesirable outcomes of incitement that we may wish to prevent. Incitement against minorities may perpetuate serious structural social wrongs that we may well seek to regulate. Moreover, there may be cases in which causal relationships are stronger, costs of enforcement significantly lower, and redeeming features nonexistent. The balance of considerations may thus shift.

Considerations for new legislation or the abolition of existing legislation are obviously very different. One should be especially careful not to legislate against speech because of populist demands: more often than not, the purpose of such legislation is to suppress and silence political minorities who are seen as a threat. In such cases, arguments against the legislation are rooted in political morality, not in the public nature of law and its enforcement. When such legislation is passed nonetheless, enforcement agencies and the courts should regard themselves as institutional guarantees against abuse. When enforcement agencies fail and respond to populist or other pressures, it is the task of the courts to protect freedom of speech against unjustified intervention. When the speech is clearly undesirable, but the law is not the proper tool because of a situation of deep controversy, the enforcement agencies must do the protecting, since the courts are in an institutional bind: conviction may reinforce the dangerous tendency of the inciters to accuse the system and delegitimate it, whereas acquittal may send an undesirable message of permissibility. What needs to be protected in such cases is not the rights of the speakers (if they are violated at all in these cases) but the integrity of the democratic system and the legal system within it. To preserve this integrity, special caution must be used in the decision to require a court of law to decide publicly on the illegality of inciting speech.

In the case of incitement law in Israel, I think the laws, although overbroad, should be left on the books for the present. I see no reason for a declaration that after the assassination it became clear that these laws are unnecessary. The question of the optimal legislation should be discussed when the political and the legal systems are not in the midst of turmoil. In the meantime, enforcement agencies should be careful not to invoke the law in inappropriate situations.[37]

I return to the issue of case versus rule. One may be tempted to say that if laws against incitement could not be enforced after Rabin's death, there will never be a case in which the law might justifiably be invoked. The conclusion of abolition seems to follow. I disagree. The Elba case may provide a case in point. I do not know of many written texts that came as close to encouraging murder as Rabbi Elba's text. It is a declaration of holy war against a whole people, far beyond shoutings of "Death to the Arabs" after a cruel terrorist activity. It is a reasoned argument, made by a religious authority, to justify and require murder of individuals simply because they are Arabs. Moreover, Elba made preparations to act in accord with his text.

Perhaps it would have been wiser to prosecute Elba only for his actions: collecting ammunition and conspiring to harm Arabs. Given the conditions in Israel, however, especially the background of Jewish violence against Arabs, and faced with a choice between declaring Elba's text illegal and protecting such speech, I believe acquittal was out of the question—it would have dealt a deadly blow to the law. Indeed, it may be that Israelis would have used more inciting language, with clearer and more immediate deadly results, had the law been different. We should not abolish laws simply because they do most of their work by guiding behavior without the need for prosecution.[38]

Rabin's murder dramatizes a case in which the argument for legal curbs may seem, in retrospect, extremely strong. Nonetheless, a detached and sober analysis at the time of the assassination could have shown what developments since then demonstrate: such legal curbs may often be ineffective and counterproductive. It is important to see why an argument that appears compelling in such dramatic and rare cases may nonetheless be misleading. It is even more important to see how crucial and central the often-disregarded institutional and systemic features of law and its enforcement are. The frustration of helplessness in the face of undesirable complex social processes may persist, but deluding ourselves into thinking that the law can solve the problem is wrong. The mistake, moreover, is not costless: the attempt to regulate such situations through law will not only fail to fight dangerous social trends, it may endanger the very ability of law to perform its distinct function in society.

The public nature of law, as a tool of the state, is relevant and important to the question of whether the law should be used to curb speech. Law, however, is a way of regulating and dealing with social problems, and these problems often have foundations that go very deep. Law's effectiveness as a tool may depend on its being used as a part of an integrated program, where all are aware of the law's strengths and limitations and the risks involved in its invocation.

Notes

1. Mill's argument in *On Liberty* (London: J. W. Parker, 1854), chapter 2, as well as Milton's, is not confined to democracies.

2. See, for example, Alexander Meiklejohn, *Political Freedom: The Constitutional Powers of the People* (New York: Oxford Univ. Press, 1965); and Thomas Emerson, *Toward A General Theory of the First Amendment* (New York: Random House, 1966).

3. I am using here a narrow meaning of *censorship* as the legal prior prohibition of speech. I am not *arguing* for this narrow usage. Under broader meanings, all legal curbs, both prior and subsequent, are called "censorship." Under yet broader meanings, all inhibitive mechanisms of speech are called "censorship," as Richard Burt seems to do in "(Un)Censoring in Detail: The Fetish of Censorship in the Early Modern Past and the Postmodern Present," pages 17–41 in this volume. For a very interesting discussion of the "meaning" of censorship see Frederick Schauer, "The Ontology of Censorship," pages 147–68 in this volume.

4. When people in power wanted to prevent publication of intimate information about them, it was often related to their wish not to create an incentive for insurrection and not to contribute to a tendency to feel contempt for the government. Legal prohibition of invasions of privacy by publication appeared, if at all, only at the very end of the nineteenth century. For a historical account of the law of defamation, see Debora Shuger, "Civility and Censorship in Early Modern England," pages 89–110 in this volume.

5. I am stressing here the speech variety of these arguments, but the same strategy is made to challenge the general belief that individuals enjoy equal freedom of action in the prelegal state. Such critiques come both from the political left, concerning economic equality, and from radical feminists, concerning the sources of the inequality of women. See Catharine A. MacKinnon, *Toward a Feminist Theory of the State* (Cambridge, Mass.: Harvard Univ. Press, 1989).

6. Liberalism is criticized for allegedly seeing pornography as a "private" matter, in which society and the law should not interfere because of Mill-type arguments. For a discussion see Ruth Gavison, "Feminism and the Public-Private Distinction," *Stanford Law Review* 45 (1992): 1.

7. See Rae Langton, "Whose Right? Ronald Dworkin, Women and Pornographers," *Philosophy and Public Affairs* 19 (1990): 311.

8. I take it that this is the attitude, both theoretical and practical, exemplified by Richard Burt (see note 3).

9. For a recent comprehensive analysis see J. Cohen, *Philosophy and Public Affairs* 22 (1993): 207–63; reprinted in David Heyd, ed., *Toleration: An Elusive Virtue* (Princeton: Princeton Univ. Press, 1996), 173.

10. Some leaders of the opposition refused to participate in these mass demonstrations because they tended to get out of control and because the participants in the main were not Likud members but settlers and members of fringe radical right-wing groups. They were also careful to maintain the delicate line between criticizing the agreements and delegitimating the government. However, many other leaders of the opposition expressed themselves less cautiously and used metaphors and analogies that were similar to those I describe here. For a long list of such pronouncements by leaders prior to the murder, see *Haaretz*, 24 Oct. 1996, p. B7 (in Hebrew).

11. For a comprehensive review see Pnina Lahav's description in Pnina Lahav, ed., *Press Law in Modern Democracies: A Comparative Study* (New York: Longman, 1985).

12. Elba's essay was included in a book titled *Baruch Hagever* ("Blessed the Man," from a Jewish prayer). The title is a pun on Goldstein's name.

13. *Elba v. State of Israel*, Cr. App. 2831/95. Ironically, the appeal was heard in court the day after Rabin's murder; the justices sat without making any comments to the attorneys' oral arguments. In a second hearing a few months later, some justices questioned the prosecutor about the compatibility of the charges with freedom of religion and religious study. The same justices, who are both identified with the religious right, voted to acquit Elba on the basis of freedom of speech and freedom of religion. The majority, including Barak, who is known as a staunch supporter of free speech, presented a tortured justification for the decision to convict.

14. *Jabbarin v. State of Israel*. Barak allowed a further hearing of this case.

15. A religious person who said on television that he was glad Rabin "the dictator" was dead, and that he hoped Arafat and Peres would have the same fate, was detained until the end of criminal proceedings against him and then indicted. After a public outcry, he was allowed to go home on bail. In July 1996 he was acquitted by the court. The judge said his words were despicable, but that the intention required for conviction had not been proven.

16. One of the accused was elected to Israel's parliament under a right-wing ticket calling for "transfer" of Israel's Arabs; his immunity must be lifted if the trial is to continue.

17. The Palestinian Authority (PA) was given control of all major cities of the West Bank with the exception of Hebron, where four hundred Jewish settlers have established an enclave. The delay in the evacuation of Hebron was agreed upon by Peres and Arafat in the wake of the terrorist attacks on Israel in February and March of 1996. Elections to the PA were duly held, and Arafat became the elected president of the new entity.

18. One member of the religious right was prosecuted for allegedly conducting

a religious ceremony tantamount to a symbolic execution of Peres. The ultrareligious press contained words depicting Peres as anti-Jewish and deserving hate and contempt.

19. Yigal Amir was convicted for Rabin's assassination and sentenced to life imprisonment. He also was convicted with his brother and another man for conspiring to kill Rabin and for acting against Arabs.

Three girls from a religious high school admitted on national television that they admired Amir and, moreover, were in love with him. After a public outcry, they apologized and explained that their words had been taken out of context. However, a study revealed that up to 15 percent of high school students in Israel agreed with Amir and that many believed that their teachers felt the same way. Since it is not "politically correct" to publicly support Amir, the actual numbers are probably higher.

20. An orthodox Jewish soldier who shot at Arabs and wounded some in the Hebron marketplace in early January 1997 enjoyed very little public support. He was later pronounced insane by a special committee.

21. The requirement that speech be censored only if it leads to bad results may be a distinctive feature of all *legal* regulation. One may well seek to discourage or criticize speech when it involves falsehood, when it is vulgar, inelegant, too noisy, frivolous, irrelevant, boring or in bad taste, and one may shun people whose speech is often of this type. All these do not seem proper reasons for invoking the power of the law, however.

22. I therefore think that the decision to prosecute the leaders of Zu Artzenu, a right-wing organization, for incitement and not for their illegal activities was a mistake.

23. When the *intifada* started, Rabin, who was then the minister of defense, said during a television broadcast that Israel should "break their bones" to teach the Arabs a lesson. I never liked this statement, but I am not sure that asking the attorney general to prosecute Rabin was the right response.

24. Early in 1996, when it was reported that Yihye Ayash, the man responsible for many terrorist activities in Israel, was killed, all Israeli leaders expressed deep satisfaction. No call was made to prosecute anyone for expressing joy at the killing.

25. Linking an action to speech may consist of two parts. One is the concession that we do not want to protect a person calling "Fire" in a crowded theater, or using "fighting words"; the other is to redefine these activities in terms of the distinction between speech and action. The second move is best seen as a rhetorical device, aimed at fitting the practical conclusion into a principle prohibiting all punishment of speech. My concern is with the practical question itself.

26. B. Fischoff and R. Beyth, "I Knew It Would Happen: Remembered Probabilities of Once Future Things," *Organizational Behavior and Human Performance* 13 (1975): 1–13. The authors argue for the existence of "the hindsight fallacy" and suggest that once a person knows that an event in fact occurred, the probability he assigns to its occurrence is much higher than the one he would have assigned had he not known the fact.

27. This may be supported by the fact that Amir had started to plan the killing very soon after the signing of the first agreement with the Palestinians. His profile is not at all that of the incited youth. He seems to be a calculating individual, and one

moved by a sense of a holy mission. Although he did participate in public protest against the political process, it is not clear whether he decided on the murder only after he became convinced that democratic protest had failed.

28. Some indeed argue that the legal system failed because it cooperated with some segments of the public to strengthen this distinction between the risks of Jews acting against Jews and those of Jews acting against Arabs by showing leniency toward the latter.

29. Thus, if the only way to regulate an industry is by extremely vague standards that are not self-executing and cannot be made clearer through litigation, and if the result is capricious and erratic policy of prosecution and judicial decisions, it may be neither just nor effective to try such a regulation.

30. After the Hebron massacre, the Shamgar Commission of Inquiry documented the failure of the legal system to deal effectively with Jewish violence against Arabs and recommended that law enforcement against Jewish violence be stepped up. This determination came as no surprise to those who followed law enforcement in the occupied territories. The close ties, both personal and ideological, between Jewish terrorism and the religious right wing of Israeli politics prevented implementation of this recommendation.

These close ties were expressed by the fact that many rabbis and political leaders openly supported members of the "Jewish underground," a group whose members shot to death Palestinian students and maimed Palestinian mayors, and who, in April 1989, were detected just before they succeeded in blowing up two Arab buses. It was extremely difficult to prosecute these people, the sentences were very lenient, and the murderers (there is a mandatory life sentence for murder in Israel) were released by presidential pardon after less than seven years, despite the fact that some of them did not express remorse. More problematic than lenient sentences is the fact that many acts of killing, harassing, and looting of Palestinians do not result in any prosecution or conviction.

31. The reaction within the religious world to the conviction of Elba was very subdued. However, when Netanyahu decided to release all Palestinian women prisoners according to the Oslo and Hebron agreements, calls were made to pardon Jews who had been convicted of murdering Arabs as well.

32. This is a danger that attends all enforcement of the law in periods of political protest. A rabbi and his wife, both from Hebron, were prosecuted in early 1995 for attacking policemen on duty. Both refused to attend the court, and subpoenas against them were issued. The wife refused to obey the order. She was carried into the court hall, refused to stand up to hear the verdict, and kept shouting that the court and the police were traitors because they had betrayed the Jewish settlers of Hebron. She was sentenced to ten days in prison for contempt of court.

33. Indeed, much of the moral force of the demand that those using "inciting" speech accept some indirect responsibility for the murder is allegedly taken away by the fact that the demand is directed against the opposition on the whole, or against the university in which the murderer studied, rather then at the elements of public and political behavior in both camps who suggest a willingness to resolve differences by force.

34. It is interesting to see what happened in Israel in the wake of the attack on the

Supreme Court and the chief justice. All circles explicitly and immediately denied any intended connection between the harsh criticism and violence. While the government was slow to denounce the criticism (since some religious members of the government repeated it), many other parts of "civil society" came out very strongly against the delegitimating speech. The speakers themselves persist, but the severance between speech and violent action has been internalized. The speech is justified as part of an attempt to change the role of the court in Israeli society, especially in the area of the separation of religion and the state, and not as a prelude to using force against it.

35. This alternative way of achieving the desired protection is not always available: such protection cannot be given to women in their families or to African Americans in bigoted neighborhoods. When the threat is more widely and diffusely spread, the case for fighting the conditions facilitating the violence may be stronger.

36. On this front, the record is not very clear, attesting to the complexities of the situation. Although some religious leaders have stressed the need to take religion out of politics, this is a minority view that is challenged by most religious political leaders. There has been no clear declaration by political and religious elites condemning Amir's analysis of Jewish law. Similarly, when asked about Elba's positions, one frequently hears that he is a radical and marginal, but there has been no serious public discussion, from a religious perspective, about his exposition of Jewish law.

37. Most observers believe that the attorney general overreacted in the period after the murder and that he has since regained composure. In late 1996, however, a right-wing person who expressed joy at the deeds of Amir and Goldstein, and made implicit threats against Netanyahu, was indicted for incitement. Many doubted the wisdom of this decision.

38. Laws that are generally unenforced (and that are very difficult to enforce effectively) create fascinating jurisprudential problems on various levels. One argument seeks correspondence between laws on the books and laws in action. This is one of the reasons that realists argue for a definition of law that will exclude unenforced laws from the realm of law. Furthermore, laws that are not regularly enforced create the danger of arbitrary and discriminating enforcement. These are reasons for abolishing them. It is not clear, however, that laws do not have expressive functions even where these functions are not reinforced by actual enforcement, and abolishing the law will prevent law enforcers from using the law against blatant violations of accepted norms. It is worth noting that the problem is not unique to the law or even to normative systems more generally. Some accept the need to deter others from serious violence as a justification for the development and possession of nuclear weapons, despite the fact that it is well understood that using such weapons is very hard, almost impossible, to justify, and that using them may well be counterproductive.

Ernst Zündel following his trial in Toronto in 1985.
Courtesy Ernst Zündel.

Policing the Past: Holocaust Denial and the Law

Lawrence Douglas

Is it possible that the antonym of "forgetting" is not "remembering," but *justice?*

—Yosef Hayim Yerushalmi[1]

The trial of Ernst Zündel in 1985 placed an unusual question before a Toronto jury: did the Holocaust actually happen? Zündel, who had made a small fortune in Canada as a photo retoucher for mass circulation magazines (his work twice had received awards from The Art Directors' Club of Toronto),[2] had arranged for the publication of *Did Six Million Really Die?*, a pamphlet that alleged the Holocaust was a Zionist hoax. Charged with violating a little-used portion of the Canadian Criminal Code prohibiting the publication of false statements "likely to cause injury or mischief to a public interest,"[3] Zündel turned his trial into a media circus, arriving at court each day in a flak jacket and hard hat emblazoned with the words "Freedom of Speech."

Yet more noteworthy than the defendant's courtroom histrionics was the case's odd procedural profile. Because the indictment charged Zündel with knowingly publishing false statements, the court reasoned that it was incumbent upon the prosecution to prove the falsity of Zündel's denial of the Holocaust. Although courts commonly take "judicial notice" of the truth of certain "notorious" and accepted facts, the trial judge reasoned that taking such notice of the Holocaust essentially would have relieved the prosecution of its burden of proving guilt. The Crown, as a consequence, was obliged to prove—in accordance with legal conventions of proof and evidence—that the Holocaust in fact occurred, a discomfiting position in a trial meant to demonstrate that certain statements are so beyond the pale of legitimate dispute as to justify the imposition of a criminal sanction.

Notwithstanding the unusual, perhaps unseemly evidentiary questions placed before the court, the Zündel trial provocatively captures the changing terms of the law's engagement with the Holocaust. The spectacular trials staged about Nazi atrocities—the first Nuremberg trial in 1945–46, the Eichmann trial in 1961, and the Barbie trial in 1987—were all centrally concerned with the problematic of responsibility: how could the conventional idiom of the criminal law accommodate the extreme evil of genocide? Half a century after the commission of the original crimes, the need to punish the perpetrators has diminished—for reasons less moral than actuarial. Yet the gradual dying off of the perpetrators does not signal the end of legal struggles to do justice to the Holocaust. As the Zündel case suggests, the problem that the Holocaust poses to the law today is less one of assigning responsibility than one of preserving responsible memory. The law has been enlisted in the project of safeguarding historical truth.[4]

Yet the Zündel case does more than merely exemplify the changing nature of the law's engagement with the Holocaust. It poses in stark terms the question that will animate this essay: is the law adequate to the task of securing the history of the Holocaust in responsible memory? The answer, I believe, is no, and I claim this not because I fear that attempts to use the law to proscribe Holocaust denial will contribute to an undesirable restriction of free speech rights. Rather, I argue that certain features that define the law as a formal discourse—such as the concept of legal harm and the epistemological conventions that control adversarial trials—should make us particularly wary about using the law to police the bounds of Holocaust representations. Finding my examples in the United States, Germany, France, and Israel, and then returning to Canada and the Zündel case, I will argue that the efforts to use legal means to safeguard the history of the Holocaust may contribute to distortions of the very historical record that the law has been asked to defend.

The claim that law can play a valuable role in making the past intelligible is a proposition accepted by most legal theorists and historians.[5] Like the discipline of history, the law remains anchored to a factual record that must be investigated and probed with an eye toward organizing events and actions into a coherent narrative embedded in a normative framework.[6] Although the murder trial of O. J. Simpson in 1996 might provide an example of the hazards of relying upon the verdict delivered in a criminal trial as a reliable source of historical instruction, both criminal and civil litigation can often serve to clarify and settle disputed history.[7] In the case of the Holocaust, the Nuremberg trial of the major war criminals was largely prompted by the Allies' conviction that open judicial proceedings could serve as tools of historical instruction.[8] The legal adequacy of the Nuremberg trial has been a continuing subject of debate, but few would deny the importance of the vast amount of historical information assembled by the prosecution and later made available to scholars.

What remains more controversial is the claim that the law can contribute to an understanding of the past by silencing or criminalizing denials of the historical record. In the United States in particular, efforts to use the law to censor Holocaust denial have been met with familiar First Amendment arguments. Alan Dershowitz, the outspoken avatar of free speech, expressed the idea succinctly.

> I am categorically opposed to any court, any school board, any governmental agent taking judicial notice about any historical event, even one that I know to the absolute core of my being occurred, like the Holocaust. I don't want the government to tell me that it occurred because I don't want any government ever to tell me that it *didn't* occur.[9]

Dershowitz's "slippery slope" notwithstanding, it can be argued that certain efforts to make Holocaust denial legally actionable are perfectly compatible with First Amendment jurisprudence. In 1985, for example, Mel Mermelstein, an Auschwitz survivor, sued the Institute for Historical Review, a California "think tank" dedicated to Holocaust "revisionism," for its failure to honor a pledge to pay $50,000 to anyone who could prove that gassings took place at Auschwitz. Claiming injury as a result of both breach of contract and, more interestingly, the intentional infliction of emotional distress, Mermelstein accepted a pretrial settlement in which the institute agreed to pay the promised original sum and an additional $100,000 in damages. Although the precedential implications of the case are less than clear as a result of the early settlement, the Mermelstein litigation suggests that the First Amendment might not bar civil suits claiming that Holocaust denial constitutes tortious conduct. While the "First Amendment recognizes no such thing as a 'false' idea,"[10] it does recognize that there is such a thing as a false fact, and if the distinction between ideas and facts has been problemized in many circles, it remains sound as a matter of law: the Supreme Court continues to maintain that "false statements of fact" deserve no constitutional protection as "they interfere with the truth-seeking function of the marketplace of ideas."[11] Thus if we agree that a statement denying the mass extermination of Jews during World War II constitutes a false statement of fact, and further, that such a statement will usually be made in reckless disregard of the truth, then it seems that, Alan Dershowitz's concerns notwithstanding, civil actions such as "intentional infliction of emotional distress" might offer a constitutionally permissible response to Holocaust denial.

Lurking beneath the doctrinal issue, however, remains the more interesting question: why seek a legal remedy to Holocaust denial? The most obvious answer seems to be the one that prompted Mermelstein to bring his suit. As Elie Wiesel has argued, Holocaust denial defames the dead and insults survivors. In this respect, Holocaust denial seems to provide an excellent example of the type of speech against which the tort of "intentional infliction of emotional distress" was meant to protect. The Mermelstein suit can thus be seen as an unremarkable effort to use legal means to seek compensation for injuries that the law was meant to redress.

In another respect, however, the turn to the law to silence Holocaust denial seems to have very little to do with the compensation of survivors. In the last decade, several Western democracies have passed laws specifically criminalizing Holocaust denial. Such laws, it would seem, serve ends distinct from the Mermelstein litigation—or, rather, they accomplish directly what

Mermelstein could achieve in this country only through indirection: they safeguard the facticity of the Holocaust from the erosion of memory itself. So understood, criminalizing Holocaust denial anticipates a time when the event will no longer remain alive in the memory of survivors, as the group of plaintiffs who could claim emotional distress will have died off. The law thus prepares us for a rapidly approaching future in which the Holocaust will have become an artifact of history.

That the facticity of the Holocaust would require such legal protection is, in a sense, remarkable. Despite the Nazis' best efforts to hide their atrocities, it is difficult to imagine an event of recent history for which the factual record is more complete. Why then do we need the law to secure the Holocaust in responsible memory, when we do not need a law to remind us that the earth revolves around the sun or that Napoleon's armies fought at Waterloo? Part of the answer seems to lie in a fear of the spread of the disbelief that Primo Levi notes first greeted news of the camps.[12] The very extraordinary nature of Nazi genocide, it is argued, renders it vulnerable to a campaign of skepticism. Harold Kaplan has observed that "disbelief [originally] was justified, for to discover its [the Holocaust's] reduction of human beings from all existential assumptions is to undermine reality."[13] Laws that proscribe Holocaust denial thus seek to contain one of the most odious features of such speech: the way it turns the very unbelievability of the atrocities into prima facie evidence of their impossibility. Moreover, Holocaust denial is a particularly invidious form of hate speech, as it typically claims that Jews—or a conspiracy of "World Zionists"—are responsible for creating and spreading the myth of their own extermination in order to extort money from Christian nations. The literature of Holocaust denial thus draws on classic anti-Semitic stereotypes of Jews as conspiratorial, money-hungry internationalists, shamelessly attempting to extract advantage from the history of their own alleged victimization.

If a shibboleth of the First Amendment counsels that the best response to odious speech is more speech, such a recipe contemplates a capitulation to the very strategies of Holocaust revisionism. As Deborah Lipstadt argued in *Denying the Holocaust,* to debate Holocaust deniers is already to accede to the force of their logic—it is to admit that the topic is one about which reasonable persons can have reasonable disagreements.[14] There is, of course, a difference between refusing to debate and turning to the law to silence those who would; in this regard, I believe it is necessary to understand efforts to proscribe Holocaust denial as born of an additional desire to safeguard this past from what Geoffrey Hartman has termed an "encroaching anti-memory," where the past is trivialized and banalized through a "culture industry that can simulate anything and everything."[15] Proscribing Holocaust denial is thus meant to except the topic from the spectacle of talk-show contention and the circulation of ambient media noise.

That groups or individuals should turn to the law to silence the voice of Holocaust denial is hardly, then, surprising. As Robert Post has observed, legal sanctions both enjoy a monopoly on physical coercion and "alone purport to define social norms in accents that are universal."[16] Post's observation, however, not only explains the turn to law but also invites us to consider the state's motives in agreeing to use *its* power to criminalize Holocaust denial. Why would the *state* provide the facticity of the Holocaust a degree of legal insulation not offered other facts? By proscribing Holocaust denial in specific, doesn't the liberal state abandon its putative neutrality in order to protect the sensitivities of a particular group within a heterogeneous community? This, of course, raises a deeper question: by criminalizing denials of the historical record, whom does the law seek to protect?

Again, we might argue that the law is protecting the memory of the camp victims, although it seems odd, if not problematic, for a liberal state to use the *criminal* law to enforce norms of decency and respect toward such a specific group. We might say that the state is attempting to protect the historical record itself, although, again, it seems odd that the state would enlist its coercive power to safeguard a particular factual statement. Perhaps, then, it can be argued that Holocaust denial does not so much offend a particular group or history itself as it insults the very notions of meaning upon which the liberal concept of public discourse is predicated.

This claim is far more foundational, for it does not insist that Holocaust denial can be silenced because it insults codes of civil behavior and speech; rather, it contends that because Holocaust denial makes a mockery of conventions of truth-testing and good faith conversation, it violates the most basic norms that make intelligible the concept of public discourse. Stipulating to the facticity of the Holocaust—an event that remains a trauma to the liberal imagination—thus serves as a litmus test of one's willingness to participate in the thinnest version of the discursive community. As such, Holocaust denial threatens less a specific group than the discursive basis of the liberal state.

The state's interest in proscribing Holocaust revisionism may seem complex if not obscure, and this complexity of motive has left its traces upon the laws that have been passed to criminalize denial. Consider the law passed by the Federal Republic of Germany in 1985 to staunch the rise of rightist and neo-Nazi disputations of the death camps. The statute, known as the "*Auschwitz-lüge*" or "Auschwitz-lie" law, criminalizes claims that the Holocaust was a phantasm of the Zionist imagination. Based on the theory of criminal libel, the law treats Holocaust denial as an insult *(Beleidigung)* punishable by up to one year in prison. This law, however, did not pioneer the concept of criminal libel in German jurisprudence. Instead, it modified the existing law to enable the state, on its own, specifically to punish Holocaust denial. Prior to these modifications, the old statute functioned as a hybrid of civil and criminal law, relying upon the insulted individual—the person who had putatively suffered the legal harm—to petition the state to initiate criminal proceedings against the alleged insulter. The old law thus functioned to protect specific groups or persons from uncivil expressions. This arrangement, however, had begged the question of who, within the meaning of the German law, could claim to be insulted by denials of the Holocaust.

As Eric Stein has shown, the answers that German courts had supplied were problematic at best.[17] A case in 1979, for example, posed the question of whether a German citizen with one Jewish grandfather could petition the state to prosecute a man who had publicly posted a leaflet attacking the Holocaust as a Zionist swindle.[18] The Bundesgerichtshof (Federal Court of Justice) concluded that the man could bring an insult claim because, though not a "full Jew," he would have been classified as a second-degree *Mischling* (mixed breed) according to the notorious Nuremberg laws of 1935 and thus subject to considerable discrimination.[19] Extending this mode of analysis, an appellate court in 1985 acquitted a defendant because the petitioner was neither a Jew nor a *Mischling* and therefore could not claim to be offended by the words of a Holocaust denier.[20] Yet the unseemliness of relying on the standards and definitions supplied by the laws that paved the way to the Holocaust to decide who may legally claim to be insulted by Holocaust denials did not signal an idiosyncratic failing of the German courts. The notion of legal harm, the concept through which the law structures its institutional capacity to redress social wrongs, inevitably thrust German courts into the position of having to decide who could legitimately claim to be insulted for the purposes of the statute.

The law passed in 1985 solved this problem by abolishing the requirement of the private petitioner, authorizing the state to initiate criminal prosecution *ex officio*. By placing the state in the position of the complainant, the statute seemed to recognize that Holocaust denial insults not only Jews as "a group singled-out by fate" but also the German state itself and its historical record.[21] Indeed, the new law seemed to commit the state to using its coercive power to preserve a singular historical truth.

The wisdom of using state force to sanction denials of the historical record, however, has not escaped scholarly and judicial challenge. The terms of these challenges are, in a sense, familiar, as they revisit the distinction between facts and interpretations—a distinction that is recognized in both Anglo American and Continental jurisprudence,[22] yet one that has been increasingly subject to challenge by scholars (in the legal academy and elsewhere) who argue that facts are socially constructed and thus prefigured by interpretation.[23] In the hands of figures such as Ernst Nolte, a controversial right-wing academic associated with the *Historikerstreit* (historians' debate) of the last decade, these arguments have been enlisted against the Auschwitz-lie law. Arguing that the Final Solution found ample precedent in Stalin's gulag, Nolte has attacked the Auschwitz-lie law not because he denies that the mass killing of Jews took place in World War II, but because he objects to the law's implicit interpretation of these facts—that is, that such killing was so unique and unprecedented that its memory deserves special judicial protection.[24] While Nazi atrocities cannot be denied, Nolte argues, the very decision to insulate this fact from debate commits the state to a particular reading of the event. Such a law, Nolte fears, might chill not only Holocaust deniers but also the work of "legitimate" scholars who question the dogma of the Holocaust's uniqueness.

Nolte's logic is suspect on its own terms: even if we agree that the law, by virtue of its singularity, implicitly commits the state to an interpretation of the Holocaust as unique, it does not follow that the law will therefore work to chill the work of serious scholars. The speciousness of Nolte's reasoning notwithstanding, his argument suggests the difficulties that would face a legislature or court trying to stipulate the content of those facts the denial of which a law could legitimately proscribe. As Dershowitz has observed, "What are we to take judicial notice of?... Certainly not the number six million; that was an approximation. Certainly not the fact that all Jews were gassed in the way that movies suggest that they were because it was far more complicated than that."[25] Indeed, one could argue that the very term *Holocaust* denotes less a historical fact than a particular understanding of this history—namely that "the mass annihilation of Jews was unique, different from other genocidal phenomena."[26]

Yet assuming, as I believe we can, that the facticity of the Holocaust can find summary in certain intersubjectively truthful and therefore legally enforceable statements, the more interesting issue lies in the idea that by legislating against the Auschwitz-lie, the German state seems committed to the position that a foundational truth deserving the protection of its legal and coercive apparatus should be the fact of the state's own criminal past. Jacques Derrida, following the lead of Max Weber and Walter Benjamin, has detailed the complex ways that states buttress their claims to legitimacy through acts of forgetting—rituals of erasure that obscure any connection to the state's foundational moment, inevitably a time of violent, lawless instantiation.[27]

In contrast, the German law demands that no one deny the state's monstrous past. In this manner, the German Federal Republic attempts to redeem its claims of legitimacy through acts of coerced remembering, in which the history of past crimes remains ever present and in which the law serves as the muscle of memory. Yet the very reliance upon the law to police responsible memory serves not only to connect the present German state to its past incarnation but also to sever such ties. Here the state's candor in admitting past transgressions appears as a legitimating virtue, and the law that proscribes insults to the historical record also serves to create a gulf that separates the present state from its reprobate precursor by adopting a posture of obsessive mindfulness of the past.

The German example thus complicates the understanding that laws proscribing Holocaust denial offer symbolic protection to the norms of public discourse. Holocaust denial, in the German context, challenges not simply these liberal norms, but the very integrity of a state whose legitimacy depends upon its confessional embrace of the past. Holocaust denial, in this regard, poses less a threat to either the principles of public speech or the survivors than to the state attempting to make good on its effort at liberal redemption.

Yet if the state is committed to acknowledging its past identity as victimizer, it also insists on a legal recognition of the German as victim, for in its final form, the Auschwitz-lie law came to proscribe more than simply Holocaust denial. Opposed by the Christian Democrats, the senior party of the ruling coalition, the bill was subtly changed in committee to win support among the government's conservative flank. In its altered and approved form, the law now criminalizes *two* distinct statements of denial: those that deny the Nazi death camps, and those that deny the forced expulsion of "ethnic" Germans from the former German provinces of Poland at the war's conclusion.[28] The law thus equates the destruction of European Jewry with the forced migration of Silesian and East Prussian Germans.

As grotesque as this may seem, it is in a sense predictable. Once the state moves beyond protecting a thin notion of public discourse and views itself as harmed by representations of the past, then the laws used to police these representations will tend to reveal more about the state's own sensitivities than about the history it seeks to protect. And once the state supplants the survivors as the object of legal harm, it should come as no surprise that the legal instrument originally meant to protect the survivors from "insults" to the historical record should itself become a source of fresh insults.

Germany is not alone in the effort to use the law to silence the voice of Holocaust denial. France passed a law in 1990 making it a crime for anyone to contest "the existence of one or several crimes against humanity as defined in Article 6 of the Statue of the International Military Tribunal."[29] The International Military Tribunal was the official name of the court that presided over the Nuremberg Trial of the Major War Criminals; Article 6 of the tribunal's charter (the "London Charter") defined crimes against humanity to include:

> Murder, extermination, enslavement, starvation or deportation and other inhumane acts committed against any civilian population, before or during the war, or persecutions on political, racial, or religious grounds in execution of or in connection with any crime within the jurisdiction of the Tribunal.[30]

By proscribing denials of the very crimes condemned at Nuremberg, the French law seems drafted with greater specificity and precedential force than the comparable law in Germany. Yet the French law also seems peculiarly insular, as it does not protect historical facts per se, as much as it protects *legal facts*, or, at the least, historical facts that were produced by the legal process. The problems with using the juridical conclusions that issued from the Nuremberg tribunal as the benchmark of historical truth can be appreciated by considering the tribunal's understanding of genocide more closely. Article 6 of the London Charter, for example, offers a significantly narrower definition of crimes against humanity than the text suggests. While the words "before or during the war" imply that the Nuremberg court enjoyed a broad power to condemn Nazi crimes, a reader of the original document finds his eye drawn to an asterisk after the word "war" and to the laconic accompanying footnote, the only explanatory note in the entire text of the charter: "Comma substituted in place of semicolon by Protocol of 6 October 1945."[31]

The consequence of this seemingly minor, last-minute substitution was that the first clause of Article 6 was placed under the control of the last: "in connection with any crime within the jurisdiction of the Tribunal." This was crucial, as the court concluded that only crimes involving the "planning, preparation, initiation or waging of a war of aggression" were "within the jurisdiction of the Tribunal." The tribunal, as a result, had no authority to condemn inhumane acts if committed unconnected to the "war of aggression." The Allies' worries that a too-robust concept of crimes against humanity would supply a potentially unattractive precedent for challenging a sovereign's control over its own domestic population found voice in a fascinating example of the power of diacritics.[32] The idea of jurisdictional competence—the notion that a court's authority to pronounce judgment is restricted geographically, conceptually, and by the knowledge that its present decisions may bind future adjudication—thus led the Nuremberg tribunal to limit the reach of its own power. In this way, jurisdictional concerns supported an understanding that viewed the Holocaust essentially as the horrific consequence of a war of aggression.

The record of the French prosecution at the Nuremberg trial further underscores the ironies produced by the 1990 French law. Responsible at Nuremberg for presenting evidence of war crimes and crimes against humanity, the French neglected to include the annihilation of European Jewry as one of the Nazis' principal offenses.[33] Indeed, the only mention of Jews in the entire French case was by prosecutor François de Menthon: "It is also well known that racial discriminations were provoked against citizens of the occupied countries who were catalogued as Jews, measures particularly hateful, damaging to their personal rights and to their human dignity."[34] Thus the recent French law, if read narrowly (and perhaps somewhat mockingly) in light of the French case presented at Nuremberg, would not even touch Holocaust denial, as the extermination of the Jews was not, judging by the evidence submitted by the French prosecution, one of the "several crimes against humanity as defined in Article 6 of the Statute of the International Military Tribunal."[35]

An Austrian statute passed in 1992 that makes it a crime if a person "denies, grossly trivializes, approves or seeks to justify the national socialist genocide or other national socialist crimes against humanity" raises similar problems.[36] While Austrian courts have not yet parsed the meaning of such potentially fraught language as "grossly trivializes" *(gröblich verharmlost)*, one could make the case—not entirely facetiously—that such a law could make actionable the performance of the respective prosecutorial teams, particularly the French, at Nuremberg. The crime of "genocide," coined in 1943 by Raphaël Lemkin, an adviser on foreign affairs to the U.S. War Department, to describe the systematic annihilation of European Jewry, is specifically named in the Nuremberg indictment under "War Crimes," but the word is never uttered at the trial itself.[37] The trial's most spectacular testimony regarding the Final Solution, the testimony of Rudolf Höß, former commandant at Auschwitz, is supplied by a witness not for the prosecution but for the defense: Höß was called for the purpose of establishing that the existence of centers of extermination was a well-concealed fact, unknown even to the senior members of the Nazi command on trial at Nuremberg.[38]

The most sustained discussion of the annihilation of Jews is presented by the Soviet and American prosecutors, but even here certain omissions and distortions remain notable. In a revealing slip, L. N. Smirnov, the Soviet chief counsel, speaks of the "excessive anti-Semitism of the Hitlerite criminals."[39] Not only does Smirnov imply that a measure of anti-Semitism may be normal, more crucially, he suggests that the Holocaust can be understood as an "excess," an uncontrolled outpouring of the same violent impulses that directed the Nazis' brutal war effort. This reasoning echoes Robert Jackson's opening statement for the prosecution, in which the Final Solution is portrayed as an expedient of "aggressive war," the chief crime for which he argued the Nazi leadership could and should be held responsible.[40] Following the Allies' restrictive definition of "crimes against humanity" in Article 6, Jackson viewed Nazi genocide as a dreadful although ancillary transgression, a consequence of belligerent militarism.

One can, of course, claim it is unfair to condemn the prosecutorial teams, burdened with shaping a vast amount of evidence into a complex juridical case in a short period of time, for failing to be fully attentive to the crimes against the Jews. Moreover, one can argue that despite its manifest shortcomings, Nuremberg "built a good foundation for including the murder of European Jews in an understanding of Nazism and the Second World War."[41] Yet the failure of the Nuremberg trial to address satisfactorily the Nazis' most spectacular crimes was not simply an example of overtaxed prosecutors revealing the same indifference to the fate of the Jews that the Allies had shown during the war. A marginalizing of the Holocaust was in some sense the inevitable result of a juridical effort whose aim was to pioneer the use of legal means to legitimate the punishment of aggressive militarism.

The Eichmann trial, by contrast, importantly corrected this defect, as it supplied a harrowing, moving, and remarkably complete record of the Nazis' largely successful effort to annihilate European Jewry. The juridical narrative that explained these crimes, however, has been the subject of numerous critiques. Hannah Arendt's *Eichmann in Jerusalem,* the most influential of these statements, documents the strenuous, and in her mind misconceived, attempts of the Israeli prosecution to render the Holocaust judicially manageable by creating a narrative of extreme human malignancy.[42] Arendt argues that the Israeli prosecution and court could not accept what she believes was the most unsettling aspect of Eichmann's defense: that he organized acts of genocide out of a spirit of *law-abidingness.* By treating Eichmann as a liar and casting him as a monster, the prosecution and the court were able to preserve the concept of *mens rea* upon which the criminal law remains largely predicated — the idea that all serious criminals have moral knowledge of the illegality of their acts.

Arendt argues that both the prosecution and the court failed to perceive the deeper, more sinister lesson of the Holocaust: that a vast apparatus of death could be administered by a group of unimaginative, craven, but not particularly cruel or pathological bureaucrats. The Eichmann trial, burdened by the need to render clear and emphatic judgment, thus misapprehended the nature and meaning of the Holocaust. One need not, of course, agree with all aspects of Arendt's critique, yet it frames the difficulties of using the law to punish misrepresentations and trivializations of the Holocaust when one can plausibly argue that the great Holocaust trials have themselves failed to do full justice to the historical record.

This line of argumentation, however, invites an immediate and stern rejoinder: there is, after all, a critical difference between failing to represent the Holocaust fully and hatefully denying that there is anything to represent. Up until now, all I have argued is that certain common elements of Western legal discourse — the concept of harm, the notion of jurisdictional competence, and the theory of criminal wrongdoing — have compromised legal efforts to do justice to the meaning and nature of the Holocaust. Yet the failure of the law to locate an idiom adequate to the task of comprehending Nazi crimes does not in and of itself supply a reason for eschewing the law as a tool for punishing outright denial. Indeed, one could argue that because the Holocaust resists efforts to secure its central horror in conventional idioms (a problem that scholars such as Saul Friedländer, Geoffrey Hartman, Lawrence Langer, and James Young have shown plagues not only the law, but history, theology, philosophy, literature, the visual arts, and so on), this redoubles the need to establish parameters of the plausible. If we cannot fully express what the Holocaust was and meant, then perhaps we can at least establish what remains beyond the pale.[43]

Just as the efforts to proscribe Holocaust denial bring the law in contact with its own troubled attempts to do justice to the Holocaust, the actual writings that such laws seek to criminalize present the law with a disturbing mimicry of its own elaborate discourse and conventions of proof. The arguments of these so-called revisionists powerfully conjure the rhetoric of attorneys practiced at the art of adversarial litigation. Many Holocaust deniers, of course, simply engage in the hysterical vituperation of undisguised hate speech. By questioning the capacities of gas chambers and the crematoria, such deniers simply recapitulate the logic of the Nazis, as genocide is taken from a moral or ontological plane and dropped to the level of technical feasibility. Even so, the more notorious of these revisionists have demonstrated if not a subtlety of argument, then at least an annoying brand of tenacious speciousness suggestive of the arguments of counsel in a trial setting.[44]

While one can understand the reluctance of serious academics to study the structure of deniers' arguments, Pierre Vidal-Naquet's *Assassins of Memory* offers a fascinating reading of the subversive hermeneutics of revisionists such as Serge Thion and Robert Faurisson.[45] Among the several principles of argument and interpretation that guide revisionist work, Vidal-Naquet specifies the following: First, any direct testimony contributed by a Jew is considered a lie (the perjurious testimony of a partisan witness) or a fantasy (the unreliable testimony of one who has suffered a war trauma). Second, any document that offers firsthand information concerning the methods of the Nazis is dismissed as forged or in some sense bogus (the prosecution has tampered with the evidence). Third, any Nazi document written in coded language is read literally, whereas any document written plainly is underinterpreted or overinterpreted.[46] Thus, terms such as *Umsiedlung* and *Sonderbehandlung* are read literally as "resettlement" and "special treatment" and not as code words for annihilation; while *das Lager der Vernichtung*, words that appear in the diary of an SS doctor at Auschwitz, are read as referring not to a "camp of extermination" but to a camp visited by a typhus epidemic.

These strategies can, of course, be dismissed as predicated upon mutually exclusive principles of reading and violative of what Francis Lieber, an early theorist of legal interpretation and international law, identified as the first principle of legal hermeneutics: reading in good faith.[47] Vidal-Naquet himself asserts that these interpretive strategies are born of, or at least are exploitative of, the renegade hermeneutics of poststructuralist critics (here he finds Faurisson's career as a scholar of French literature instructive), but I would claim that the arguments of revisionists are less suggestive of Paul de Man than of Johnnie Cochran and Robert Shapiro.[48] Indeed, Vidal-Naquet's analysis of the structure of revisionist arguments strongly indicates the way such works fix upon legalistic standards of proof as the preferred method for evaluating historical truth—at the same moment that they try to discredit any fact that has been produced by the legal process. The testimony of Höß at Nuremberg cannot be trusted, for example, because Nuremberg was a victor's trial (and in this way revisionists exploit the critiques of Nuremberg advanced by legitimate scholars such as Hans Kelsen). Any knowledge produced by a legal proceeding whose legal adequacy is open to challenge cannot be trusted. Yet, in the same gesture that revisionists dismiss the factual findings of any criminal trials conducted by the Allies, they champion, as a formal matter, the criminal trial—and its elaborate rules of evidence—as the model of truth-seeking inquiry.

Clearly there is something wrong with viewing adversarial jurisprudence as an efficient tool for arriving at the truth. As the legal scholar Marvin Frankel has observed, "we know that others searching after facts—in history, geography, medicine, whatever—do not emulate our adversary system."[49] Indeed, criminal justice, in both Anglo American and Continental contexts, has long been dedicated to values such as protecting the dignity and autonomy of the accused that may actually disable the pursuit of truth in a particular case.

(To take an example from American law, the "exclusionary rule," which suppresses the use of highly relevant evidence if illegally obtained, subordinates truth to other goals.) By casting the trial as a truth-seeking device, the revisionists are able to justify strategically their appropriation of the rhetorical conventions of counsels arguing in an adversarial context. In so doing, they are able to present the most tendentious and partisan hyperbole as a proper contribution to public debate and historical instruction.

The very distinction between Holocaust revisionism and zealous adversarial advocacy vanishes in the statement of Jacques Verges, who served as Klaus Barbie's defense attorney at the 1987 Lyons trial: "Barbie was not a Nazi. What is a Nazi? We are all Nazis."[50] The statement recalls Freud's famous example of the response of the defendant accused of breaking his neighbor's teakettle: "The defendant asserted first, that he had given it back undamaged; secondly, that the kettle had a hole when he borrowed it; and thirdly, that he had never borrowed a kettle from his neighbor at all."[51] Whereas Freud uses his example as a trope for the overdetermination of the psyche's pleas for innocence, Verges's statement aims at global incrimination, seeking less to acquit the specific defendant than to cover the accusers with the pall of guilt.

Verges's statement calls attention to a final similarity between trial advocacy and revisionist rhetoric. Like the defense counsel in a criminal trial, the revisionist is less interested in proving the Nazi state innocent of systematic extermination than in tainting the accuser and in planting seeds of doubt about the Holocaust through a systematic campaign of radical skepticism. Indeed, revisionists in the United States have mastered the technique of dressing up such arguments in the rhetoric of the First Amendment, claiming that they seek not to silence or foreclose dialogue but to subject the historical understanding of the Holocaust to "robust scrutiny" and "open debate"—the very catch phrases that lie at the heart of liberal defenses of free speech. Even if these appeals fundamentally misstate the doctrinal commitments of the First Amendment (as we have observed, false statements of fact, uttered in reckless disregard of the truth, hardly enjoy robust constitutional protection), they remain rhetorically effective. Deborah Lipstadt, for example, has described how numerous American university newspapers believed that they were obligated to run advertisements paid for by the Institute for Historical Review—accepting, as they did, the institute's argument that the refusal to do so would have constituted censorship of an unpopular viewpoint.[52]

By making actionable the lies of the revisionists, statutes proscribing Holocaust denial seek to punish those who have mastered the subversive hermeneutics of trial advocacy and the doctrinal pieties of free speech jurisprudence. But because revisionists often strategically exploit legal styles of argumentation, the very norms that control adversary criminal justice render the law an extremely awkward tool for punishing revisionists. This point gains support by a consideration of the trial of Ernst Zündel. As the case required the Crown to show that Zündel's denials of the Holocaust were in fact "false," the Canadian trial court found itself functioning as a tribunal burdened with determining the truth of the Holocaust according to legal conventions of proof and evidence.

This made for several unseemly problems. First, Anglo American jurisprudence's bar against hearsay testimony (that is, testimony in which a witness describes as fact events that he or she has not personally observed but that have been reported to him or her by a third party unavailable to the court) rendered many Holocaust narratives either unavailable to the trial or available only through evidentiary loopholes. When Zündel appealed his conviction, the Canadian appellate tribunal had to decide whether the testimony of Raul Hilberg, the eminent Holocaust historian, had been improperly admitted during Zündel's trial.[53] While the appellate court conceded that Hilberg's testimony was technically hearsay, it reasoned that exceptions to the hearsay rule "are based upon (a) necessity, and (b) the circumstantial trustworthiness of the evidence to which the exception applies."[54] Here the criterion of necessity was satisfied, as the question of whether the Holocaust ever occurred had to be demonstrated by the Crown to sustain its burden of proving the guilt of the accused. The turn to expert—that is, hearsay—testimony was further necessitated, the court reasoned, by the unlikelihood that "living witnesses could be obtained":[55]

> The events sought to be proved by Dr. Hilberg's opinion occurred more than forty years ago, and while there are survivors of the Nazi concentration camps, some of whom were called as witnesses, it is unlikely that living witnesses responsible for formulating the policy of the Nazi government or carrying out the policies in relation to the events alleged, could be obtained.[56]

Although survivors could offer eyewitness accounts about conditions in specific camps, presumably they could not, the court reasoned, offer firsthand testimony about what happened at the Wannsee conference. Thus the court concluded that the prosecution could legitimately present this hearsay testimony as evidence of the deeper architecture of the Final Solution.

Hilberg's work also satisfied the second criterion of trustworthiness, as it was based upon "material to which . . . any careful and competent historian would resort."[57] Yet the notion that such historical studies can be admitted only as *hearsay exceptions* vaguely echoes revisionist arguments and carries the further suggestion that the very facticity of the Holocaust will diminish as eyewitnesses continue to die. The court's discussion thus captures the temporal vulnerabilities of litigation that remains dependent, for its normative force if not its legal adequacy, upon the testimony of survivors.

This observation is strengthened by the fact that the court permitted the defense to respond to Hilberg's expert testimony by calling its own expert, the notorious Faurisson.[58] Faurisson's certification as an expert witness by the court was not lost upon revisionists, who later publicized the judicial recognition that had been implicitly conferred upon one of their ilk. This circumstance remains, then, exemplary of a larger phenomenon, as the formal evidentiary agnosticism of adversarial jurisprudence may have the ironic effect of contributing to the erosion of the very boundary between truth and fiction that the law attempts to police.

Consider as well the court's conclusion that a documentary film compiled by the United States Army's Signal Corps (under the direction of George Stevens, the respected Hollywood director), which chronicled the liberation of Nazi concentration camps in Western Europe, had been improperly shown to the jury at Zündel's first trial. Because the nameless screenplay writer and narrator were unavailable for cross-examination, the documentary failed under rules of hearsay. Although the film had been shown at Nuremberg as one of the centerpieces of the prosecution's case and ostensibly produced direct visual information about the depicted historical event, the court concluded that because the makers of the narrative were not present for adversarial confrontation at the time of the film's screening at Zündel's trial, the film could not be accepted as a trustworthy window upon the disputed history.[59] (Here Zündel's successful career as a photo retoucher creates discomfiting resonances.) Despite the testimonies of Hilberg and the survivors, the admission of the Signal Corps documentary, along with other procedural defects in the first trial, led the court to throw out the original conviction.[60]

Zündel's second trial (which lasted from mid-January until early May 1988) differed from the first in one dramatic respect: the judge in the second trial agreed to take judicial notice of Nazi genocide. Dismissing the objections of Zündel's counsel, the judge directed the jury to accept that "the mass murder and extermination of Jews in Europe by the Nazis during the Second World War is so notorious as not to be subject of dispute."[61] The judge did not, however, "take judicial notice of the facts alleged in the appellant's pamphlet."[62] Indeed, as Zündel's attorney argued in his final address to the jury, the judge's instructions did not necessarily contradict his client's thesis:

> His Honour will tell you what he says is reasonable for reasonable men to contest. But it won't include the six million, it won't include the gas chambers and it won't include an official plan. That's basically what this book is all about.[63]

The attorney's arguments notwithstanding, Zündel was found guilty in the second trial and sentenced to nine months in prison.

His legal odyssey, however, had not reached its end. In 1992, the Canadian Supreme Court declared unconstitutional the section of the Criminal Code under which Zündel had been convicted — the section that proscribed the publication of false statements likely to cause mischief to a public interest.[64] Against a vigorous dissent, the majority reasoned that the statute was unconstitutionally overbroad, as it relied upon "concepts as vague as fact versus opinion or truth versus falsity in the context of history."[65] The court thus accepted the instability of the distinction between fact and interpretation, an argument that, as we have seen, has been used by rightist scholars to attack the Auschwitz-lie law in Germany. Here, of course, the court did not polemically deny the distinction between facts and opinions; instead, it questioned the institutional competence of juries and judges to distinguish between truth and falsity, and, as a further matter, suggested that even false statements might not be without value:

> A given expression may offer many meanings, some of which seem false, others, of a metaphorical or allegorical nature, which may possess some validity. Moreover, meaning is not a datum so much as an interactive process, depending of the listener as well as the speaker.[66]

Even a publication as crude as Zündel's, the court argued, "illustrates the difficulty of determining its meaning," as the text may stand for the idea "that the public should not be quick to adopt 'accepted' versions of history, truth, etc."[67] Although the court here seemed to confuse significance and meaning, an important distinction in certain hermeneutic circles, its argument remains familiar, echoing John Stuart Mill's canonical defense of false speech in *On Liberty*. Yet the decision was also deeply insular, as the court revealed itself to be understandably less concerned with the truth of the Holocaust than with the legitimacy of the law. Preoccupied as it must be with how its decision would serve as precedent, the court treated the Holocaust in precisely the fashion rejected by so many scholars—as just another historical event about which unpopular claims can be made. Whether the challenged law can reliably serve to protect the history of the Holocaust from distortion is a question that did not concern the court. Instead, in a remarkable rhetorical inversion, the court decried the law as itself Hitlerian in its control of speech. By making possible conviction "for virtually any statement which does not accord with currently accepted 'truths,'" the challenged law could be used, the court warned, in a manner akin "to totalitarian states like the Nazi regime in Germany."[68]

The court's conclusion that the statute was unconstitutionally vague and overbroad does not mean that a law drafted with the specificity of the German, French, or Austrian laws might not pass constitutional muster. Canada's own hate crime law, a statute that has passed constitutional challenge, supplies fresh legal ammunition against Holocaust deniers. Yet, as I have tried to suggest, the problem with using the law to proscribe Holocaust denial is not, as free speech advocates would argue, that one runs the risk of chilling speech that one should protect; it is that the law, as a formal discourse, cannot do justice to the history it has been enlisted to protect. As the *Zündel* case exemplifies, when the law intervenes to protect the Holocaust from the charge that it is all falsehood, the law's evidentiary constraints and its concerns with its own legitimacy may demand that it approach the past from a position of formal agnosticism—a peculiarly weak position from which to defend the integrity of the historical record. Indeed, the law's need to view the past agnostically may inadvertently lead to the erosion of the very distinction between historical fact and falsehood that the law has been asked to support.

This, however, raises a final issue, one that returns us to our point of departure. If, as is commonly accepted, the law often can serve as a tool of historical instruction, how can we understand a conclusion that questions the wisdom of relying upon legal means to safeguard the facticity of the Holocaust? Part of the answer, I believe, has already been suggested: at least in the case of criminal trials, we do not expect the law necessarily to provide a transparent or responsible account of the historical record. Historical accuracy is sometimes subordinated to other values, such as the dignitary rights of the accused. Thus, when the state attempts to silence Holocaust deniers by criminalizing their statements, it pursues a path that obligates it to defend norms that place claims upon the law that are superior to the claim of historical truth. This becomes particularly problematic, as we have seen, when the law is confronted with hateful lies that have been structured specifically to exploit its obligation to pursue justice at the expense of truth.

This, however, is not intended to suggest that civil remedies remain the more efficacious tool for silencing the voice of Holocaust denial. As already noted, the impulse to silence denial is borne less of a desire to compensate survivors than to prepare for a day when the Holocaust has passed from memory into history. It aims less to protect the dignitary concerns of a specific group or to enforce codes of civil speech than to define the frontier beyond which public discourse ceases. Thus, while we might look to the civil law to tell us whether General Willam C. Westmoreland was libeled by CBS, such an example is inapposite to the present case.[69] In this regard, we are reminded of the difference between using the law to clarify or elucidate the historical record and relying upon the law to police a history that has already been adequately clarified. The former seeks to use the power of the state as a tool of discovery, the latter seeks to dictate the terms of responsible memory through an act of legal will.

This effort is destined to fail not because the state is corrupt and any truth supported with a legal sanction is tainted. Rather, the law will fail to do justice to the memory of the Holocaust because the law ultimately will remain less interested in safeguarding history than in preserving the conditions of its own complex normativity and discursive neutrality. This does not mean that efforts to proscribe the Holocaust necessarily disturb this neutrality. Yet it does suggest that in attempting to preserve the terms of its neutrality, the law's effort to silence the hateful voice of Holocaust deniers will create a new obligation to listen.

In his parable "The Witness," Jorge Luis Borges writes, "There was a day in time when the last eyes to see Christ were closed forever."[70] Fifty years after the liberation of the death camps, Borges's words find a grim echo. In the not too distant future, the last eyes to have seen Auschwitz—from the inside—will close forever. Their closing, however, will not bring to an end the law's troubled attempts to find an adequate response to the extermination of European Jewry. Half a century after the first juridical effort to condemn these crimes, the law still struggles with their legacy. But the memory that haunts legal efforts to police the bounds of Holocaust representations is not simply the lingering evidence of crimes that have never been adequately comprehended by the law. Efforts to proscribe Holocaust denial remind us that the very legal grammar of harm, jurisdiction, culpability, and proof that permits the law to order our social world effectively, may frustrate the law's efforts to speak reliably on behalf of that world's most difficult histories and most traumatic memories.

Notes

I would like to thank the members of the seminar on censorship and silencing for their helpful comments; I would like to express special thanks to Robert Post. In addition, Robert Burt, Frank Couvares, Owen Fiss, Alexander George, Nasser Hussain, Nancy Pick, Austin Sarat, Martha Umphrey, and James Young offered valuable comments on an earlier, substantially different draft of this essay that appeared as "The Memory of Judgment: The Law, the Holocaust, and Denial," *History and Memory* 7 (1996): 100–120. William Connelly, Research Librarian at the United States Holocaust Research Institute, and Stephen Porder provided valuable research assistance. My research and writing were generously supported by a Karl Loewenstein Fellowship in Jurisprudence at Amherst College.

1. Yosef Hayim Yerushalmi, *Zakhor: Jewish History and Jewish Memory* (Seattle: Univ. of Washington Press, 1996), 117.

2. See Manuel Prustchi, "The Zündel Affair," in Alan Davies, ed., *Antisemitism in Canada: History and Interpretation* (Waterloo, Ontario: Wilfred Laurier Univ. Press, 1992), 255.

3. *R.S.C. (Revised Statutes of Canada)*, ch. C-34 § 177 (1st Supp. 1970). The statute provided that "every one who willfully publishes a statement, tale or news that he knows is false and that causes or is likely to cause injury or mischief to a public interest is guilty of an indictable offense and is liable to imprisonment for two years."

4. Given the work of thinkers such as Pierre Nora, who has articulated the differences between history and memory, the association of historical truth with responsible memory may seem problematic, just as the term "responsible memory" may seem something of an oxymoron. The concept of responsible memory is meant, however, to suggest a fidelity to the historical record that remains normatively invested in maintaining a direct and organic link to the past. See Pierre Nora, "Between History and Memory: Les Lieux de Mémoire," *Representations*, no. 26 (1989): 7–25.

5. See, for example, the essay by Sanford Levinson, "The Tutelary State: 'Censorship,' 'Silencing,' and the 'Practices of Cultural Regulation,'" pages 195–219.

6. See, for example, John T. Noonan, *Persons and Masks of the Law: Cardozo, Holmes, Jefferson, and Wythe as Makers of the Masks* (New York: Farrar, Straus & Giroux, 1976); and Hayden White, *The Content of the Form* (Baltimore: Johns Hopkins Univ. Press, 1987).

7. *The People of the State of California v. Orenthal James Simpson* (Superior Court, Los Angeles County). For a valuable examination of the efficacy of using the

criminal law to cultivate public memory, see Mark J. Osiel, "Ever Again: Legal Remembrance of Administrative Massacre," *University of Pennsylvania Law Review* 144 (1995): 463–704.

8. See Telford Taylor, *The Anatomy of the Nuremberg Trials: A Personal Memoir* (Boston: Little, Brown, 1992), principally chapter 2.

9. Quoted in Gerald Tishler, "Holocaust Denial and Group Libel: Comparative Perspectives," *Boston College Third World Law Journal* 8 (1988): 65–90, 71.

10. *Gertz v. Robert Welch, Inc.*, 418 U.S. 323 (1974), 339.

11. *Hustler Magazine v. Falwell*, 485 U.S. 46 (1988), 52.

12. Primo Levi, *The Drowned and the Saved*, trans. Raymond Rosenthal (New York: Summit Books, 1988), 11–12.

13. Harold Kaplan, *Conscience and Memory: Meditations in a Museum of the Holocaust* (Chicago: Univ. of Chicago Press, 1994), 44.

14. Deborah E. Lipstadt, *Denying the Holocaust: The Growing Assault on Truth and Memory* (New York: Free Press, 1993), 1–29.

15. Geoffrey Hartman, "Introduction: Darkness Visible," in idem, ed., *Holocaust Remembrance: The Shapes of Memory* (Oxford: Blackwell, 1994), 11.

16. Robert Post, *Constitutional Domains: Democracy, Community, Management* (Cambridge: Harvard Univ. Press, 1995), 147.

17. For a valuable history and analysis of the law, see Eric Stein, "History Against Free Speech: The New German Law Against the 'Auschwitz'—and Other—'Lies,'" *Michigan Law Review* 85 (1986): 277–324.

18. 75 *BGHZ (Entscheidungen des Bundesgerichtshofes in Zivilsachen)* 160; 33 *NJW (Neue juristiche Wochenschrift)* 45 (1980); see also Stein (see note 17), 301–5.

19. 75 *BGHZ* 160 (see note 18), 166.

20. Decision of 30 January 1985, *OLG (Oberlandsgericht)* Celle, No. 1 Ss 126/84–10 Js 228/80 Sta; see also Stein (see note 17), 304.

21. 75 *BGHZ* 160 (see note 18), 162.

22. An excellent teasing out of the conceptual distinction is provided in Post (see note 16), 153–63.

23. See, for example, Kim Lane Scheppele, "Facing Facts in Legal Interpretation," in Robert Post, ed., *Law and the Order of Culture* (Berkeley: Univ. of California Press, 1991).

24. Letter from Professor Dr. Ernst Nolte, in "Correspondence on the 'Auschwitz Lie,'" *Michigan Law Review* 87 (1989): 1026–32, 1029. See also Ernst Nolte, *Der europäische Bürgerkrieg, 1917–1945* (Berlin: Propylaen Verlag, 1987).

25. Quoted in Tishler (see note 9), 72.

26. Uriel Tal, "On the Study of the Holocaust and Genocide," *Yad Vashem Studies* 13 (1979): 7–52.

27. Jacques Derrida, "Force of Law: The 'Mystical Foundation of Authority,'" in Drucilla Cornell, Michael Rosenfield, and David Gray Carlson, eds., *Deconstruction and the Possibility of Justice* (New York: Routledge, 1992), 3–64.

28. The relevant sections of the bill (passed as *Einundzwanzigstes Strafrechtänderungsgesetz* [Twenty-first Law Modifying the Criminal Law] on 13 June 1985) were modified to criminalize insults to persons who have suffered persecution under

National Socialism "or any other form of despotism and tyranny." See Stein (see note 17), 307–10.

29. The full text of the statute appears in Stephen J. Roth, "Denial of the Holocaust: An Issue of Law," *Institute of Jewish Affairs Research Reports,* no. 2 (1994): 4.

30. "Charter of the International Military Tribunal," reprinted in *Proceedings of the Trial of the Major War Criminals before the International Military Tribunal* (hereafter *IMT*), 42 vols. (Nuremberg: Secretariat of the International Military Tribunal, 1947), 1: 11.

31. Ibid.

32. For a more extended discussion of the redrafting of Article 6, see Taylor (see note 8), 75–77.

33. See *IMT* (see note 30), 5: 368–426.

34. Ibid., 5: 412. See also Taylor (see note 8), 293–98.

35. When French prosecutors had an opportunity to revisit these issues in the Klaus Barbie trial, they managed once again to marginalize the crimes of the Holocaust, conflating the Nazis' execution of captured members of the resistance with the extermination of Jewish children. See Alain Finkielkraut, *Remembering in Vain: The Klaus Barbie Trial and Crimes Against Humanity,* trans. Roxanne Lapidus (New York: Columbia Univ. Press, 1992).

36. For a more complete text of the law, see Roth (see note 29), 5.

37. See Tal (see note 26), 7–52.

38. *IMT* (see note 30), 11: 396–422.

39. Ibid., 8: 294.

40. Ibid., 2: 98–155.

41. Michael R. Marrus, "The Holocaust at Nuremberg," *Yad Vashem Studies,* forthcoming.

42. Hannah Arendt, *Eichmann in Jerusalem: A Report on the Banality of Evil* (New York: Viking, 1963). Arendt's argument has, of course, been sternly rebuked. Yet most of these critiques focus more upon her discussion of the role that the various Judenräte played in helping to organize the Final Solution and less upon her banality thesis. See, for example, Jacob Robinson, *And the Crooked Shall Be Made Straight: The Eichmann Trial, the Jewish Catastrophe, and Hannah Arendt's Narrative* (New York: Macmillan, 1965).

43. See, for example, Saul Friedländer, ed., *Probing the Limits of Representation: Nazism and the "Final Solution"* (Cambridge: Harvard Univ. Press, 1992).

44. Ironically, the term *revisionist,* first prominently used in a juridical context to describe those who agitated for a revision of the verdict against Dreyfus, is now used as an appellation for Holocaust deniers. See Robert L. Hoffman, *More Than a Trial: The Struggle Over Captain Dreyfus* (New York: Free Press, 1980).

45. Pierre Vidal-Naquet, *Assassins of Memory: Essays on the Denial of the Holocaust,* trans. Jeffrey Mehlman (New York: Columbia Univ. Press, 1992).

46. Ibid., 21–24.

47. Francis Lieber, *Legal and Political Hermeneutics* (Boston: Little, Brown, 1839).

48. Cochran and Shapiro led the defense team in the murder trial of O. J. Simpson (see note 7).

49. Marvin E. Frankel, "The Search for the Truth: An Umpireal View," *University of Pennsylvania Law Review* 123 (1975): 1032.

50. In an interview with director Marcel Ophuls in his documentary film, *Hotel Terminus* (Los Angeles: Samuel Goldwyn Pictures, 1988).

51. Sigmund Freud, *The Interpretation of Dreams,* trans. and ed. James Strachey (New York: Basic Books, 1955), 120.

52. Lipstadt (see note 14), 183–208.

53. *Regina v. Zündel,* 31 Canadian Criminal Cases (3d) 97 (Ontario Appeal Cases, 1987).

54. Ibid., 145.

55. Ibid., 144.

56. Ibid.

57. Ibid., 148.

58. Without further explanation, the trial judge "ruled that Dr. Faurisson should be permitted to testify as an expert witness on the same basis as Dr. Hilberg was allowed to testify, namely, whether the German Government [sic] from 1933 to 1945 deliberately embarked on a scheme to exterminate the Jews in Europe." Ibid., 142.

59. See *IMT* (see note 30), 2: 431–34. Ironically, an examination of the film's use at Nuremberg reveals that it was used not as proof of the extermination of European Jewry, but as evidence of the Nazis' brutal treatment of prisoners of war and political prisoners. See Lawrence Douglas, "Film as Witness: Screening *Nazi Concentration Camps* Before the Nuremberg Tribunal," *The Yale Law Journal* 105 (1995): 449–81.

60. The other defects included an improper *voir dire* regarding pre-trial publicity and improper jury instructions regarding the mental state of the defendant. *Regina v. Zündel* (see note 53), 89–102, 124–5.

61. Leonidas E. Hill, "The Trial of Ernst Zündel: Revisionism and Law in Canada," in *Simon Wiesenthal Center Annual* (Chappaqua, N.Y.: Rossel Books, 1989).

62. *Regina v. Zündel,* 75 Canadian Criminal Cases (3d) 449 (Supreme Court Reports, 1992), 456.

63. Ibid.

64. For a discussion of the trial, see Lipstadt (see note 14), 157–182.

65. *Regina v. Zündel* (see note 62), 506.

66. Ibid., 509.

67. Ibid., 510.

68. Ibid., 519.

69. See *Westmoreland v. CBS,* 596 F. Supp. 1170 (S.D.N.Y.1984) Even here we should recall Robert Post's argument that "we would certainly rather trust the verdict of infinite generations of historians than the verdict of any given jury on questions such as whether General William Westmoreland gave orders to intelligence officers to underestimate enemy troop strength during the Vietnam War"; Post (see note 16), 381.

70. Jorge Luis Borges, "The Witness," in idem, *A Personal Anthology,* ed. Anthony Kerrigan (New York: Grove Press, 1967), 178.

Civility and Censorship in Early Modern England

Debora Shuger

In 1599 the Archbishop of Canterbury and the Bishop of London, in their capacity as licensers of the press, issued a laconic edict forbidding, among other things, all publication of satires. This edict, known as the Bishops' Ban, presents the most sweeping and stringent instance of early modern English censorship. No other official document outlawed a whole category of literary production. Although the bishops offered no rationale for their decision, modern scholars generally view the ban as an attempt to silence "pointed and articulate" social critiques that had ventured "too close to the truth for comfort."[1]

The ban provoked surprisingly little contemporary comment, in contrast to the widespread murmuring when, two decades later, King James tried to prohibit any discussion of his unpopular foreign policy. The only extended responses to the Bishops' Ban are three poems, collectively known as the *Whipper Pamphlets,* published in 1601. Contrary to modern assumptions about the relation between poets and censors, however, two of the poems support its blanket condemnation of satire. Both poems criticize late Elizabethan satirists, not because satires reprehend social or political corruption, but because they purvey "plain-lies"; they maliciously defame their victims, who "shall causeless ill opinion have"; and they violate the basic norms of Christian love, uncovering "with malignant spite / . . . all the frail infirmities of your weak brethren to the wide world's sight"—"a course of little charity."[2]

This is, from a modern perspective, a strange way of thinking about censorship. For us, censorship primarily implies state-sponsored repression of individual liberty (the liberal or "Whig" paradigm). This model governs our understanding of censorship except with respect to a narrow band of issues specific to late twentieth-century pluralist democracies—in particular, hate-speech and pornography—issues in which individual liberties conflict with social equality. In these debates, censorship presents itself as a last-ditch expedient against the insidious "freedom" the dominant culture possesses to intimidate and humiliate marginalized groups (what might be called the "multicultural" paradigm). Both ways of framing censorship tend to ignore the more general social operations of language, the ways in which words function to knit—or sever—the political and moral ligatures that collectively bind a people into community. Hence defenders of both find it difficult even to

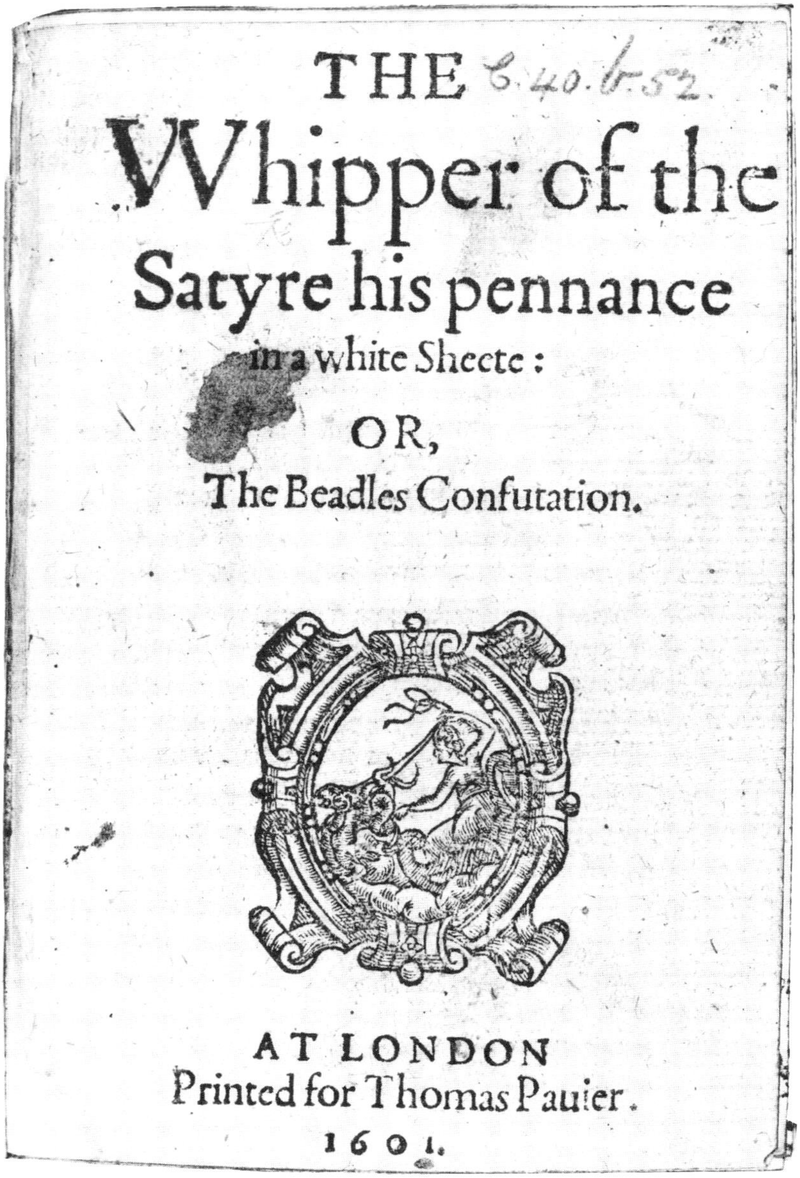
THE
Whipper of the
Satyre his pennance
in a white Sheete:
OR,
The Beadles Confutation.

AT LONDON
Printed for Thomas Pauier.
1601.

Title page from *The Whipper of the Satyre*, published in the *Whipper Pamphlets*, 1601. Courtesy British Library.

pose the question of what genuine dangers to the whole social body censorship might attempt to avert—or, conversely, what cultural goods it might safeguard. On the liberal paradigm, freedom of expression trumps both official and communal values, so that censorship becomes illegitimate almost by definition.[3] On the multicultural one, sensitivity to divisions and differences within a pluralist society casts heavy suspicion on any appeal to totalizing concepts like "cultural goods" and "whole social body," the rhetoric of the whole being perceived as an attempt to mask the conflicts among its parts.

As the *Whipper Pamphlets* suggest, early modern English persons, who did not think in terms of categories like individualism, racism, and sexism, construed censorship differently. While this means that Tudor-Stuart censorship practices have no *direct* bearing on current debates, the early modern understanding of censorship repays study precisely because it attends to functions and effects of language that our cultural assumptions render invisible. This chapter attempts to describe Tudor-Stuart censorship, not to solve current public policy issues. It most assuredly does not recommend a return to the early modern licensing system which required all manuscripts to be vetted by state-appointed licensers prior to publication (a system that did not, even then, work very well). Investigating Tudor-Stuart censorship does not answer, but rather poses, questions—I think important ones—about the relation between freedoms and virtues, between the power of language and the power of the state, between doing things with words and doing things to people.

Generalizations in the humanities are not scientific laws; they need not account for every relevant case, just for a significant number of them. In early modern England, texts might be censored for a dozen reasons: the playwright quarreled with a Privy Councillor's servant, an ambassador complained about affronts to his monarch's honor, a nobleman resented praise heaped on a rival. Nevertheless, it seems to me that, in general, Tudor-Stuart censorship is best understood as a way of coping with threats to what the first of the *Whipper Pamphlets* terms "the Law of all Civility"—what we now call "civility rules."[4]

Libelous Politics

"Trust," as Steven Shapin remarks in his *Social History of Truth,* is the "great civility."[5] Four centuries earlier, Montaigne had reached a similar conclusion: "We are men, and hold together, only by our word.... If it deceives us, it breaks up all our relations and dissolves all the bonds of our society"; for this reason "lying is an accursed vice."[6] And lying, politically motivated falsehood, has a good deal more to do with early modern censorship than is usually supposed.

Most studies of censorship in Tudor-Stuart England assume that its primary object was "to prevent the circulation of dangerous ideas," "controversial opinions," and other "attempts to deliver the truth."[7] Yet the Elizabethan proclamations condemning seditious books—which, unlike the Bishops' Ban, did explain why a given text had been outlawed—insist upon the untruthfulness of the proscribed works, not their ideological perversity.[8] Thus the proclamation issued in 1579 attacking John Stubbs's *Gaping Gulf* (1579)—a Puritan denunciation of Elizabeth's proposed marriage to the French Duc d'Alençon—vehemently objects to its "heap of slanders . . . bolstered up with manifest lies," its "fardel of false reports" and rehearsal "of hearsays uncertain or of vain guessings and suposals . . . maliciously forged against manifest truth." A Roman Catholic libel on William Cecil, *A Treatise of Treasons* (1572), provoked a 1573 proclamation objecting to its "most notorious false assertions," "false calumnies," "feigned and surmised tales," "manifest untruths." Cardinal William Allen's incendiary *Admonition to the Nobility and People of England* (1588)—numerous copies of which were carried by the Spanish Armada to foment a Catholic uprising concomitant with the invasion—are likewise condemned as "most false and abominable lies" designed "to slander and dishonor her majesty."[9]

We may, of course, suspect that these accusations are themselves false, mere doublespeak for the Crown's fear of dangerous truths and revolutionary ideologies. Yet if one examines the works cited in these proclamations—the works, that is, against which the state turned the full force of its censorship arsenal—one finds oneself confronted by what can only be described as a "fardel of false reports." Moreover, these works seem surprisingly devoid of ideological substance or anything that might be construed as political *theory*. Rather, they attack specific individuals. They are, that is, libels—attempts to discredit political opponents by defaming their motives and morals. Character assassination remains an effective tactic today, but it would have been particularly so in an era without reliable, independent sources of news and without the "hard" evidence of fingerprinting and photographs. Such lies presented a serious political danger because they would have been virtually impossible to refute.

Tudor-Stuart censorship, in turn, cannot be understood apart from the threat posed by this sort of libelous politics, by the circulation of defamatory attacks on the ruling elite—a danger often ignored in modern discussions of this subject. In his ground-breaking *Freedom of the Press in England*, Fredrick Siebert thus explains that Stubbs's *Gaping Gulf* made Elizabeth "furious" because the author had dared "to discuss in public print . . . [a] matter of state policy."[10] What Stubbs had done, in fact, was considerably less innocuous. He began his criticism of the proposed match by explaining that the Duc d'Alençon is "not Satan in body of a serpent, but the old serpent in shape of a man." We later learn that Alençon's "strange incredible parts of intemperancy" pass the "worst of Heliogabalus." Equally bad, the gentleman comes from France, and "the French," as it turns out, "do account as fair virtues all foul lies, treasons, poisonings, massacres, and turning of realms upside down." And to cap matters, Stubbs claims to have discovered that Alençon really had no intention of marrying Elizabeth at all but was secretly planning to wed Mary Stuart, after which the pair would together lead a rebellion to usurp the English throne.[11] This is not "discussing public policy," at least not in the current sense of the phrase, but *scandalum magnatum*—inventing or spreading "false news" about the monarch, royal ministers, or chief peers—the crime for which Stubbs was convicted and which cost him his right hand.

The majority of texts condemned by the Elizabethan proclamations are, like Stubbs's, stuffed with defamatory lies. Many are products of the Roman Catholic slander machine on the Continent, which seems to have been operating at capacity throughout the late sixteenth and early seventeenth centuries. Cardinal Allen's *Admonition* may serve as a representative instance. Concerning the queen's relation to the Earl of Leicester, Allen relates that "she took [him] up . . . only to serve her filthy luste, whereof to have the more freedom and interest; he (as may be presumed, by her consent) caused his owne wife cruelly to be murthered." Nor was Leicester the queen's only paramour; rather with "divers others she hathe abused her bodie . . . by unspeakable and incredible variety of luste . . . whereby she is become notorious to the worlde." When her peers beg her to marry, Elizabeth replies "in contempte and rebuke of all the states of the realme" that "none should so muche as be named for her successor duringe her life, savinge the naturall, that ys to saie bastard borne childe of her owne bodie." Allen then supplies the moral to be drawn from these fables: the English queen "deservethe not onelie deposition, but all vengeaunce bothe of God and man."[12]

The first of Allen's accusations repeats calumnies previously detailed in *Leicester's Commonwealth* (1584). Neither modern scholars nor sixteenth-century polemicists can, of course, *know* whether Leicester had his first wife, Amy Robsart, murdered; she was found dead at the bottom of some stairs, and the coroner's jury ruled "death by mischance." D. C. Peck's meticulous study of *Leicester's Commonwealth,* however, finds the charge against Leicester distinctly implausible: at the time of her demise Robsart was dying of breast cancer; if Leicester had wished her dead, he need only have waited a few months. Peck thinks it more likely either that she committed suicide or that her spine collapsed—a result of her spreading cancer—causing the fall.[13] Like Allen's *Admonition, Leicester's Commonwealth* is the work of exiled recusants. Its allegations probably derived from rumors spread by the Howard clan, whose members blamed Leicester for their own political eclipse; recognizing that his "power depended upon attractive personal qualities, [they] sought to make him unattractive."[14] Like so many of the texts that the Elizabethan authorities sought to suppress, the work is a "heap of slanders . . . bolstered up with manifest lies."

The accession of James did not interrupt the Roman Catholic libel campaign against the English monarchy.[15] More significant, at least in hindsight, was the steadily increasing stream of Protestant oppositional discourses. Since these contributed to Parliament's triumph over Stuart absolutism, and since this has generally been viewed as a positive outcome, most historians and literary scholars have viewed these critiques favorably. Yet their tactics differ little from those employed by sixteenth-century Catholic propagandists. The hotter sort of Jacobean Protestants attacked the proposed match of James's son Charles to a Spanish princess with the full arsenal of defamation, forgery, and partisan distortion. By the 1620s the anti-Catholic–anti-Spanish party was circulating bitterly slanderous attacks on the Jacobean court, whose allegations spread rapidly across the country, raising dark suspicions among the king's Protestant subjects.[16]

The most scurrilous fantasies occur in the verse libels of the period, which, as Alastair Bellany notes, exhibit considerably more interest in the sex life of leading courtiers than "threats to habeas corpus or to the subject's liberties." One, for example, recounts how the elderly Countess of Buckingham played "the fucking game" with Bishop Williams (an advocate of the Spanish match), along with similar information about the female relatives of various pro-Spanish noblemen.[17] Early seventeenth-century diaries preserve similar verse libels, as well as tendentious reports of court intrigue and Catholic plots. William Davenport's journal thus transcribes a newsletter implicating the Earl of Somerset and various Catholic noblemen in treason, together with two related documents—both Puritan forgeries—exposing the perfidious machinations of Spanish diplomats.[18] Newsletters, both printed and manuscript, likewise warned of impending Catholic massacres, of the king's imminent submission to Rome, of powerful courtiers betraying their country to the Antichrist for Spanish gold.[19]

Forgery seems to have been a particularly effective political weapon. Thomas Scott, a Puritan minister, was the undisputed master of this genre; two of the items Davenport copied into his news-diary—the council speech of Archbishop Abbot and the Spanish king's letter—were Scott's work. His other accomplishments include a "Dutch" pamphlet describing Spanish aggression in the Netherlands, a list of secret articles agreed upon by the College of Cardinals, and the brilliantly effective *Vox populi* (1620) and *The Second Part of Vox Populi* (1624), both "translations" of reports allegedly delivered by Count Gondomar, the Spanish ambassador to England, recounting his numerous successful efforts to trick the English king into compliance with Spanish interests.[20] Scott, of course, fabricated the reports—out of what cannot always be ascertained. One of the few modern historians to investigate the matter concludes that Scott was "in no position to have any accurate notion of what was going on"; the two parts of *Vox populi* (and similar tracts) mix "exaggerations, errors of fact, and ludicrous excesses... to stir up anti-Spanish and anti-Catholic hatreds."[21] They are, in fact, masterpieces of conspiratorial paranoia.

The *Vox populi* tracts, it is important to note, were widely accepted as genuine. Simonds D'Ewes, a university-educated Puritan gentleman, noted in his journal that the "discovery of his [Gondomar's] villainous practices" had been "generally approved of, not only by the meaner sort... but also by all men of judgment that were loyally affected to the truth of the Gospel."[22] The success of these tracts, in turn, lent plausibility to subsequent conspiratorial fantasies, which played upon the same fears. Thus in 1641, on the eve of the Civil War, John Pym warned the Long Parliament of schemes "woven by Jesuits, bishops, popish courtiers and prelates acting in concert," informing the Commons that the French were preparing to invade Portsmouth, assisted, "as by good information appears," by "divers persons of eminency about the Queen." Similar rumors spread panic in the localities: the Mayor of Norwich told the Privy Council of receiving information that 12,000 papists were poised to attack the city, while a gentleman from Derbyshire reported that Catholics had been stockpiling hatchets with which to slaughter their Protestant neighbors.[23] In the wake of the Irish revolt, lurid reports of atrocities committed against Ulster Protestants intensified this crisis of trust; as Richard Baxter would later recall, the horrific stories of Irish cruelty

> filled all England with a fear both of the Irish and of the Papists at home . . . insomuch that when the rumour of a plot was occasioned at London, the poor people, all the countries over, were ready either to run to arms or hide themselves, thinking that the Papists were ready to rise and cut their throats. And when they saw the English Papists join with the king against the parliament, it was the greatest thing that ever alienated them from the king.[24]

Parliamentary newsletters told of "enormous and largely mythical reinforcements of savage Irish Catholics . . . hurrying to join the King," of cavalier banners bearing "the Popes Motto," of crucifixes invariably found on royalist corpses. Sinister rumors spread across the country that Henrietta Maria, Charles's wife, and perhaps even Charles, had ordered the Irish massacres.[25]

While we cannot finally know, as Robert Darnton cautions, what makes a value system rupture—we cannot, that is, measure the extent to which works like *Vox populi* eroded the great civility of trust—the bleak possibility remains that a considerable portion of the English people took up arms against the king in 1641 because they believed widely disseminated rumors, written or spoken, that implicated Crown and Church in sinister popish plots.[26] The atmosphere of panic and mistrust spread by these anti-Catholic libels became, as a recent historian puts it, the "cloud of unknowing through which contemporaries blundered into civil war."[27]

The works discussed thus far—*Gaping Gulf, An Admonition, Leicester's Commonwealth,* and *Vox populi*—typify the standard mode of early modern political dissent. Most Tudor-Stuart oppositional writing relies heavily on defamation, malicious conjecture, and what Holinshed termed "the pestilent precept of Medius . . . to nip boldlie, and to bite with store of slanders. For (quoth he) although he that is bitten should be cured of the wound, yet the skar at the least will still remaine."[28] But precisely because these works target individuals, they have rarely attracted much notice. Modern scholars have tended to identify subversion with ideological critique and thus to regard the whole issue of defamation as only marginally relevant to early modern *politics.*

But this distinction between defamation and politics seems to me singularly unhelpful in any attempt to understand either Tudor-Stuart political discourse or the attempts made to regulate it. As recent historians have pointed out, blood ties rather than ideology fastened political groupings well into the Jacobean age; consequently, opposition to authority was far less a matter of generalized principles than "rights, grievances, and personalities."[29] "Personalities" is crucial here. For the ruling classes, personal reputation constituted "the very essence of their ability to govern."[30] As Edward Coke rhetorically queried, "What greater scandal of government can there be than to have corrupt or wicked magistrates to be appointed and constituted by the king?"[31] Defamation became an effective political weapon, precisely because in early modern England the political was personal. It is, as Darnton notes, "easy to underestimate the importance of personal slander . . . because it is difficult to appreciate that politics took place at court, where personalities counted more than policies"; "nothing sapped legitimacy more effectively than the literature of libel."[32]

The nightmares of early modern English persons—the foreboding shadows cast by historical memory—unfurled grim scenarios depicting the breakdown of a sociopolitical order based, somewhat precariously, on personal authority and allegiances. But insofar as authority depended on reputation (and a dog, *pace* Lear, is not always obeyed in office), it needed the protection of robes and furred gowns. As the British sociologist F. G. Bailey observed, "authority requires a mask," in part because the mask symbolizes "the community and its fundamental values," but also because, by concealing the leader's human failings, the mask protects charisma from contempt.[33] Attempts to subvert authority, in turn, do so by stripping—or claiming to have stripped—off its "lendings," by calling into question the motives and morals of the man behind the mask. As Darnton remarks, this sort of seditious libel proved "dangerous propaganda. . . . It severed the sense of decency that bound the public to its rulers."[34] At the close of his *Life and Reign of King James I,* published in 1653, Arthur Wilson similarly called attention to the link between the "strange Monstrous Satyrs against the King's own Person" and the fall of the Stuart monarchy.

> And the Tongues of those Times more fluent than my Pen, made every little Miscarriage (being not able to discover their true Operations, like small Seeds hid in earthy Darkness) grow up, and spread into such exuberant Branches, that evil Report did often pearch upon them. So dangerous it is for Princes, by a remiss Comportment, to give Growth to the least Error: for it often proves as fruitful, as Malice can make it.[35]

Wilson's genealogy summarizes basic early modern assumptions about the form and content of oppositional discourse: that it attacked persons rather than ideas, that it was composed of malicious and often mistaken conjectures, and that princes had reason to fear the "dangerous" fruit such "evil Report" might bear.

Tudor-Stuart censorship attempted to contain the quite real threats posed by these reports. In sixteenth-century common law neither holding nor publishing dissident opinions (other than heresy) constituted a punishable offense.[36] Language became actionable only if it involved treason, *scandalum magnatum,* or defamation.[37] The laws governing discourse suggest that what troubled the ruling elites of early modern England was less political critique *simpliciter* than politically motivated slander. But given the pervasive coupling of dissent and detraction in antigovernment writings, the silencing of dissent remained throughout the period inseparable from the enforcement of fundamental civility rules—which may help explain the puzzling phenomenon Blair Worden once noted, namely, that virtually no one in seventeenth-century England, radical or royalist, defended freedom of the press per se.[38]

Hence, with the exception of Milton's *Areopagitica,* the collapse of the licensing system in 1641 did not occasion general rejoicing over the new freedom of self-expression; instead, writers across the political spectrum voiced deep misgivings. In 1642 Thomas Fuller thus lamented the "scurrilous scandalous papers" issuing from the unregulated press: "they cast dirt on the faces of many innocent persons, which dryed on by continuance of time can never after be washed off."[39] Later in the century Baxter offered an equally disillusioned verdict.

> The prodigious lies which have been published in this age . . . doth call men to take heed what history they believe. . . . In this age there have been such things written against parties and persons whom the writers design to make odious so notoriously false as you would think that the sense of their honour at least should have made it impossible for such men to write.[40]

The circulation of printed falsehood disturbed even radical factions like the Levellers, who protested that the Long Parliament allowed the press "to print, divulge and disperse whatsoever books, pamphlets and libels they please, though they be full of lies."[41] Early modern English persons would not have had difficulty grasping Stephen Greenblatt's observation that power *is* the "ability to impose one's fictions upon the world."[42] They had less concern for the freedom of the press than do we precisely because they recognized the potency of falsehood.

The Morality of Language

I have argued thus far that early modern libelous politics threatened the great civility of trust in two ways: it attempted to destroy people's trust in their rulers, and it neglected the habits of truthfulness on which trust—and, in consequence, human community—depend. State censorship targeted political libels because they endangered the very premises of civil society.

There is, however, a further and more subtle link between early modern censorship and civility. As previously noted, the laws regulating language, whether spoken or written, focus on the problem of defamation. But defamation law, as Robert Post acutely remarks, presupposes—and therefore embodies—"an image of how people are tied together, or should be tied together, in a social setting."[43] In the most literal sense, defamation law concerns civility: how people should behave toward each other. It is the means by which a society protects the social and religious "sacredness" of its members, shielding them from insult, contempt, and degrading exposure.[44]

Post focuses on contemporary American jurisprudence, but his reading of defamation law as a mechanism for enforcing civility has striking affinities with the standard early modern view of censorship. Throughout the Tudor-Stuart period, constraints on individual expression—constraints imposed as much by self-censorship as legal sanctions—presupposed a link between use of words and relationships among people. They embodied, that is, a *morality* of language—not, however, our morality. Throughout the period, there seems to have been a fairly widespread consensus that some news was not fit to print, an attitude that no longer finds much support. We tend to assume that one of the free press's primary functions is to expose precisely the information that someone (or everyone) wishes to hide: *The Pentagon Papers,* for example. Early modern persons seem to have viewed the ethics of disclosure somewhat differently, subordinating the public right-to-know to the moral prohibition against exposing one's neighbors' failings. Thomas Fuller, a moderate royalist and Anglican priest, thus deplored "scurrilous scandalous" pamphlets because, even granting "the things true they jeer at," Christians ought not "to play upon the sinnes and miseries of others."[45] A Puritan biographer similarly explained that he had not attempted to record his subjects' "weaknesses, [or] to discover their shame, for this is a poysonous disposition."[46]

The term most often used for such reticence is not, however, *civility* but *charity*. The 1559 *Injunctions for Religion,* which enact the Elizabethan licensing system, open by condemning "slanderous words and railings whereby charity, the knot of all Christian society, is loosed."[47] The church courts treated defamation as a violation of "harmony and charity within the Christian community"; hence in ecclesiastical defamation law, as in criminal, truth was no defense.[48] While shaped by Christian values, such constraints on telling the whole story did not, it should be added, express a narrowly clerical viewpoint. Samuel Daniel, a deeply intelligent and much underrated poet, thus avers that "*gratitude, and charity* / ... keepe no note, nor memory will haue, / Of any fault committed."[49] Even a sophisticated and disillusioned courtier like Fulke Greville similarly insists that "bashfull Truth vayles neighbours errors too"—a particularly interesting line, since "Truth" here must mean troth, not veracity.[50]

In a moving passage from his *Autobiography,* Baxter makes explicit the relation between these precepts of charity and the practice of censorship; reviewing his own literary output, he concludes,

> I have a strong natural inclination to speak of every subject just as it is, and to call a spade a spade.... But I unfeignedly confess that it is faulty ... especially because

> ...I know that there is some want of honour and love or tenderness to others; or else I should not be apt to use such words as open their weakness and offend them. And therefore I repent of it, *and wish all over-sharp passages were expunged from my writings,* and desire forgiveness of God and man.[51]

One omits certain facts not to avoid legal reprisal but to maintain the spiritual bonds of community. Moreover, as Baxter's conjunction of "honour and love" suggests, the specifically Christian regard for the sacredness of all persons—the precepts of love or charity—overlapped the secular honor code with its almost obsessive insistence on the sacredness of a gentleman's good name. A popular sixteenth-century catechism thus invokes the intertwined religious and social values grounding early modern defamation law: "everie man is bound to have a charitable opinion and good conceit of his neighbour, with a desire of his good name and credit."[52]

Such attitudes would have encouraged considerable self-censorship. On occasion, they may also have influenced government regulation of the press. Most notable in this regard are the directives in the Bishops' Ban that condemn satires, epigrams, and the *opera omnia* of Thomas Nashe and Gabriel Harvey, whose public quarrel violated moral strictures against playing upon the "sinnes and miseries of others"—as did the satires explicitly named in the ban. The first of the *Whipper Pamphlets* thus commented on the ban and its victims:

> Was not one hang'd of late for libeling?
> Yes questionless. And you deserve the same:
> For you before whole volumes forth did bring
> and whom you pleas'd, did liberally defame.[53]

At least for the author of this work, the Bishops' Ban did not prohibit "open and explicit criticism" of government policy[54] but the public mockery of another's "good name and credit."

The hermeneutic counterpart to the demand that authors conceal what it would be uncharitable to disclose is the legal rule that words should be interpreted *in mitiori sensu.* This rule held that if a statement could be construed in both a defamatory and an innocent sense, the latter should be considered its true meaning: *"verba semper accipienda sunt in mitiori sensu."*[55] *Mitior sensus* was a common law hermeneutic, devised in the late sixteenth century to adjudicate the rapidly increasing numbers of defamation cases, many of which the judges considered spiteful fabrications and hence attempted to discourage by refusing to label defamatory any statement that could possibly be given a more charitable interpretation.[56] Poets and playwrights subsequently transposed this axiom to defend their own words against what Ben Jonson called

> . . . the sinister application
> Of the malicious, ignorant, and base
> Interpreter: who will distort, and straine
> The generall scope and purpose of an authour,
> To his particular, and priuate spleene.[57]

The dramatists' reiterated attacks on readers who quarry dangerously topical meaning from their works — their insistence that the works should be held innocent unless guilty beyond reasonable doubt — invoke *mitior sensus*. Like the legal and ecclesiastical authorities, the playwrights treat charity as a hermeneutic norm.

Accusations of topical reference could, of course, expose an author to legal sanctions, but one finds numerous instances of self-censorship for reasons other than fear of punishment. In particular, writers explicitly indicate that they have "tread . . . tenderly on the graves" of departed noblemen,[58] in whom "no power remaines . . . to hold / The tongues of men, that will be talking now."[59] The terrible vulnerability of these once-powerful figures to slanderous attack haunts Daniel's elegy on the Earl of Devonshire (1626), for "the Lyon being dead euen Hares insult." Yet, Daniel continues,

> The worthier sort, who know we do not liue
> With perfect men, will neuer be so vnkinde;
> They will the right to the disceased giue,
> Knowing themselues must likewise leaue behind,
> Those that will censure them. . . .
> And will not vrge a passed error now,
> Whenas he hath no party to consult,
> Nor tongue, nor aduocate, to shew his minde.[60]

Sir Robert Naunton's *Fragmenta Regalia* — a series of thumbnail biographies of Elizabethan statesmen and courtiers written in about 1630 — likewise announces its unwillingness to publicize the "passed error" of these dead lions, since "modesty . . . forbids the defacement of men departed." As he quite elegantly puts it:

> I had rather incure the censure of abruption than to be conscious . . . of sinning by eruption and in trampling on the graves of persons at rest which living we durst not look in the face or make our addresses to them otherwise than with due regard to their honors and reverence to their virtues.[61]

Such self-confessed abruption is less a response to government censorship than an affirmation of the moral and social values that authorized such restrictions. We may or may not consider this reverence for dead noblemen legitimate, but numerous early modern writers apparently did — and were, moreover, perfectly explicit about the silences this respect imposed. The "cultural bargain between writers and political leaders," to which Annabel Patterson has called attention, that allowed the former to offer political and social criticism *if* decently veiled, was perhaps, as Patterson herself notes, less a bargain than a "joint project"—one that proved, on the whole, mutually satisfactory because both parties thought the communal bonds of honor, troth, and charity worth protecting.[62] That the legal restrictions on speech and print embodied widely shared cultural sentiments may help explain why several of the most notorious victims of early modern censorship—for example, Stubbs and Scott—were not radicalized by this experience: Stubbs entered the service of Lord Burghley, writing (presumably with his left hand) anti-Catholic pamphlets in his patron's defense; even the incendiary Scott remained chaplain to the English garrison at Utrecht until his death.

The protocols of charitable interpretation were intended to foster civil harmony, which sufficiently explains their appeal to Tudor-Stuart authorities. However, their cultural plausibility also rested, at least in part, on specifically Christian assumptions about human nature and human knowledge, in particular the possibility of moral and spiritual transformation and the impossibility of intersubjective scrutiny. The interrelation between these postulates is implicit in Richard Hooker's restatement of what he terms "the safest axioms for charity to rest itself upon": "It becometh not us during this life altogether to condemn any man, seeing that (for any thing we know) there is hope of every man's forgiveness, the possibility of whose repentance is not yet cut off by death." No person, he continues, has "sufficient means to comprehend" nor "leave to search in particular" the state of other men's souls, this knowledge having been reserved "only unto God, who seeth their hearts and understandeth all their secret cogitations."[63]

These axioms of charity suggest why claims to have uncovered secret faults or to have made windows into men's souls might seem deeply suspect, and why scrutinizing people's motives and morals—what we regard as the legitimate aim of serious journalism, history, and biography—could be perceived as defamatory fabrication. They establish a theological right to privacy.

Such axioms entail that some matters be passed over in silence; yet, as Michel Foucault has pointed out, constraints are not merely inhibitory, for power also produces: "it produces reality; it produces domains of objects and rituals of truth."[64] If charity forbids certain ways of writing about people, it fosters others. In particular, the axioms of charity link censorship practices to the peculiar conventions for representing character typical of Tudor chronicle histories and history plays—genres the authorities policed with special vigilance and which therefore supply crucial evidence concerning what, under the early modern regime of censorship, *was* permissible to print or perform.

Significantly, neither historians nor playwrights extenuate the sins of kings and magistrates; they do, however, deal generously with their souls. In Robert Fabyan's early Tudor *Chronicles* (1516), Edward II, although formerly dominated by "the appetite and pleasure of his body," after his deposition "tooke great repentaunce of his former lyfe."[65] Even the tyrannical Richard III is extended the possibility, albeit remote, of repentance; Holinshed thus grudgingly refrains from passing final judgment: "but to God, which knew his inward thoughts at the houre of his death, I remit the punishment of his offenses committed in his life."[66] The discontinuities in Marlowe's portrayal of Edward II and Shakespeare's depiction of Richard II and Wolsey—all of whom become markedly more sympathetic in their plays' last scenes—presuppose the discontinuous selfhood of pastoral theology as well as the axiom of charity it underwrites.

Like the theologians, the chroniclers tend to shrink from analyzing the motives impelling their characters. Sir George Buc thus concludes his history by invoking the "divine epigram": "Leave secret things to God, who knows all hearts."[67] Holinshed's *Chronicles* (1587) registers the same conviction that the heart is not available for human inspection; rather, the historian's gaze reaches only to matters "publicklie doone" and "the truth of that outward act."[68] As Worcester's ghost complains in *Mirror for Magistrates* (1559), "Thus story [that is, history] writers leave the causes out, / Or so rehears them, as they wer in dout"[69]—a complaint echoed in Gabriel Harvey's disparaging remark that Tudor chroniclers knew nothing of "the art of depicting character."[70]

The chroniclers do not, however, altogether refrain from alleging possible motives for things "publicklie doone," but they evince considerable discomfort with such explanations, often citing several incompatible motives for the same act to emphasize their conjectural status. This incorporation of divergent voices does not, I think, obliquely advocate "the idea of an open society in which dissent must be spoken," as Patterson has suggested.[71] It seems rather to register the chroniclers' sensitivity to the problem of defamation, their awareness that motives cannot be known but only imputed, and that such imputations may be slanderous. Such concerns suffuse Holinshed's account of the death of King John's nephew, Arthur:

> But now touching the maner in verie deed of the end of this Arthur, writers make sundrie reports.... Some have written ... [that] he fell into the riuer of Saine, and so was drowned. Other write ... [that] he pined awaie.... But some affirme, that king Iohn secretlie caused him to be murthered ... but verelie king Iohn was had in great suspicion, whether worthilie or not, the lord knoweth.[72]

The historian must perforce rely on contemporary witnesses, "but such was the malice of writers in times past" toward King John that every unfortunate occurrence "was still interpreted to chance through his default, so as the blame still was imputed to him." Whatever John's failings, "yet to thinke that he deserued the tenth part of the blame wherewith writers charge him, it might seeme a great lacke of aduised consideration in them that so should take it."[73] The chronicler sets down the incriminating allegations found in his sources because some may have been true, but, like the narrator of *Paradise Lost,* he attempts to educate his readers to consider advisedly charges purveyed by talking snakes.

The chroniclers' peculiar formulae for depicting character—the sudden repentance of wicked rulers, the unselective rehearsal of contradictory interpretations, the unwillingness to probe the occulted causes impelling the "outward act"—assume the possibility *(gratia assistente)* of radical moral change and the impenetrability of "the soul's most subtle rooms."[74] These assumptions underwrite the chroniclers' efforts to deal gently and generously with the souls of famous men, as well as the legal hermeneutic of the *mitior sensus* and the charitable protocols of self-censorship. Such reticence seems to have been emphasized during the Tudor-Stuart era in response to political concerns, but these were concerns apparently shared by authors and authorities over the uncivil depredations of what Edmund Spenser called the Blatant Beast, a monster whose battle with the knight of courtesy occupies the final canto of the *The Faerie Queene* (1596). This creature, whose thousand tongues "spake reprochfully, not caring where nor when," spits forth

> licentious words and hatefull things
> Of good and bad alike, of low and hie;
> Ne kesars spared he a whit, nor kings,
> But either blotted them with infamie
> Or bit them with his banefull teeth of injury.

But as the monster rails at his opponent "with bitter termes of shamefull infamy; / Oft interlacing many a forged lie," the knight of courtesy, in what might almost be read as an allegory of censorship, "did him suppresse, and forcibly subdew."[75] The Blatant Beast does not, of course, signify unlicensed printing but simply defamation, yet it was precisely the conviction that the latter profoundly threatened the foundations, both ethical and religious, of civil society that made it possible to perceive early modern censorship as a discipline of the Spenserian courtesy that "spreds it selfe through all civilitie."[76]

This is not how we typically regard censorship. Yet the premise behind Spenser's allegory—that words can hurt as much as sticks or stones—seems remarkably close to the central thesis of new historicism: that texts are "forms of power."[77] If, however, words have the power to hurt, then, as with handguns, the state would seem to have a legitimate interest in regulating their use—the conclusion toward which Spenser's allegory points.

There is something admittedly odd about pairing censorship with gun control, at least in part because we think of texts as menacing orthodoxies rather than individuals. As I have now argued at length, early modern persons thought differently. In *The Use of the Law; For Preservation of Our Persons, Goods, and Good Names,* Francis Bacon thus lumps together verbal attacks with physical assault. As the title itself suggests, for Bacon the state is equally responsible for securing "men's persons from death and violence" as "their good names from shame and infamy." Hence, he continues,

> if any man beat, wound, or maim another, *or give false scandalous words that may touch his credit,* the law giveth thereupon an action of the case for the slander of his good name; and an action of battery, or an appeal of maim, by which recompence shall be recovered, to the value of the hurt, damage or danger.[78]

For Bacon, scandalous falsehoods are the verbal equivalent of battery: they wound people.

We should not, moreover, read such violence as strictly metaphoric, since words could easily lead to bloodshed. Thus, as part of his campaign to suppress the English nobility's often fatal enthusiasm for dueling, in 1613 King James outlawed "the publishing of any reports or writings of Duels," since

> when as We shal have taken the paines to cause Our Marshals to agree a Quarrell, whereupon Wee and all honest men have reason to accompt it as utterly extinct[,] upon such publication . . . the parties shall againe fall out who before were agreed . . . [and] even their friends, and peradventure other friends who had nothing to doe with the matter, must upon that backe reckoning fall by the eares together. . . . And so shall Quarrels become immortal, and their memory renew, whereas the best remedy against all sinnes and offences is Forgetfulnesse.[79]

Scandalum magnatum and the libel laws criminalized defamation for much the same reason: because it posed a quite literal threat to "harmony and charity within the Christian community." Censorship, on this view, is very much like gun control.

The Bill of Rights would also seem to associate censorship with gun control. But it, of course, repudiates both. In guaranteeing—and conjoining—freedom of the press and the right to bear arms, the Bill of Rights presupposes a model of sociopolitical relations that differs in fundamental respects from the typical early modern outlook. The Founding Fathers were not particularly interested in protecting communal charity, Christian or otherwise; they were, however, concerned to guard individual liberties from the encroachments of state power. Events of the past two centuries have repeatedly validated this concern, and I have no wish to minimize it. Yet our preoccupation with the dangers of hegemony has made it difficult for us to think about freedom of the press except in terms of individual freedom. We tend, perhaps, to underestimate the extent to which a hermeneutic of suspicion acts as a powerful solvent not only on the masks of power but also on the fabric of decency: the civility rules that secure an individual's standing within the community as well as the mutual trust and forbearance that make community possible. I do not mean by this to recommend censorship—as Baxter wisely remarked, "to persecute men and then call them to charity is like whipping children to make them give over crying"[80]—but only to suggest that calling men to charity might still be a good idea, and that how to do so *without* persecuting them is still a good question.

Notes

1. Richard McCabe, "Elizabethan Satire and the Bishops' Ban of 1599," *Yearbook of English Studies* 11 (1981): 191–92. See also Lynda Boose, "The 1599 Bishops' Ban, Elizabethan Pornography, and the Sexualization of the Jacobean Stage," in Richard Burt and John Michael Archer, eds., *Enclosure Acts: Sexuality, Property, and Culture in Early Modern England* (Ithaca: Cornell Univ. Press, 1994), 196–98; and G. B. Harrison, "Books and Readers, 1599–1603," *The Library,* 4th series, 14 (1933): 14.

2. [John Weever], *The Whipping of the Satyre,* ll. 295, 748, 805–7; [Nicholas Breton], *No Whippinge,* l. 281. Both poems are reprinted in *The Whipper Pamphlets* (1601), 2 vols., ed. A. Davenport (Liverpool: Univ. Press of Liverpool, 1951). I have modernized the spelling, orthography, and punctuation throughout.

3. See Robert Post, "The Social Foundations of Defamation Law: Reputation and the Constitution," *California Law Review* 74 (1986): 734.

4. [Weever] (see note 2), l. 586; Post (see note 3), 710.

5. Steven Shapin, *A Social History of Truth: Civility and Science in Seventeenth-Century England* (Chicago: Univ. of Chicago Press, 1994), 36.

6. Montaigne, "Of Liars" and "Of Giving the Lie" (1580), quoted in Shapin (see note 5), 10.

7. Christopher Hill, "Censorship and English Literature," in idem, *The Collected Essays of Christopher Hill: Volume One: Writing and Revolution in 17th-Century England* (Amhurst: Univ. of Massachusetts Press, 1985), 32–33; Anne Castanien, "Censorship and Historiography in Elizabethan England: The Expurgation of Holinshed's Chronicles," Ph.D. diss., Univ. of California at Davis, 1970, 34; Annabel M. Patterson, *Reading Holinshed's Chronicles* (Chicago: Univ. of Chicago Press, 1994), 263.

8. Moreover, it is evident that unorthodox or transgressive political theory was not prohibited, since the principal texts of classical republicanism were available in English translation by 1641.

9. See vol. 2 of *Tudor Royal Proclamations,* 3 vols., ed. Paul L. Hughes and James F. Larkin (New Haven: Yale Univ. Press, 1964–1969), 21 Eliz. I, 15 Eliz. I, 30 Eliz. I; and Matthias A. Shaaber, *Some Forerunners of the Newspaper in England, 1476–1622* (Philadelphia: Univ. of Pennsylvania Press, 1929), 93. Note, however, that the proclamations against heretical books employ quite different categories; thus some separatist pamphlets are banned not only as "seditious" but also "schismatical, and erroneous" (25 Eliz. I).

10. Fredrick Seaton Siebert, *Freedom of the Press in England, 1476–1776: The Rise and Decline of Government Controls* (Urbana: Univ. Illinois Press, 1952), 91.

11. John Stubbs, *Gaping Gulf, with Letters and Other Related Documents,* ed. Lloyd E. Berry, Folger Documents of Tudor and Stuart Civilization (Charlottesville: Univ. Press of Virginia, 1968), 3, 71, 80–81.

12. Quoted in Frederick C. Chamberlin, *The Private Character of Queen Elizabeth* (London: John Lane, 1922), 185–87.

13. *Leicester's Commonwealth: The Copy of a Letter Written by a Master of Art of Cambridge* (1584), ed. D. C. Peck (Athens: Ohio Univ. Press, 1985), 81, 265–67.

14. Ibid., 50–51.

15. The most notorious example being the *Corona regia,* printed in the Low Countries in 1615 (the author, publisher, and place of publication given on the title page are fabrications); on James's reaction to this virulent satire, see Winfried Schleiner, "'A plott to have his nose and eares cutt of': Schoppe as Seen by the Archbishop of Canterbury," *Renaissance and Reformation* 26 (1990): 48–57.

16. Significantly, between 1603 and 1619 James issued only two proclamations dealing with censorship—one condemning, at Parliament's behest, John Cowell's *Interpreter* (issued 25 March 1610), the other prohibiting reports of duels (15 October 1613); between 1620 and 1624, however, four separate proclamations banned seditious, slanderous, and/or schismatic books—they are reprinted as numbers 208, 218, 247, and 256 in *Stuart Royal Proclamations,* 2 vols., ed. James F. Larkin and Paul L. Hughes (Oxford: Clarendon Press, 1973).

17. Alastair Bellany, "'Raylinge Rymes and Vaunting Verse': Libellous Politics in Early Stuart England, 1603–1628," in Kevin Sharpe and Peter Lake, eds., *Culture and Politics in Early Stuart England* (London: MacMillan, 1994), 287; Thomas Cogswell, *The Blessed Revolution: English Politics and the Coming of War, 1621–1624* (Cambridge: Cambridge Univ. Press, 1989), 46–47.

18. Quoted in Richard Cust, "News and Politics in Early Seventeenth-Century England," *Past and Present* 112 (1986): 73–74, 80, 83.

19. Robin Clifton, "Fear of Popery," in Conrad Russell, ed., *The Origins of the English Civil War* (London: MacMillan, 1973), 157–60, 165; Cogswell (see note 17), 24, 31, 35; Siebert (see note 10), 154.

20. Thomas Scott, *The Workes of the Most Famous and Reverend Divine Mr. Thomas Scott* (Utrecht, 1624).

21. Charles Carter, "Gondomar: Ambassador to James I," *The Historical Journal* 7 (1964): 191–92.

22. Quoted in Louis Wright, "Propaganda against James I's 'Appeasement' of Spain," *Huntington Library Quarterly* 6 (1943): 152–53. See also Shaaber (see note 9), 72; and Margot Heinemann, *Puritanism and Theatre: Thomas Middleton and Opposition Drama under the Early Stuarts,* Past and Present Publications (Cambridge: Cambridge Univ. Press, 1980), 156.

23. Kevin Sharpe, *The Personal Rule of Charles I* (New Haven: Yale Univ. Press, 1992), 939, 910.

24. Richard Baxter, *The Autobiography of Richard Baxter, Being the "Reliquiae Baxterianae" Abridged from the Folio* (1696), ed. J. M. Lloyd Thomas (London: Dent, 1925), 32.

25. Clifton (see note 19), 144–45, 162. See also J. S. Morrill and J. D. Walter, "Order and Disorder in the English Revolution," in Anthony Fletcher and John Stevenson, eds., *Order and Disorder in Early Modern England* (Cambridge: Cambridge Univ. Press, 1985), 147–48; and Lucy Hutchinson, *Memoirs of the Life of Colonel Hutchinson,* ed. James Sutherland (London: Oxford Univ. Press, 1973), 52.

26. See Robert Darnton, *The Forbidden Best-Sellers of Pre-Revolutionary France* (New York: Norton, 1995), 238; Sharpe (see note 23), 911, 939; and Clifton (see note 19), 161.

27. Peter Lake, "Anti-popery: The Structure of a Prejudice," in Richard Cust and Ann Hughes, eds., *Conflict in Early Stuart England: Studies in Religion and Politics, 1603–1642* (London: Longman, 1989), 73.

28. Quoted in Castanien (see note 7), 291.

29. Mervyn James, *Family, Lineage, and Civil Society: A Study of Society, Politics, and Mentality in the Durham Region, 1500–1640* (Oxford: Clarendon Press, 1974), 184–85.

30. Anthony Fletcher, "Honour, Reputation and Local Officeholding in Elizabethan and Stuart England," in Fletcher and Stevenson (see note 25), 92, 115; see J. A. Sharpe, *Defamation and Sexual Slander in Early Modern England: The Church Courts at York,* Borthwick Papers 58 (York: Univ. of York Press, 1972), 2; W. S. Holdsworth, *A History of English Law,* 3rd ed., 9 vols. (Boston: Little, Brown, 1922–26), 5: 207.

31. Edward Coke, *The Reports of Sir Edward Coke, Knt.,* 7 vols., ed. and trans. George Wilson (London, 1776–77), 3: 125r; see Holdsworth (see note 30), 5: 209.

32. Robert Darnton, *The Literary Underground of the Old Regime* (Cambridge, Mass.: Harvard Univ. Press, 1982), 203–4; and his *Forbidden Best-Sellers* (see note 26), 216.

33. F. G. Bailey, "The Management of Reputations and the Process of Change," in F. G. Bailey, ed., *Gifts and Poison: The Politics of Reputation* (New York: Schocken Books, 1971), 291–94.

34. Darnton, *Literary Underground* (see note 32), 205.

35. Sir Arthur Wilson, *The Life and Reign of King James I* (1653), reprinted in *The Complete History of England,* 3 vols., ed. White Kennett (London, 1706), 2: 792.

36. While seditious doctrine per se could be prosecuted under special felony statutes, these, as Philip Hamburger notes, proved paper tigers, and after lapsing at Elizabeth's death were never reenacted. Philip Hamburger, "The Development of the Law of Seditious Libel and the Control of the Press," *Stanford Law Review* 37 (1985): 671.

37. Throughout the period, *defamation* (whether civil or criminal), *libel,* and *slander* were used as synonyms; the same laws thus covered printed, manuscript, and spoken defamation. See Hamburger (see note 36), 669–71; Holdsworth (see note 30), 5: 207; and Coke (see note 31), 3: 125r.

38. Blair Worden, "Literature and Political Censorship in Early Modern England," in A. C. Duke and C. A. Tamse, eds., *Too Mighty To Be Free: Censorship and the Press in Britain and the Netherlands* (Zutphen: De Walburg, 1987), 47.

39. Thomas Fuller, *The Holy State* (1642), in idem, *Thomes Fuller: Selections,* ed. Edmund Kemper Broadus (Oxford: Clarendon Press, 1928), 59.

40. Baxter (see note 24), 126–28.

41. Quoted in Worden (see note 38), 47. Pierre Bayle proposes an interesting sort of typographical censorship to deal with the similarly mendacious French *chroniques scandaleuses:* these, Bayle complains, "are a mixture of fictions and truths, half romance, and half history," making it extremely difficult "to distinguish fiction from true matter of fact"; this being the case, Bayle concludes, "I believe the civil powers will at last be forced to give these new romancers the option: either to write pure history, or pure romance; or at least to use crotchets to separate the one from the other,

truth from fiction." Quoted in Michael McKeon, *The Origins of the English Novel, 1600–1740* (Baltimore: Johns Hopkins Univ. Press, 1987), 55.

42. Stephen Greenblatt, *Renaissance Self-Fashioning from More to Shakespeare* (Chicago: Univ. of Chicago Press, 1980), 13.

43. Post (see note 3), 693.

44. Ibid., 962.

45. Fuller (see note 39), 59–60.

46. Samuel Clarke, *A Collection of the Lives of Ten Eminent Divines* (London, 1662), A3(r).

47. In *Tudor Royal Proclamations* (see note 9), 2: 128. According to Melanchthon, *"tribuunt christiani sapientiam et iustitiam magistratui.... Deinde huc pertinet etiam errata legum et magistratuum tegere, excusare et mitigare. Haec epieikeia, cum in privata conversatione necessaria sit, multo magis necessaria est in publica societate erga magistratus, sicut scriptum est: 'Dilectio omnia perfert'... item: 'Omnia delicta tegit dilectio'"* (Christians ascribe wisdom and justice to the magistrate.... This extends, moreover, to covering, excusing, and mitigating the defects of both laws and magistrates. Such equity, while necessary in private relations, is much more necessary in public conduct toward the magistrate, as it is written: "Love endures all things patiently"... and likewise "Love covers all faults"). Philipp Melanchthon, *Commentarii in epistolam Pauli ad Romanos* (1532), in idem, *Melanchthons Werke,* 7 vols., ed. Gerhard Ebeling and Rolf Schaefer (Tübingen: Gütersloh, 1964), 5: 324–25.

48. Martin Ingram, *Church Courts, Sex and Marriage in England, 1570–1640,* Past and Present Publications (Cambridge: Cambridge Univ. Press, 1987), 294–95.

49. Samuel Daniel, "A Funerall Poeme Upon the Death of the Late Noble Earle of Devonshire (1606)," in idem, *The Complete Works in Verse and Prose of Samuel Daniel,* 5 vols., ed. Alexander B. Grosart (London: Hazel, Watson & Viney, 1885–1886), 1: 184, ll. 345–47.

50. Fulke Greville, "An Inquisition upon Fame and Honour," in idem, *Certaine Learned and Elegant Workes* (1633), (Delmar, N.Y.: Scholars' Facsimiles, 1990), l. 24.

51. Baxter (see note 24), 131.

52. Cited in Sharpe (see note 30), 2.

53. [Weever] (see note 2), ll. 331–34.

54. McCabe (see note 1), 193.

55. W. S. Holdsworth, "Defamation in the Sixteenth and Seventeenth Centuries," *Law Quarterly Review* 40 (1924): 407.

56. Ibid., 404–7.

57. Ben Jonson, *Poetaster* (1602), in idem, *Ben Jonson,* 11 vols., ed. C. H. Herford, Percy Simpson, and Evelyn Simpson (Oxford: Clarendon Press, 1925–52), 5.3.137–44. A seventeenth-century jurist uses similar terms to characterize the majority of actions for defamation facing the courts: they serve largely to "vent the spleen of private jars and discontents among men"; Holdsworth, "Defamation" (see note 55), 404n. See also Pope's magnificent curse on the "babbling blockhead" who "reads but with a lust to misapply, / Makes satire a lampoon, and fiction, lie." Alexander Pope, "Epistle to Dr. Arbuthnot," in idem, *The Poems of Alexander Pope,* ed. John Butt (New Haven: Yale Univ. Press, 1963), 607, ll. 301–4.

58. Samuel Daniel, "Epistle Dedicatory," in *The Collection of the History of England* (1626), in *Complete Works* (see note 49), 4: 78.

59. Samuel Daniel, "Funerall Poem," in *Complete Works* (see note 49), 1: 173. Grosart prints these lines, which appear only in the manuscript version, in a footnote to his edition of the poem. After 1606, libels against the dead could be prosecuted as *scandalum magnatum*.

60. Ibid., 1: 184–85, ll. 353–62.

61. Sir Robert Naunton, *Fragmenta Regalia, or Observations on Queen Elizabeth, Her Times & Favorites* (written ca. 1630), ed. John S. Cerovski (Washington, D. C.: Folger Books, 1985), 86.

62. Annabel Patterson, *Censorship and Interpretation: The Conditions of Writing and Reading in Early Modern England* (Madison: Univ. Wisconsin Press, 1984), 7, 11–15.

63. Richard Hooker, *Of the Laws of Ecclesiastical Polity,* in idem, *The Works of Mr. Richard Hooker* (1888), 7th ed., 3 vols., ed. John Keble, R. W. Church, and F. Paget (New York: Burt Franklin, 1970), 5.49.2, 3.1.2.

64. Michel Foucault, *Discipline and Punish: The Birth of the Prison,* trans. Alan Sheridan (New York: Random House, 1979), 194.

65. Robert Fabyan, *The New Chronicles of England and France* (1516), ed. Henry Ellis (London: F. C. & J. Rivington, 1811), 417, 431.

66. Raphael Holinshed, *Holinshed's Chronicles of England, Scotland, and Ireland* (1587), 6 vols. (London, 1807–1808), 3: 447.

67. Sir George Buc, *The History of King Richard the Third* (1619), ed. Arthur Noel Kincaid (Gloucester: Alan Sutton, 1979), 193–94.

68. Quoted in Castanien (see note 7), 198.

69. *The Mirror for Magistrates* (1559), ed. Lily B. Campbell (New York: Barnes & Noble, 1960), 198; Patterson (see note 7), 265.

70. Ibid., 15.

71. Gabriel Harvey quoted in Patterson (see note 7), 265

72. Holinshed, *The Third Volume of Chronicles, beginning at Duke William the Norman* (1587), 165b; quoted in A. R. Braunmuller, "King John and Historiography," *English Literary History* 55 (1988): 316.

73. Holinshed quoted in ibid., 321.

74. George Herbert, "The H. Communion," in idem, *George Herbert and Henry Vaughan,* ed. Louis L. Martz (Oxford: Oxford Univ. Press, 1986), 45.

75. Edmund Spenser, *The Faerie Queene* (1596), in idem, *The Complete Poetical Works of Spenser,* ed. R. E. Neil Dodge (Boston: Houghton Mifflin, 1908), 6.12.27–33.

76. Ibid., 6.preface.4.

77. Stephen Greenblatt, "Introduction," in idem, ed., *The Forms of Power and the Power of Forms in the Renaissance,* Genre Special Topics 7 (Norman: Univ. of Oklahoma Press, 1982). See also Jean Howard, "The New Historicism in Renaissance Studies," *English Literary Renaissance* 16 (1986): 25, 27; and Margot Heinemann, "Political Drama," in A. R. Braunmuller and Michael Hattaway, eds., *The Cambridge Companion to English Renaissance Drama* (Cambridge: Cambridge Univ. Press, 1990), 177.

78. Francis Bacon, *The Works of Francis Bacon,* 10 vols. (London, 1826), 4: 81 (emphasis mine). Coke draws a similar analogy between libel and, interestingly enough, poisoning. See Coke (see note 31) 3: 126v.

79. *Stuart Royal Proclamations* (see note 16), 1: 295–96 (13 October 1613).

80. Baxter (see note 24), 17.

"An Immoderate Taste for Truth": Censoring History in Baudelaire's "Les bijoux"

E. S. Burt

In May 1949 a French Court of Appeals reversed an 1857 decision condemning six poems from Charles Baudelaire's *Les fleurs du mal* for obscenity, in a signal case of a public lifting of a ban against lyric poems.[1] Not the least of the several interesting features to the case is the decision to proceed against the work in the first place. Lyric poetry does not appear an attractive target for censorship, for its subject matter and formalism remove it far from the experience of most readers. Gustave Flaubert, fresh from his troubles with the court over *Madame Bovary,* expressed his surprise at the government's attack: "This is new," he wrote to Baudelaire, "this pursuit of a volume of verse."[2] Although his comment was in point of fact inaccurate, Flaubert put his finger on a problem worth considering.[3] Here *Les fleurs du mal* would seem to be naturally exempt from state intervention by virtue of its deliberate retreat from risky political subjects and the inaccessibility of the genre, yet it was censored nonetheless by the state. Can anything be learned about "normal" state censorship from this exceptional case?[4]

A key factor in the government's decision to pursue the book, according to the prosecutor Ernest Pinard, was that Baudelaire's poetry might prove accessible to a large audience: "An immoral book that had no chance of being read or understood would not be pursued," he states.[5] In his argument, as in the judgment by the court that the condemned poems "lead necessarily to the exciting of the senses by a coarse realism offensive to modesty," the assumption is that the work is extraordinarily available and its pictures immediately referable to ordinary experience.[6] In the six condemned poems, language is judged to be not a veil but a tool, and a sex tool at that. "Despite an effort of style," the poetic setting—that of the boudoir in most of the poems—is painted in a language deemed insufficiently flowery.[7]

A second interesting feature in the case is that when the decision was reviewed in 1949, during de Gaulle's Fourth Republic, the court summarily dismissed the 1857 judgment of coarse realism as just one possible interpretation, and a forced one at that. Instead, the court found that the poems are self-referential, symbolic entities that do not represent ordinary experience:

> If some pictures, on account of their originality, were able to alarm some minds upon first publication and appeared to the first judges as offensive to morality,

> such an appraisal, attaching itself only to a realistic interpretation of the poems and neglecting their symbolic meaning, has proved to be of an arbitrary character, unratified by public opinion or by the judgment of the literary world.[8]

The representations that were considered outrageous in 1857 were in 1949 understood to deliver the Wordsworthian "shock of mild surprise" by which we recognize an original work of art. In 1949, the poems had become precious artifacts; their language was not realistic but symbolical, and the language's sensuous forms revealed an inner, spiritual meaning.

A crucial resemblance can be discerned between the actions taken by the two courts: both make their judgments in terms of a "reading pact," a set of "artificial rules" that are presumed to govern reading and to have currency in the context. *Les fleurs* was policed in the name of this generic purity, with Pinard calling the judge "a sentinel who must not let the border be crossed"; the decision in 1949 said something similar when it confirmed the opinion of the literary world that the poems' supposed transgression against public morality was actually a transformation of the rules regulating the narrow confines of lyric poetry.[9]

This concern that texts be framed by a reading pact aimed at constraining their interpretation is worth considering by any who would like to move the discussion of censorship from the level of pragmatics to that of theory. It leads to queries about the possibility of getting rid of state censorship entirely and about the state's interest in the institutionalization and enforcement of such reading pacts. It raises the issue of an ambiguity in the role played by the literary establishment, which can be seen most often acting in collusion with the state on this matter of generic purity. That is partly a matter of empirical fact. In the case of *Les fleurs du mal,* literary journalists brought the whiff of scandal to the state's attention in 1857; in 1949 it was a Society of Learned Men who brought the suit to rehabilitate Baudelaire's memory and literary critics who provided expert testimony as to what Erich Auerbach called the work's "aesthetic dignity."[10] It also touches on a region where censorship law flows over into copyright law, with the rights to profit from a work's reproduction and dissemination entailing, besides the responsibility to publish the names and coordinates of author, publisher, and printer, an implied directive not to mislead readers as to the literary genre to which the work belongs. As for the works themselves, they can presumably collaborate with as easily as infringe upon the state's attempts to regulate linguistic indeterminacy. Where they help maintain the border between referential and self-referential language uses, they are presumably complicitous with the state and form a perfect mirror of its ideology.

The point I will pursue is a somewhat different one, albeit related, and it requires a bit of preliminary introspection. I suspect that part of the attraction of studying cases of state censorship for a critic like myself is that one can point to such cases as tangible proof that literature does matter, that it sometimes does leave its ivory tower to touch the world. The state is hit in a vital spot, as if the work lays open some secret that censorship laws try to rebury. This is thrilling to critics, this notion that the state is somehow imperiled by a literary work. It vindicates literary activity, which turns out not to be pointless after all, but is instead invested with urgency and relevancy.[11]

I cast this in the form of a confession because I am somewhat suspicious of the drama of the scenario. It neatly pits a beleaguered text or author against the monolithic authority of a state threatened by and threatening to the literary work.[12] The reality of censorship is less reassuringly centralized; it is more diffuse, more disseminated, and less univocal in its functioning than such a scenario would suggest. Censorship's most repressive acts never can do more than partially or temporarily screen the offensive material. Nor are works ever all black or white: their complicity with the state on matters of textual hygiene is also at least partial.

Nevertheless, the scenario of the state censoring Baudelaire's poems helps focus our inquiry, for it distinctly centers attention on the threat posed by textual indeterminacy as it spills over to disturb the presumed unity and stability of its context. In the case of *Les fleurs,* poems which the state rehabilitated once they were found to have a legible address and mode of meaning, the point of contention is the relation of the literary work to experience, memory, and history.

The prosecutor in 1857 provides the first hint that memory is the stake when he complains that the poems do not remove us from past sensuous experience but instead *produce* and even *model* it. He says the poems have the effect of "giving back their senses to those who can no longer feel."[13] Into the experience of reading—an experience considered reflective and removed from the senses—intrudes a new kind of remembering: the sudden revival of deadened senses. This experience of memory as transgressive recollection has been analyzed by the eminent critic of Baudelaire, Walter Benjamin, in a discussion relevant enough to merit a brief summary.

Discussing Theodor Reik's distinction between memory and remembrance, Benjamin explains that remembrance protects and preserves impressions whereas memory destroys and disintegrates them. Remembrance is a present act of retrieval that relies upon a forgetting of "what has not been experienced explicitly and consciously, what has not happened to the subject as an experience."[14] It thus conserves the past as past, subordinating it to the present act of consciousness, and confirms the view that the gain of understanding more than compensates for whatever the present has lost in terms of immediacy or in proximity to natural experience.

As for memory, it recalls uncollected and as yet unexperienced fragmentary impressions connected to the memory trace, that is, the "writing" that records and preserves sense impressions in the mind. It is apparent from Benjamin's analysis that memory disintegrates at least two structures for parrying what he calls the *shock* made in the imprinting of sense impressions. First, it calls into question the everyday experience of a subject by showing that conscious life is an artificial construction, reliant on decisions and exclusions such as those in which vision (with its tendency toward seizing an experience as a totality in an idealized image) is privileged over the other senses. Second, it disrupts the temporal assumption of remembrance, which preserves the past as past with respect to its act. Memory is an experiencing *for the first time* of left out impressions—for instance, the repressed sensations of the body as a tangle of parts and disconnected senses. Such a past has not taken place until it emerges, shattering the stability of the present in the act of recollection. The knowledge provided by memory can be termed "negative knowledge," since in recalling what is left out by consciousness in remembrance, one is faced with understanding the limits of the understanding. If, as Benjamin quotes Reik as saying, "becoming conscious and leaving behind a memory trace are processes incompatible with each other in one and the same system," memory forces consciousness to engage in a desperate and open-ended struggle of recalling traces that it never can fully assimilate but upon which its survival depends.[15]

Benjamin's analysis of Baudelaire calls into question the view that literature depicts a prior model, whether that model is found in nature, in other works, or in the author's transforming imagination. In such a view, the work of art preserves the image produced by the artist as a faithful remembrance of his act; it stands as a memorial to the mental activity of a conscious subject. For Benjamin, however, Baudelaire's poems situate the work of art in respect to an experience that requires writing in order to happen. Benjamin's argument implies that Baudelaire's poems act against what Lawrence Douglas calls "preserving responsible memory."[16]

Responsible memory, translated into the terms of our discussion, would be remembrance and memory working together dialectically. In a dialectic, the undoing of the mystified images of the past would occur with the ultimate aim of incorporating the findings of the critique into a more satisfying image or pointed narrative. Remembrance and memory would together produce a version of events that not only would preserve the past (and could thus be termed a *memory*) but also would answer the demand for truth (and could thus be termed *responsible*). If Benjamin's Baudelaire acts against responsible memory, it is not because he is irresponsible, but rather because, as a poet, he is interested in language, which is always more and less than a serviceable medium of exchange and is thus, like the refuse impressions rejected by remembrance, never fully accounted for by a dialectical interpretation.

Baudelaire's poems reveal a forgetfulness in the space of public monuments. Such monuments—among them would be those stockpiles of acquired knowledge called archives and libraries—tell us that past events and past theories are over and done with; they try to place the past of remembered events in a stable relation to the present of their interpretation. They shelter the present from the past, making the past so distant as to be unlikely to erupt into the present as unassimilated shocks. Baudelaire's library is, rather, a cross between a heap of incomprehensible ruins and a fireworks factory set down in the midst of the bustling modern city. In his view, memory and history are open-ended, future-oriented projects of recalling the conditions and limits of consciousness and of any history that would be modeled as a coming into consciousness. Small wonder that poems publicizing a fault line in the archive should be relegated to the Hell *(L'enfer)* of the National Library, where French courts sent censored texts in the nineteenth century.

My hypothesis is that the question of how the text enters history lies at the heart of the censoring of *Les fleurs du mal.*[17] That is the problem I will discuss here, first nuancing the state's position on the text as public monument, and then pursuing, through the reading of a poem, the notion of a disintegrating, inventive memory available in obscene writing that is incompatible with public, preserving memory. It is this disintegrating memory that explains the uneasy relation of the state to the literary work: as disintegrating, its violence is perceived as a threat; as inventive, it is oriented toward the future and has a productive energy to be exploited. Since the poet's ultimate responsibility as poet is to the language, it is history carried in language that will provide the lens for my analysis.

Writing Between the Lines: Remembering Language

Leo Strauss's "Persecution and the Art of Writing" provides a good starting point to complicate the state's position. Strauss's discussion of censorship is guided by a complex understanding of the relation of philosophical texts to history. As products of their time, philosophical texts preserve and pass on the opinion of that time; but they also engage in conflictual dialogue with opinion, and as such, transmit less a content than a critical method distinguished by a negative moment. Where state censorship has gotten in the way of the explicit expression of this dialogue between opinion and its critique (as it did in much of eighteenth-century Europe, for example), philosophical writers have had to resort to elaborate strategies of indirection, called by Strauss "writing between the lines," to transmit their philosophical method.[18] To write between the lines is to write a text that, read as statement, is entirely orthodox but that, by the arrangement of the statements, devices of argument, and strategic asides, is revealed as criticizing the orthodoxy.

The recognition that the means of saying can intervene actively in signification allows Strauss first to formulate a critique of historicism as interpretative method. Historicism, he says, had as its principle that

> no term of any consequence must be used in the interpretation of an author which cannot be literally translated into his language, and which was not used by him or was not in fairly common use in his time. The only presentations of an author's views which can be accepted as true are those ultimately borne out by his own explicit statements.[19]

By such methods, teaching texts like those of Plato, Averroes, Kant, or Rousseau were diminished to documents transmitting the most platitudinous orthodoxies. Against historicism, Strauss presents a theory of history as an ongoing process of interpretation of fundamental texts. Its method is that of active, self-critical dialogue over orthodox doctrine, a dialogue made available in works written in time of persecution by way of a disjunction between a statement and its mode of presentation—or, as we would nowadays say, by way of a disjunction in an utterance between its force as a constative or statement and its force as a performative affirming or denying the truth of whatever it states. Strauss can thus distinguish the true interpretation of a work from the merely correct, historicist one: the true interpretation is neither the orthodox nor the heterodox opinion *qua* opinion; it is rather the interpretation that, having taken strategy into account, can teach a dialectical method to "the young men who love to think."[20]

What is most relevant in this account for our question is that the recollection that language actively affects meaning serves as a teaching moment, a privileged moment of progress and liberation from mere doxa. A crucial double effect on the concern of the liberal state with freedom of expression can be extrapolated from Strauss's theory of history and of writing between the lines.[21] If his young men—the "puppies of the race"[22]—progress by recalling language, then a liberal state interested in the fostering of its puppies and the furtherance of progress must tolerate to a certain degree the disruptiveness identified with Benjamin's disintegrating memory. We have to revise the simple opposition that pits the censoring state against the individual author, the public space of pious preservation of a heroic past against a private space where memory can be free to be disintegrative. Revealed here is a gray area of possible production and education where public and private interests overlap, where friendly disagreement of groups of reasonable citizens with one another and with a state founded on reason can take place, and where agreements can be forged. The content of texts, statements *qua* statements, are in themselves shown to be unthreatening. Once an opinion has value only insofar as its truth is confirmed or belied by the force of its language, a state conceived along Straussian principles can easily liberalize its censorship of content. Paradoxically, however, this state would tend to tighten its control over the means of expression, hoping to limit the negative power of language to what can be assimilated as positive knowledge. In his essay Strauss notes the need to find such limits, discussing the need for "criteria for distinguishing between legitimate and illegitimate reading between the lines."[23]

Censorship in such a state would hardly merit the name: its aim would be to shelter the means as inventive and educative, while limiting the potential for disruption. The aim is simply accomplished by the determination of those limits as those of knowledge. Any monological text whose structures confirm the liberal orthodoxy by saying what they mean would be allowable, in that it would provide knowledge of a content. Any dialogical text whose presentation has a force discrepant with respect to the views it states would provide a lesson on method to the alert few. In either case, the relation of performative to constative enables education, but revelation of a potential, momentary discrepancy contributes the most by promising a dynamic, progressive education in which action and knowledge in the long run coincide. The axiomatic statement that "virtue is knowledge . . . and thoughtful men as such are trustworthy and not cruel" would allow a Straussian state conceived along liberal principles to reduce the arena for positive censorship almost to nothing. The only texts offensive to public morality, and thus excisable, are those that provide for knowledge and action that do not confirm the axiom.[24]

The very few cases that could still fall under a positive censorship can be found in Strauss's essay in the form of deafening silences on issues germane to his topic. One silence is on playful modes of writing between the lines—literature, especially poetry—where indirect expression is not a teaching method but an art.[25] Another silence is on obscenity, a language use that falls outside the interpretative scheme defining the work as the intentional act of a moral being.[26] Nor do any young women who love to think make an appearance in Strauss's essay: there is no thought of woman at all in his dreamed-of future; the only love moving "thoughtful men" is for the male "puppies of the race."[27]

The reading of obscene writing, "profitable," in Baudelaire's words, "only to those minds possessed by an immoderate taste for truth," leads in another direction.[28] It demands that we take into account a dimension of language that may not ultimately confirm the harmonious convergence of knowledge and action. An *immoderate taste* for truth is the taste of someone who has not stopped with the revelation of the truth of method and of history as progress, but has developed an unhealthy appetite for revelation irrespective of whether it leads to positive knowledge. Obscene writing thrusts in our face a certain repetitive material and a certain pleasure to be gotten from the material that are rejected when writing is conceived in teleological terms. To recall obscenity is to threaten more than a prohibition on certain *topoi.* It threatens the very fundamental, convening assumption of the Straussian version of the liberal state that "virtue is knowledge." Its censorship, we may hypothesize, would constitute an attempt to keep the neglected material from returning to affect the public space of the liberal state, which is built by respectful, preserving remembrance and by the state's tolerant encouragement of a limited amount of disruption by disintegrating memory.

Dirt for Dirt's Sake

Let me gather some support for my understanding of obscenity, and start filling in the gaps left in Strauss's discussion, by reference to a case settled in the American courts in 1933, the case of James Joyce's *Ulysses,* where we see an enlightened judge hard at work interpreting a literary work as productive of knowledge. Because it is a work of fiction that is in question, it is the language as used by its speakers that is the object rather than logic and method, but the same axiom is still operative.

John M. Woolsey's ruling on the question of whether *Ulysses* could enter the United States became famous outside legal circles because it was printed in several editions of the text as its foreword. In his discussion of the "dirty words" that pepper the text, Judge Woolsey explains what he takes to be Joyce's nonpornographic intent. It is a sincere and honest one, proper to the artist, of "show(ing) exactly how the minds of his characters operate." For Woolsey, the artistic intent of bringing out "not only what is in the focus of each man's observation of the actual things about him, but also in a penumbral zone residue of past impressions," carries with it demands and responsibilities. Joyce, he says, would have "funked its necessary implications" had he not told fully what his characters think. Woolsey explains away the dirty words: Joyce's "attempt sincerely and honestly to realize his objective has required him incidentally to use certain words which are *generally considered* dirty words."[29]

For Woolsey, in this specific context—given the framing intent and the creative technique—words generally considered dirty are not really dirty. They are determined otherwise, as the words that the author in all honesty must use. We might call them *honest dirt,* for they symbolize the sweat exuded from the brow of the inventing artist. In the specific context of *Ulysses* they have ceased to be filthy. The artist reconfigures the language, with the expletives as the clue.

The author does not really "use" the dirty words at all—he uses them, as Woolsey says, "incidentally." For a term to be judged obscene, it is clearly not enough that it refer to a sexual or excretory organ or function. Otherwise, any talking about such functions, never mind any talking about talking about such functions, would be forbidden, and obscenity trials themselves would become impossible.[30] The key to obscenity lies in the way language is being used. Like *tree* or *table,* dirty words are literal, referential terms properly designating entities in the physical world. If they nonetheless offend good linguistic hygiene, it is because when we use them we break the rule set forth in the work of empiricists like Locke or Condillac that dictates a one-to-one correspondence between the ideas we get from our senses or our reason and the terms designating them. In obscenity (as in certain theological discourses) the terms reserved to name a single referent—physical or metaphysical—proliferate, and a reserve of words piles up that can be substituted for or added to one another without loss or gain in meaning. Obscene terms guard one door to a secret place of play in language, where the substitution of names unregulated by meaning, unaccountable to knowledge, can occur and where we can take pleasure in words for their own sake.[31] Language's public virtue as enabler of education is contested by the use of expletives (*explere,* to fill out)—forceful verbal filler.

When Woolsey says Joyce does not use obscene terms except incidentally, I take it that he means the author does not himself commit the abuse. Rather, he collects and pins these obscene words into his text purposively, as *examples* of language abuse. Obscenities, Woolsey says, clutter the minds and speeches of Joyce's characters, but they are always quoted so far as the author himself is concerned.[32] He mentions them to fulfill his obligation to provide a full picture of the language. Quoting a dirty word partially launders it by making it an example of a general possibility of language. It brings the prohibited material and the prohibition forward as objects of knowledge. Framed obscenity obtrudes the sheer physicality of language on us, but at a distance. By it the writer signals his debt and promise to represent the language in its entirety.

Quotation marks, literal or implied, are critical in Woolsey's discussion. They are laundry marks added by the artist which let him represent the whole body of language without reserve.[33] The judge gives a glimpse of the stakes when he reminds us that the words that Joyce has reclaimed are "old Saxon words known to almost all men, and, I venture, to many women."[34] Behind Woolsey's brief statement lies a rationale that can be spelled out as follows: Joyce accepts our English language as is, soiled by overuse and abuse, in parts reserved and shameless, with the aim of restoring its ideal Saxon integrity and purity; he takes terms eroded over time to the value of filler and makes them signify as examples of the transformation to which language is subject; by this move he arrests and even reverses the work of time; language *shown* to be shopworn is language *revealed* to be subject to unacknowledged historical processes and is thus language brought into a certain conformity with the Straussian axiom: virtue is knowledge.

The point is worth tarrying over, for Woolsey is revealing an attitude toward the function of the work of art in purifying language by reversing the corrosion of time. In their account of the trial, Morris Ernst and Allen Schwartz insist that the explanation of "each four-letter word in historic terms" was the turning point in the battle.[35] Counsel for *Ulysses* gave etymological arguments that persuasively carried the terms back to a time before they had been set aside as obscene. These etymological arguments are in point of fact *a*historical, for they try to fix the term in an imagined pristine state, before any figurative extension, before any reserve or repetition. Counsel states of the word *fuck,* for instance, that:

> One etymological dictionary gives its derivation as from *facere*—to make—the farmer fucked the seed into the soil. This, your honor, has more integrity than a euphemism used every day in every modern novel to describe precisely the same event.[36]

Everything is revealing here: the definition, the example, the vague "this," the appeal to "your honor," the emphasis on the integrity of the past as opposed to modern prudishness, and so on. Most interesting is the example. Here we have the sort of man who might have minted the term to name his work, which is that of a farmer sowing his seed. This is an Adam before the fig leaf, who would have called things by their proper names, before figurative extensions, reserves, or euphemisms. *Fuck* was as innocent and honest a word as any in the English language. Counsel provides a glimpse of a nascent, agrarian people whose language was as fresh and virginal as the soil they planted. In contrast, the modern situation shows the same event of making, but everywhere repeated, banalized, and degraded. The cause of corruption is overuse and unacknowledged quotation, and the veil of euphemism is interposed to hide it. Joyce partially reclaims the term by an acknowledged quotation that frames a mythic picture of a language once virginal but now prostituted, whose exemplary tale can serve as a warning about the rest of the language, which is still meaningful and still capable of being used with decency and respect.

Woolsey signals that he agrees with this recall to hygiene as a valuable service performed by the work of art. He does so partly by a slip, clumping the four-letter word *fuck* with the others, as criticized terms that are actually "old Saxon words." To say that *fuck,* which counsel had just derived from the Latin *facere,* is a Saxon word is, at the very least, to wipe out the Norman Conquest and the large-scale importation of Old French into the English language. It is to assume that there was a moment when the English language was entire, before contamination by suspect foreign influence, by transports this way and that. In the name of race, nation, people, and some ideology of the proper, the judge is going along with what he takes to be the artist's function with respect to the language: cordoning off the ruined parts from the living language and restoring the ideal of a language as an intact whole.

Judge Woolsey also considers the same dirty words from the perspective of the world of the diegesis, in terms of the internal consistency of the characters depicted. Here, the quotation marks function somewhat differently. The obscene terms, he says, are "such words as would be naturally and habitually used . . . by the types of folk whose life, physical and mental, Joyce is seeking to describe. . . . It must always be remembered that his locale was Celtic and his season Spring."[37] From the perspective of the internal world of the novel, these dirty words are, so to speak, *natural dirt,* compost from which flowers might spring. We are not surprised when Woolsey suggests that Joyce is truly inventive, in that he opens up the unconscious of his characters by way of this dirt. Any other terms would have been euphemisms, the censored language of conscious thought, and would have kept locked the door to the world within the world of the novel which is that of the unconscious. As words from its unknown language, they point beyond the visible world of literal language and the spiritual world revealed by metaphor to a third world, ordinarily repressed, that obeys the logic of a logorrheic stream-of-consciousness. But that means that they are not really spoken by the characters. The latter are ventriloquized by them. These words that erupt from the mouths of the characters are the terms of an unfamiliar language; they are pronounced by the characters, as one would pronounce the words of a text written in a language one does not know. The obscene terms are the written language of the unconscious.

Placing the disruptive utterances in quotation marks, implied or literal, helps contain the violence. A mouth of a single character or class of characters opens at a single moment to express the unconscious. Woolsey is very clear that this kind of talk is that of "persons of the lower middle class living in Dublin in 1904."[38] Joyce's framing techniques isolate, as in a sick ward, those utterances that are not spoken by conscious subjects from the normal utterances of that character the rest of the time, as well as from those uttered in the world outside the fiction. The marks are internal dikes in the elongated sentence that is the novel; they let us differentiate, say, between Molly Bloom's soliloquy and Judge Woolsey's prefacing opinion. Mentioning dirty words launders them doubly: first, by preserving them as ruined terms recalling the originary state of the language in its integrity and propriety; second, by a partial censorship, a separating of the disruptive talk from ordinary utterances.

Joyce's partial censoring provides a clue to a third kind of dirt, a dirt neither honest nor natural, potentially afflicting the whole of the language. Had Woolsey found it in *Ulysses,* he *would* have termed it obscene. He says of *Ulysses,* "although it contains ... many words usually considered dirty, I have not found anything that I consider to be *dirt for dirt's sake.*"[39] This third kind of dirt is rejected as unreclaimable excess. The phrase Woolsey uses—"dirt for dirt's sake"—tells us what is unreclaimable: it is dirt unendowed with a purpose; it is dirt as an index, just more of the dirt that it stands for. Dirty dirt puts the tautological and repetitive in the place of the teleological at the outset; it threatens Woolsey's myth of language at its origin as an intact whole. Woolsey says that *Ulysses* expels such dirt. He knows that by the purging effect the work has on the reader: "My considered opinion, after long reflection, is that whilst in many places the effect of 'Ulysses' on the reader undoubtedly is somewhat emetic, nowhere does it tend to be an aphrodisiac."[40] The dreck the work of art cannot purify it must cause to be expelled. *Ulysses* induces vomiting rather than pleasure; it makes its readers sick of sex.[41]

The case of *Ulysses* supports the contention that the censoring of obscenity operates according to a different logic than that of the censorship of philosophical texts. In the literary text, where knowledge of language use is the stake, the representation of obscenity can be seen as necessary. The judge, representative censor, lifts the quarantine on *Ulysses* because he finds it to be good for linguistic hygiene: it purifies and reclaims the language for use where it can by quoting, and purges dirt where it cannot.

Note the juridico-political situation of the literary text vis-à-vis the censor. Where message-oriented texts are concerned, the arena for legal censorship can be greatly restricted. Strauss's censor is bound by the law, which demands proof of an author's intent and of his vigilance over all his expressions. Structurally speaking, the author is less intelligent than a writer even of average intelligence.[42] Where it is a matter of fictional texts whose aim is to represent the language, however, the protection of the law does not seem to apply. Implicit in Woolsey's argument is the view that artists have a duty to draw the line anew between those words and images that can be reassigned meaning and those that are unreclaimable. Theirs is the Herculean task of mucking out the Augean stable of language made dirty by overuse and excessive euphemism. Artists thus stand open to the accusation of obscenity precisely insofar as they try to keep their promise as artists.

As for the censor's limits, it seems that the judgment of obscenity ought to stand on the success or failure of the work to reclaim the language as a whole. But since no one is or could be in a position to judge on such a matter, it relies instead on the intelligence and courage of the censoring judge. Judges are required to be informed about things that, for structural reasons, they cannot know. For instance, they have to know when an author is exemplifying language, by placing a term in quotation marks, and when she is using it, by speaking in her "own" voice.[43] Judges have to know when obscene talk is quoted to clean up and contain the dirt and when such quoting is just a pleasurable, and guilty, manipulation of sensuous language—repetition without transformation.

As for the definition of obscenity, it is entirely problematic.[44] More than one author complains of the lack of any objective criteria to follow.[45] If the work is indeed engaged in the redefining of obscenity, first by reclaiming "foul" language for meaning, and second in causing to be regurgitated as excess what it cannot so reclaim, then it follows that the judge never could approach a new work armed with a prior definition but would always have to rely on the work to provide a dividing line. To the extent that the work manages to assimilate "dirt," it defines it in terms of a purpose. To the extent that it cannot assimilate it to that purpose, to the extent that it expels it, it is mere tautology. By definition, *as* tautology, the obscene falls outside definition. Indeed, Woolsey's own attempt at defining obscenity, which is one that enjoyed a certain currency in the writings of the mid–twentieth century on obscenity laws—"dirt for dirt's sake"—is really less a successful definition than a phrase coined to renounce definition. It gives up on determining a concept of dirt and gives in by just reiterating the term.[46] It indicates a symptomatic moment of breakdown, of unreclaimable excess in Woolsey's writing. Because it fills in for a missing definition with a word that adds nothing, we can call it an expletive, a swear word in its own right: for dirt's sake, dirt![47]

These problems—the special risk and license of the artist, the special requirements of the censor, the necessary time lag in the law that makes it so no author could know when she was breaking the law before having been called to account for it, the impossibility of defining obscenity—make the problem of censorship much murkier in the case of obscenity and the work of art than in the rather optimistic case that Strauss presents for the philosophical text.[48]

Nonetheless, despite their differences, Strauss and Woolsey do agree on the teleological nature of the understanding as mirrored in texts, with censorship legitimated as the act of reason overseeing transgressions against its rule. Woolsey's account can be said to complete Strauss's account, since it awards the work of art the function of reclaiming language to make it susceptible of bearing meaning. A question arises. Is this official view of the work of art as upholding the border between telos and tautos actually consonant with the nature of literary language?

Art for Art's Sake

To address this question, we require an example. What better place to look than in the texts of Baudelaire, the self-proclaimed theorist of "Art for Art's sake"? We may as well start with the slogan *"l'art pour l'art,"* coined by Victor Cousin, imitated by Woolsey, and picked up by Baudelaire in defiance of Hugo's *"l'art pour le progrès."* Does Baudelaire mean by his slogan the opposite of what Hugo says—namely, that art does not serve an ideology outside itself but is responsible to its own truth, to no idea but that of autotelic beauty and formal perfection? Certainly, the preposition *pour* (for) can express purposiveness and suggest a religion of art and a celebration of symbolic language. But a coined phrase comes with two sides. *Pour* can also state an equivalence between two different interchangeable things, as in *"j'ai eu un pain pour cinq francs"* (I got a loaf of bread for five francs), or even among similar exchangeable things, *"œil pour œil, dent pour dent"* (an eye for an eye, a tooth for a tooth). The problem expressed by *l'art pour l'art* in such a reading would be to find two arts that are interchangeable: one art for another art, say *poetry* for *painting.* Baudelaire often does call attention to this underside of the poetic economy, where the poet is engaged in sniffing out terms that are equivalent as terms—rhyme words, words of equal syllables, words with alliterative possibilities, or the like. With *l'art pour l'art,* Baudelaire may be pointing away from the teleological toward the tedious labor of the artisan with his material.

With this duality to the work in mind, let us look at one of the poems condemned by the 1857 court, "Les bijoux" (reproduced at the end of the essay). The poem was polemically rebaptized by the prosecutor with a descriptive title, "Naked woman, trying on poses before her fascinated lover,"[49] and its opening lines, as translated by J. McGowan, seem to support the point: "Knowing my heart, my dearest one was nude, / Her resonating jewellry all she wore, / Which rich array gave her the attitude / Of darling in the harem of a Moor."[50] The artifices by which the woman attracts the lover and the epithet *"la très chère,"* which ironically suggests that the dearest one is very dear indeed, in that the jewels she displays may have been purchased by some rich lover, contribute details that might have served the prosecutor's contention that Baudelaire attempts to "give senses back to those who no longer can feel."[51] McGowan has pushed the poem in this direction by translating the impersonal *"la très chère"* (literally, the very dear one) as the more intimate "*my* dearest one," and the rather sinister *"les esclaves des mores"* (literally, the slaves of Moors), to whom she is likened, as the more innocuous "*darling* in the harem of a Moor." The poem is turned into a representation of an intimate moment between lover and expert courtesan, a moment that the poet—something of an exhibitionist as well as a voyeur—is letting us share. In this reading, the poem blatantly contradicts some of Baudelaire's strong statements of preference for draped women over the nude. In *Le peintre de la vie moderne,* for instance, he writes that woman is a general harmony, not only in her bearing and the movement of her limbs, but also in the muslins, the gauzes, the vast and shimmering clouds of material with which she envelops herself, and which are, as it were, the attributes and pedestal of her divinity; in the metal and the mineral that snake about her arms and neck, that add their sparkle to the fire of her eyes, or that chatter softly at her ear. What poet would dare, in the depiction of the pleasure caused by the appearance of a beauty, to separate a woman from her costume?... [The disinterested enjoyer of beauty makes of] the two, the woman and the dress an indivisible totality.[52]

The stark nudity of the woman in most readings of "The Jewels" contrasts with this refusal to separate woman from her dress.[53]

With this in mind, another reading of the first lines emerges, one that would be more in keeping with an accent on the enveloping garb: "The very dear one was... a cloud, and knowing my heart, she had reserved only her sonorous jewels." *La nue,* from *nubes,* is a term for "cloud" that a working poet, one concerned with the formal requirements of the alexandrine or of a rhyme scheme, would do well to have in mind.[54] The poem, in this translation, would contain a daring metonymy representing the dearest one by her dress. It would be playing on something of a commonplace of mid-century Parnassian poetry, the topos of the cloud-wrapped goddess descending from her mountain retreat, eagerly awaited by her priest-celebrant.[55]

We can thus give two readings to the female figure: the first, the crude and fleshy nude, *"la très chair"* (flesh), that links the poem to those addressed to the courtesan Jeanne Duval; the second, a veiled and enthroned idol, *"la très chaire"* (throne or chair), a figure close to that glimpsed in "La beauté," who "reign(s) in the azure" *("trône dans l'azur").*[56] Whichever reading one starts from, it is shadowed by the other.

The problem is not which reading is the right one, since the poem can and does make sense of both. The problem is rather how the poet presents the relationship of meanings in the singular gift that is the poem. That relationship is puzzling. The poet quite deliberately does not provide an obvious itinerary, say by exploiting the protean shape of the cloud as a metaphor for desire and then stripping away the cloud cover to reveal the nude.[57] In "Les bijoux" such an avenue is not available: no natural landscape is provided. We are in a room illuminated by an uncertain fire, with occasional light refracting from the "clairvoyant" eyes, polished limbs, and sonorous jewels. It takes an act of the mind, an observation finer than that of the eye, to find in the fleshy nude a relation to a cloud-enveloped deity. The poet has to bypass visible nature and its analogies; he has to find an allegory.[58] If "Les bijoux" is an allegory, what does it allegorize?

One allegory is that of the poem itself, as engendered from the homonym. Take the seemingly insignificant detail of the sonorous jewels on which the poet fastens for the length of two stanzas. Whether we consider the poem as inspired by goddess or courtesan, "sonorous jewels" points away from resemblances based on what we can see (and thus to the signified) to analogies prized for their sound alone. The jewels have the audibility of signifiers, and in celebrating them the poet celebrates analogies based on sound. A nude courtesan can substitute for a cloud-wrapped goddess if one must rely only on one's ears.

This is remarkable and, in a way, scandalous. Here is a poem that takes the representation of a gentleman eyeing a nude courtesan, an image on a dirty postcard, and the representation of priest awaiting a goddess and treats them as indistinguishable. Not only that, but the poet, who is writing a poem for poets, is only interested in the double image as one possibly owed to a homophony. Allegory (which gets its "didactic effectiveness," according to Paul de Man, by making "one forget the vices it sets out to represent") is the right term to use for a poem that sets aside so quickly the pleasures of sex and religion in favor of a discussion of poetic form.[59] This is the sort of quotation of an obscene image that Woolsey might approve, since it lets us know that it is *language's* sensuous existence that is being depicted, not "dirt for dirt's sake." Read as an allegory, the central conflict of the first two stanzas concerns whether the poet's attention to the sensuous signifier is degrading or elevating. On the outcome of this conflict rides a second question: whether the homonym is ultimately to be understood in terms of the sounded signifier.

On the one side in the conflict, we have the reading of *nue* as a nude courtesan who has (kept on) "*gardé*" only her sonorous jewels. The attention of the poet-as-John is distracted from the nude to the jewels; the poet's concupiscent eye intent on seizing its pleasure gives way to the ear. The ear, always open to the word of the other, is here the organ of conscience that starts to turn the voyeur poet away from pleasure, to contemplate such questions as the evanescence of things (stanza five), the state of his soul (stanza six), a new form of art (stanza seven), and even his own death (stanza eight). The ear can overhear words differently, as saying something other than what the speaker means by them. These chance words are not just places where cultural differences are revealed, where one group of speakers of a language systematically misunderstands another group apparently speaking the same language—as when a visitor from England overhears an American parent bewailing the "potty talk" on a school playground and comes away with the impression that madness is rampant among the American elementary school set.

Chance words can also awaken us to consider the disorienting possibility that language speaks about itself through us, in the very utterances that we think reveal us as subjects. At the beginning of the second stanza, the poem provides an instance of a word received as if from on high, where "*son bruit vif et moqueur*" stands out as significant. In context, in terms of the figure visualized, the phrase is easily translated as a description of an attribute of the courtesan's jewelry, "its lively and mocking noise." Given the invitation to listen to sound, however, and given the proximity of the term for noise, "*bruit,*" we could easily read "*son*" not as the possessive adjective, "its," but as the homonym, the noun "sound." The rest of the line becomes an apposition, offering a sort of definition: "sound, lively and mocking noise." The sound of the words of the statement interferes with the statement that is made about the value of sound to the poet. The interruption reveals a meaning that is more "elevated," poetically speaking, than is the mere pleasure taken in the sensuous signifier, since here the signifier can plausibly be said to have *produced* meaning by spinning off a theoretically sound definition of what sound is. It does not emerge from the poet, who receives it rather as a listener, but seems to come from the poem itself, as if it were "divinely inspired." The poet-as-John is shown distracted away from the sensuous pleasures associated first with the eye and then with the ear, toward an increasingly elevated mood of introspection. The possibility is that the play of the signifier—language in its independent action—recovers an earlier state of language when words shed light by their sound.

Conversely, the *nue* can be read as the cloud-veiled goddess anticipated by her priest-celebrant. Here things take place very differently. Awaiting her imminent manifestation, the priest gets so impatient as to start hearing sounds of her approach before they occur. In keeping with her muted advance, she has *"gardé"* (kept back, in reserve) her sonorous jewels, and yet the poet starts to celebrate his furious love for sound. This is a rapid degradation: eagerly anticipating the arrival of the goddess, the poet is distracted and thinks only of his own senses. A movement of falling can be traced throughout the poem, down through the final stanzas where the priest, as a connoisseur in deities, compares his idol to other goddesses (stanza seven), until finally, letting the sanctuary light go out, the poem closes with a euphemistic veil partly drawn over the final sex act.[60]

Instances of sound play in the first stanza support this movement of degradation. The line describing the effect of the sonorous jewels, *"Dont le riche attirail lui donnait l'air vainqueur,"* means "whose rich array gave her the conquering air." It also adds, distractingly, a homophone, a word that sounds the same as *dont* (whose): *don* (gift). It suggests that the priest, talking about the air the jewels give her, is giving her another gift: *don(t) . . . don(nait)*. The gift is not as innocuous as it looks, or the priest is drunker than he first appears, for he says *"don . . . don."* A *dondon* is an onomatopoeic term of some vulgarity meaning "fat lady," and it would be a wounding insult from a priest officially charged with celebrating the cult of "the dear one." The excess carried by the chance words of the sounded signifiers gets in the way, threatening the overall meaning of celebration. The poem thus diverts our attention from its meaning, which in this reading states that it is the play of the signifier that threatens meaning and leads to mental distraction *("fureur")*.[61] Here the play of language does not tend toward an ideal reconciliation of sound and meaning, of force and signification, but is instead disruptive. It leads toward the ventriloquizing of the very words in which the priest tries to celebrate his deity.

What then is the outcome of the conflict between the two readings? Does Baudelaire evaluate this play with the signifier as a divinely inspired means for producing meaning, or as a dangerous, degrading fall away from Art into sensualism? This question requires that we consider what the *poem* means about poetic language independent of the poet's wishes or thoughts on the subject. Whatever the reason for this distraction—excess of pleasure, madness, or divine inspiration—it is a key that his statements are those of a literally absent-minded poet. Something else (which we are calling the poem) seems to speak momentarily through him.

In one of its more remarkable moves, the poem discards the question as a false question derived from the mistaken idea that poetic language is voiced, phenomenalized language or, as popular wisdom has it, that poems are "meant to be read aloud."[62] There are several places where it is evident that the poem labors against the poet to reject sound patterns as a source of meaning or pleasure. Consequently we may conclude that the homophony is a diversion from the *written* homonym as a figure for the poem. In the first line of the second stanza, the poet explains that he loves "this radiating world of metal and stones . . . [w]hen it throws off in dancing its lively and mocking sound." The line summarizes the problem succinctly by way of the ambiguous term "*jette,*" which can mean "emit" or "throw out," with the sensuous poet celebrating the jewels as emitting sound, and also "throw off" or "discard," with the meditative poet celebrating the jewels as producing meaning in the shedding of sound. But the dilemma is dispensed with quickly once we understand that dancing is not the actual situation of the poem. The poet loves this world "[w]hen . . . dancing," but the poem knows that "when" is hypothetical. It is not now. The *mundus mulieribus* does not now emit or discard any noise at all. The hypothesis, with all the razzle-dazzle of the signifier producing meaning, is a fiction indicating the actual situation of the poem, which is one of stillness and deprivation—of voice, sensation, presence, sentiment, mobility, and so on.[63]

The poem is, after all, a poem of mourning. It commemorates the stilling of the spoken language and lays to rest any interpretation that seeks to exploit the sounded signifier. The poem's jewels mock sound to obtrude their actual silence on our notice. For what reason should the poem insist on reminding us of its existence as a written artifact? The simplest reason is that it cannot help but do so. However powerfully it charms us into believing that some subject, or language itself is murmuring lessons in our ear, it can only exert its charm because it is written down. The meaning of the homophone is only available because the phoneme (*ny*) is written down in a memorandum as *nue,* not said and heard but quoted and read, reiterated and reiterable as it appears. Of course, the poem makes a virtue of necessity by forcing a comparison between the poem desired (as a spoken, intelligible communication between subjects) and the poem received (as a written, legible legacy from the past). That comparison requires us to consider the relationship of the language's intelligibility to its legibility.

A surprise likeness shows up between the spoken word and the written word: both are historical products. Instead of asking what Baudelaire means, we are obliged to ask what historical accidents have happened to make *nue* indistinguishable from *nue*. The answer—that the difference between the *b* of *nubes* and the *d* of *nudus* has been eroded and forgotten by usage[64]—is less important than the fact that writing is necessary both to pose the question and to answer it. Homonyms appear as dead spots where the historical character of the so-called living language is in evidence. Differences also surface—for instance, between the rates and sorts of transformations to which spoken and written language systems are subject. The living language appears as smoothly continuous with the past, as having evolved slowly. But the writing system, which preserves that language, is an addition subject to other kinds of losses and rates of loss: to surprise gains and irrecuperable collapses, to its own calculations and regulations. Worms eat books; censors delete passages from them, laws regulate and sometimes prohibit their publication, libraries get set up to preserve them, and sometimes—fortunes of war, acts of God, deliberate repressions—libraries get burnt. Writing systems can lose their legibility, in parts or wholly. Or, someone can force a comparison between meaningful and legible language and recover a huge terrain. In short, the poem quotes or mimes a speaking, and in doing so, it makes us ask what is added and what is lost by its quoting.

The collapse and withdrawal of the homonym, foreseen by the poem, is then significant. "I follow in vain the withdrawing God," Baudelaire says in "Le coucher du soleil romantique," and that movement is quite literally what he has seized here.[65] In 1877, the *Littre* still sees *nue* as a cloud, a synonym for *nuage* and *nuée*.[66] By the end of the century, when Mallarmé writes "She, dead *nue,* in the mirror," he is already taking into account the fact that *nue* is dead as a common term for cloud.[67] A new *âge* has dawned; *nuage,* already the usual term for Baudelaire, has entirely taken over in ordinary speech about the cloudscape. The *Trésor de la langue française* consecrates this change, saying the term *nue* is "archaic, poetic and literary" and subsists in only a few clichés in common parlance.[68]

Clearly, from the perspective of the referent, it does not matter whether one calls a cloud a *nue* or a *nuage*. What does matter is that in this poem access to the allegory is only available if the figure remains legible as a metonym for the goddess figure. The homonym is the key to the riddle of writing that reduplicates (for preserving remembrance) and deprives (as disintegrating memory) the speech act of its originary force; its loss spells the possible end of the poem's legibility. The poem takes a snapshot of a little fissure in the archive, a fracture that by our period has so widened that the chief problem of the poem is nearly inaccessible. It tries to capture in its snapshot the moment of collapse, when the very memory of the departing *nue* is getting lost and, with it, the memory of writing as redoubling the spoken language as it originates. Far from providing a reader's pact against which to measure the value of each of its enunciations, the poem is concerned with its inability to transmit meaning without depriving itself of legibility. However we interpret *"nue,"* we are forgetting that the poem, as given in the speech act, is preserved in a writing whose legibility is already in doubt.

This little fragment provides evidence that the act of reconfiguring the language as a whole, healthy body entails a partial loss of its legibility. That it is a small piece is not comforting, since with it goes not only the poem's discussion of the idol of the time and the lesson on the play of the signifier as leading to madness but also what the text has to say about a creeping sclerosis affecting the living language. In poems it is possible to ask where the language is in its process of becoming, as André Chénier says, "an antique writing and no longer a language."[69] In determining language as meaning, in terms of consciousness, we become estranged from our archive.

The poem is indeed concerned with the issue of history at work in the language, just as Woolsey's *Ulysses* is, but to very different effect. In Woolsey's view, Joyce quotes obscenity to give us back the language in its pristine state. In Baudelaire's poem, a fissure shows language ruined at the outset. Obscene language reveals the truth that language never was a virgin, and by it we learn that language is always already affected by deprivation. It is not a whole body but a catalog of parts.[70]

The poem knows that this history is working to render illegible its bicephalous figure. In an ensuing crucial section of the poem (stanzas five and six, the stanzas that came under direct fire in the 1857 trial), the verbs *"Passaient"* and *"S'avançaient"* establish the meditation as concerned with the past and future of the language.[71] In this section, the examination of the double-sided figure and the development of the allegory proceeds in the relative calm provided by the knowledge that the poetic figure is stilled. She lies mute on her couch, and the term *"couchée,"* which means "prone," "abed," but which also can mean "consigned" or "inscribed in a text," again points to the textual allegory. Something disturbs the quiet, however, and we are given a second glimpse of the poet, no longer distracted and awakened by the poem to an awareness of the historical character of the language as represented by the movements of the central figure. The poet's love has turned contemplative. With the idea of an eventual intervention, he contemplates the movements of the allegorical figure. The movements, the movements of history, are doubly evaluated: a potential for evolution, for continuing metamorphosis and renewal is seen, but a rather threatening fracturing is also evident, as certain body parts recede or are thrust forward.

In the fifth and sixth stanzas, the poet differentiates between those parts of the figure that pass away before his serene surveying glance and those that advance — belly and breasts — to trouble his repose. In terms of the poetic allegory, these body parts are details that draw our attention to the structural parts of the poem: the organization of its stanzas and its syntax. The poem provides a striking instance of such structuring parts in the coordinating conjunction *et*, made visible by dint of its being repeated no fewer than nine times in eight lines, three times in positions of stress.

And has two distinct grammatical functions in the fifth stanza. It adds together like things: body parts — "arms and . . . leg, and . . . thigh and . . . loins," and "belly and . . . breasts." It also adds together things considered in their difference. It adds the two verbs—"And ... Passed ... and ... Advanced"—so as to present the widely different effects of the parts on the poet. He is "serene" in his mastery over the parade of some passing parts, yet "troubled" by the advancing belly and breasts. We have to be able to tell the difference between *et* as enumerating like things and *et* as enumerating different things to understand the dramatic shift in the stance of the poet.

The poet is considering the corrosive work of usage on the parts of the language. He furthers the erosion of certain articulations by repeating and polishing them to the point of near liquefaction—they are "polished as with oil." This stream of conventional, polished parts is passing away, and the poet views it with serenity, for he sees that other articulations still have meaning. The use of *et* is exemplary. It makes no difference to interpretation and could almost be replaced by commas in the list of body parts. In the list of verbs, however, it makes a very big difference by making available *as different* the serene and the troubled poet. The poet knows himself to be engaged in a double process. He speeds up the polishing of *and* by repeating it, and he slows down that work by reactivating the differentiating function of the conjunction.

Things change in the sixth stanza. Here *and* plays, in addition to its grammatical role, a properly poetical role in the formal organization of the stanzas. It links the sixth stanza to the fifth, finishing out a pattern set in the fifth stanza by the opening words of the lines: *"Et ... Polis ... Passaient ... Et ... S'avançaient ... Pour ... Et."*[72] Formal questions are not accidental in the sixth stanza, which is thematically concerned with the dominance of Poetry over the poet, with Poetry's ability to shake the poet's tranquil assumption of mastery and, thus, with his subservience to her in certain matters like those of stanza organization. If we ask what function this *and* serves in terms of meaning, moreover, we would have to say it is a negative or subtracting function. The poet indulges in what can only be called a pleonasm, a needless repetition, when he says that breast and belly advanced to trouble his soul's repose and to disturb it off its crystal rock *("pour troubler le repos où mon âme était mise / Et pour la déranger du rocher de cristal")*. This *and* does not add like or different things—it adds the same thing, said again in different words. Half of the stanza is an exercise in redundancy, with the poet forced, as it were, by the demands of formal unity to finish out the stanza despite his failing inspiration.

My point is not that Baudelaire is a bad poet who ekes out his stanza by repeating in other words thoughts he has articulated before. Clearly, the stanza is concerned with this issue, and Baudelaire is so good a poet because, knowing that it is a possibility plaguing any poet, he acts out a loss of poetic inspiration before the poem is finished, to ask after its effect on poet and poem. The effect is dramatically negative with respect to the interpretation that makes the poet a contemplative surveyor of the scene of language, picking parts to polish off and parts with a differential value worth reactivating. This master is knocked off his perch by the poetic demand for formal order *regardless* of meaning. The term *and* enacts the fall. It is an *and* deprived of its additive function altogether, having the value of a minus sign. Nothing is added by this pleonastic *and* except formal symmetry, unless one considers a verbal gesture dramatizing in advance the poet's fall into poetic senility a fresh addition.

It could be objected that *and* can sometimes be used emphatically, at the beginning of a sentence, to introduce something startlingly original.[73] Baudelaire's poem has an example of such an *and* in the last stanza, where he introduces a view of the room that appears unconnected to the earlier stanzas, which concentrate on the female figure. It is not farfetched to interpret stanza six in the same way. Throughout the poem, whenever the poet is talking about his own passion, his speech inevitably is about "the very dear one," and he could again be speaking of her, instead of the more immediate referent *"mon âme,"* when he states that her breasts and belly advance *"pour la déranger"* (to disturb *her*).[74] In that case, what the poem says is something quite different: not that the poetic form overturns the poet by forcing him to repeat his utterances; rather, that the poem advances against itself, pushing Poetry off her pedestal. The stilled figure gets mobility. Poetry thrusts herself forward against the poet's tranquil ideal of "Art for art's sake," to posit the value of the work as that of "Art against art," as *anti-work*. The androgynous figure emerging in the seventh stanza represents the poem as self-divided in exactly this way.

Reading the stanza as disruptively self-toppling makes sense in the light of earlier patterns. Everything has had to be read twice: the naked figure / the veiled goddess; its lively and mocking noise / sound, lively and mocking noise, and so on. It is not surprising that the poem should repeat the pattern of doubling at the level of these lines. What is disruptive is that the poem does what it says in a new way, inventively: it states, "And to disturb *her* off her rock," but it can do so only if the overriding pattern of doubling is advanced to cover the utterance. This is an unconventional performative. It is blind in that it neither confirms nor denies a truth presumed to be prior to it: the blind performative posits a truth that only becomes a truth as a result of its act of positing. The poem only ceases to have the immobility of an idol when it and if it thrusts forward the disruptive reading. It is impossible to determine the legitimacy of this reading, which is at once inevitable, because it is in keeping with earlier formal patterns and is radically unauthorized because it has emerged without the poet's say-so, in the very enunciation where his claim is that of a technician making concessions to sheer form. The poem makes use of the poet's attempt to resolve a purely formal problem as the occasion to impose its law. Like a Straussian interpreter, the poet is alerted to the fact that structure can produce meaning. But whereas Strauss's puppy cut his teeth on a work received from a thoughtful author whose structures are calculated to teach, the putative author stumbles in his text over a lesson still to be read about the nonconvergence of meaning and structure.

However we look at it, "Les bijoux" outrages the axiom that makes virtue converge with knowledge. It does so by bringing to the fore problems of reading and writing centered on the memory trace. On the one side, it commemorates the supplanting of a spoken language by silent writing and transmits a lesson about the differing modes of memory and forgetfulness attached to each. It situates itself at the fracture line that disconnects the text's capacity to transmit knowledge from its capacity to be read, bearing the gloomy awareness that determining language for interpretation is forgetting "the writing on the wall"—that is, the writing system and the accidents that affect the legibility of the archive. By censoring the poem in 1857, the court agreed with the prosecutor that the court's job was to keep from view what the poem had to say about disintegrative memory and a destabilizing fault line in the archive. In this light, the action of the court in 1949 consisted less of a liberal, uncensoring move than of a confirmation that, with the loss of the homonym from the lexicon, the poem's shocking secret—the redoubling at the source of the poem—had become a secret.

The advance of the poem against its own ideal of formal unity discloses another side to the predicament. By reproducing its pattern, the poem produced something new. It produced a certain reading, a certain future for itself as anti-poem or self-toppling symbol. Here the poem is still lively. If we need any proof of that, the court's deciding opinion in 1949 that Baudelaire's poems are to be interpreted symbolically can provide it. The attempt to regulate the means of expression by imposing a reading pact on the poem and the attempt to relegate the realistic interpretation of the poem to the dustbin of history as erroneous are both attempts to recover the poem for "responsible memory" by a partial veiling of the destabilizing, wild performative that advances the poem against itself, and that certainly has more than one realistic referent in modern life.

The free agency of human subjects with respect to linguistic structures, their ability to determine whether those structures are referential or symbolic, is in doubt in this poem. The rationale for the state's attempt to limit access to such a possibility is obvious enough: where freedom of expression is a fundamental right, there is need for a convention assigning to an individual like Baudelaire the authorship of his speech acts, and not, as in this case, assigning to the poem the authorship of its reader, Baudelaire.[75] At the same time, there is need to incorporate alternatives like the one glimpsed here, where the individual's freedom of expression turns out to be limited by a nonexpressive side to language. Otherwise, the rather threatening future given by this poem written in the age of revolution—the future of a repetitive toppling of old ideologies by new acts of blind positing—might well be ours. Our modern states, after all, have come into existence on the basis of blind performatives positing interpretations that were not true before their positing.[76] It is reasonable to suppose that their survival depends in part on their ability to mask or limit partially the public visibility of violent acts like the one by which they came into existence. Following the evidence of the poem, which showed the unconventional performative emerging in the midst of the poet's attempt to confine the independent force of language to a matter of form, the attempt to limit access too much could well provide the occasion for the realization of the threat. The move the poem makes that orients it toward the future, that makes it inventive and liberating with respect to the old ideology, is the one that questions the poet's agency. It asks for greater publicity for the dilemma in which "freedom of expression" becomes a statement that describes a text's independence from its author, even more surely than it refers to a right guaranteed an individual.

The analysis of the poem from *Les fleurs du mal* reveals a challenge to laws against obscene writing. Its censoring deprived us of a poem that provided negative knowledge of a disintegrating memory at work in the archive without restraining the process of ruin. As for the obtrusive blind performative—an open secret in this text—to restrict access to it is to seek to foreclose on a source of invention as well as a source of threat. The challenge is to find ways to legislate that take into account those areas of speech where the axiom that virtue is knowledge does not pertain, where freedom of an individual's expression is limited and extended by writing, and where the agency and autonomy of the reasonable, conscious subject are in question. The state has a vested interest in the pasts and futures given by the blind performative; it has need to extend more protection to those having developed "an immoderate taste for truth," and to obscene writing as one place where those pasts and futures obtrude.

Les bijoux

La très-chère était nue, et, connaissant mon cœur,
Elle n'avait gardé que ses bijoux sonores,
Dont le riche attirail lui donnait l'air vainqueur
Qu'ont dans leurs jours heureux les esclaves des Mores.

Quand il jette en dansant son bruit vif et moqueur,
Ce monde rayonnant de métal et de pierre
Me ravit en extase, et j'aime à la fureur
Les choses où le son se mêle à la lumière.

Elle était donc couchée et se laissait aimer,
Et du haut du divan elle souriait d'aise
A mon amour profond et doux comme la mer,
Qui vers elle montait comme vers sa falaise.

Les yeux fixés sur moi, comme un tigre dompté,
D'un air vague et rêveur elle essayait des poses,
Et la candeur unie à la lubricité
Donnait un charme neuf à ses métamorphoses;

Et son bras et sa jambe, et sa cuisse et ses reins,
Polis comme de l'huile, onduleux comme un cygne,
Passaient devant mes yeux clairvoyants et sereins;
Et son ventre et ses seins, ces grappes de ma vigne,

S'avançaient, plus câlins que les Anges du mal,
Pour troubler le repos où mon âme était mise,
Et pour la déranger du rocher de cristal
Où, calme et solitaire, elle s'était assise.

Je croyais voir unis par un nouveau dessin
Les hanches de l'Antiope au buste d'un imberbe,
Tant sa taille faisait ressortir son bassin.
Sur ce teint fauve et brun le fard était superbe!

—Et la lampe s'étant résignée à mourir,
Comme le foyer seul illuminait la chambre,
Chaque fois qu'il poussait un flamboyant soupir,
Il inondait de sang cette peau couleur d'ambre!

The Jewels

Knowing my heart, my dearest one was nude,
Her resonating jewellery all she wore,
Which rich array gave her the attitude
Of darling in the harem of a Moor.

When dancing, ringing out its mockeries,
This radiating world of gold and stones
Ravishes me to lovers' ecstasies
Over the interplay of lights and tones.

Allowing love, she lay seductively
And from the high divan smiled in her ease
At my love—ocean's deep felicity
Mounting to her as tides draw in the seas.

A tiger tamed, her eyes were fixed on mine,
With absent air she posed in novel ways,
Whose candour and lubricity combined
Made charming all her metamorphoses;

Her shoulders and her arms, her legs, her thighs,
Polished with oil, undulent like a swan,
Passed by my tranquil and clairvoyant eyes;
Then belly, breasts, those clusters on my vine,

Came on, tempting me more than devils could
To break the peace my soul claimed as its own,
And to disturb the crystal rock abode
Where distant, calm, it had assumed its throne.

Her waist contrasted with her haunches so
It seemed to me I saw, in new design,
A boy above, Antiope below.
The painting on her brown skin was sublime!

—And since the lamp resigned itself to die,
The hearth alone lit up the room within;
Each time it uttered forth a blazing sigh
Flushed with tones of blood her amber skin.

Notes

1. The decision was made possible by a law passed in 1946 allowing a judgment on a book to be appealed after twenty years had passed.

2. Letter to Charles Baudelaire, 15 August 1857, in *Correspondance de Gustave Flaubert,* 4th ser. (1854–1861), (Paris: Louis Conard, 1927), 214.

3. The popular rhymster Pierre Jean de Béranger was successfully prosecuted in 1821, for instance. According to Jean Pommier, although Béranger was pursued for *"outrage à la morale publique et religieuse,"* his aim was "political provocation." The first attacks in the press came from the Ultras, who noted the greater freedom of expression enjoyed by verse:

> Here we must admire the marvellous privilege of rhyme: it is doubtless as powerful as the letters of inviolacy enjoyed by our Deputies, for an unprotected citizen who had said *in prose* what M. Béranger has said in verse would certainly have had a bone to pick with the King's Prosecutor.

Cited in Jean Pommier, *Autour de l'édition originale des "Fleurs du mal"* (Geneva: Slatkine Reprints, 1968), 7, 9.

In his work *Obscenity and the Law* (London: Secker and Warburg, 1956), which draws heavily on English cases, Norman St. John-Stevas remarks on violent attacks in the press against Keats, Byron, Shelley, Tennyson, and Swinburne. As a rule, these attacks did not lead to legal problems. St. John-Stevas cites only a pirated edition of *Queen Mab* as prosecuted for blasphemy. Indeed, while deploring the attacks, St. John-Stevas nonetheless finds reason to take heart in the fact that to attack poetry is to acknowledge it as an important social force. "Critical excesses are indefensible," he writes, "but the assumption of the value and relevance of poetry to the life of the community which determined their approach was sound" (49).

4. Walter Benjamin, "On Some Motifs in Baudelaire," in idem, *Illuminations,* ed. Hannah Arendt, trans. Harry Zohn (New York: Schocken Books, 1969), 155.

5. Quoted in Charles Baudelaire, *Œuvres complètes,* 2 vols., ed. Claude Pichois (Paris: Gallimard, 1976), 1: 1208. I have drawn heavily on Pichois's account of the trial reproduced in the notes of this edition. Because the laws of the time forbade the reporting of trials, the statements of the prosecution and the defense were not published until 1885. Evidence suggests that they may well have been written near the later date. Pinard explains that the government does not lose its freedom to pursue a given work because it has not pursued others equally offensive. If the government is reserved in some cases, it is because it judges that the work will have "no chance of being read or understood" and that "to bring it to justice would be to indicate it to the public and perhaps assure to it the day's success it would not have had without that" (1: 1209).

6. Ibid., 1: 1208.

7. It is this paradoxical situation of poems whose style removes them from ordinary experience the better to make them represent modern experience that is the point of departure for Benjamin's analysis in "On Some Motifs in Baudelaire" (see note 4).

8. St. John-Stevas (see note 3), 249.

9. The two charges brought against the total of eleven poems were "offense to public morality" and "offense to religious morality." Only the first charge was upheld in the condemnation of six of these poems.

10. "The Aesthetic Dignity of 'Les Fleurs du Mal'" is the title of an essay by Erich Auerbach that is roughly contemporaneous with the 1949 decision. See Erich Auerbach, *Scenes from the Drama of European Literature* (Minneapolis: Univ. of Minnesota, 1984), 201–6.

11. There is a resemblance to be noted between the critic and Baudelaire's figure for the reader in "Au lecteur," the monstrous Ennui who dreams of dramatically violent deeds while yawning and smoking his dope; see Baudelaire (see note 5), 1: 5–6.

12. This is somewhat the scene as Pinard paints it. He is acutely aware that he is cast in the role of persecutor by the world of letters, and he boasts of his (anti-) heroism in laboring for the good of the public nonetheless.

13. In Baudelaire (see note 5), 1: 1208.

14. Benjamin (see note 4), 160. Benjamin distinguises *Gedächtnis* (remembrance) from *Erinnerung* (memory). I am following Harry Zohn's translation.

15. Ibid.

16. Lawrence Douglas, "Policing the Past: Holocaust Denial and the Law," page 68 of this volume.

17. A recent writer in *The New York Times,* writing of billboards plastered with sexually explicit imagery and of lone artists (Robert Mapplethorpe, Merry Alpern) targeted for censorship, supports my point that it is the medium and not that message that is the lightening rod here. Vicki Goldberg writes: "The sensationalistic images that flood the visual environment appear far more frequently and get immeasurably greater distribution in the popular culture than they ever do in art. Yet art bears the brunt of public attacks"; Vicki Goldberg, "Testing the Limits In a Culture of Excess," *The New York Times,* 29 October 1995, 40.

The recent show of Alpern's photos that is the occasion of the article bears the Baudelairian title, "Dirty Windows." Speculating from the title and the single photograph that is shown in the *Times,* we can ask whether Alpern is not breaking the rule that an artwork view things through colored windows (roseate or not), whereas in ordinary commerce we are to see things through clear windows, that is, transparent language. What Alpern does in giving us *dirtied* windows is to note the presence of "color" in the apparently transparent windows of real-life sexshop bathrooms. This is subversive and makes the show a worthy successor to Baudelaire's "Mauvais Vitrier."

18. Leo Strauss, "Persecution and the Art of Writing," in idem, *Persecution and the Art of Writing* (Glencoe, Ill.: Free Press, 1952), 24.

19. Ibid., 26–27.

20. This is the source of Gadamer's interest in Strauss. See Hans Georg Gadamer, *Truth and Method,* translation ed. Garrett Barden and John Cumming (New York: Crossroad Publishing, 1975), 482–91. See also Paul de Man, "Dialogue and Dialogism," in idem, *The Resistance to Theory* (Minneapolis: Univ. of Minnesota Press, 1986), 106–14, for a discussion of Strauss and Bakhtin.

21. I am extending Strauss's argument by suggesting its consequences for the liberal state.

22. Strauss (see note 18), 36.

23. Ibid., 32

24. Ibid., 25. All this is well known; discussion of silencing and hate speech—concentrated as it is on the discursive situation as on the exclusion of certain groups and speech acts from the scene of "friendly" dialogue—can only take place because it is acquired. If I rehearse it here, it is as the background necessary to raise two points. The first is that the Straussian liberal state gains an astonishing flexibility and durability as a result of its disregard of content. Once the state ceases to occupy itself with dictating what can be said, the positive content of its history, the details of a moral education, and so on, it can occupy itself instead with what Judith Butler calls the "formation" of its subjects in "Ruled Out: Vocabularies of the Censor" (see page 253 of this volume). It produces, for instance, normal citizens as those who state their opinions freely and explicitly, who say exactly what they mean (although what they mean is never more than mere opinion). As for those who make use of parody or irony to write between the lines, their heterodoxy may be suspect, but it is indulged on account of the inventive energy released in the unrepressing of the performative aspect. The liberal state goes out of the business of censoring messages; instead it feeds off the energy released by such unrepressions. The second point concerns the limits that Strauss effectively places on writing between the lines by determining it as educational. A writing that appears to state an opinion in order to criticize it is a writing whose use of parody, irony, strategy, and so on, has been limited to what can be recuperated as critique, according to a teleology in which the formation of subjects is the end. It can be asked, however, whether this limitation on the subversiveness of writing between the lines does not, as it were, leave out leaving out—censor its own censorship—and, in doing so, lose sight of aspects of writing that do not lead to education, construed positively.

25. Strauss (see note 18) mentions Homer, but it is only to quote the cliché "even Homer nods from time to time" (26). Milton is also mentioned, but in the *Areopagitica*. Literary works provide a stock of images to help out in Strauss's exposition, but do not figure as instances of texts persecuted.

26. Strauss (see note 18) is actively repressive of one aspect of language, figurative language. He remarks, for instance, that persecution teaches good writers to avoid flowery utterances when it is a matter of uttering the hidden doctrine ("he would silently drop all the *foolish excrescences* of the liberal creed," 25), and, on the contrary, to display a flowery style when it is a matter of uttering the orthodoxy being criticized ("The attack, the bulk of the work, would consist of *virulent expansions* of the most *virulent utterances*," 25).

27. Ibid., 36.

28. "La fanfarlo," in Baudelaire (see note 5), 1: 555.

29. In James Joyce, *Ulysses* (New York: Random House, 1961), ix. Since 1934 Woolsey's remarks have been published as part of the prefatory material in the Modern Library edition.

30. Morris L. Ernst and Alan U. Schwartz cite a case lost when the defense lawyer felt unable to "mention in court or print in his brief an Anglo-Saxon word used in the novel several times by one of the characters"; *Censorship: The Search for the Obscene*

(New York: Macmillan, 1964), 95. The lawyer's inability to mention the term showed the term to be censorable. At the other extreme, the defense attorney for Baudelaire spent most of his time reading long quotations from various literary sources, with the aim of defusing the effect of shock Pinard made by his abbreviated textual "clippings." The length or brevity of quotations is a recognized ploy of argument.

31. That is true of expletives, for instance, where the names for the sexual organs or functions are not used as names but as meaningless signifiers allowing the speaker to vent feeling in language freed from referential constraints. A "mother-fucking verb paradigm" is an abusive use of terms that are properly used to describe an Oedipal situation and are carried over instead to express the speaker's frustration at having to learn a difficult Latin verb. Obscene language shocks by virtue of an abusive transfer of a term valued as a name to express the pleasure or anger the speaker feels at language being so unanchored. It is as though by taking a name in vain one *made* naming in vain. It is obscene to persist in substitution where metaphor as an exchange of names between entities on the basis of an observable resemblance is no longer possible.

32. In lieu of quotation marks, which are of course literally absent from *Ulysses,* Joyce has made use of a multitude of techniques for marking and blurring the distinctions between what characters say and their accompanying thoughts, hesitations, automatic actions, and so forth. He is a master at wielding dashes, paragraphs, italics, parentheses, blanks, and spaces, as well as at standing standard English syntax and spelling on its head. One effect is that the language appears defamiliarized and at the center of the action. Woolsey appears to have picked up on these techniques that frame Joyce's language as slightly foreign, the language of another, or, as we are asserting, as quoted.

33. Woolsey says: "Each word of the book contributes like a bit of mosaic to the detail of the picture which Joyce is seeking to construct for his readers." In Baudelaire (see note 5), xii.

34. Ibid., x.

35. Ernst and Schwartz (see note 30), 94.

36. Ibid.

37. In Baudelaire (see note 5), x.

38. Ibid., ix.

39. Ibid., x.

40. Ibid., xii.

41. A somewhat similar view, reported in St. John-Stevas (see note 3) as that of Havelock Ellis, is the theory that obscene books are not aphrodisiacs but "safety valves protecting society from crime and outrage" (189).

42. Strauss (see note 18), 26.

43. They have also to judge the extent to which the work is successful at transforming custom. It was twenty years after *Ulysses* was published that Woolsey decided to let it into the United States. It took ninety years, and a new law allowing cases of "offense against morality" to be reheard, for the *Fleurs du mal* to be acquitted. These cases merely dramatize the time lag that is a necessary feature of obscenity cases, where one cannot know until after the publication whether an offense is felt and, until

long afterward, whether custom has been effectively transformed. Writers on the subject of obscenity laws in America and in England consistently deplore the fact that the shock that the artist must deliver in order to be true to her art opens her to accusation by any reader, however untutored, who happens to pick up the work and, equally, to the unjust verdicts of fearful or unknowing judges. Alan Herbert makes this point in his introduction to *Obscenity and the Law:* "Any private person can start (a prosecution), any old lady who unluckily picks out of a twopenny library a book which shocks her." See St. John-Stevas (see note 3), xiii. In Baudelaire's case, journalists raised the wind. Another writer, discussing the situation in America in 1976, deplores the inability of most judges to discriminate between works allowable to artistic license and hard-core pornography. See Felice Flanery Lewis, *Literature, Obscenity, and Law* (Carbondale: Southern Illinois Univ. Press, 1976), 247.

44. The U. S. Supreme Court Justice Potter Stewart once said, for instance, that "he knew hard-core pornography when he saw it but was unable to define it"; Lewis (see note 43), 247. This is a recurrent theme. Ernst and Schwartz (see note 30) ironically entitle one chapter "The Word Obscenity 'Defies Misunderstanding,'" and they cite the dictionary to show that the terms *lewd, lascivious, indecent,* and *obscene* are synonyms that do not help determine the concept, but repeat it.

45. Ernst and Schwartz (see note 30) state the problem:

> Not all law is as untidy as the Law of the Obscene. Lawyers and jurists have always had trouble defining in a courtroom words such as "negligence" or "reckless," or drawing a picture of "The Reasonable Man." But even "reckless," for example, has some objective definable outlines. "Reckless" driving can be described in terms of speedometer reading, condition of the road, density of population in the area and traffic on the road, infirmities of the driver, condition of the vehicle, and hundreds of factors on which factual testimony might be taken. Not so with censorship of the obscene.... When man has had fears of such concepts as blasphemy, impiety, or obscenity, law attempts avoidance rather than solution. (244–45)

46. Woolsey's *bon mot* gets cited and recited, on both sides of the Atlantic, as if it were a definition; see, for instance, St. John-Stevas (see note 3), xiv.

47. See Richard Sieburth's very interesting Foucaultian analysis, "Obscenity in Baudelaire and Swinburne," in Anna Balakian, ed., *Proceedings of the XXth International Congress of Comparative Literature* (New York: Garland, 1985–1987), 464–71.

48. It is a picture not without its irony, since the peculiar exposure of the work to accusation from the public offended is such as to make censorship laws protective of individual authors from discrepant readings.

49. In Baudelaire (see note 5), 1: 1208.

50. *The Flowers of Evil,* trans. James McGowan (Oxford: Oxford Univ. Press, 1993), 47.

51. Baudelaire (see note 5), 1: 1208

52. Baudelaire (see note 5), 2: 714.

53. This is a consistent theme in Baudelaire. Women are always flashing clothing. We could cite "A une passante" and "Avec ses vêtements ondoyants et nacrés." Even "A une mendiante rousse" spends more time looking at the holes in the dress as signs of her poverty and beauty than peering through them for a glimpse of skin. As for "Le serpent qui danse," its very skin is a shimmering fabric, not just because of its light, but presumably because it can be discarded like a dress. For Baudelaire, nudes are clothed. In this he follows André Chénier: *"C'est par ses vêtements qu'elle est nue à tes yeux"* (By her clothing she is nude / cloud to your eyes). André Chénier, *Œuvres complètes,* ed. Gerard Walter (Paris: Gallimard, 1958), 459.

54. At the end of *Mon coeur mis à nu,* Baudelaire cites a sonnet by Théophile de Viau that rhymes *nue* with *nue.* De Viau's homonym explains a state of error, in which a dreamer takes as an airy illusion what is actually a substantial shadow: "I dreamt... that Philis returned... Wanted her phantom to make love again, / And that, like Ixion, I should embrace a cloud. // Into my bed her shadow slides all naked." *("Je songeais ... que Philis revenue... Voulait que son fantôme encore fit l'amour, / Et que, comme Ixion, j'embrassasse une nue. // Son ombre dans mon lit se glisse toute nue.")* See Baudelaire (see note 5), 1: 708.

55. Leconte de Lisle, in "Le manchy," a poem much appreciated by Baudelaire and roughly contemporaneous with the *Fleurs du mal,* starts out his description of the approaching Muse as follows:

Sous un nuage frais de claire mousseline
Tous les dimanches au matin,
Tu venais à la ville en manchy de rotin,
Par les rampes de la colline.
La cloche de l'église tintait.
(Beneath a fresh cloud of clear muslin
Every Sunday morning
You came to the town in a rattan palanquin
Down the slopes of the hill.
The church bell rang out.)

The approach in a swirling cloud of muslin, with a poetic fanfare of exotic terms like "palanquin" *("manchy")* and "rattan" *("rotin"),* the attention called to sound, makes "Le manchy" a near cousin of Baudelaire's "Bijoux," with its sonorous jewelry, enveloped woman, and exotic Moorish detail. See Leconte de Lisle, *Œuvres de Leconte de Lisle,* ed. Edgar Pich (Paris: Belles Lettres, 1976–1978).

"La fanfarlo" contains a description of a deity in a "ravishing hovel, that owed at once to the place of ill-repute and the sanctuary." The "radiant and sacred splendor of her nudity" is rejected by the poet, who wants her back as Colombine, "with her fantastic get-up and her clown's blouse"; Baudelaire (see note 5), 1: 576–77.

56. The poem, numbered 20 in the first edition, occupied the transitional position between the cycle of idealized representations of Beauty and the Jeanne Duval cycle. The two poems that Baudelaire wrote to replace "Les bijoux" both insist on the double face of Beauty. In "Le masque" (1: 23–24), the statue turns out to be wearing a

mask and is called a "bicephalous monster." As for the Beauty of "Hymne à la beauté" (1: 24–25), a series of questions states her origin to be undecidably divine or satanic, her nature that of "Angel or Siren." Both poems help us read "Les bijoux"(1: 158–59) as concerned with a redoubled face, as the execrable pun, *bi-joues,* supports.

57. That is the itinerary followed in "Le voyage" (1: 129–34), which starts out in a natural landscape, and relies on a perceivable resemblance between the forms of cloud and woman.

58. It was against the argument that the *Fleurs du mal* are redeemed by way of an allegorical intention of this sort that the prosecutor Pinard directed his heaviest fire in the 1857 trial. Without naming allegory as such, he took it upon himself to refute the claim that the work teaches by way of a counterexample. Certain arguments would have it, states Pinard, that the "author wanted to depict evil and its deceitful caresses, for the sake of preserving against them"; in Baudelaire (see note 5), 1: 1207. Pinard is a more sophisticated reader than are many modern-day censors who assume that the representation of a vice automatically leads, by the seductive power of resemblance, to its imitation.

59. Paul de Man, *Allegories of Reading: Figural Language in Rousseau, Nietzsche, Rilke, and Proust* (New Haven: Yale Univ. Press, 1979), 74.

60. It is presumably this sort of rapid degradation that so shocks the prosecutor in this poem that he claims, against the argument that the poem provides a didactic allegory, that it makes grown (male) readers "pick up easily a taste for lascivious frivolities"; in Baudelaire (see note 5), 1: 1208.

61. In the essay on Tassaert in the *Salon de 1846,* Baudelaire (see note 5), comments on the reverse tendency of obscene literature toward degrading the divine. "Genius sanctifies everything, and if these subjects were treated with all the care and self-collection necessary, they would not be soiled by that revolting obscenity that is rather a *flourish of trumpets* than a truth." In an aside, "revolting obscenity" is associated with the miserable drawings we find hanging above the *"pots fêlés et les consoles branlantes"* of a prostitute's room. The double entendre of *branlantes* ("shaky," but also the slang for "masturbating") provides another example of the way that the excessiveness of the signifier interferes with the meaning production (2: 443). Baudelaire identifies puns, tautology, expletives—whatever draws attention to the signifier and interferes with meaning—as the obscene sanctified by genius.

62. Baudelaire's observation in *Mon coeur mis à nu* (see note 5), about the trial, as about the reading of the *Flowers of Evil,* is apposite: *"Histoire des Fleurs du mal, humiliation par le malentendu, et mon procès"* (2: 682). *"Malentendu"* means "misunderstanding," but it is the sort of misunderstanding to which the ear exposes one (*mal-entendre*—"mis-hear").

63. Once again the *Salon de 1846* has a parallel. Baudelaire (see note 5), tells us that melancholy is the proper attitude in front of erotic drawings: "Has it happened to you, as it has to me, to fall into great melancholy after having spent long hours leafing through erotic engravings?" (2: 443). In other places, Baudelaire mimes noisemaking the better to discuss the seduction that consists in giving voice to what has none. In *Fusées,* for instance, he says, "Do you hear these sighs . . . these wails, these cries, these death rattles?" (2: 651). He thus draws attention to the lack of any such lively sound

around, and to the figural means by which the poet can make the mute text appear as speaking.

64. Note that the poem spends a good deal of time collecting *b*'s and *d*'s, as if to draw attention to the crucial missing letters.

65. "Le coucher du soleil romantique," in Baudelaire (see note 5), 1: 149.

66. Emile Littré, *Dictionnaire de la langue française* (Paris: Gallimard & Hachette, 1961).

67. Mallarmé writes the line in the 1887 revision of the 1868 sonnet we know as "Sonnet en-yx." The 1868 version had no *nue*. See Stéphane Mallarmé, *Oeuvres complètes*, ed. Henri Mondor (Paris: Gallimard, 1945), 68–69.

68. Centre Nationale de la Recherche Scientifique, *Trésor de la langue française: Dictionnaire de la langue du* XIX*e et du* XX*e siécle (1789–1960)* (Paris: Centre Nationale de la Recherche Scientifique, 1971–1994).

69. "Hermès," in Chénier (see note 53), 405.

70. In "A une passante" (see note 53), the fascinating widow is afflicted with a statue's leg; here, the "dear one" displays a museum-full of polished members.

71. The poem is written in the past tense, and it stands out from the poems in the Jeanne Duval cycle, which are mainly in the present tense, and from the poems of the cycle on beauty, which are also in the present tense. The commentators have not known what to make of the historical vision implied. Leakey speaks of the poem as "the recollection of a privileged moment of deep intimacy," but gives no account of the rather terrifying *"Passaient devant mes yeux clairvoyants et sereins,"* with its suggestion that the poet is watching a pageant of transitory forms passing before him and vanishing. See F. W. Leakey, *Baudelaire: Collected Essays, 1953–1988* (Cambridge: Cambridge Univ. Press, 1990), 388.

72. Michael Riffaterre is certainly right when he reproaches Claude Lévi-Strauss and Roman Jakobson for noting more formal patterns than are perceptible to readers in their classic analysis of "Les chats." With a poet like Baudelaire, however, who is so insistent on the effects of the *labor* of poetry on the poem, one has to take into account the possibility that he may have considered the potential interference of readable as well as perceptible poetic patterns on the meaning of the poem. See Michael Riffaterre, "La Description des structures poétiques: Deux approches du poème de Baudelaire, *Les chats*," in idem, *Essais de stylistique structurale* (Paris: Flammarion, 1971), 305–64.

73. The first chapter of the King James version of Genesis contains striking cases of the English *and* with this force: "And the Spirit of God moved upon the face of the waters. And God said, Let there be light: and there was light." Each phrase translates the disruptiveness of God's creative positing.

74. The reading is all the more plausible because Baudelaire has a habit of using the vocative "my soul" as a term of ironic endearment, so that the problem would be that of a Galathea coming to life to disturb the poet's earlier tranquil assumption of the idol's immobility and his own agility. See "Une charogne," in Baudelaire (see note 5), 1: 31.

75. Pinard's recommendation of indulgence for Baudelaire, "who is a troubled and unbalanced nature," and of condemnation for a work that tries to "paint every-

thing, describe everything, say everything" confirms this point; in Baudelaire (see note 5), 1: 1209.

76. See Jacques Derrida's discussion in "Declarations of Independence," *New Political Science* 15 (1986): 7–15, specifically of the wild performative bringing into legal existence "the good people" that did not exist before its positing.

CRESCENT CITY WHITE LEAGUE
SEPT. 14 1874
COL. W. J. BEHAN
MAJOR W. E. HUGER
CAPT. W. T. VAUDRY SEC. A
" GEO. H. LORD " B
" S. H. BUCK " C
" ARCH MITCHELL " D
" R. B. PLEASANTS " E
" THOS McINTYRE " F
" D. M. KILPATRICK " G
" R. S. DENNEE 2 WARD
" J. R. SELLECK 3 "
" GEO. W. DUPRE 6 "
TENNISON 7 "

Discourse: The Tutelary State

A protester tries to cover an inscription on the Liberty Place Monument during a demonstration in March 1993. Copyright 1993 The Times-Picayune.

The Ontology of Censorship

Frederick Schauer

People once knew what censorship was, even if they were unsure whether it was good or bad. Until the twentieth century, censorship was understood as a system requiring preclearance for all publications, but even as this conception broadened to include a larger range of state sanctions against the spoken or printed word, debates focused not on the nature of censorship but on the extent to which those sanctions were beneficial or harmful. Today the situation is different. It remains possible to describe an act of censorship and then proceed to praise it, but just barely. In the last thirty years, the word *censorship* has become dominantly pejorative, and to praise an act of censorship is to verge on committing a linguistic mistake.

With this shift in connotation has emerged a commensurate uncertainty about what it is that so deserves this condemnation. More and more frequently, attempts are made to attach the negative implications of the word *censorship* to a broader range of activities, as when citizens who complain about the books in a library's collection are described as "censors" and when the decision of a newspaper or magazine not to print an article or letter is called "censorship." Even broader is the argument, increasingly made, that censorship may come from discourse itself, as when forms of discourse discourage people from speaking, or when the rules of discourse make certain utterances impossible. Although we have replaced the uncertainty about whether censorship is good or bad with a widespread belief in censorship's undesirability, we have at the same time moved to a point of considerable uncertainty about what censorship is. When censorship might include not only state licensing and state punishment but also activities as diffuse as the way in which some discourses marginalize others by displacing them, it is time to step back and consider just what censorship is, for without such a conception it is impossible to decide whether whatever it is is something that we wish to praise or condemn. To be more specific, when it is argued that an act of censorship might emanate not just from the regulatory apparatus of the political state but also from the everyday conditions of social life, it is time to examine the relationship of the censored to the uncensored, and thus of the constrained to the unconstrained, the coerced to the uncoerced, and the externally imposed to the internally generated.

Consider in this regard the laws against cannibalism. The laws of my state, like the laws of most others, prohibit me from engaging in cannibalism. Even if the object of my culinary desire has died from natural causes, the law orders me to refrain from eating the flesh of my fellow human beings and threatens me with harsh punishment if I do not comply. Yet if Massachusetts were to repeal its laws against cannibalism, the repeal would have no effect on my behavior. Unlike the repeal of laws requiring me to pay income taxes or to obey the speed limit on clear dry days, the laws prohibiting cannibalism change my preferences and behavior not one whit, for cannibalism is simply something I do not wish to do. That it is also against the law is, at least for me, a matter of total irrelevance, as is, I might add, the fact that cannibalism is the subject of great social disapproval. As I perceive it, I avoid cannibalism neither because it is unlawful nor because it is unpopular. I simply do not fancy it.

That my avoidance of cannibalism strikes me as endogenous could well be a case of adaptive preferences or false consciousness. I do not know, and cannot know, whether I would be a cannibal in a world in which cannibalism was legally and socially accepted. The counterfactual is just too "counter" for me to grasp its possibilities. In the world I do inhabit, however, cannibalism is a practice I consider personally ineligible, its ineligibility a function neither of legal nor of social sanctions. And in this world that I do inhabit, the difference between how I see the prohibition of cannibalism and how I see the prohibition of tax avoidance connects directly with the deepest and hardest issues surrounding the subject of censorship. The traditional conception of censorship suggests external constraint, coercion, and agents interfering with what would otherwise be our expressive, communicative, artistic, and informational preferences. Yet what if, like cannibalism, the antecedent determinants of our own preferences were at least as important as the external constraints on those preferences? In that case we might be well advised to train our attention on the sources of those preferences rather than on the possibly epiphenomenal forces that interfere with our ability to put those preferences into practice.

Indeed, the issue is more difficult yet. Cannibalism, understood as the practice of consuming the flesh of our fellow human beings, is a practice that can be defined largely by reference to physical phenomena. We can describe the practice of cannibalism by exclusive resort to the language we would use to describe bodily movements. Human cannibalism is in many respects similar to cannibalism among crocodiles (a species within which the practice flourishes), and it is no more conceptually or definitionally dependent than is crocodilian cannibalism on the institutions created by human beings. Yet when we consider the range of activities that we might call communicative, expressive, artistic, or informational—when we speak of speaking, to oversimplify—the language of physical movement is spectacularly inadequate. As with John Searle's distinction between the constitutive and the regulative, some activities are intrinsically social and inherently rule-dependent or institution-dependent.[1] Insofar as art and language are prototypical examples of such institution-dependent activities, our artistic and linguistic preferences are themselves a function of the artistic and linguistic possibilities constituted by and dependent on the activities of others. Consequently, what we can say and how we can express ourselves is significantly a function of what others do. Our preferences are thus in important ways both externally influenced and fragile, dependent on and changeable by the practices of others.[2]

To the extent that preferences themselves are at least partially externally determined, the question of censorship becomes accordingly less tractable. At one level of analysis, that of the most traditional picture of the idea of censorship, our preferences are endogenous and antecedent, and identifying the external agent as censor is unproblematic. At the next and deeper level of analysis, a level quite common in contemporary thought, our preferences themselves are subject to constitution and control by others; thus it is, so it is said, important to identify the censorious and silencing capabilities in the very actions that determine our expressive possibilities, rather than looking only to the actions that might restrict antecedently generated expressive preferences. When the discourse of others can silence us, it is argued, and when the actions of others create structures and institutions that stifle our expressive capabilities, it is important to see such activities as censorious in much the same way as we see the more overt restrictive actions of the state as censorious.

Once we acknowledge that our abilities to express and to communicate are so dependent on the actions of others, however, to continue to speak of some of those actions as censorship appears odd. That is why I shall argue that at a third, deeper level of analysis it is not that censorship appears in unexpected places, but rather that the very concept of censorship is problematic. For if the use of the word *censorship* presupposes that censorship is a relatively identifiable subset of the set of human activity, then it makes no sense to identify as such a subset something that is part and parcel of all human activity. When we think about just what it *is* to censor—when we think about the ontology of censorship and not just about the epistemology that enables us to identify it—we may discover that the very idea of censorship collapses. We may find that there is no subset of human behavior that we can identify solely because it restricts our communicative possibilities, since all human behavior both constitutes and restricts our communicative possibilities.

This, at least, is what I shall try to show here. I will not be content with unraveling the concept of censorship, however, for that is too easy. When so much of the world is ontologically comfortable with a problematic concept, it is possible that it is the world that is confused. But it is also possible that something else is going on, and that, I believe, is the case with censorship. Although censorship may be problematic as a descriptive concept for reasons I have suggested above and will argue for below, the word *censorship* may instead be ascriptive, marking the conclusion that some things are to be treated differently from others. I will devote the conclusion of this essay to sketching the distinction that it appears to be the function of the misleading language of censorship to mark.

The traditional American libertarian picture of censorship, the picture we encounter when we open the mailbox to find today's apocalyptic direct mail solicitations from the American Civil Liberties Union and the People for the American Way, is premised on a particular ontology: the traditional picture is based on a contestable but unarticulated view about what censorship is, and the traditional account then proceeds to identify and to condemn censorship so conceived whenever and wherever it appears. According to the ontology on which the traditional picture is founded, an act of censorship is an act of external interference with the internally generated communicative, expressive, artistic, or informational preferences of some agent.[3] Moreover, the traditional ontology tracks not only the standard liberal conception of the public-private distinction but also the state action requirement of the Constitution of the United States,[4] thereby identifying as a paradigm case of censorship one in which the external interference with an individual preference comes from the government or those directly dependent on it. So when the Contemporary Arts Center in Cincinnati decides (the word is crucial) to exhibit the photographs of Robert Mapplethorpe, and the state through its criminal law initiates a prosecution against the center and its curator Dennis Barrie, we see the clearest form of censorship under the traditional conception.[5] So too when a member of the Chicago city council physically removes from the walls of the School of the Art Institute of Chicago a painting depicting the late Mayor Harold Washington clad in women's undergarments, thus interfering with the preferences of both the artist and the museum. In both cases these actions could lead the museum (we do not know about the artist) to stifle other preferences in order to forestall a recurrence of the same type of official action. In these and similar cases, the internal preference is taken to be antecedent, and the external interference comes from the state or its agents. To put basically the same idea in different language, the initial preference is seen as uncoerced and the subsequent interference as an act of coercion.

The traditional ontology of coercive governmental interference has in recent years become sufficiently inclusive to recognize that government may often operate (and thus restrict) indirectly as effectively as it operates directly. If it is accepted that most artists are dependent on government largesse (grants from the National Endowment for the Arts, most prominently) to support themselves and their work, then withholding that largesse from artists like Karen Finley and Andres Serrano, and, more important, from artists who aspire to be as provocative as Finley and Serrano, achieves the desired effect of governmental restriction on what would otherwise be the expressive preferences of these artists.[6] If public libraries are dependent on municipal funding for their operations and individual librarians are dependent on that same municipal funding for their employment, then a threat to withhold funding for libraries that do not exclude *Heather Has Two Mommies, Daddy's Roommate,* and Madonna's *Sex* from their collections has the same effect. From the traditional perspective, the threat to withhold funds to induce departure from what would otherwise be the collecting and distributing preferences of librarians can be seen as roughly equivalent to a criminal or civil penalty.

A further variant on the traditional picture recognizes, at least as a matter of social reality even if not American constitutional doctrine, that coercive interference with endogenous communicative or expressive preferences may often be nongovernmental rather than governmental.[7] Although General Motors commits no constitutional wrong in dismissing those of its employees who publicly criticize the reliability of Chevrolet automobiles, General Motors is still engaged in what appears to be an external limitation or punishment of the employee for indulging in self-generated communicative preferences, and thus General Motors is seen as thwarting or distorting the communicative preferences of others. So too with the decision of a newspaper editor (or television network) to "spike" what a reporter has written, or the decision of the organizers of a political debate to exclude a so-called fringe candidate, or the decision of a curator to exclude a work of art from a museum because it will offend large donors or even because in the curator's own judgment it is an inferior work. In all these cases the external agent—editor, network, curator, large donor—is not the state, but the agent nevertheless uses some form of greater social, political, or economic power to interfere with the communicative preferences (which include both location and audience) of someone with less social, political, or economic power.[8]

Even in its most expansive form, the form that recognizes that censorship can be indirect as well as direct and also that it can be nongovernmental as well as governmental, the traditional ontology of censorship leaves the distinction between the internal and the external untouched. Recently, however, theorists from varied disciplines and with equally varied perspectives have sought to broaden our conception of censorship by recognizing the external influences on what we might desire to communicate.[9] These theorists have recognized that it is a mistake to think of communicative or expressive preferences as uninfluenced by external forces and thus have sought to identify external influences at the stage of preference formation and not just at the stage of preference frustration. Feminist theorists, for example, especially but neither necessarily nor exclusively in the context of arguments about pornography, have sought to develop the idea of silencing, a perspective that is important politically and rhetorically as well as conceptually and theoretically.[10] The political and rhetorical importance comes from the fact that in the contemporary United States freedom of speech appears to have a firmer political and rhetorical pedigree in public discourse than does equality, so it is often the case that appeals to freedom in general, and to freedom of speech in particular, have more persuasive effect (this is strictly an empirical claim) than appeals to equality, especially when filtered through the common (albeit erroneous) belief that speech is largely a self-regarding act.[11] In the political and rhetorical battle of free speech against equality, free speech often appears to come out ahead.[12] But if speech itself can be characterized not only as denying equality but also as denying speech, the argument from silencing moves to the rhetorically higher ground of seeing the speaker as censor, the talker as silencer. The political and rhetorical cachet of appeals to free speech makes it important to characterize, if at all possible, one's claims as based on the right of free speech. (If we had the Second Amendment but not the First, it might be important to try to characterize speech as a weapon, and if we had the Fourteenth Amendment but neither the First nor the Second, it might be important to transpose many existing free speech claims into equality claims.)[14] As a matter of rhetorical strategy, the silencing argument can be seen as an attempt to compete for the high ground of anticensorship in the free speech versus equality debate.

The argument from silencing has considerable intrinsic merit to accompany its occasional strategic advantages. As a *psychological* matter, it should come as no surprise that one who fears verbal abuse or linguistic belittling would, at least at the margin and often elsewhere, refrain from speaking or would say things other than what she might have said under different conditions. If during the first session of a class I point out the silliness of some student's comments, I can be confident I will not hear again from that student for the remainder of the course. That speech can inhibit speech should come as no surprise. If we can understand this phenomenon, then it is only a small step to recognize the more pervasive but more subtle phenomenon under which general environmental cues about who is important and who is not, who is worth listening to and who is not, whose ideas are picked up and whose are dropped are powerful determinants of who speaks and who remains silent. Speech is often the instrument of choice in the process of social acceptance, and thus it is often the weapon of choice in the process of social exclusion or marginalization.[14]

In addition to the psychological dimension of silencing, some theorists have focused on the *conceptual* dimension, and have stressed the way in which the language of others can silence by making forms of discourse less possible than they otherwise would have been. Rae Langton, most prominently, employs a speech act analysis to provide the conceptual support for the concept of silencing by speech.[15] If the authoritative words of others (as those words are used to create institutions that in turn create illocutionary force) are necessary to give performative effect to "I hereby christen thee" or "I now pronounce you husband and wife," for example, then so too can authoritative words give or take meaning from the words of others. It is largely words that make it possible for a woman's "No" to be understood as "Yes," and thus it is largely words that can make it difficult or impossible for a woman to make the noise "No" and have it convey the illocutionary significance of negation. This is the phenomenon that Langton calls "illocutionary disablement," and she observes, correctly, that it is all around us.[16]

Although Langton's point about the possibility and the frequency of illocutionary disablement is sound, it may be sounder than she supposes. Like others who seek to recognize that the occasions of censorship are more frequent and more pervasive than the traditional liberal ontology assumes, Langton still sees the silencing effect of words as a form of censorship and as an external and coercive interference with a speaker's communicative opportunities and preferences.[17] She and others who identify new forms of silencing and new domains of censorship see the silencing and the censorship as aberrations on an uncensored ideal. Indeed, by continuing to describe the phenomenon she reconceptualizes as "silencing" and as "censorship," Langton presupposes the existence of the unsilenced or the uncensored and thus necessarily presupposes the existence of language whose meaning is uninhibited by the language of others.

I want to insist (well, maybe only to suggest) that whether the analysis be in the language of speech acts or in the language of psychology or in the language of postmodern analyses of power, the persistence of a view about censorship as an eliminable (in theory) aberration or pathology is puzzling. Language—all language and not just the language that silences—is essentially and not just aberrantly a phenomenon of the other. The language of others may at times make it less possible to say today what I could have said yesterday or what I might say tomorrow, as Langton and others argue. But what I could have said yesterday and what I might say tomorrow is no less dependent on the language of others, for that is just what makes it a language. And if what I could have said yesterday and could say tomorrow, and what I could not have said yesterday and cannot say tomorrow, is as dependent on the language of others as what I can and cannot say today, then it seems odd to see the limitations on my communicative possibilities today as an epiphenomenal censorship or silencing.

Moreover, the very possibility of language, the particular languages that exist within that possibility, and the particular meanings that exist within a language depend not only on the language of others but also on the way in which the language of others creates rules that make language possible precisely by making some language impossible. When someone says, "fringulation begets commonly," and I say "Huh?," have I censored, or have I just done my part in reinforcing the rules that enable language to exist? Or have I done both, since what some would marginalize and condemn as censorship is part of the mechanism that allows communication to take place. The language of others can make "No" mean "Yes," but it is also the language of others that can make "No" mean "No." In fact, the language of others is necessary to make "No" mean "No." If this is so, then the attempts by Langton and others appear only half right. They are correct in identifying and conceptualizing the idea of silencing, but by persisting in the language of censorship, they may underestimate the import of their original insight. It is not censorship to which they object, but the particular substance of the censorious acts that are necessary for the maintenance of language as we know it.

Consider the genre commonly referred to as "appropriation art." Actually, the term has two denotations in the jargon of contemporary art theory. One, the narrower, refers to art, such as the work of Sherrie Levine and Mike Bidlo, that quite literally appropriates other art in order to highlight and put at issue concepts such as ownership, originality, copying, and creativity.[18] When in an exhibit of supposedly original works of art by Bidlo I see what is obviously a Picasso and a Brancusi, and when in a Levine show I see photographs by Edward Weston and Walker Evans and drawings by Willem de Kooning and Egon Schiele, I wonder what makes an original an original and what makes a copy a copy, and I begin to question the ease with which we assign the very categories of "original" and "copy."

This conception of appropriation art is interesting and important, and not irrelevant here, but a broader and occasionally seen conception of appropriation is more intriguing and more relevant still. Consider now the art that seeks to take away (to appropriate) the ease with which we routinely accept as natural the existing forms of representation. We have, for example, a moderately workable distinction between what we call literature and what we call visual arts. But when we see a work by Jenny Holzer in a museum—words and only words in a place allegedly devoted to the visual arts—we wonder. Holzer, as well as others like Barbara Kruger and Bruce Nauman, has appropriated from the world of literature a form that the world of literature thought was *theirs* and put it somewhere else. Similarly, when we see a Holzer as a T-shirt or as a moving sign in Times Square (or when we see a slogan on a T-shirt and are *told* that this is a work of art by the famous artist Jenny Holzer), we consider the possibility that Holzer has appropriated something from the museum or the gallery. It is not that she has removed a work of art from the museum or the gallery, it is that she has taken away from the museum part of their claim of distinctiveness. If I stand (on public property) in front of Bijan on Rodeo Drive giving away Bijan perfume that I received as a gift, I have in a very real economic sense taken money away from Bijan. Just as money can be appropriated in this way by the lawful actions of others, so too can reputation, prestige, or exclusivity be appropriated by the actions of others. Insofar as what we have is dependent on social institutions (like price, for example), we live in continual jeopardy that what we have will be taken away by the perfectly lawful actions of others. If my neighbor, in the exercise of his First Amendment rights, paints a ten-foot iridescent penis on the side of his house, I have lost something that cannot be measured exclusively in the precipitous drop in the value of the house.

What Holzer does by appropriating from the world of literature its monopoly on language as art, and by appropriating from museums and galleries their monopoly on the location of the visual arts, is to remind us of the way in which our representational lives are not our own. Holzer's message is thus of a piece with what so much of the best art (or at least the best of the self-conscious art of the last hundred years or so) does: it challenges us to recognize the contingency of the settled artistic conventions whose very conven-

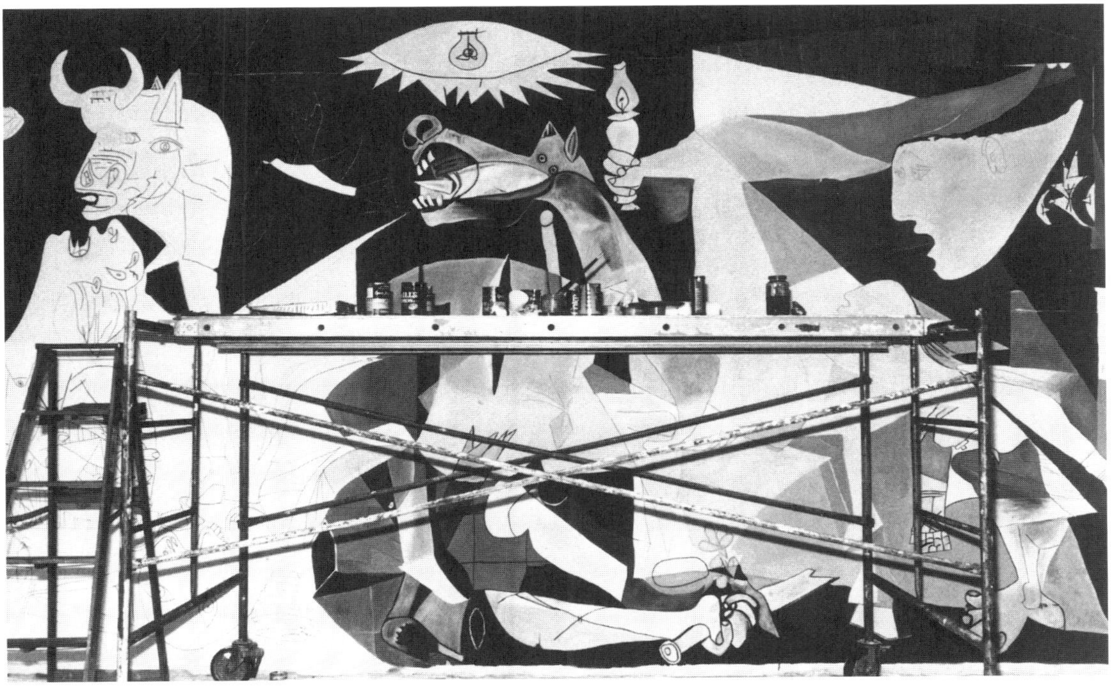

Mike Bidlo,
Guernica: A Work in Progress.
Courtesy Gagosian Gallery.

Jenny Holzer,
Signs, 1986.
Photo copyright 1986 by Lisa Kahane.

tionality becomes so encrusted that we perceive it as fixed and noncontingent. What Picasso does with perspective, what Manet does with the relationship between viewer and image, what Cezanne and Seurat do with our sense of surface, what Magritte does with the concept of representation, what Dada in general and Duchamp in particular do with the concept of art, and what surrealism does (or attempts to do) with the concept of reality ("*Ceci n'est pas une pipe*"), to take just a few examples, is to put into flux what we had previously thought to be fixed, to unsettle the settled, and to highlight the contingency of, and the human agency in, what we had hitherto perceived as inevitable and natural.[19]

Consider what happens when artists like these are effective. Having seen Duchamp's moustached *Mona Lisa,* can I ever see the "real" *Mona Lisa* in the same way as I saw it before? Maybe it is just me, but to see Leonardo's *Mona Lisa* knowing about Duchamp's *Mona Lisa* is an experience accompanied by a slight chuckle and wondering where the moustache is.[20] Does a smooth surface appear quite so smooth to me again after understanding Dubuffet? What is perspective after De Chirico, and what do the borders of a photograph mean after reading Sontag's *On Photography*?[21] One of the things that Warhol presumably wanted to do was change the way I experience the soup aisle in the supermarket, and he has done so. On numerous occasions, therefore, the best artists succeed in transforming artistic understanding, but in doing so they have not only made possible ways of seeing that were not possible before, but they have also censored or silenced ways of seeing that used to be possible.[22]

The phenomenon, of course, is hardly limited to art. By calling themselves "Queer Nation," the members of this gay and lesbian activist group seek to take something away from the homophobes; the subsequent and far broader use of the word *queer* by gays and lesbians to describe themselves and to describe an intellectual agenda is designed precisely to do the same. The self-conscious use of the word *queer* in this manner seeks to transform the meaning of someone else's expression without the someone else actually having to *do* anything, just as the speech of others may turn "No" into "Yes." Queer Nation and its successors want to convert a pejorative into something more positive. The nonpejorative or ironic use of someone else's pejorative (consider also the rap group NWA—Niggers With Attitude—or, more broadly, the plainly nonpejorative use of the word *nigger* within parts of the African American community) is often a quite effective way of drawing the sting from someone else's language. It is also, however, a way of denying to someone else a communicative possibility that they otherwise would have had.[23]

Consider the following: You are at a public event, sitting there, minding your own business, communicating by your inaction little more than politeness and respectability. Someone stands and says, "Now let us all bow our heads and pray." No longer does your inaction convey politeness and respectability. Now it conveys Godlessness, or rebellion, or arrogance, or something you may have preferred not to convey. You have been forced to speak, and you have

Members of Queer Nation staging a protest during the Academy Awards ceremony in Los Angeles, 1994. Copyright Ted Soqui.

spoken without moving a muscle. To have expressed admiration in 1975 for the work of Martin Heidegger or Paul de Man was simply to make a philosophical or literary or academic judgment. To do the same thing now, the Nazi sympathies of both having been exposed, is possibly to be understood as taking a position about Nazism, or at least to be understood as taking a position about the relevance of Nazi sympathies to understanding and appreciating these men's scholarly contributions. Unlike the state of affairs a few years ago, to consume a bottle of French wine now is, possibly, and in some social circles, to make a statement about nuclear testing. Insofar as it was possible a few years ago to make a statement about French wine whose clarity was unencumbered by the "noise" (in the economist's sense of additional data or additional complicating factors) of a simultaneous statement about nuclear testing and the personality of the French people, it is now far less possible to make such a statement. Those who would wish to do so, therefore, are deprived of the possibility of making a statement they previously could have made. In that sense, they have been silenced. They appear to have been censored by world events and by the reaction of certain people to those events.

The examples I give are relatively dramatic, just because they are often transformative in a "Eureka!" sense. But my point is not about the occasional transformative experience. It is instead about the continuous and gradual transformations that are a much larger part of our representational lives. The examples I use are simply among the more dramatic instances of the way in which our communicative existence is dependent on the rules, conventions, and understandings over which we as individual communicators have only the smallest amount of control. At some times more vividly than at others, our ability to speak—or not to speak—is largely in the hands of our fellows.

With our communicative capacities so much out of our control, the idea of communicative preferences as overwhelmingly endogenous seems strained, and that makes the idea of identifying censorship with the exogenous seem equally strained. Without an idea of the internal there seems little point in talking about the external, and without the idea of the external the idea of censorship itself seems fragile. Put less extremely, if so much of what we can say is necessarily in the hands of others, what if anything demarcates the category we routinely, even if problematically, refer to as "censorship"? Although recognizing the dependence of our discourses on the discourses of others is a staple of contemporary thinking in many disciplines, many who hold this view continue to insist that there is a discrete category of the censorious and that censorship in this deeper way is problematic.[24] Instead, it appears, censorship in this sense is part and parcel of our communicative existence, and the conclusion is not, contrary to some of the modern (in the nontechnical sense of that word) wisdom, that this variety of censorship is more present than we think, but rather that because this type of censorship is everywhere, it is, as Richard Burt suggests, nowhere at all.[25]

Yet this is too hasty. We have learned from J. L. Austin, Gilbert Ryle, and other leaders of Anglo-American philosophy in the 1950s not only that speech acts are important but also that we should not be too quick to reject the categories and distinctions embedded in ordinary language. It may not be, as Wittgenstein put it, that "ordinary language is all right"[26] or that "it is in order as it is,"[27] but ordinary language is still a highly reliable marker of categories and distinctions that most often serve a purpose. Our task, therefore, should be to try to ascertain what this purpose is before we reject a category or distinction out of hand. When faced with the persistence of a category — in this case, censorship — that seems on closer inspection to be so expansive as to be empty, we ought first to see if something else is going on.

Implicit in what I say is the belief that standard usage of the word *censorship* tends to be ascriptive rather than descriptive, that it is a conclusion masquerading as an analytic device.[28] Indeed, this point is not dependent on the more extreme version of what I argued in the previous section. Even under a more conventional conception of censorship, we see the word *censorship* applied when library boards of trustees decide to exclude books from public libraries but not when librarians exclude them, when office buildings exclude works of art they believe will not appeal to the residents of the building but not when gallery owners exclude works they believe will not appeal to the visitors to the gallery, and when political journals exclude works that espouse unpopular political opinions but not when literary journals exclude works that espouse unpopular literary opinions. It is censorship when the tobacco industry induces a television network to tone down its criticism of smoking, but it is editing when the producer asks the same thing of the writer.

All too often, what is at times characterized as censorship seems to be quite similar to what at other times is characterized as editing, or choice. At times it is "simply" speech, as when pundits blithely characterize the words of Salman Rushdie as the target of censorship and the words of the Ayatollah Khomeni in calling for a *fatwa* against Rushdie as censorship, even though, like Rushdie, words were the only things that the Ayatollah employed.[29] When confronted with these and numerous similar examples, I am tempted to conclude that the word *censorship*, which is largely even if not exclusively pejorative (and that is why censors always deny they are censoring, even when they are censoring for good purposes),[30] does not describe a category of conduct, but rather attaches an operative conclusion (ascribes) to a category created on other grounds. Yet why is it that the operative conclusion (condemnation) attaches to some acts and not others, if all are equally deserving of the label "censorship" in a strictly descriptive sense?

Consider again the case of the library. With some frequency, professional librarians describe as "censorship" those cases in which political institutions (including elected boards of library trustees) urge not only the removal of a book but also its initial nonselection. Indeed, professional librarians are prone to characterize as censorship even citizen complaints — usually organized but sometimes not — about the books that have been selected. Yet those same professional librarians rarely see censorship in their own deacquisitions and their own nonselections, even where those choices are based on content or even on point of view. Numerous libraries with no history of pressure of any kind on their selection policies routinely subscribe to *People* but not to *Hustler,* magazines of roughly similar literary content and roughly similar potential demand, but only one of which is sexually explicit and glorifies violence against women. When this selection decision is made by professional librarians it is not censorship but choice. When it is made by elected officials it is not choice but censorship.

So too with museums and galleries. If an assistant curator placed on the exhibition wall of the School of the Art Institute of Chicago a painting that the head curator had explicitly rejected as being of inferior artistic quality and the head curator had removed the painting in response, in just the same way that the city council member had removed the painting of Mayor Washington, we would be inclined to characterize this as an appropriate response to insubordination, not an act of censorship. When at the prompting of Hitler and Goebbels in 1937 the Archäologisches Institut in Munich staged its famous exhibition of "Degenerate Art," it engaged in what is now routinely taken to be an act of censorship, even though the work of the "degenerate" artists such as George Grosz, Max Beckmann, Emil Nolde, Lyonel Feininger, and Oskar Kokoschka was shown rather than hidden.[31] Yet when a museum now shows some inferior art precisely so its patrons might see the difference between the good and the bad, we hardly think of this as an act of censorship.

The same phenomenon exists within educational institutions. The decisions that teachers and professors make about what to teach are necessarily based on content and are often based on viewpoint, and this is rarely viewed as censorship. When faculty members choose to stress the advantages of affirmative action over its disadvantages or argue that Claude Monet was a better painter than Sam Francis, we do not see them as censors (at least of their own content, although we might see them as potential censors of student comments), but if the dean suggests the same thing and urges the faculty members to act on the suggestion, we rise up in arms and shout "academic freedom," which is within some circles an even better rallying cry than opposition to censorship. At one remove, if deans or faculties require that constitutional law be taught while admiralty is dropped or that there be three offerings in contemporary art and only one in classical art, we think of this as a matter of choice. If university administrators, or worse, trustees, or worst of all, elected officials require the same thing, the heavy artillery of anticensorship and academic freedom rhetoric is wheeled into action.

In the previous paragraph I coupled the language of academic freedom with the language often employed to oppose censorship. I did so because the language of academic freedom is, with particular overtness, the language of professional prerogative and the language of autonomous decision making. The claims of academic freedom thus remind us of what is at issue in all the cases I have described. Having recognized the omnipresence of censorship, we look for something that suggests the deeper distinction that the use and nonuse of the language of censorship is designed to mark. What the academic freedom case suggests most clearly, and what the library, museum, and gallery examples reinforce, is that it is professional competence (or, more skeptically, guild prerogative) rather than censorship or noncensorship that is at issue. Censorship is inevitable, necessary, and desirable—but it is less inevitable, necessary, or desirable that this group rather than that group do it. Librarians—and curators and professors—are not objecting to censorship so much as claiming the office of censor. The process by which we set and enforce standards, by which we establish and modify the norms of evaluation, is inevitably a process that in a differentiated society falls, by topic or domain, more into the hands of some than of others. As suggested by Niklas Luhmann, differentiation and autonomy are paired thoughts.[32] As the world of art is differentiated from the world of politics, as the world of the academy is differentiated from the public at large, as the world of librarianship is differentiated from the world of religion, inhabitants of these differentiated institutions will often, and often wisely, seek to preserve the autonomy of their institutions and the autonomy of the decision making that takes place within them.

The language of censorship is thus the language of professionalism, the language of expertise, the language of institutional competence, the language of separation of powers.[34] It can also be, more maliciously, the language of turf. Yet in suggesting that censorship is the language of power, I do not mean to suggest that power or turf is an end in itself. For some people and groups power may be, and for some theorists power is, the primary and irreducible component of human interaction. This view, however, is not mine. People often, and often correctly, see their own claims of power as justified by larger social interests. Although cynics may see claims of academic freedom, for example, as claims that are largely self-interested, this is often not the perception of the academics who make those claims. Instead, they see their claims as premised on the *social* interest of granting to academics a degree of autonomy in their decision making. So it is too with the claims of artists to artistic freedom and of librarians to freedom from political control. Again, these claims may often be infected with a not inconsiderable degree of self-interest, but the forms in which the claims are made call forth a non–self-interested value (the value to society of artistic creativity, for example) to which the claimed autonomy is thought to be instrumental.

From the perspective of a society deciding whether to accept these claims to autonomy, therefore, the fact that such claims may be tinged with the self-interest of the claimants is excessively reductionist. The task facing a society in its role as institutional designer is to decide whether these claims of autonomy—these claims to be free of a certain form of institutional constraint—are justified. The question then is not whether artists should be censored. The question is whether the judgments of curators should be preferred to the judgments of the state and whether the forces of the market should be preferred to the forces of politics. In the context of funding for the arts, the question is whether the judgments of artistic peers, themselves infused with the politics of art as well as the judgments of professionals, should be preferred to the judgments of public officials, which are equally infused with a politics of a different kind and equally premised on judgment of a quite different type. With respect to libraries, the question is whether the judgments of professional librarians as to what to include and what to exclude should be preferred to the judgments of elected officials. And in making these determinations we cannot avoid the most difficult questions of what functions the institutions are supposed to serve and whose judgments and whose autonomy are most conducive to serving those functions.

In trying to transform the question that society should ask from one about the presence or absence of something called "censorship" into one about the appropriate locus of content-determining authority, I seek to focus attention on the content-determining capacities of supposedly uncensored agents and institutions and on the pathologies as well as the virtues of specialization. Currently existing artistic mores, norms, and standards, for example, exert considerable influence over the creative choices of individual artists, an influence often obscured by the language of censorship. It may be that this influence is for the good, and certainly some of it is necessary (how could art challenge the conventions of representation if there were no conventions to challenge?), but some of this influence is likely stifling, and some of this influence exists in domains in which it is plausible to consider whether it should be entrenched or ameliorated.

The peer review panels employed by the National Endowment for the Arts, for example, seem plainly (to me, at least) preferable to decisions by Senator Jesse Helms or his allies, yet once we recognize that these peer review panels also serve to entrench the content-determining and content-stifling norms of a particular subculture, we might well consider whether alternative approaches would be better. A panel consisting of one artist and two representatives of the nonvisual arts (a poet and a musician, for example) might be more conducive to the autonomy of individual artists than is the system that now exists... or perhaps not. Without some even deeper analysis of the likely factors that such a body would employ, we are ill-equipped to evaluate this alternative. My only point here is to suggest the ways in which the language of censorship may blind us to the content-determining effects of numerous social institutions and to suggest as well that in many contexts there are choices that are not about whether content should be determined, but are rather about which people and which institutions should be involved in the determination.

The language that I would substitute for the language of censorship is thus the language that we might use in making social decisions about the allocation of content-determining authority and the language that a society might use in negotiating competing claims for the right to exercise that authority. Such language would identify whose choices we as a society wish to privilege and whose choices we wish to suspect. And although we may often make the wrong choices in deciding which censors to privilege, we often make the right ones as well. The lesson that comes out of a deep look at the ontology of censorship is not that there is more bad censorship than we ever realized, nor is it that all censorship is good. Instead, we realize that censorship per se is not as ontologically useful a category as we have often thought. By recognizing this, we can focus on more ontologically useful categories, of which the category of autonomy, the category of differentiation, the category of institutions and institutional competence, and the category of separation of powers are ones that quite quickly rise to the surface.[34]

Notes

This chapter was prepared for the Seminar on Censorship and Silencing at the Getty Research Institute for the History of Art and the Humanities, 15–16 December 1995. Much earlier versions were presented as a lecture at the Art Institute of Chicago in July 1991 on the occasion of the opening of the "Degenerate Art" exhibition, at the Asia Society Galleries in October 1991 on the occasion of the opening of the "Undercurrents in the Floating World: Censorship and Japanese Prints" exhibition, and as the first Martha Boaz Lecture in Intellectual Freedom at the University of Michigan School of Information and Library Studies in September 1994. For useful comments I am grateful both to the participants in the Getty seminar and to the audience at a faculty workshop at the University of Chicago Law School, where a later version was presented on 23 January 1996.

1. John R. Searle, *Speech Acts: An Essay in the Philosophy of Language* (Cambridge: Cambridge Univ. Press, 1969), 33–42. I am inclined to agree with Raz that the distinction is less one of different types of *rules*, as Searle argues, but is rather between different types of practices, some (like bidding a grand slam) requiring human institutions for their existence and definition, and others (like coughing) being largely institution-independent. See Joseph Raz, *Practical Reason and Norms* (Princeton: Princeton Univ. Press, 1990), 108–17. This idea is also captured by Searle (see above) 50–53, in his distinction between brute and institutional facts.

2. On preferences as partially exogenous to the preferrer, see Cass R. Sunstein, *The Partial Constitution* (Cambridge, Mass.: Harvard Univ. Press, 1993), 164–79, 190–92; Cass R. Sunstein, "Constitutions and Democracies: An Epilogue," in Jon Elster and Rune Slagstad, eds., *Constitutionalism and Democracy* (Cambridge: Cambridge Univ. Press, 1988), 327–53, at 348 ff. Sunstein, however, gives law a large place in the exogenous determination of preferences, a claim with which I disagree and which is, in any event, immaterial to my argument here. For somewhat less law-dependent claims about the social sources of individual preferences, see Jon Elster, *Sour Grapes: Studies in the Subversion of Rationality* (Cambridge: Cambridge Univ. Press, 1983).

3. The phrase "communicative, expressive, artistic, or informational" is cumbersome, but I want to emphasize that the preferences to which I refer might be preferences about what to receive as well as what to send, and about how to distribute an

idea as well as what idea to distribute. Similarly, I do not want anything to turn on contested communicative, informational, or aesthetic theories, such as the dispute about whether art is expressive, or communicative, or both.

4. The First Amendment opens with "Congress shall make no law," which, although now well understood to encompass all instrumentalities of the government, does not include nongovernmental entities. And the Fourteenth Amendment, through which the First Amendment is applied to the states, contains the similarly interpreted language, "nor shall any state." Although nongovernmental entities that have been entrusted with essentially governmental responsibilities are subject to the constraints of the First Amendment (*Marsh v. Alabama,* 326 U.S. 501 [1946]), the basic rule is that nongovernmental entities, even ones with great economic and social power, are beyond the reach of the constitutional protections of freedom of speech and freedom of the press. See *Hudgens v. National Labor Relations Board,* 424 U.S. 507 (1976).

5. There is a historical usage of the word *censorship,* one still important today outside of the United States, in which the word is reserved for the licensing boards (which were the exclusive preoccupation of John Milton in the *Areopagitica* and William Blackstone in the *Commentaries*) or other forms of preclearance or prior restraint. Little in contemporary usage (or contemporary American law) so limits the word—or the idea itself.

6. This is, technically, the problem of *unconstitutional conditions,* which, as a matter of legal doctrine, is less sensitive to the censorious capacities of withholding funds than the contemporary proponents of the traditional liberal picture would desire. See Seth Kreimer, "Allocational Sanctions: The Problem of Negative Rights in a Positive State," *Univ. of Pennsylvania Law Review* 132 (1984): 1293–1356; Kathleen M. Sullivan, "Unconstitutional Conditions," *Harvard Law Review* 102 (1989): 1413–1506.

7. In his contribution to this volume, "Pornographizing, Subordinating, and Silencing," pages 285–311, Leslie Green suggests a category of *coercive public action* slightly broader than the category of the governmental. The extent to which what I say in the text overlaps with Green's point is a function of what Green means by the idea of the "public."

8. As Sanford Levinson has suggested to me, the term *self-censorship* is especially curious. We do not use it when describing the choices of an agent unafraid of legal or social sanctions, even though we are constantly censoring ourselves for numerous reasons unrelated to a fear of legal or social repercussions. But when we censor ourselves precisely because of those fears, it is hard to see what makes *self-censorship* different from *censorship,* as commonly understood. The standard use of the word *censorship* applies it to the nonspeech of an agent whose non-speech is a function of fear of imprisonment, fine, civil damages, or social ostracism. If so, then appending the descriptor *self-* adds nothing to what is typically suggested by the word *censorship* standing alone.

9. In addition to various works discussed below, see Pierre Bourdieu, "Censorship and the Imposition of Form," in idem, *Language and Symbolic Power,* ed. John B. Thompson, trans. Gino Raymond and Matthew Adamson (Cambridge, Mass.: Harvard Univ. Press, 1991); Richard Burt, ed., *The Administration of Aesthetics: Censor-*

ship, Political Criticism, and the Public Sphere (Minneapolis: Univ. of Minnesota Press, 1994); and Robert Justin Goldstein, *Political Censorship of the Arts and the Press in Nineteenth-Century Europe* (London: Macmillan, 1989).

10. The *locus classicus* is the work of Catharine A. MacKinnon. See especially the essays collected in *Feminism Unmodified: A Discourse on Life and Law* (Cambridge, Mass.: Harvard Univ. Press, 1987). For various attempts to work out the basic idea, see, for example, Rae Langton, "Subordination, Silence, and Pornography's Authority," pages 261–83 in this volume; Rae Langton, "Speech Acts and Unspeakable Acts," *Philosophy and Public Affairs* 22 (1993): 293–330; Frank Michelman, "Conceptions of Democracy in American Constitutional Argument: The Case of Pornography Regulation," *Tennessee Law Review* 56 (1989): 299–334; and Melinda Vadas, "A First Look at the Pornography/Civil Rights Ordinance: Could Pornography Be the Subordination of Women?" *Journal of Philosophy* 84 (1987): 487–514. For responses, see, for example, Ronald Dworkin, "Liberty and Pornography," *New York Review of Books* 15, no. 12 (1991): 12–15; Ronald Dworkin, "Women and Pornography," *New York Review of Books* 21, no. 16 (1993): 36–42; Daniel Jacobson, "Freedom of Speech Acts? A Reply to Langton," *Philosophy and Public Affairs* 24 (1995): 64–79; and Leslie Green, "Pornographizing, Subordinating, and Silencing" (see note 7).

11. For the argument supporting the parenthetical assertion, see Frederick Schauer, "The Phenomenology of Speech and Harm," *Ethics* 103 (1993): 635–53.

12. That the American press is hardly a disinterested reporter of issues touching on the First Amendment is hardly irrelevant to this phenomenon.

13. As my colleague Bill Hogan puts it (I do not know if it is original with him or not), if you have a hammer, every problem looks like a nail.

14. See Catharine A. MacKinnon, *Only Words* (Cambridge, Mass.: Harvard Univ. Press, 1993), 31.

15. Langton expands on this argument in this volume (see note 10). For related ideas, see Andrew Altman, "Liberalism and Campus Hate Speech," *Ethics* 103 (1993): 302–17; Jennifer Hornsby, "Speech Acts and Pornography," in Susan Dwyer, ed., *The Problem of Pornography* (Belmont, Calif.: Wadsworth, 1995), 220–32; and Vadas (see note 10), 487–511.

16. I take Leslie Green's identification of authority as a necessary condition of the phenomenon to be correct, but not inconsistent with the basic point. See Green (see note 7).

17. See Lawrence Lessig, "The Regulation of Social Meaning," *The University of Chicago Law Review* 62 (1995): 943–1045.

18. See Jeanne Siegel, ed., *Art Talk: The Early 80s* (New York: Da Capo Press, 1990), 191–96, 245–56.

19. Under one view, it is just the purpose of modern art in particular, and the avant-garde in general, to engage in this type of unsettling with respect to the distinction between the beautiful and the ugly. See Renato Poggioli, *The Theory of the Avant-Garde,* trans. Gerald Fitzgerald (Cambridge, Mass.: Harvard Univ. Press, 1968), 80–84.

20. Maybe what I think is the real Mona Lisa is not a Leonardo da Vinci, but is instead a Duchamp with the moustache removed.

21. Susan Sontag, *On Photography* (New York: Dell Publishing, 1978).

22. Robert Hughes notes:

> Today, surrounded by art that rejects formal grace in the interest of narrative, contradiction, and hyperbole, we are conditioned to see a different Manet. In eyes that have viewed de Chirico's train stations, for instance, Manet's painting of a woman and child at the Gare St.-Lazare acquires a strangeness that contradicts his intention of painting a peaceful urban scene.

Robert Hughes, *Nothing If Not Critical: Selected Essays on Art and Artists* (New York: Viking, 1992), 136. "Now that [Robert Hughes] has pointed out the formal correspondence between Nazi rallies and Hollywood musicals I will never be able to look at *Babes on Broadway* in quite the same way"; Wendy Steiner, *The Scandal of Pleasure: Art in an Age of Fundamentalism* (Chicago: Univ. of Chicago Press, 1995), 10.

23. And this is why Leslie Green is correct in noting that a discourse of freedom of speech may itself undercut some of the illocutionary force of an utterance, since the discourse of freedom of speech may diminish the claim of a speaker to speak from or with authority. See Green (see note 7).

24. A good example is Sue Curry Jansen, *Censorship: The Knot That Binds Power and Knowledge* (New York: Oxford Univ. Press, 1988). Jansen, whose work has influenced a fair amount of the preceding few pages, urges us to recognize the *constitutive censorships* that exist alongside of and behind the more familiar *regulative censorships*. See also Jonathan Miller, *Censorship and the Limits of Permission* (London: Oxford Univ. Press for The British Academy, 1971), 11–14. But Jansen's conclusion, that we be as concerned about and hostile to constitutive censorships as we are to regulative censorships, is a far more cautious conclusion than her own analysis would suggest.

25. Richard Burt, "(Un)Censoring in Detail: The Fetish of Censorship in the Early Modern Past and the Postmodern Present," pages 17–41 in this volume.

26. Ludwig Wittgenstein, *The Blue and Brown Books* (Oxford: Basil Blackwell, 1958), 28.

27. Ludwig Wittgenstein, *Philosophical Investigations*, 3rd ed., trans. G. E. M. Anscombe (Oxford: Basil Blackwell, 1958), sec. 98.

28. On ascription, see H. L. A. Hart, "The Ascription of Responsibility and Rights," in A. G. N. Flew, ed., *Logic and Language, First Series* (Oxford: Basil Blackwell, 1951), 145–66. Hart later recanted some of his claims about the extent of ascription in the legal system, but the basic distinction between the descriptive and the ascriptive remains sound. See H. L. A. Hart, *Punishment and Responsibility: Essays in the Philosophy of Law* (Oxford: Clarendon Press, 1968), v.

29. For an example of the phenomenon, particularly ironic because of the author's insistence on the separation of words and conduct, see Steiner (see note 22), 94–127.

Relatedly, consider the current debates about "political correctness." Although many of the people who worry about the phenomenon of political correctness worry about speech codes and related formal disciplinary sanctions for using speech of a certain kind, even more pervasive is the concern that in the contemporary university "climate," certain words or ideas cannot comfortably be articulated. At times we hear the phenomenon described as censorship, and people claim that they are censored in their ability to, for example, oppose affirmative action, or question the concept of date rape, or whatever. Yet in most cases it appears that what makes it difficult for them to do so is simply the words of others. Why is the person who, using only words, condemns someone as insensitive a censor rather than a speaker?

30. There is an important rhetorical difference between "this is not free speech" and "free speech must give way to other interests." In popular discourse, to have admitted that something *is* a free speech case is to have given away most of the game, even though in more academic settings the idea of rights being overridden in exigent circumstances (compelling interests, clear and present dangers, and the like) is a commonplace. See Robert Nozick, "Moral Complications and Moral Structures," *Natural Law Forum* 1 (1968): 1–44; Frederick Schauer, "A Comment on the Structure of Rights," *Georgia Law Review* 27 (1993): 415–34; Frederick Schauer, "Can Rights Be Abused?" *Philosophical Quarterly* 31 (1981): 227–36; and Judith Jarvis Thomson, "Some Ruminations on Rights," in idem, *Rights, Restitution, and Risk: Essays in Moral Theory,* ed. William Parent (Cambridge, Mass.: Harvard Univ. Press, 1986), 49–65.

31. See Stephanie Barron, ed., *"Degenerate Art": The Fate of the Avant-Garde in Nazi Germany* (Los Angeles: Los Angeles County Museum of Art, 1991).

32. See, for example, Niklas Luhmann, *Soziale Systeme: Grundriss einer allgemeinen Theorie* (Frankfurt: Suhrkamp, 1984); and Niklas Luhmann, *The Differentiation of Society,* trans. Stephen Holmes and Charles Larmor (New York: Columbia Univ. Press, 1982).

33. I believe my central point is different from that in Robert C. Post, "The Management of Speech: Discretion and Rights," *The Supreme Court Review,* 1984, 169–236, but we share an interest in seeing the domains of speech control in institutional competence and separation of powers terms.

34. Part of my goal here is to connect some of the more sophisticated discussions of personal autonomy to currently less sophisticated discussions of institutional autonomy. For an example that represents the first category, see Meir Dan-Cohen, "Conceptions of Choice and Conceptions of Autonomy," *Ethics* 102 (1992): 221–43.

Public Funding for Science and Art: Censorship, Social Harm, and the Case of Genetic Research into Crime and Violence

David Wasserman

Introduction

Can a government committed to funding biological and social science refuse to fund research into genetic predispositions to impulsive, violent, or antisocial behavior, not because such research is scientifically unsound or uninteresting, but because it may offend, denigrate, or threaten social harm to individuals or groups in the society? Can recent debates on public funding for the arts shed light on this issue?

A variety of current research programs investigate genetic influences on impulsive, aggressive, and criminal behavior. Some attempt to tease out genetic from environmental influences by studying twins and adoptees; others employ the latest genetic technology to search for markers, and ultimately genes, associated with crime and violence. Still others study the neurobiology of human behavior in laboratory and clinical studies. Although they differ greatly in method and ambition, these programs share the assumption that it makes scientific sense to look for genetic influences on morally or legally significant categories of human behavior.[1] Most researchers also believe that the identification of such genetic influences would be socially beneficial, because it would permit interventions that would be more humane and effective than criminal prosecution.[2]

Although most mainstream researchers do not look for, or expect to find, racial or other group differences in genetic predisposition, and, although most deny that their findings would support mandatory screening, forced medication, or harsher sentences, opponents argue that their research reinforces public perceptions of criminal behavior as an essentially biological problem, affecting some races more than others, diverts attention from the social and economic conditions that breed crime, and promotes repressive policies. Some opponents have demanded that genetic research in this area be "defunded" or stopped by more "radical" means; more moderate opponents have called for a moratorium on the public funding of such research.[3]

Many critics challenge the research on scientific grounds. In their view, we do not need to address the question of whether the research should be denied funding despite its scientific merit, because it lacks merit. Some argue that the very idea of genetic predispositions to socially defined behavior is confused; others say that there is no reason to expect differences in such predispositions among individuals *or* groups. But these claims are not accepted by many equally well-credentialed biological and social scientists.[4] Since I do not believe that the nonscientists who must decide on public funding in a democratic society can confidently dismiss all such research as scientifically unsound, I think we must consider whether the state can refuse to support it on grounds other than its lack of scientific merit.

I will address this issue in the context of a larger debate over government funding for art and science—that is, whether it is constitutionally or morally permissible for the state to award funds on any basis other than artistic or scientific merit, as judged by independent peer review. I will question the way in which policy alternatives have been framed in much of this debate: either that it is improper to give any consideration to potential offense, denigration, or social harm in making funding decisions because such consideration unduly burdens freedom of expression or violates government neutrality, or that it is permissible to give those concerns as much weight as the government chooses because funding for art and science is an entirely discretionary exercise of public largess.

Two arguments are often raised against restrictions on public funding for potentially offensive or denigrating art or science: that such restrictions violate an individual right to expression by unduly burdening its exercise, and that they violate government neutrality in the management of public debate. Although these arguments have generally been deployed against restrictions on government funding for art, I will examine their relevance for government funding of science. I will claim that both arguments fail with respect to the funding of science, for somewhat different reasons than they fail with respect to the funding of art.

With respect to the first argument: Even if funding restrictions would significantly interfere with the freedom of researchers to pursue questions of interest to them, and even if the restrictions were intended to have that effect, they would not violate any expressive rights of the researchers. The government has the prerogative to decide what types of scientific inquiry it should underwrite and what constraints it should impose on those inquiries. With respect to the second argument: If the government is to manage the public debate responsibly, it cannot maintain neutrality, and one way in which it must violate neutrality is by deciding what factual inquiries advance the public debate on critical issues. It cannot leave to scientific experts the ultimately moral and political questions of whether the knowledge sought by certain types of research is worth acquiring or whether its potential value is outweighed by the danger of offense, denigration, or other social harm.

If, however, the decision about the funding of research whose findings or applications threaten vulnerable individuals or groups should not be left to scientific experts, neither should it be left to legislative or popular whim. The decision requires a sustained dialogue among scientists, policy makers, and representatives of affected interests. That dialogue, I believe, will yield a principled basis for conditions on funding for genetic research on crime and violence, with different consequences for research on individual and group differences.

The Right to Free Expression

For the purpose of examining the threat to freedom of expression posed by restrictions on the public funding of scientific research, my point of departure will be the debate over "content restrictions" on the public funding of art. That debate focused on the funding restrictions proposed by Senator Jesse Helms in 1990 in response to public controversy over National Endowment for the Arts (NEA) grants for several projects: exhibits of Robert Mapplethorpe's work on gay sexuality; Andres Serrano's photograph *Piss Christ*, showing a crucifix in a jar of urine; and productions by such performance artists as Karen Finley.[5] The Helms amendment prohibited the use of NEA funds to "produce or disseminate" work (1) that is "obscene or indecent," (2) that "denigrates the objects or beliefs of the adherents of a particular religion," or (3) which "denigrates . . . a person, group, or class of citizens on the base [sic] of race, creed, sex, handicap or national origin."[6]

The objection raised by liberal opponents of Helms's amendment was categorical: that it would be a violation of freedom of expression to deny funding on the basis of potential affront and offense.[7] While this objection was generally framed as a constitutional claim, it could also be understood as a moral claim, and I will treat is as such. The liberals' argument is that because content restrictions involve the violation or infringement of an important right when they are applied to the arts, they are not subject to the kind of cost-benefit calculation that might favor content restrictions in other circumstances. The right to artistic expression, to adopt a now-standard locution, "trumps" the utilities involved in the prevention of offense and denigration.

The objection was explicitly directed at sections 1 and 2 of the Helms amendment, which denied funding to obscene and sacrilegious works of art. But it applies to *all* funding restrictions based on the content of the proposed work, including restrictions based on section 3, which denies funding to art that "denigrates . . . a class of citizens on the base of race."[8] The offense taken by bluenoses at "obscene" or "indecent" art produced or displayed with public subsidies may pale when compared with the insult given to vulnerable minorities by publicly subsidized racist art. But if content restrictions do infringe a right to free expression, then these significant psychological and moral differences are irrelevant to funding decisions, because the right trumps the affront in either case. If restrictions based on section 1 constitute censorship, so do restrictions based on section 3. Moreover, the liberal objection to content restrictions would apply not only to the blanket funding restrictions found in the Helms amendment but also to the mere consideration of offense or denigration as one factor in funding decisions. To make a decision based on offensiveness, even to break a tie between proposals of equal merit, would smack of censorship.

There are two general strategies for finding a threat to free expression in content restrictions. These strategies reflect two distinct and sometimes conflicting justifications for freedom of expression. One regards that freedom as an individual right, required for personal autonomy or flourishing; the other regards freedom of expression as a collective or social interest, required for full and open deliberation in a democratic society.[9]

Freedom of Expression as an Individual Right

One way of finding a violation of an individually based right to free expression in content restrictions is to treat the denial of funding on that basis as the same kind of wrong as that associated with a criminal prosecution: an imposition (admittedly a lesser one) on the expression of a view. An obvious problem for this approach is that someone denied public funding is still "free" to pursue his project with private funding.

Any claim that freedom of expression in contemporary society has a "positive" dimension, requiring not merely forbearance but support, faces the obvious objection that it would give a moral or legal grievance to the vast majority of grant applicants who are denied public funding. Either the state would have to fund everyone who applied, or it would have to award grants randomly as the only alternative in the face of scarcity. Both seem absurd. At most, a concern for interference with expression would be appropriate where the denial of funding could be plausibly construed as an *act* of interference—for example, the withdrawal or suspension of funds that had already been awarded.[10]

A more promising way of finding the violation of individual rights to free expression may be to consider content restrictions as "unconstitutional conditions." Under this judicial doctrine, of broad but uncertain scope, the government's discretion to deny a benefit altogether does not permit it to condition that benefit on restrictions of the recipients' constitutional rights—for example, the government cannot make payment of welfare benefits contingent on the recipients' adherence to speech restrictions.

One standard argument is that such conditions are unconstitutional because they are coercive: the waiver of the constitutional right is not truly voluntary. The problems with this approach are well illustrated by its application to content restrictions. Artists in this country are not literally starving, and their acceptance of content restrictions on their art cannot be regarded as coerced by hunger or some other biological imperative. We might instead, like some recent political philosophers, see coercion as a normative rather than a psychological concept,[11] and regard a condition as coercive because it is unjustifiable, not because it is irresistible. That, however, only defers the question of whether content restrictions are unconstitutionally coercive, since we could only regard them as coercive if we had already concluded, on independent grounds, that they were not justifiable.

Most recent accounts of the doctrine of unconstitutional conditions regard it as serving to limit the power acquired by an activist state through its financial support of an increasing range of its citizens' activities.[12] In one of the most persuasive of these accounts, Kathleen Sullivan argues that the doctrine should be understood to bar offers by the state whose primary purpose or effect is "to pressure recipients to alter a choice about exercise of a preferred constitutional liberty in a direction favored by government."[13] It could be argued under this interpretation that even though the state is free to provide no funding for art and science, it cannot condition funding on the absence of affront or offense in the proposed projects. To do so would be to engage in an unacceptable manipulation of the self-expression of its citizens in a direction favored by the government.

It is not clear, however, that conditioning grants on a lack of offense or affront would constitute unacceptable manipulation in this sense. The purpose of Helms's conditions was not, arguably, to pressure grant applicants to exercise their "preferred constitutional liberties" in less offensive ways, but to ensure that taxpayers would not have to subsidize projects they regarded as offensive.[14] This purpose would be fully satisfied even if the net effect of the Helms amendment were to increase the production of offensive work—for example, by liberating private funds for offensive art or science.

It is, of course, debatable whether the purpose of the Helms amendment was so limited. It could certainly be argued that the Helms amendment, like the Hyde amendment, which withheld federal Medicaid funding for most abortions, was really a rearguard action against a constitutionally protected activity, intended to discourage not merely government subsidies but the activity itself. The *effect* of the Helms amendment, however, would have been far more limited than the effect of the Hyde amendment. Daniel Shapiro observes that NEA funding in 1989 was a small fraction of the $114.7 billion in private giving for the arts that year. Shapiro speculates that, given the adversary posture of the private arts community, the overall funding prospects for the kind of works targeted by the Helms amendment may actually have improved.[15]

These considerations about the purpose and effect of funding conditions appear to cut the other way for scientific research. It seems clear that many, if not most, critics of genetic research on criminal behavior want to see an end not merely to government subsidies for such research but to the research itself. While government support may increase the threats posed by the research, by suggesting official approval of genetic explanations and raising the specter of coercive applications, few critics would find the research acceptable if it were carried out under strictly private auspices.

Moreover, the adverse effect of restrictions on public funding would be considerably more severe for scientific research than for art. Although public funding is only a small part of total funding for the arts, public funding for science has recently been estimated to constitute more than 60 percent of all spending for science in the United States.[16] Few major research programs could be carried out without government funding.

Despite the greater dependence of scientific research on government support, however, it is not clear that the doctrine of unconstitutional conditions should apply to the public funding of science. The principal evil the doctrine seeks to avoid is not present in this setting because the choices the government seeks to influence are made in a domain where the individual's own preferences lack sovereignty. Scientific research may have once been a personal expression of the researcher's intellectual curiosity or conviction, but, because of its increasing cost and social importance, it has become a collaborative undertaking in the public domain. Whole areas of scientific research, from nuclear fission and fusion to artificial intelligence, have been midwifed, if not created, by intensive government sponsorship.[17] Although an individual's choices about what research areas to pursue, and what hypotheses to test, are in one sense private, those who apply for research grants choose to enter an area of activity that has long been regarded as public. In seeking to shape individual choices about what research areas to pursue and what hypotheses to test, the government is following a two-hundred-year-old, bipartisan tradition of selective government support for research and development.[18]

Art also has a long history of public sponsorship, but it is more entrenched in the private domain. While artists, like researchers, must often seek public funding to carry out their work, artistic creation is too closely tied to individual expression to be regarded as an entirely public activity. It is also more difficult in science than in art to make a distinction that Sullivan finds critical: between subsidies, in which the government has no direct interest in the product, and commissions, in which it does. Although most science grants are formally subsidies, the government's involvement in the research and its interest in the results are so strong that these awards often have the character of commissions. Much research is done "intramurally," by government scientists, and is often closely integrated with research funded "extramurally," by competitive grant. In this and other respects, the government often demonstrates a more direct interest in the subject matter and methods of the scientific research it funds than in the content and techniques of publicly subsidized art.

And yet, even if scientific research is securely within the public domain, there is something troubling in the government's declining to fund certain areas of inquiry that are of interest to the scientific community because of their potential for offense or social harm. More troubling still is the specter of government sponsorship of research designed to serve a narrow partisan or ideological agenda. The focus of these concerns, however, is not the rights of individual researchers, but the duty of government as a public steward.

Freedom of Expression as a Collective Interest

The second general strategy for treating content restrictions as a violation of free expression is informed by a "collectivist" view, which justifies freedom of expression in terms of its contribution to democratic deliberation. Here the objection to content restrictions is not that they violate an individual right to free expression, but that they impair the quality of public debate by excluding relevant information and argument: "Keeping ideas and information from the public, not the unfair treatment of the speaker, is the gist of the constitutional wrong."[18] For Owen Fiss, the leading contemporary exponent of this approach, the failure to promote the expression of unpopular ideas constitutes a violation of the government's obligation to be neutral among its citizens' competing viewpoints:

> The ideal of neutrality in the speech context not only requires that the state refrain from choosing among viewpoints, but also that it not structure public debate in such a way as to favor one viewpoint over another. The state must act as a high-minded parliamentarian, making certain that all viewpoints are fully and fairly heard.[20]

Whatever the merits of this approach as a general account of freedom of expression, it may seem particularly apt in evaluating public funding for art and science. Because it grounds freedom of expression in the collective good of "robust and wide-open" debate, it does not encumber the state with even a presumptive duty to subsidize the expressive activity of all citizens. Yet because it stresses the importance of breadth and diversity in the public forum, it offers, or seems to offer, strong protection for unpopular views:

> In the allocative context, the state's decision will necessarily have an impact on which viewpoints are heard by the public, and the state's obligation of neutrality requires that it make certain that the public debate is as rich and varied as possible.... [A] court must ascertain whether the allocative decision would contribute to a debate on national issues that is "uninhibited, robust, and wide-open," or whether its effect would be just the opposite.[21]

If certain views have been ignored or neglected because of the offense they give, the government may have all the more reason to promote their expression. In effect, Fiss regards neutrality as a matter of nondiscrimination among viewpoints, which may require "affirmative action" to assure a fair hearing for viewpoints that have been ignored or marginalized.[22]

There are, however, serious problems in this effort to find a denial of free expression in the funding agency's failure to promote a public debate "as rich and varied as possible." First, even if a funding agency is committed to supporting unpopular viewpoints, it will inevitably make poor judgments on specific cases that detract from the breadth and vigor of public debate. Fiss surely would not want to treat such unavoidable lapses as First Amendment violations. But it is not clear how he would distinguish venial from mortal sins without recourse to the agency's intentions in rejecting a proposal—a "neutrality of intent" standard that Fiss rejects as too easy to satisfy and too difficult to enforce.[23]

But the more basic question for Fiss's account is how the state can maintain neutrality among competing viewpoints while assuring the richness and vigor of public debate. Neutrality among competing viewpoints may not be compatible with what Fiss takes to be the overarching goal of a system of free expression: the promotion of democratic deliberation.

The neutrality of "high-minded parliamentarians" which Fiss takes as a model is usually understood in strictly procedural terms: the Speaker of the House of Commons makes sure that members speak in turn, use the proper forms of address, and so on. The procedural neutrality demanded of them is also required of funding agencies: agencies must consistently enforce deadlines and avoid conflicts of interest. But such procedural neutrality assures neither the full and fair presentation of marginalized viewpoints nor a rich and vigorous debate. Significantly, real parliamentarians are not held responsible for the *quality* of the debate, but only for its procedural regularity and civility.

Fiss recognizes that something more than procedural neutrality is required of those who moderate democratic deliberation. There is also a need for

> a sense of the public agenda, a grasp of the issues that are now before the public and what might plausibly be brought before it, and then an appraisal of the state of public discourse, not to decide who is right or who is wrong, but to see whether all the positions on the issue are being fully and fairly presented so that the people can make a meaningful choice.[24]

Fiss does not regard these kinds of judgments as compromising neutrality; he appears to believe that a moderator can maintain her neutrality merely by declining to "decide who is right and who is wrong." But the mere refusal to decide among opposing viewpoints does not assure neutrality. Structuring a public debate requires threshold judgments about what issues should be addressed, how they should be addressed, and who should address them—all of which are nonneutral judgments about urgency, relevance, and credibility.[25]

More broadly, there is a tension in the conception of a democratic moderator offered by Fiss, between the commitment to a public debate that promotes "meaningful choice" and the commitment to a neutrality that requires that "all the positions on an issue [be] fully and fairly presented." The very idea of presenting "all the positions on an issue" is problematic: it is unclear how we would identify all the positions on any given issue, and the demand that all the positions be presented is perverse.[26] It would oblige the moderator to secure the full and fair presentation of obscure, implausible positions that no one in the community actually holds by, for example, paying skilled advocates to present them. Surely this is an obligation that Fiss would reject.

But if the moderator has no such obligation, why should she be obliged to present "all the positions" that happen to be held by members of the community? It might seem wise to adopt the presumption that any position held by someone in the community is worth presenting; in this way, the moderator might reduce the real dangers of complacency and insularity. But the presumption is surely rebuttable. Anyone who has listened to a late-night call-in show will appreciate that some views, however deeply held, can only confuse the debate. A commitment to ensuring meaningful democratic choice through rich and robust public discussion may thus conflict with a commitment to presenting all the positions, especially if time and resources are limited.

I suspect that some of the appeal of the requirement that "all the positions" be presented arises from a confusion between neutrality and equality. Thus, Fiss contends that Mapplethorpe's work presents the viewpoint of a marginalized community and that the refusal to fund his work reinforces the orthodoxy responsible for its marginalization.[27] This may well be a valid point, but as an argument for funding Mapplethorpe's work it is not consistent with the neutrality Fiss demands. Some regard the marginalization of the gay community as a good thing, and to treat it as a bad thing, and to make its rectification a high priority, is to take a strong substantive position on a controversial issue.

These tensions in Fiss's approach surface in its application to state funding of research on genetics and crime. The issue, in Fiss's terms, is whether it would enhance the vigor and breadth of public debate on the causes and control of crime to investigate whether genetic differences among individuals or groups contribute to a predisposition for violent or predatory behavior. That decision can hardly be made on neutral grounds. Those who support such research insist that its pursuit would enhance the public debate, not only because it would help explain crime and facilitate humane interventions but also because the very idea that there are significant genetic factors in criminal predisposition has been dismissed or marginalized in the recent debate. Those who oppose the research argue that its pursuit would only confuse and polarize the public debate and that the claim of individual or group differences is a red herring, diverting attention from the overwhelmingly environmental causes of crime and treating a social and political problem as a medical one. The state cannot decide whether to fund research on genetics and crime without taking sides.

Finally, the underlying appeal Fiss makes to the pursuit of substantive equality as a basis for public funding is double-edged. Fiss claims that equality is served by art that presents the perspectives of marginalized communities; others claim that equality is threatened by scientific research that searches for genetic variations in behavioral disposition among individuals or groups. Whether or not these specific claims are valid, the government's commitment to greater equality may give public agencies reason to oppose some artistic and scientific projects even as it gives them reason to support others.

The Peer Review Process

If the government cannot achieve the neutrality of a high-minded parliamentarian in its funding of art and science, perhaps it can satisfy a less demanding standard of procedural neutrality by deferring to the usual arbiters of merit in these domains — the art and science establishments — and the peer-review process by which they assess merit. David Cole argues that although such deference cannot achieve the substantive neutrality demanded by Fiss, it does prevent the government from monopolizing the public debate.[28] Although the agencies that decide which artistic projects and research programs to fund are hardly neutral in their points of view, they are insulated from direct political pressure by their employment of an independent peer-review process.

On this view, peer-review panels function like juries in assuring that decision making is decentralized and subject to only limited review. To impose content restrictions on the review process from outside is to compromise the independence that keeps this process from being dominated by propaganda and partisan agendas. This objection to content restrictions is based on the dangers of government "speech," not the threat to individual expression.[29]

Cole's call for procedural deference, however, ignores the extent to which political interests already shape the structure of public funding. The mandates and budgets of the public funding agencies, as well as their research agendas and funding priorities, often reflect the views of successive administrations and Congresses about what subjects should be open to artistic exploration or scientific inquiry.

The stamp of politics and ideology is particularly evident in government funding of research that investigates the causes and control of impulsive, aggressive, and criminal behavior. On the one hand, conservative scholars like James Q. Wilson have complained that since the World War II, administrations committed to the proposition that human behavior is largely determined by environmental conditions and modifiable by environmental interventions have discouraged the funding of research that would explore genetic and biological differences in behavioral dispositions, as well as genetic and biological constraints on their malleability.[30] Scholars like Wilson see the willingness of recent administrations to fund such research as restoring a balance and reducing the sway of ideology over public funding.

On the other hand, liberal and radical scholars see something disturbing if not sinister in government support for such research: a cynical attempt to account for the failure of half-hearted social reforms by looking to the genetic or biological recalcitrance of their beneficiaries. These scholars point to a long history of government-sponsored research into alleged biological differences whose existence was supposed to justify differences in political and social status. Given the conflicting agendas and cross-purposes of government agencies, there is likely to be some truth to conservative and liberal claims alike. This very ambivalence, however, reduces the threat Cole perceives in government speech: if the government speaks out of both sides of its mouth, it can hardly have a monopolistic impact on public discourse.

Moreover, Cole's procedural approach may be inappropriate even if there is a significant threat to public discourse from government speech. Research strategies and priorities often raise issues of public importance that are not appropriate for resolution on a case-by-case basis by independent agencies. It is instructive to compare two sets of issues that are resolved in this way with one that has not been: human subject protection and demographic representativeness, on the one hand, and fetal tissue research, on the other. In the former areas there is an existing or emerging social consensus on general policy: researchers should minimize risks to human subjects and should not put those subjects at significant risk without their fully informed and voluntary agreement, and researchers should examine the benefits and risks of new treatments to all major population subgroups.[31] Decisions about whether risks to subjects have been minimized, whether consent has been adequately informed, and whether the benefits and risks of a new treatment may differ for different subpopulations are appropriately left to expert committees.

In contrast, there is a widely shared conviction that the decision about whether, or under what conditions, to permit fetal tissue research should not be left to scientific experts. It is generally agreed that the moral status of embryos and gametes and the moral constraints on their use are outside the province of expert judgment and can be adequately resolved only by interdisciplinary dialogue and public debate. Whether the actual resolution of those issues by recent administrations has been satisfactory, public interest in, and influence on, government policy in this area is entirely warranted.[32]

In some respects, research on genetics and criminal behavior would seem to warrant the same kind of public and interdisciplinary debate. Expert panels can hardly be expected to resolve, on a case-by-case basis, deep disagreement about whether such research has any appropriate role to play in explaining and controlling criminal behavior. Furthermore, many of the risks posed by such research are related to its perception and appropriation; they can be mitigated only slightly, if at all, by the efforts of individual researchers. Finally, decisions about the propriety of pursuing such research cannot be based on an *ad hoc* weighing of benefits and burdens. There is a seductive, but, I think, misleading analogy to the courtroom rule which permits a judge to suppress relevant evidence if its "probative value" is outweighed by its "potential for confusion and prejudice." It is far easier to assess, and compare, these opposing considerations in a trial than in society at large.

It might be argued, however, that the harms anticipated from genetic research on social behavior are of a different sort from those contemplated in the debate about fetal tissue research and that their very consideration is antithetical to the values that underlie the public funding of science. The debate about fetal tissue research concerns the appropriate means of acquiring knowledge; the debate about behavioral genetic research concerns the very desirability of acquiring knowledge. Public funding of science is, arguably, premised on the view that acquiring scientifically interesting knowledge is a good thing, even if its acquisition may be properly limited by restrictions on means. To refuse to fund research because of fear about the direct or indirect impact of its findings belies the moral commitment to the pursuit of knowledge on which the public funding of science is based. This raises the issue that I will pursue in the remainder of this paper: whether a society whose funding policies appear to recognize the value of unfettered scientific inquiry has a principled basis for refusing to fund or impose restrictions on the funding of certain areas of research.

Equality versus Scientific Inquiry

In the related area of government funding for the arts, Robert Post has suggested that the state's participation in public discourse through its funding activity gives rise to a tension between the values the government seeks to promote through its participation—in particular, artistic excellence—and the neutrality we generally demand of the government in the realm of public discourse, which requires that it refrain from promoting particular values out of deference to the autonomy and self-determination of its citizens.[33] Post sees the conflict as unavoidable if the government is to fund art at all, since that use of government funds is predicated on values that not all citizens share or can reasonably be expected to share.

The conflict about government funding for scientific research cannot be framed in quite the same way. The values in conflict—the pursuit of scientific knowledge and the achievement of political and social equality by vulnerable minorities—do not neatly align with Post's constitutional norms of democratic self-government and community self-determination.[34] In the apparent conflict between scientific inquiry and equality for vulnerable groups, both sides can invoke both of Post's constitutional norms. Vigorous scientific inquiry and the knowledge it yields appear critical for democratic self-government, but so does equality of respect for the participants in the deliberative process. Similarly, the pursuit of science and the achievement of social and political equality are both deeply held but not universal values in American society.

Fortunately, we do not need to resolve the conflict between the two apparently conflicting values in the controversy over science funding by deciding which has greater weight or closer association with constitutional norms. A critical examination of both values suggests possibilities for reconciliation. We may find that political equality is not threatened by the possible findings of human genetic research or that our commitment to the pursuit of scientific knowledge rests on assumptions or beliefs that require consideration of its social impact: on a rebuttable assumption of its general utility or on its contribution to democratic self-rule.

Rationales for Public Funding

It could be argued that there is a categorical reason for a liberal-democratic society to refuse to fund any research into individual or group differences in genetic features that appear relevant to the functions of citizenship. To fund research that looks for significant congenital differences in the capacity to reason or to obey the law would be to support a challenge to the empirical premises of a liberal-democratic society. Although the state must permit individuals to offer such challenges, it need not subsidize them.

One obvious response to this argument would be to deny that a liberal-democratic society rests on empirical assumptions that would be challenged by the results of individual- or group-difference research. The assumption of moral and political equality is compatible with significant differences in intelligence and temperament. Contemporary democratic theory holds that meaningful participation requires only limited intelligence, psychometrically defined; contemporary moral and legal theory treats people as capable of, and responsible for, self-control, even if they are congenitally impulsive or aggressive. Research revealing large individual or group differences in intelligence or temperament would clarify, not undermine, our commitment to moral and political equality.

But although political equality may be consistent with the recognition of large differences in intelligence and temperament among individuals or groups, the denial of political equality has often been based on the invocation of such differences. Starting with Francis Galton, many genetic researchers have claimed to find an evolutionary hierarchy among humans and have presented their findings as having profoundly illiberal political implications. Current genetic-difference research may not have the same political agenda and may yield far more modest claims of relevant differences, but it may still contribute to the recalcitrant conviction that people lack sufficient biological commonalities for political equality.

That conviction lies near the heart of discriminatory institutions and practices in the United States. As Andrew Koppelman argues, the ultimate target of civil rights legislation is the pervasive belief that some people deserve less concern and respect, political power and social privilege, because of their race, gender, or other "ascriptive" characteristics.[35] This belief has received, and may continue to receive, aid and comfort from research that investigates differences in intelligence and temperament associated with those characteristics. Can the destructive potential of such research be taken into account in funding decisions in a way that is consistent with our strong public commitment to the support of scientific inquiry?

In contemporary America, scientific research receives support from at least three sources: a commitment to the more complete understanding of the natural and social worlds, and thus to scientific knowledge for its own sake; a belief in the social utility of scientific knowledge; and a conviction that democratic self-rule requires that government actions and policies be guided by scientific research and subject to scientific evaluation. These are all public values with strong, if ambivalent, public support. All three values can be seen as fragments of a more comprehensive Enlightenment faith in science and rationality.[36] The first value, which I will call "epistemic," preserves the Enlightenment reverence for scientific knowledge as an end in itself; the second, which I will call "utilitarian," evinces an Enlightenment optimism about the beneficence of scientific discovery; the third, which I will call "deliberative," is heir to the Enlightenment tradition of rationality in government, valuing science for its contribution to informed decision making. In a democratic society, this requires not only that the information yielded by the research be useful to the decision maker but that it contribute to, or at least not subvert, the democratic character of the decision-making process.

These rationales for the public funding of science are not freestanding. Few people support science funding on one of these grounds alone; most support it on all three. But in the late twentieth century, we have become painfully aware of the possibilities for conflict among, and within, these rationales. Research that has great explanatory power may also have terrible destructive potential; research that promises great social benefit may also threaten grave social harm; research that provides valuable information for democratic decision makers may also be used, or understood, in ways that polarize or undermine democratic decision making.

The three rationales differ in how they accommodate concerns about the harmful effects of scientific research. An epistemic rationale is the least amenable to balancing scientific knowledge against social harm, since it values scientific knowledge for its own sake. Even though it is committed to the pursuit of scientific truth, however, it need not treat all scientific truths equally. Knowledge that deepens and enlarges our understanding of the natural and social world is more valuable than knowledge that merely fills in gaps or supplies minor details. Thus, although the epistemic rationale does not provide for balancing, it does discriminate among different types of scientific inquiry on the basis of their theoretical interest.

A utilitarian rationale values scientific research for its potential benefits, but it is committed, at least in theory, to taking account of its potential harm as well. In its optimism, however, it may treat all scientific inquiry as presumptively beneficial and be reluctant to curtail it except in the face of the most serious and imminent harms. Moreover, in its reliance on interpersonal comparisons of welfare, it may not take adequate account of less concrete and quantifiable harms. It does recognize the need for some kind of balancing nevertheless.

If an epistemic rationale does not give equal weight to all scientific knowledge, and a utilitarian rationale allows, and may require, an assessment of social benefits and costs, a deliberative rationale takes account of some, but not all, harmful consequences in assessing the potential of the research for promoting or impairing public debate. In Fiss's terms, the issue is whether the research findings will enhance or diminish the vigor, breadth, and richness of democratic deliberations. Even if research were highly relevant to public deliberations, it might be likely to confuse, inflame, or polarize public debate. Even if it did not have a direct effect on the tenor of public debate, it might impair the democratic character of that debate by discouraging or marginalizing minority participation.[37]

Thus, only an exclusively epistemic rationale would ignore the harmful effects of scientific research. Divorced from any concern about social utility or democratic self-government, however, that rationale carries little weight. Although it remains an important element of public support for science, the commitment to scientific truth for its own sake has been tempered by doubts about the objectivity of scientists and the objective character of scientific knowledge. Even though few people, including academics, embrace a comprehensive skepticism about scientific knowledge, there is a broad recognition that scientific theories are often underdetermined by the available data and that scientific judgments are profoundly influenced by the assumptions, sensibilities, and interests of the larger society of which scientists are a part. This recognition is reinforced by diminished expectations about the explanatory power of science, as many fundamental questions, like the origin of the universe, seem more elusive or less empirical than they once appeared. Although scientific truth may be a somewhat devalued currency, it is still possible to imagine a hard choice about the funding of research with great theoretical interest but destructive social potential. This choice is not presented, or so I will argue, by public funding for genetic research into crime and violence.

Group-Difference Research

I begin with what I think is the easier case: research that looks for differences in behavioral genetic predispositions among racial or ethnic groups (which I will refer to as group-difference research). It is tempting to dismiss such research on strictly scientific grounds: the vagaries of racial and ethnic classification severely limit the scientific value of studying racial or ethnic groups as biological categories or of looking for genetic differences among those groups. Noam Chomsky makes this point with respect to research into a genetic basis for racial differences in IQ:

> In the present state of scientific understanding, there would appear to be little scientific interest in the discovery that one partly heritable trait correlates (or not) with another partly heritable trait. Such questions might be interesting if the results had some bearing, say, on hypotheses about the physiological mechanisms involved, but they do not.[38]

There is no reason to think that the state of scientific understanding in this area has changed in the generation since Chomsky wrote. As Martin Zuckerman concluded in 1990, "generalizations about the innate intelligence or social responsibility of large and genetically diverse segments of the population . . . serve no important scientific purpose, given the present ambiguities in the definition of the independent variables and immense sampling problems."[39]

This lack of theoretical interest significantly diminishes the appeal that group-difference research has on an epistemic rationale. If such research has little potential for contributing to our understanding of the natural and social worlds, its pursuit requires less deference. To decline to fund research into the genetic basis of racial differences in intelligence or behavioral disposition is not to block our understanding of important general truths.[40]

The lack of theoretical interest of the research also figures in a utilitarian weighing of its social benefits and costs. Ned Block and Gerald Dworkin argued a generation ago that the social value of knowledge about the genetic basis, if any, for racial differences in IQ was outweighed by its social costs:

> [I]t is true that knowledge of a genetic component to racial differences would be relevant to our expectations of the effect on reducing differences of giving everyone, for example, a middle-class environment. No doubt, having realistic expectations about such things is better than not having them, but it seems a small benefit compared with the harm ... that might flow from investigating genotypic racial differences.[41]

The benefits are likely to be even more limited, and the harm greater, for research on genotypic racial differences in criminal predisposition. Any official use of "positive" results from racial-difference research by the criminal justice system—for example, in the predictive models used for sentencing and parole decisions—would be morally and constitutionally unacceptable. The potential for harm is obvious. Many Americans now see violent crime mainly as an African American problem, in part because of the disproportionate number of African Americans in prison and the inordinate media attention to "black-on-white" crimes, in part because of deeply embedded prejudices that make violent crime appear more characteristic of blacks than whites and that obscure the enormous differences in behavior and disposition within groups. Needless to say, a claim that African Americans are more predisposed genetically to crime than are other racial or ethnic groups would greatly reinforce a stereotype that already inflicts terrible damage on the lives of all young African American men. Even if there were genetic differences between races, there is no reason that such differences should affect our treatment of individuals, but there is every reason to fear that they would.

I come to a similar conclusion with respect to the deliberative rationale. We can put the question in Fiss's terms by asking if the knowledge such research seeks would advance the public debate on the causes and control of crime. No reasonable person denies the dominant role of social factors in creating racial disparities in crime rates; no reasonable social policy needs to assume the absence of any genetic differences among groups in relevant traits.[42] To deny group-difference research any relevance to the public debate, liberals should be willing to let go of the assumption that *any* difference in rates of offending is due to social injustice. They do not need that assumption to argue convincingly that current disparities in rates of offending reflect egregious injustice. No remotely plausible claim of genetic differences could explain either the magnitude of those disparities or their massive increase over the past thirty years.

A deliberative rationale would consider not only the slight relevance of group-difference research for public debate on the causes and control of crime but also its adverse effect on the tenor and fairness of public discussion. The mere fact that certain racial or ethnic groups are "under investigation" for a genetic predisposition to criminal or violent behavior would deflect attention even further from the causes of crime that are within the control of a liberal-democratic society and would make it even harder for those racial and ethnic groups to take part in the discussion about crime on equal terms.

Given the limited theoretical interest, practical value, and policy relevance of group-difference research, the denial of government funding for that research does not present a significant conflict between the public commitments to scientific inquiry and to social and political equality. The public values underlying the public support of scientific inquiry lend, at most, slight and ambivalent support to that research. Government support of the research would evince either an insensitivity to the interests of the vulnerable minorities who are threatened by it or a mistaken belief that it really has significant theoretical importance, social utility, or policy relevance.

Individual-Difference Research

Research on individual differences in genetic predisposition fares better than research on group differences on an epistemic rationale because it has greater theoretical interest. Many scientists who oppose group-difference research support individual-difference research on this basis. Zuckerman, for example, argues that "a more important task" than investigating possible group differences "is to discover the biological and social bases of individual differences in personality and intelligence within populations."[43] Arguably, research on genetic and biological differences among individuals is required for an adequate assessment of the contribution made by social and environmental differences; the failure to study the former would distort our picture of the forces that shape human behavior.

The theoretical interest of the research is not dispositive, however. On a utilitarian rationale, we also need to consider the social benefits and harms of the research. Defenders of individual-difference research argue that it will promote less-punitive responses to crime and that the research will eventually yield an array of preventative measures and treatments more humane and more effective than incarceration. Critics, however, see the rise of a therapeutic response to crime as an ominous development, threatening a massive expansion of social control. They argue that it would be reckless, or at least premature, to attempt to develop biological techniques for predicting and "treating" juvenile delinquency or adult criminality, especially when those techniques would be placed in the hands of educational and criminal justice institutions that have shown so little capacity to serve their clients humanely or to respond appropriately to the array of social conditions that provoke misconduct. While the forced medication of boisterous and disruptive children—the specter raised by radical critics—seems unlikely in light of our constitutional scruples, it is not difficult to imagine genetic testing and medical treatment being made a condition of probation or parole or being "offered" to disruptive or unreliable employees as an alternative to termination. Other pharmacological treatments, from anabuse to lithium, have been introduced in this way, setting a strong and dangerously seductive precedent.

Nevertheless, we may be able to impose, and enforce, an indefinite moratorium on some of the more clearly problematic uses of individual-difference research, such as genetic testing by public school or juvenile justice systems. And we can reasonably hope that our society will someday become fair and humane enough to make conscientious use of the findings of such research for education, counseling, and environmental modification.

Finally, a deliberative rationale offers some support for individual-difference research. Defenders of this research argue that its findings may contribute to the public debate on the causes and control of crime. Consider the familiar conservative claim that the appalling conditions of the contemporary urban ghetto do not deprive its occupants of a meaningful choice about whether to commit violent crimes because, after all, so many of them do not. This use of the "moral majority" to reproach the minority assumes that there are no other differences between the two groups that affect their capacity for self-control. That assumption would be challenged by evidence that those in the criminal minority were more likely to have some genetic factor that predisposed them to impulsive or aggressive conduct. Such evidence, however, would be double-edged: it would also challenge the assumption, more congenial to liberals, that what separates the criminal minority from the law-abiding majority is entirely environmental: worse family circumstances, greater material privations, or stronger social pressures. In such ways, evidence about individual genetic predispositions may sharpen and focus the public debate on crime, responsibility, and punishment. Of course, any such refinement in the public debate must be weighed against its potential to increase racial polarization.

On both a utilitarian and deliberative rationale, the greatest concern may be the public perception of the research. Any evidence of individual differences in behavioral genetic predispositions, however slight, environmentally mediated, or mutable, is likely to be seen as evidence of the recalcitrance of serious offenders and the incapacity of the educational, social welfare, and criminal justice systems to divert or reform them. Worse, much of the public will regard the identification of *any* genetic predisposition as implicating the black community, whatever the researchers' disclaimers.[44] Still, it is important to recognize that this risk arises from the misunderstanding of research findings. To return to the language of the Helms amendment, I do not think individual-difference research can be said to "denigrate a class of citizens on the basis of race," even if it increases the risk of denigration by third parties. While this distinction may not be reflected in a standard cost-benefit analysis, it strikes me as having an important bearing on the question of whether the government should fund such research.

Although it seems unreasonable to ignore the potential for abuse or misunderstanding, it also seems fundamentally unfair to decline to fund proposed research solely on that basis. To do so would confer a "demagogue's veto" on those who deliberately misappropriate or misrepresent research despite the researcher's best efforts to limit its use or clarify its findings.[45] I do not think there is a general solution to this conundrum, except to suggest that the responsibility for preventing abuse and misrepresentation should be shared by the researcher and the funding agency and that a public funding agency deciding whether to fund a sensitive project should be able to take account of the researcher's commitment to preventing or mitigating abuse and misrepresentation.

Conclusion

Research on individual genetic differences in criminal predisposition fares better than does research on group differences under all three rationales for the public funding of science. But although it seems possible to reconcile the pursuit of scientific inquiry in this area with the protection of vulnerable minorities, the issue is close enough to warrant further consideration. The question, however, is what form that consideration should take: should it simply be a factor in decisions on individual grants, or does it require a more general, and more public, resolution?

This appears to be an issue on which interdisciplinary dialogue is critical. The risk of oppressive social control (if not of stigmatization) depends to some extent on what is likely to be found by the research—for example, how easy it will be to screen for genetic variations associated with criminal or violent behavior and what such variations will really predict. Such questions are as speculative as they are important, and genetic researchers are needed to make educated guesses. At the same time, researchers may not be well equipped to assess the risks of social harm: they may be insufficiently sensitive to those risks or unduly optimistic about the prospects for reducing them.

Although the standard review process for science funding has an interdisciplinary component—scientific "peers" first judge the merits of proposed research, then a council of scientists and laypersons decide how well those projects serve the purposes of the funding program—the issues raised by genetic research on crime and violence do not seem amenable to such case-by-case resolution. Questions about how this research would fit into the "portfolio" of federally funded science, and how to manage its presentation and application, would be better addressed on a systematic basis.

Two blue-ribbon panels have already examined the portfolio of federally conducted and funded research on genetic and biological factors in violent and criminal behavior and absolved them of the most serious charges, including racial targeting, made by some critics.[46] And a National Research Council Report on understanding and preventing violence has called for more studies of genetic and biological factors within integrated programs of biosocial research.[47]

I hesitate to recommend yet another multidisciplinary panel. Yet I do not think that any of the three panels that have met thus far have adequately addressed the broader social harms threatened by individual-difference research. Nor have they developed adequate guidelines for presenting results to the popular media, responding to misrepresentations, and limiting research applications. More important, none of these panels even considered the issue of what potential uses of research findings, especially by the educational and criminal justice systems, are unacceptable. It would be prudent to have an enforceable moratorium on certain uses in place before the rush to apply the research findings begins.

So I think we do need another panel, one with a more comprehensive mandate, similar to the panels on human subject protection and informed consent formed in the 1970s, to give the greatest possible scope to its deliberations and the greatest authority to its recommendations. If it did approve genetic and biological research on individual differences in behavioral predisposition, it would face the difficult task of deciding how to incorporate safeguards into case-by-case review. This, however, is a challenge that has been met before.

If such a panel concluded that the substantial risk of misunderstanding and abuse should not preclude funding for individual-difference research, it might still impose significant restrictions on funding sources and applications. It may be unwise for genetic research on crime and violence to get funding from agencies that are seeking results of immediate practical value. It may be more appropriate to consider funding this research as basic genetic and neurobiological science, judging it by its potential contribution to those areas rather than by its potential value in controlling crime and violence. If, as the researchers maintain, their rationales have significant explanatory potential in these areas, their projects should flourish under this funding rubric; if, as critics claim, the research has little scientific value, it should lose out in the competition.

Researchers who receive funding for individual-difference research will surely have an obligation to prevent or mitigate any harm associated with their work. They must publicly challenge distorted media reports on, or questionable applications of, their findings. A public funding agency should demand assurances that the researcher will take this obligation seriously, and assess its fulfillment in any performance audit.[48]

I have argued that the state may properly consider the risk of social harm associated with such research, and I have examined some of the complexities in assessing the risk. Decisions on whether to fund specific research projects despite that risk will ultimately depend on judgments about which reasonable people will differ: about the value of the proposed research to basic or theoretical science, the magnitude of the social harm that may follow from such research, and the feasibility of measures to mitigate that harm.

Notes

1. See, generally, Adrian Raine, *The Psychopathology of Crime: Criminal Behavior as a Clinical Disorder* (San Diego: Academic Press, 1993); Albert J. Reiss, Klaus A. Miczek, and Jeffrey A. Roth, eds., *Understanding and Preventing Violence: Volume 2: Biobehavioral Influences* (Washington, D.C.: National Academy Press, 1994).

2. See, for example, Diana Fishbein, "Prospects for the Application of Genetic Findings to Crime and Violence Prevention," in "Symposium: Genetics and Crime," *Politics and the Life Sciences* 15, no. 1 (1996): 91–94.

3. See David Wasserman, "In Defense of a Conference on Genetics and Crime: Assessing the Social Impact of a Public Debate," *The Chronicle of Higher Education,* 23 September 1992: A44; see also the introduction and commentaries by Evan Balaban, Roger Masters, and David Wasserman in "Symposium: Genetics and Crime" (see note 2).

4. For a sense of the debate, compare Richard C. Lewontin, "All in the Genes?" in idem, *Biology as Ideology: The Doctrine of DNA* (New York: Harper Collins, 1993), with Raine (see note 1). See also the commentaries by David Comings, Balaban, Gregory Carey and Irving Gottesman, David Goldman, and Wasserman in "Symposium: Genetics and Crime" (see note 2).

5. The 1989–1990 controversy over NEA funding is described by Owen M. Fiss in "State Activism and State Censorship," *The Yale Law Journal* 100 (1991): 1087–2106, 2088–96, and by Daniel Shapiro, "Free Speech and Art Subsidies," *Law and Philosophy* 14 (1995): 329–55, 329–30.

6. The provisions of the Helms amendment are discussed in Fiss (see note 5) and in Harry Brighouse, "Neutrality, Publicity, and State Funding of the Arts," *Philosophy and Public Affairs* 24 (1995): 35–63, 59.

7. Shapiro (see note 5), 330 n. 3, points out that such claims were made by many of the writers in two collections of essays on government funding for the arts that appeared shortly after the controversy.

8. See notes 5 and 6 for discussions of the Helms amendment.

9. Robert Post distinguishes self-governance and managerial rationales for free expression: the former value free expression for its role in political autonomy and democratic self-government; the latter for its role in the efficient resolution of practical political problems; see, for example, Robert Post, "Managing Deliberation: The Quandary of Democratic Dialogue," *Ethics* 103 (1993): 654–78. I would classify both of Post's rationales (or families of rationales) as collectivist because they value freedom of expression for its contribution to a collective political project. An individual-rights rationale as I understand it is not instrumental even in this limited sense. It regards limits on state interference with speech as a matter of respect for each person's dignity as a rational agent; it is concerned with autonomy in a Kantian sense, as opposed to the political autonomy of democratic self-government.

10. It might be argued that there was an act of interference not only in a funding agency's withdrawal or suspension of funds but also in its departure from its usual merit-based criteria for awarding grants. A "meritorious" grant rejected only because of potential offense could be regarded as suppressed rather than merely denied. Even if this claim were plausible for current funding decisions, it would no longer be plausible if a measure like the Helms amendment, which would change the standard criteria for awarding grants, were adopted. Content restrictions would then be embedded in the review process, rather than superimposed on it.

11. The outlines of a normative analysis of coercion were laid out by Robert Nozick in "Coercion," in Sidney Morgenbesser, Patrick Suppes, and Morton White, eds., *Philosophy, Science, and Method: Essays in Honor of Ernest Nagel* (New York: St. Martin's, 1969).

12. Notably, Seth Kreimer, "Allocational Sanctions: The Problem of Negative Rights in a Positive State," *University of Pennsylvania Law Review* 132 (1984): 1293–

1397; Kathleen M. Sullivan, "Unconstitutional Conditions," *Harvard Law Review* 102 (1989): 1415–1505.

13. Ibid., 1499–1500.

14. The added insult would be felt whether or not government funding of research were seen as endorsing it; see Fiss (see note 5), 2106 n. 42. The members of a vulnerable minority group could reasonably feel insulted at having to pay for research that denigrated their group even if the state were not seen as endorsing that research.

15. Shapiro (see note 5), 335, 344.

16. Stephen Goldberg, "Culture Class: Law and Science in America," *Yale Law Journal* 106 (1996): 151–95.

17. Ibid., 134–39, 154. Moreover, since virtually all scientists depend on outside funding, the imposition of the conditions does *not* burden some but not others on the basis of economic class and thereby does not create or reinforce "constitutional castes"; see Sullivan (see note 12), 1497–99.

18. Fiss (see note 5), 2100.

19. Ibid.

20. Ibid., 2101.

21. Ibid.

22. Ibid., 2100. The emphasis on neutrality also suggests one reason why it may be harder to justify funding restrictions on science than on art, although it is not a reason that Fiss would accept. The decision to fund any art may already involve a departure from the neutrality many liberal theorists require of the state, between all reasonable conceptions of the good. Harry Brighouse (see note 6) has recently argued, for example, that the public funding of art may violate neutrality, because it is not required for distributive justice, general welfare, or any other objective endorsed by all reasonable conceptions of the good (35–79).

It is, however, easier to make a case for the neutrality of funding scientific research, either in terms of its urgency—the claim made for medical research and the Manhattan Project—or in terms of its broad economic and social value—the claim made for basic theoretical research. As Stephen Goldberg (see note 16) points out, there is a broad consensus among liberals and conservatives, economists and humanists, that scientific research is of general benefit and that its benefit is most fully realized by leaving the decision about what research to fund to the scientists (38).

23. Fiss (see note 5), 2098–2100, 2102.

24. Ibid., 2101.

25. Fiss (ibid.) claims these kinds of judgments "are analogous to the judgments made by the great teachers of the universities of this nation as they structure discussion in their classes." But, as the recent controversies over "great books" curricula, Afrocentrism, and creationism make clear, such pedagogic judgments are deeply value-laden and controversial.

26. There may be indeterminacy and conflict about the delineation of possible positions. The assumption that a moderator can identify, let alone fully and fairly present, "all the positions" seems at least as controversial as the assumption, made by some defenders of the principle of indifference, that the set of alternative outcomes can be uniquely specified.

27. Fiss (see note 5), 2101.

28. David Cole, "Beyond Unconstitutional Conditions: Charting Spheres of Neutrality in Government-Funded Speech," *New York University Law Review* 67 (1992): 675–749.

29. Ibid., 702–17, 727–28.

30. Commentary delivered at a symposium on "The Debate over 'Genetics and Violence': The Silencing of Socially Charged Science," California Institute of Technology, 26 January 1995, one of a series of symposia on "Censorship and Silencing: Practices of Cultural Regulation."

31. President's Commission for the Study of Ethical Problems in Medicine and Biomedical and Behavioral Research, *Summing Up: A Final Report on Studies of the Ethical and Legal Problems in Medicine and Biomedical and Behavioral Research* (Washington, D.C.: U.S. Government Printing Office, 1983)

32. For a brief history of the ban on fetal tissue research and its partial lifting, see Joseph Palca, "Hurdles Remain for Embryo Researchers Seeking NIH Grants," *The Journal of NIH Research* 6 (1994): 40–41.

33. Robert Post, "Subsidized Speech," *Yale Law Journal* 106 (1996): 151–95.

34. It is not that the values underlying the funding of science are universal—the controversy over creationism makes it clear that they are not—or that the moral and political equality of minority groups is universally accepted.

35. Andrew Koppelman, *Antidiscrimination Law and Social Equality* (New Haven: Yale Univ. Press, 1996).

36. The Enlightenment roots of American public support for science are pointed out by Goldberg (see note 16), 26–28.

37. The three rationales for the public support of scientific research differ in whom they would assign authority to decide which scientific research to fund. With its premium on theoretical knowledge, the epistemic rationale favors the scientific community as the final arbiter of merit, especially as scientific knowledge becomes more esoteric. There may be difficult questions about how narrow or broad the relevant scientific community is, but this threshold question is one that must be resolved by the larger scientific community. Although a utilitarian rationale values useful knowledge, it recognizes that the utility of scientific information may not always be obvious to impatient laypersons. Thus, while it makes public officials the ultimate arbiters of scientific merit, it advises them to defer in most cases to the scientists' own judgments. A deliberative rationale also makes public officials the arbiters of scientific merit. Although the scientists themselves are in the best position to assess specific research strategies and techniques, they are not well equipped to decide whether research is relevant to public deliberation.

The issue of decision making authority becomes more complicated if the scientific community internalizes social norms. Deborah Johnson, for example, argues that science should be viewed as a profession, owing its authority and prerogatives to an implicit social compact to produce knowledge for the good of humanity. Forbidding the acquisition of certain knowledge on the grounds that it would not serve the good of humanity may not only be consistent with the norms of science; it may also be responsible professional conduct. So, while scientists may be the best decision makers for epistemic purposes, they may not take a strictly epistemic rationale in their decision making.

38. Quoted by Ned J. Block and Gerald Dworkin in "IQ, Heritability, and Inequality, Part 2," *Philosophy and Public Affairs* 4 (1974): 40–99, 96.

39. Marvin Zuckerman, "Some Dubious Premises in Research and Theory on Racial Differences: Scientific, Social, and Ethical Issues," *American Psychologist* 45 (1990): 1297–1303, 1301.

40. The limited theoretical interest of research into racial differences also makes the researchers' motives suspect and deepens their complicity in the scientific legitimation of racial injustice. If such racial-difference research cannot yield findings of great theoretical interest and causes obvious distress to the groups alleged to be weaker in intelligence or self-restraint, why pursue the research, except to make the case that existing disparities in academic achievement or criminal offending are "natural"?

41. Block and Dworkin (see note 38), 85.

42. Parallel arguments can be made, and have been, with respect to genetic research on race and IQ. No reasonable person denies the dominant role of social and economic conditions in accounting for racial disparities in income and achievement. The possibility of a genetic contribution would be relevant only against a claim that *any* disparity in income or achievement resulted from social or economic conditions. As Block and Dworkin (see note 38) recognize, "to the extent that arguments are advanced for proportionate-to-population quotas that rely on assumptions about the distribution of genotypic abilities, it becomes relevant to assess the validity of such assumptions" (85). The strongest arguments for affirmative action do not rely on such assumptions, however, and those who support affirmative action policies would be wise to forswear them. This seems a small price to pay for denying relevance to research on group differences in genetic endowment.

43. Zuckerman (see note 39), 1301.

44. Moreover, if researchers were to find genes or genetic markers associated with criminal behavior in individuals, other researchers inevitably would try to compare the incidence of those genes or markers in different racial and ethnic groups, with or without public funding. (The material for such comparisons may even be found within the research on individual predispositions if it studies multiracial populations and codes subjects by race.) There are good reasons to doubt that the researchers would discover significant group differences, or that the differences they found would correspond to differences in present rates of offending, but the very investigation of such hypotheses would, as I have argued above, reinforce invidious racial stereotypes.

45. There are interesting parallels to this issue in the controversy that gave rise to the Helms amendment. In the dispute over NEA funding of "obscene" and "indecent" art, much of the offense was secondhand, arising not from viewings of the disputed art but from lurid descriptions contained in mass mailings to the "religious right." Donald Wildmon, a leading crusader against NEA-funded art, mailed out blowups of pornographic images taken from very small fragments of very large collages done by David Wojnarowicz, who successfully sued Wildmon for misrepresenting his work. Incidents like this raise the question of how far the opponents of a work of art should be held accountable for creating or amplifying the offense on which they base their opposition.

46. Daryl A. Chamblee et al., *Report of the Panel on NIH Research on Antisocial, Aggressive, and Violence-Related Behaviors and Their Consequences* (Bethesda: National Institutes of Health, 1994).

47. Albert Reiss and Jeffrey Roth, eds., *Understanding and Preventing Violence: Volume 1* (Washington, D.C.: National Academy Press, 1993).

48. This is not to deny that there are limits to the safeguards and restrictions the government can impose. The gag order found unconstitutional in *Stanford v. Sullivan,* 773 F. Supp. 472 (D.D.C. 1991), may well have been too comprehensive, but it is hard to imagine a constitutional objection to a grant that required the recipient to cooperate with the funding agency in correcting any significant misrepresentations of the research to appear in the scientific or general media.

The Tutelary State: "Censorship," "Silencing," and the "Practices of Cultural Regulation"

Sanford Levinson

It is probably a sign of our postmodernist times that I choose to begin this chapter by focusing on problems raised by the title itself, which reflects the title of the seminar at which the paper was presented. In thinking about censorship, especially if one is a traditional liberal who emphasizes the limited role of the state, one almost reflexively calls up the basic drama of the state invoking its legal powers—including the threat of punishment underlying the law—to suppress, and thus to silence, "private" parties who wish to express themselves.[1] If this is the paradigm case, then the almost paradigmatic response for most liberals is to express appropriate dismay about the threat posed by the state and to adopt a corrective notion of the state as limited to presiding over—and seeking to safeguard—a "free marketplace of ideas." What this means, especially for Americans imbued in the tradition of Justices Oliver Wendell Holmes and Louis Brandeis, is that the state simply sets neutral procedural rules for the otherwise unfettered competition of ideas. What is foregrounded in this approach is the view of the state as a disinterested and somewhat distant *regulator* of the intellectual and cultural marketplace; concomitantly, what is pushed to the margins is recognition of the state as an active *participant* in that market. A canonical statement of this ideal is Owen Fiss's:

> The ideal of neutrality in the speech context not only requires that the state refrain from choosing among viewpoints, but also that it not structure public debate in such a way as to favor one viewpoint over another. The state must act as a high-minded parliamentarian, making certain that all viewpoints are fully and fairly heard.[2]

To be sure, neutral regulation may have consequences for particular speech. To deny a group the right to block traffic in order to mount a demonstration is to make it less likely that the group's views will in fact be communicated to an audience, but, or so the standard doctrine has it, the basis of this regulation is "content neutral," targeted not at *what* is said but only at *how* it is said. The state would presumably suppress the hindrance of traffic even were the demonstrators rallying in favor of the most popular of causes.

This view of the state as merely the benignly neutral traffic cop presiding over "robust" exchanges between and among private citizens is, I believe, quite naive, in part because it fails to pay adequate attention to the extent that the state itself speaks. Steven Schiffrin and Mark Yudof led the way within the legal academy by focusing on the specific phenomenon of "government speech," when the state becomes an active participant within the intellectual marketplace.[3] State authorities, whether they are presidents giving major policy addresses or teachers using state-mandated textbooks within the public school system, regularly articulate, in behalf of the state, highly contestable—and completely unneutral—views about important political and cultural matters. The danger of "silencing" those who disagree with the state's views comes, most often, not from any plausible fear of classic censorship—the overt punishment for offering views repugnant to state authorities—but, rather, from being "drowned out" in the marketplace by the superior resources often available to the state. Fiss, indeed, is quite aware of this: in an essay dealing in part with public funding of the arts, he condemns the "denial of a grant" to controversial projects on the ground that this "would impoverish public debate because it would reinforce the prevailing orthodoxy on an issue of great public importance."[4] Fiss's ideal "neutral" state in fact turns out to be self-consciously antagonistic to a congealed conventional wisdom.

The state may benefit from having more economic resources to devote to articulating its position than do its opponents, but one should be aware that an important resource that is also and uniquely available to the state is its ability to *legitimate* certain arguments merely by virtue of state endorsement. To adopt the influential philosophy of language associated with J. L. Austin, the state can sometimes speak with *illocutionary* force and thus call into being, through this "speech act," a new social reality.[5] From this perspective, the main threat posed by the state is that it will become an overweening *tutor* of the public, molding a distinct consciousness and subtly (or not so subtly) delegitimizing others who would wish to play a similarly tutelary role. In any event, one might well fear a state that so dominates the marketplace that alternative conceptions of the public good will find themselves not so much silenced—at least in the specific sense of becoming legally unsayable—as relegated to the margins of the social order because they are incapable of competing with the state's preferred vision.[6]

Those fearful of a tutelary state may even suggest that state speech be subject to censorship on occasion, although, from a traditional liberal perspective, it sounds willfully paradoxical to speak of the state as the object of censorship rather than the agency that (usually illegitimately) censors others. To be sure, there is one possible setting where censorship of the state makes sense even within the framework of liberalism: a "sovereign" state, after all, can consent, by treaty or other international agreement, to limit its own rights. At that point, from the traditional perspective, it is no longer a "perfect" sovereign because it is subject to the legal rule of some higher institutional realm that can legitimately claim the power to regulate—and thus possibly to censor—the speech of the subordinated state entity. Consider in this context the covenant in the Treaty of Peace between Israel and Jordan to "abstain from hostile or discriminatory propaganda against each other."[7] It seems accurate to describe this provision as an acceptance by these states that they will be open to significant and legitimate criticism (even if, as a practical matter, there are no formal legal sanctions available) should they articulate certain views, however sincerely held, when those views fall within the status described by the respective covenants.

It is even possible to read the U. S. Constitution as similarly limiting the power of either the national or a state government to state certain views. The easiest example would involve the First Amendment's ban on the "establishment" of religion. A majority of the current Supreme Court, led by Justice Sandra Day O'Connor, has interpreted this as, at the very least, prohibiting the "endorsement" by the state of explicitly religious points of view.[8] Thus, I think most (although in fact not all) constitutional scholars would agree that Congress could not constitutionally legislate the addition of "In Christ Is Our Redemption" to the flag or the coinage.[9] Lawyers would be much more hesitant to condemn as unconstitutional the addition of "Devoted to White Supremacy" to the U. S. or a state flag, although one could certainly make a nonfrivolous argument that this, too, would violate the antisubordination principle that many view as the core of the Fourteenth Amendment or the Due Process Clause of the Fifth Amendment.[10] To the extent that we are indeed founded on a principle of "equal concern and respect" for all members of the polity, then any such expression in the name of the state would be not only censurable, but, more to the point, also the proper object of judicially mandated (because constitutionally mandated) censorship.

However genuinely interesting the legal and theoretical dimensions of such censorship might be, my focus here is elsewhere. I want to explore some of the ramifications of the fact that "cultural regulation" occurs not only—indeed, increasingly rarely, at least in the United States—through the negative acts that overtly silence by threatening to punish those with given views, but, perhaps more significantly, through *affirmative* acts of the state that speak in behalf of the people, or "community," in whose name the state commonly claims to rule.[11]

As already suggested, *regulation* is an ambiguous term. We often speak of "*a* regulation" in the sense of a mandatory requirement or prohibition. Yet we also refer easily, especially if we have been influenced even in the slightest by Michel Foucault, to an unarticled "regulation" as a means of defining what is "regular" or, ultimately, "normal," within a given political-cultural order. Formally interdictive norms are only one method—and not necessarily the most important one—by which a state "regulates" and helps to manufacture what will count, in the language of our day, as "politically correct."

In the age of the activist state, governmental speech, even when lacking the formal status of law, is a pervasive method of regulation, and we have yet to achieve any theoretically satisfying way of coming to terms with it. It has become a cliché of contemporary social theory that political communities are the products of imagination, constructed by a variety of sociocultural projects, many of which are sponsored by the state.[12] The setting for the creation of these political communities is, almost always, what the detached social scientist would readily describe as a fractionated social order—sometimes "multicultural" or "multinational," sometimes divided along class or ideological grounds—whose centrifugal pressures may well put any notion of a unified polity under great stress. One might suggest, therefore, that a central task of the state is, by apt speech, to draw together an otherwise fractured community and thus, as promised by our own national motto, create *"e pluribus unum."*

This is, of course, one rationale for a highly self-conscious program of "civic education," where the metaphor of the state as tutor becomes most clearly instantiated.[13] As Rousseau put it in *Emile,* the state must, in educating children, "direct their tastes and their opinions till they are patriotic by inclination—by instinct—by necessity."[14] Benjamin Rush, one of our nation's founders, spoke of the task facing the American republic as the creation through education of "republican machines" committed to the new political order being constructed in the United States.[15] More moderate, but nonetheless in the same spirit, is the statement of Abraham Lincoln that every child receive "at least a moderate education, and [be] thereby enabled to read the histories of his own and other countries, by which he may duly appreciate the value of free institutions."[16]

The most obvious forum for such education is the public school; it is no coincidence that Rush made his comment in a 1786 tract titled *A Plan for the Establishment of Public Schools and the Diffusion of Knowledge in Pennsylvania; to which are added Thoughts upon the Mode of Education, Proper in a Republic.* We are all familiar with ever more bitter debates coursing through our society that concern state regulation of public education and its ostensible censorship of unpopular views. Fundamentalist Christians tend to focus on such issues as the failure to engage in respectful presentation of the claims of creation science, whereas some of those who speak in the name of contemporary multiculturalists angrily scrutinize public school textbooks to determine if enough space was devoted, with the proper attitude, to their favorite groups.[17]

However important formal schooling may be, it is certainly not the only example of self-conscious civic education designed to create, or at least to maintain, a privileged notion of community identity. Indeed, I want to address some of the ways in which the phenomena of public monuments serves (or at least are intended) to tutor citizens and thus to create social meaning—not to mention contestation—in a multicultural society.[18] As Will Kymlicka writes in his recent book *Multicultural Citizenship,*

> governmental decisions on languages . . . , public holidays, and state symbols unavoidably involve recognizing, accommodating, and supporting the needs and identities of particular ethnic and national groups. The state unavoidably promotes certain cultural identities, and thereby disadvantages others.[19]

States privilege certain understandings of the community, and thus inevitably disadvantage alternative understandings, in specific ways—regardless of whether "silencing" is the best metaphor for their actions. Consider such a mundane practice as the naming of streets and other public areas "in honor" of individuals. Surely my hometown of Austin, Texas, is not the only community to have renamed streets after Martin Luther King and Cesar Chavez. Think also of the successful attempt in New York City to name an area in front of the United Nations after Raoul Wallenberg. How, one wonders, can a devotee of neutrality like Owen Fiss easily accept such acts by the state? One would have to limit the names of public streets to completely nonideological numbers, tree names, and the like. One should be aware that "neutrality" for Fiss is a complex notion, for on egalitarian grounds he would allow the state to use its power to bring before the public "viewpoints and options that otherwise might be slighted or ignored."[20] This would, presumably, create a level playing field between these ideas and those more popular ideas that threaten to swamp them in the general marketplace of ideas. Perhaps, then, he would allow the naming of a street after, say, Louis Farrakhan, but he surely would consider it far more problematic to reinforce a preexisting public orthodoxy by honoring, say, Jackie Robinson, at least in 1997. If one finds these suggestions bizarre, then perhaps this suggests the limits of neutrality, even given Fiss's modification, as a comprehensive approach to the role of the state in structuring the ideological marketplace.

Kymlicka is undoubtedly correct in suggesting the impossibility of imagining a state that does *not* try to structure some set of privileged—some might call them constitutive—understandings of the society it purports to represent. This is true even of a liberal state that tolerates the expression by ordinary citizens of direct attacks on those understandings. Not least among these constitutive understandings, of course, is the legitimacy of the state structure itself. In any event, the establishment of public monuments, especially those that designate through illocution communal heroes or sacred communal events, has throughout time been a way by which regimes, formally democratic or not, take on a material form and attempt to manufacture a popular consciousness conducive to their survival. As Kirk Savage somewhat laconically remarks,

> Public monuments do not arise as if by natural law to celebrate the deserving; they are built by people with sufficient power to marshal (or impose) public consent for their erection.... The public monument represents a kind of collective recognition—in short, legitimacy—for the memory deposited there."[21]

"Legitimacy" is a classic scarce resource; no social order bestows it promiscuously (even though many bestow it unwisely).

Consider in this context the fascinating case of *United States v. Gettysburg Electric Co.*, which involved the condemnation by the United States of land belonging to the electric company in order to build a variety of monuments to the Battle of Gettysburg.[22] The question was whether using the land as a venue for monuments constituted a "public use" that is a predicate condition to condemnation of private property by the state.[23] Writing for a unanimous Supreme Court, Justice Rufus Peckham, surely one of the great devotees of property rights ever to serve on the court, had no difficulty agreeing that the electric company could be forced to turn over its property to the state (after receiving "just compensation," of course). The monuments to be erected were "so closely connected with the welfare of the republic itself as to be within the powers granted Congress by the Constitution for the purpose of protecting and preserving the whole country."[24] Why is this the case? The answer is that monuments will provide "proper recognition of the great things that were done there on those momentous days. By this use the government manifests for the benefit of all its citizens the value put upon the services and exertions of the citizen soldiers of that period."[25]

This is no idle obeisance to the past. The efforts of these citizen soldiers to preserve the republic "is *forcibly impressed* upon every one who looks over the field."[27] Congress's willingness to expend public funds and construct the monuments touches the heart, engages the imagination of all citizens, and greatly tends to enhance their love and respect for those institutions for which these heroic sacrifices were made. The greater the love of the citizens for the institutions of their country, the greater is the dependence properly placed upon citizens for the defense of these institutions in time of necessity, and it is to such citizens that the country must look for its safety.[27]

There is, to put it mildly, nothing neutral about this "public use" any more than there is in the desire of Senator Daniel Patrick Moynihan, in creating the Pennsylvania Avenue Development Commission, to encourage buildings of "monumental quality" that will "provide visual testimony to the dignity, enterprise, and vigor of the federal government."[28] Rousseau could not have put it better than did Peckham or Moynihan.

"Public," in this context, refers primarily to the placement and ideological function of the objects in question. Quite often, of course, as in the *Gettysburg* case, they will be funded by the taxpayers and will be "public" in that very fundamental sense as well.[29] But the most "public" of all public monuments are those occupying a culture's "sacred space," such as capitol grounds, official cemeteries, or important parks or streets.[31] They serve as the icons within the civic religion that, as Rousseau argued, helps to maintain any political order. As David Chidester and Edward Linenthal write, "sacred space anchors more than merely myth or emotion. It anchors relations of meaning and power that are at stake in the formation of a larger social reality."[30] It occasions no surprise, then, that the placement of a statue or commemorative plaque in these public settings can be a source of intense controversy. Indeed, Chidester and Linenthal note that "sacred space is inevitably *contested* space, a site of negotiated contests over the legitimate ownership of sacred symbols."[32] At the very least, one might well censure the state for some of its choices on decidedly nonaesthetic grounds, whether or not one has the power formally to "censor" the state's exercise of choice.

I offer two examples of what interests (and perplexes) me when reflecting on the state's role as a cultural regulator and constructor of social meaning. The first is rather broad, taken from the final days of the Soviet Union. Fans of political semiotics certainly appreciate the significance of toppled statues, which mark the attitude of an aroused populace whose members visibly remove symbols of their oppression from the pedestals on which they are mounted.[33] Thus *The New York Times* rightly emphasized the importance of the moment in August 1991, during the popular revolution that was shortly to overthrow Communist control of what was then the Soviet Union—and, indeed, lead to the demise of the Soviet Union itself—when, in the aftermath of the aborted coup against the government of Mikhail Gorbachev, a crowd in Moscow toppled the statue of the founder of the Soviet secret police, Felix Dzerzhinsky.[34] The statue had stood for many years in front of the Lubiyanka prison, itself the instantiation of the secret police and, therefore, of the worst excesses of Communist tyranny. In a fascinating *New Yorker* article, Lawrence Wechsler notes that "monuments all over the country—fierce icons of the longtime socialist-realist hegemony—were being toppled and carted off" and, presumably, in many cases destroyed.[35]

One might assume that anyone who viewed this as a great moment for the cause of human freedom rejoiced as the symbols of the ideological walls came tumbling down. This was not exactly the case. Even some strong anti-Communists confessed to a deep ambivalence at the destruction of these important cultural signifiers. Wechsler quotes Vitaly Komar, whom he describes as "formerly among the ancien regime's most notorious dissident artists":

> "This is a classic old Moscow technique: either worship or destroy. Bolsheviks topple czar monuments, Stalin erases old Bolsheviks, Khrushchev tears down Stalin, Brezhnev tears down Khrushchev, and now this. No difference. Each time it is history, the country's true past, which is conveniently being obliterated. And usually by the same people! In most cases, there weren't passionate crowds doing tearing down—it was cool hand of officials, by bureaucratic fiat. Same guys who used to order our shows bulldozed now arranging these bulldozings."[36]

Perhaps state officials should have used their power to prevent the destruction of the statues or, at the very least, not called in state-owned bulldozers to collaborate with the inflamed mob.

Can it possibly be the case that the Muscovite political authorities were legitimately subject to criticism for failing to offer a more vigorous defense of the earlier regime's tribute to Dzerzhinsky, even if not, presumably, of the secret police system that he was praised for creating? This is simply to ask, though, what one *ought* to think of the toppling of the monuments, and to ask as well if the abstract concepts surrounding standard notions of "censorship" are at all helpful in providing any answers. In a *New York Times* dispatch about the legacy of Enver Hoxha, "the brutal, eccentric, isolationist dictator of Albania for more than four decades," Philip Shenon notes that

Crowds surround a toppled statue of Stalin,
Hungary, 1956.
Courtesy Regnery Publishing, Inc.

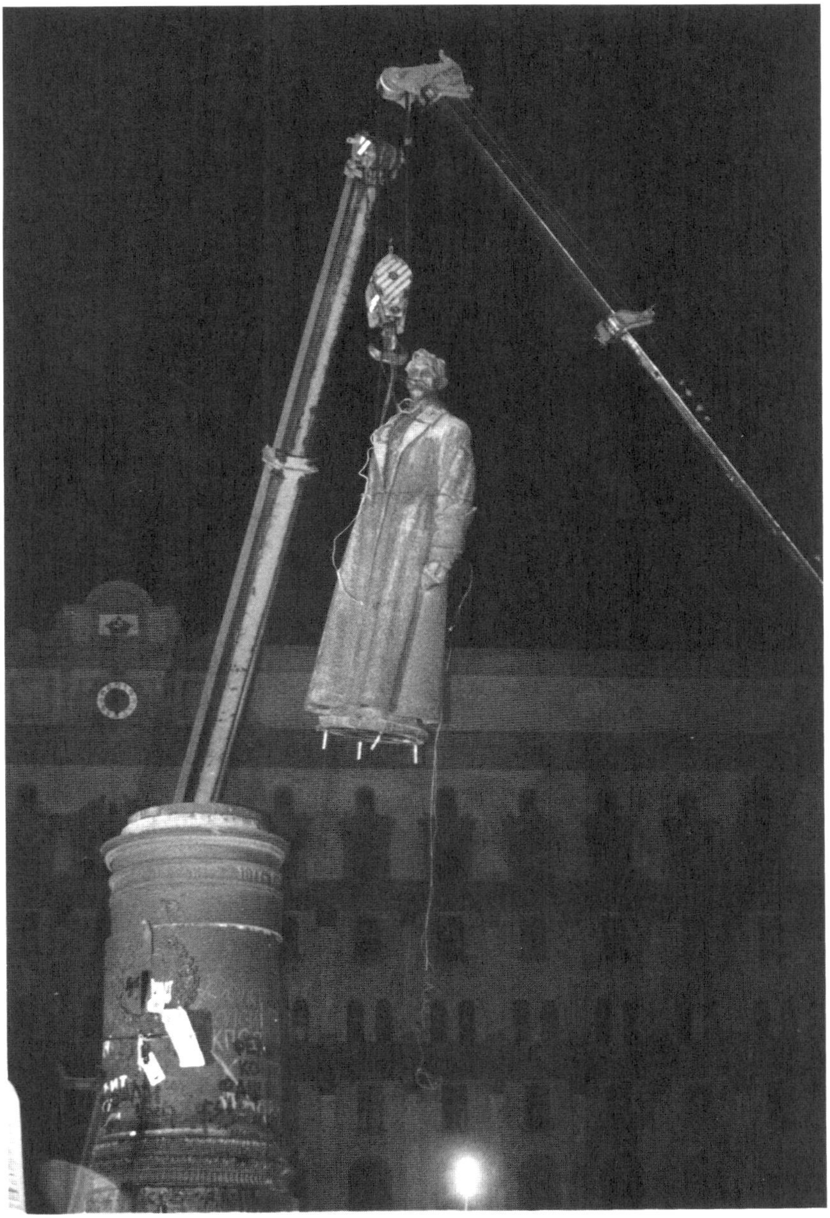

The statue of Felix Dzerzhinsky is hoisted from its pedestal in front of the former KGB headquarters in Moscow, 23 August 1991.
Copyright AP World Wide Photos.

"Albanians have spent much of the last decade [since his death in 1985] doing their best to erase any memory of his crazed dictatorship. Statues of Mr. Hoxha were smashed and photographs burned."[37] Ought the Albanians have been more respectful of the statues and photographs, at least as a way of acknowledging its past rather than trying to "erase" or, as a Freudian might well say with wonderful double entendre, to "repress" it? Do we, then, wish to praise post-Communist Berlin for maintaining at least some continuity with its past by retaining on the Alexanderplatz not only statues of Marx and Engels, but also "six stainless-steel obelisks engraved with photos from communist revolutions around the world"?[38]

We must come to terms with the transformation (or lack of same) of the public landscape of such cities as Moscow, Tirana, and... The ellipsis refers to an issue linked with the destruction of physical monuments: the very *naming* of public spaces. Should one write "Leningrad" or "St. Petersburg"? And who, if anyone, is authorized to offer a definitive answer to this question? Some of us are old enough to remember Secretary of State Dean Rusk's insistence on using "Peiping" as the name of the Chinese capital, given that it was the then unrecognized Peoples Republic of China that had changed the name to Beijing. In any event, Leningrad, which survived a 900-day siege by the Nazis during World War II, did not survive the downfall of the Soviet Union; it has disappeared on contemporary maps, and the city's name has been restored to its pre-1917 rendering as St. Petersburg. (One wonders if Shostakovich's great "Leningrad Symphony" will be similarly renamed, or will Russian youngsters be taught that, as with the morning and the evening star, there is a common referent for Leningrad and St. Petersburg?) Is the change of name a censurable act of state-sponsored cultural silencing, the extirpation of seventy-five years of Russian history, or do we instead describe it as state-sponsored cultural liberation, the (re)claiming of a different cultural heritage that itself had been ruthlessly silenced by those who wished to impose a Communist hegemony over Russian culture? These hegemons, after all, had displayed no hesitation in changing St. Petersburg's name when they deemed it ideologically useful. And the decision to name it "Leningrad" obviously takes on a wholly different valence from one to name it, say, "Nevagrad," after the Neva River that flows through the city. How, though, does one tell the difference, in such contexts, between silencing and liberation? Is it like trying to achieve neutral definitions for "terrorists" and "freedom fighters"?

The second example is far more specific, not to mention much closer—ideologically and geographically—to our concerns as Americans. In New Orleans stands what for most persons is an obscure monument to an obscure incident. The Liberty Monument celebrates the 1874 Battle of Liberty Place, described by an admiring local historian as "The Overthrow of Carpet-Bag Rule in New Orleans—September 14, 1874."[39] Members of the appropriately named White League engaged in the violent overthrow of the existing Louisiana government, which was composed of an alliance of Republican whites and newly enfranchised African Americans. Thirty-two lives were lost on both sides, with about three times that many persons injured. The ousted Republican administration of William Pitt Kellogg was in fact restored by force of federal arms, but it was only a matter of time until the Compromise of 1877 resulted in the full-scale restoration of the conservative white rule sought by the White League, with attendant consequences for the future of African Americans.[40]

Immediately following the battle, with the partisans of the White League in apparent control of the state (of which New Orleans was then the capital), the New Orleans *Daily Picayune* saluted the downfall of "the Kellogg regime": "Big, inflated, insolent, and overbearing, it collapsed at one touch of honest indignation and gallant onslaught."[41] This leading voice of New Orleans also called for the erection of a memorial to the eleven whites who had died in behalf of the insurgency. The New Orleans City Council formally agreed in November 1882, when it passed an ordinance that renamed the area of the battle as "Liberty Place" and authorized the erection of a monument "in honor of those who fell in defense of liberty and home rule in that heroic struggle of the 14th of September, 1874."[42] In 1891 these hopes were achieved with the completion of an obelisk near the Mississippi River at the foot of Canal Street, a principal street in the city.[43] The Liberty Monument included the names of the White Leaguers who gave their lives in the attack against the hated mixed-race government, as well as the names of some of the league's leaders (see page 144). It is perhaps needless to add that the members of the Metropolitan Police and of the largely African American militia who died fighting the White League were not memorialized. According to Judith Kelleher Schafer, a leading historian of the incident, the 1891 dedication of the monument on September 14 initiated what became an annual event: a parade, followed by a wreath-laying ceremony to honor the civic heroes.[44]

Lest anyone unaccountably fail to get the intended message, in 1934 the city used artisans supplied by the federally funded Works Progress Administration to make two additions to the monument which set out the official version of events: chiseled into one side of the base was "United States troops took over the state government and reinstated the usurpers but the national election in November 1876 recognized white supremacy and gave us our state"; on the opposite side appeared "McEnery and Penn, having been elected governor and lieutenant governor by the white people, were duly installed by the overthrow of the carpetbag government, ousting the usurpers Gov. Kellogg (white) and Lt. Gov. Antoine (colored)."[45]

As one might expect, the Liberty Monument has remained a source of controversy in New Orleans, especially as African Americans have become a dominant political force in the city. In 1974, for example, Mayor Moon Landrieu agreed to the placement by the monument of a bronze plaque describing the battle as an insurrection and noting that the controversial language had not in fact been part of the original 1891 monument. Most important, no doubt, was the plaque's additional statement, that "the sentiments expressed are contrary to the philosophy and beliefs of present-day New Orleans." This statement itself raises delicious political and philosophical questions: is New Orleans an entity that can have "philosophy and beliefs," and, if so, how precisely does one identify what they are, and who is authorized to speak performatively as to their content? One wonders also if it is possible that the statement, whatever its accuracy at the time of installation, was designed to *create* the consciousness that it purports to describe. Still, there can be no doubt that New Orleans adopted an overtly tutelary role in attempting to limit the pernicious consequences upon the untutored who might otherwise have been tempted to treat the words on the monument—placed there, after all, at public expense—as an authoritative enunciation of the meaning of the event that was being commemorated.

When Ernest Morial became the first black mayor of the city in 1981, he attempted to remove the monument, but was stopped from doing so by the mostly white city council, which forbade the moving of any monuments without its consent. (Does the council therefore merit an award for fending off the forces of censorship?) The council did, however, authorize the removal of any offensive wording on the monument. (Maybe it doesn't deserve an award after all.) Smooth granite slabs were placed over the 1934 additions, which also allowed removal of New Orleans' latter-day plaque, since there was no longer any statement to renounce. In the late 1980s, the administration of the second black mayor, Sidney Barthelemy, tried to remove the monument permanently when it was taken down from its Canal Street location during the course of a general riverfront reconstruction. An interesting alliance of traditionalists, historical preservationists, and white supremacists successfully blocked the effort. Nevertheless, the monument was ultimately moved from its quite prominent Canal Street spot to a decidedly more obscure setting about a block away, where it now languishes out of the sight of most of the tourists who crowd Canal Street to visit its fine shops, casinos, and the municipal aquarium and to enjoy vistas of the Mississippi. Indeed, it remains in the area only because of an agreement between the city and the State Historic Preservation Office that is based on federal historic preservation laws; these laws require that such monuments remain in the general area of the battle.

Once again, though, the "official" story changed, for in 1993 yet another large plaque was placed on the monument itself: "IN HONOR OF THOSE AMERICANS ON BOTH SIDES OF THE CONFLICT WHO DIED IN THE BATTLE OF LIBERTY PLACE. A CONFLICT OF THE PAST THAT SHOULD TEACH US LESSONS FOR THE FUTURE." What these lessons are is left wholly unarticulated. The voice of the tutor is quite muffled, leaving the monument to "speak for itself," without elaboration. One can, I believe, wonder if this really represents progress over the point and counterpoint that developed in 1974, which at least alerted observers to the ideological stakes behind the ascription of meaning to the Liberty Monument.

During this period of highly intense controversy in New Orleans, the noted Yale historian Robin Winks attacked those who counseled destruction

A crowd of demonstrators march around the Liberty Place Monument in March 1993.
Copyright 1993 The Times-Picayune.

of the monument. In an article in the New Orleans *Times-Picayune,* Winks took direct issue with those who viewed the struggle over the monument as a "clash between those who look to the future and those who hang on to the past, or even more sharply put, between racists and those who regard race as irrelevant." Instead, he opined, the struggle is really about the nature of historical memory, noting that "different concepts of history are at war." The first "holds that society should never forget any part of its past," that "it is wrong to purge the record" of past events. Winks evokes the classic negative example of the "Great Soviet Encyclopedia," which was much revised based on the desires of the given ruling elites: "history became what the written texts said it was" instead of history as it actually happened.[46]

Winks, however, is much too sophisticated to stay with this polarized opposition. "We all know," he writes, that "history is, simultaneously, three things: what actually happened, what historians choose to record, and what the people—and people, some people, these people, those people—believe to be true about the past."[47] Were he writing for a more academic audience, Winks might well have segued into a language about the existence of "discourses" that compete for cultural hegemony and that are championed by their partisans, who attempt to privilege their favored discourses through the use of the state apparatus. He might also have contrasted the versions of history predominant within the academy, at any given point, with those held by the untutored or, perhaps more precisely, by those who accept as their tutors uncertified amateurs instead of the credentialed academy.

"The past," Winks points out, "is also what is commemorated by monuments and markers, plaques and parades, historic sites and museums. Almost always a monument is an attempt to interpret an event in which those who have erected it take pride." Monuments are ways by which a specific culture names its heroes, those "people who made us what we are in a prideful way."[48] There is, I believe, a link between Winks's comment and Catharine MacKinnon's argument that

> words and images are how people are placed in hierarchies, how social stratification is made to seem inevitable and right, how feelings of inferiority and superiority are engendered, and how indifference to violence against those on the bottom is rationalized and normalized. Social supremacy is made, inside and between people, through making meanings.[49]

The Liberty Place Monument, then, is a monument whose origin was the desire to honor those who took up arms against a multiracial government and whose present meaning for many, even 120 years later, is to pay homage to the racist culture for which the insurgents fought.[50] It is worth noting, incidentally, that some supporters of the monument, such as the Louisiana White Citizens Council, and some opponents as well, like the local NAACP, essentially agree on this point (apart from the fact, one presumes, that the former refuse to describe the ancien regime as "racist"). If one rejects what the Citizens

Council (and the White League that was in a significant sense its predecessor) represents, why *not* emulate the Russians in tearing the monument down and proclaiming through the very act of destruction a commitment to a new, and presumably better, vision of reality?

Winks demurs. "The monument *must* go back up."[51] Escalating his rhetoric and adopting one of the most censorious epithets in an intellectual's vocabulary, he says that "not to put it back up would be an act of the clearest Stalinism, of intellectual vandalism." This scarcely concludes Winks's discussion. For him the real issue is not whether to keep the monument standing but, rather, *where* to place the statue. He agrees that it is not appropriate to retain its position near the historic Canal Street setting, whatever the arguments of the historic preservationists. There it would serve primarily as "an insult to most of the present population of New Orleans, . . . rub[bing] salt in open wounds not yet healed"; a decent political order can presumably act to remove the source of such hurt and to silence the message it sends.[52] Interestingly enough, Dr. Clifton Johnson, director of the Amistad Research Center, which specializes in materials relating to African American history, disagrees with Winks and agrees instead with David Duke, a former Grand Wizard of the Ku Klux Klan, that it should be remain at its Canal Street location. "Racism is part of our history," Dr. Johnson explains. For him the monument is a symbol of "racism's shame" and a reminder of the courage of all who participated in the civil rights movement and led the fight against those who wished to perpetuate the values of the White League.[53]

Winks's solution is instead to encapsulate the monument within a museum, where it would presumably take on a different semiotic status. In some museums a monument's status might be that of "aesthetic object," in which form is substantially separated from content. But no one defends the undistinguished Liberty Monument as art. Winks suggests that the monument be placed in a museum devoted particularly to history. The message, presumably, is that the object in question would be (safely) displaced to the past, at some distance—both emotional and intellectual—from the exigencies of the present. It should be obvious that this is hardly less tutelary than retaining the object within the sacred space of a public setting.[54]

Winks offers the example of Zimbabwe, which upon its creation as the successor state to Rhodesia was faced with the issue of what to do with the "great statues of Cecil Rhodes, Lord Salisbury and others who dreamt of empire" that filled "the central squares of Salisbury," Rhodesia's capital: "Of course the new civil servants of Zimbabwe did not wish to walk past larger-than-life figures of Cecil Rhodes or Lord Salisbury as they went to their new jobs." They did not, however, destroy the statues or otherwise "deny the significance of Cecil Rhodes to the history of modern Zimbabwe." Instead, they moved the statues from the great public spaces of the city "and carefully and skillfully put them once again on the grounds of the nation's new national archives and museum, a clear statement that the figure spoke to the past, not to the future."[55]

Presumably the movement of the statues, together with the change of the country's name and the capital's name from Salisbury to Harare, served to desacralize them, turning them into detached objects of historical reflection rather than icons of an ongoing civil religion. Moreover, I strongly suspect that not *all* of the memorials to Rhodes and Salisbury were moved to historical museums. There were, I assume, just too many of them; this was clearly the case in the former Soviet Union, where far more statues of Lenin were produced than could possibly be absorbed by museums. So, presumably, most of the statues were in fact destroyed even if the aesthetically best or most publicly prominent statues were given a type of immortal life in museums.

Even if one agrees with Winks that complete destruction of these monuments is unwise, whether or not "Stalinist," one might wonder if the state should be content to rely on placements within museum settings to convey the "proper message." Perhaps the state should play a much more active tutelary role in articulating a particular moral for those viewing the statues. It would be remarkable (assuming, of course, it were possible) for the state to profess to be truly neutral or indifferent to the social meaning inferred by viewers of any given statue; it might also, under many circumstances, be pernicious.

I presume that Winks would counsel the new government of South Africa to follow Zimbabwe's example and place the public monuments to their oppressors in museums. Afrikaners should presumably still be able to see mighty monuments to their ancestors, although not in the great public squares. Perhaps one would similarly advise the new governments of Russia, Poland, and other countries formerly ruled by Communists to place various statues of Lenin, Stalin, and others in the equivalent of Communist theme parks, where parents could take their children and teach them whatever lessons they wished. It takes little imagination to extend the comparison to Germany and Japan: would one have been altogether comforted had their replacement regimes moved public statuary of Hitler, Tojo, and their minions to the carefully tended grounds of a state museum where they would stand, without further adornment or explanation, for the presumed edification of onlookers?

Ian Buruma has written powerfully, in *The Wages of Guilt: Memories of War in Germany and Japan,* of the remarkable differences between the state apparatuses of these two countries in regard to their willingness to tutor their citizens as to the realities (or should it be, in the best postmodern fashion, "realities"?) of World War II.[56] In particular, the Japanese educational system has resolutely refused to emphasize the responsibility played by that country in the onset of the war (and, therefore, the extent to which the bombing of Hiroshima and Nagasaki is, even if one opposes what was done, something other than a story of abject victimization of innocents). One would, therefore, have no confidence whatsoever that adoption of the Zimbabwean solution would necessarily be beneficial to extirpating the ultranationalist sensibilities for which Tojo and others stand as symbols. To the extent that the Zimbabwean solution works even in Zimbabwe—and I have no idea of the nature of the present status (1997) of the statues of Rhodes and Lord Salisbury—I suspect it is because of the willingness of the state to adopt a highly active tutelary role in regard to these men and their actions, which leaves all Zimbabweans in little doubt as to the official view. Whatever else Rhodes may be, I suspect he is not an official hero of the Zimbabwean people, however much he remains part of their formative history.

As already noted, the primary venue of tutoring, at least for the young, is without doubt the school. It is clear, though, that many other institutions financed and operated by the state serve such tutelary functions, including museums. To the extent that one is worried about the public schools becoming vehicles of political indoctrination, should one also have concerns about state museums? It surely occasions no surprise when statuary within such museums is accompanied by various "educational" plaques and other materials that specify who is to be considered heroic and who villainous.

Anyone who has drunk from the postmodernist well (or, perhaps, simply anyone with common sense) knows how easily these official stories can be subverted by viewers. Unreconstructed Southerners (or Afrikaners, Communists, and so on) might well continue to treat even "museumized" statuary as iconic and teach their own children quite different lessons from those desired by state authorities. Indeed, the tutelary inscriptions might be pointed out to the young as direct *evidence* of hegemonic oppression rather than offered as the right way to understand the monuments. "Political correctness," the desire for which is a part of all political regimes, including liberal ones, is easily subverted.

How then should a contemporary nonracist respond to the Liberty Monument, or an anti-Communist to statues of Josef Stalin or Felix Dzerzhinsky?[57] My immediate answer is: "With caution." I remain highly uncertain that there are any useful general norms that offer much help. I have little doubt that the removal of villains' statues from public spaces—or, for that matter, canceling a traditional "official" parade or wreath-laying ceremony—*is* designed as a form of regulation to inculcate in the citizenry a "correct" civic consciousness. I am less sure that this should be described as silencing, for "private" individuals and organizations presumably remain free to organize marches and other ceremonies on their own, just as they can place monuments on private property. In any event, I cannot cogently offer general criticisms of states that engage in such regulation (or silencing), for I cannot imagine a state that does not devote at least some of its energies to performing exactly such tasks, even if it otherwise tolerates relatively unfettered private discourse. Moreover, I am happy with the state's playing a tutelary role—at least, that is, as long as I am happy with the state's substantive decisions as to whom to honor (or dishonor).

That, obviously, is the rub. Does it simply boil down to whose ox is gored or cultural symbol honored? One would like to say "No," especially if one is a liberal yearning for suitably neutral standards that enable us to transcend our own substantive politics when considering who is fit for public honor. But I do not know what these standards are. I find myself thinking of Justice

Holmes's reminder that "general propositions do not decide concrete cases" and joining this with the contemporary emphasis, often linked with postmodernism, on the importance of paying careful attention to the specific circumstances of a given situation.[58] What this means, among other things, is that there *are* times when the proper response to the sacred symbols of a prior political regime is to destroy them, and that we are certainly *not* obligated to preserve them in places of honor or, perhaps, even in the disinfected space of a museum.

While writing this piece, I found myself imagining a divorced couple—or, perhaps more accurately, *two* such couples. The first is torn asunder by the abusive practices of one of the spouses. In this instance, I assume that we would surely not criticize the victimized party for taking down pictures of his or her former spouse and giving away or even destroying other material representations of the discarded spouse, perhaps in a ritualized setting surrounded by friends offering appropriate toasts.[59] This could indeed be a most healthy step in "getting on with one's life." Our understanding of, or even sympathy with, such acts would not, however, mean that we might not wish to cheer the second couple who, having decided on an "amicable divorce," prove able to honor their past lives and to retain material representations of those lives together within their now separate homes.

Similarly, one might hope that within new regimes the partisans of change would be able to recognize that their now supplanted predecessors were not without valuable qualities and are perhaps worth honoring by public monuments or even commemorative stamps. Such pacific and ideologically generous attitudes are almost certainly the exception rather than the rule (as may be the case with truly amicable divorces). To my knowledge, there are no public monuments within the United States of George III or of Benedict Arnold (even though Arnold, as the successful general for the American revolutionaries in the Battle of Saratoga, may be said to have been an essential contributor to American independence). The British have never published a stamp commemorating Oliver Cromwell, nor have the French so honored any of their former kings. It would presumably, and, more importantly, *properly* occasion international scandal if Germany, as part of a process of "normalizing" its history, put out stamps with the portraits of Hitler, Goering, or any other of the Nazi leaders. Indeed, one suspects that the atmosphere would become heated if a German philatelic series of great generals included Erwin Rommel, who was by all accounts a military master.

What, then, should one say about the fact that the United States Postal Service in 1995 issued a set of stamps commemorating various figures of the Civil War (or, as printed in lower-point type, "The War Between the States")? There, on official documents of the United States of America, appeared Robert E. Lee (in what was in fact his third appearance on a commemorative stamp), Jefferson Davis, and "Stonewall" Jackson, among other Confederates. I confess to being more than a bit ambivalent about such commemoratives. I personally have no wish whatsoever to honor Jefferson Davis in however limited a way, any more than Catharine MacKinnon would easily agree to place Hugh Hefner on a stamp. I presume that she would readily acknowledge that Hefner is one of the truly significant shapers of contemporary American culture, just as Davis certainly made an impact on American life in his own time, but it surely seems obvious that such causal significance is not enough to merit public homage, even the relatively limited homage of being placed on a stamp. To commemorate is to take a stand, to identify a hero or a heroic event worthy of emulation or, less frequently, an event that was so terrible that it must be remembered forever after as a cautionary note.

To be sure, the semiotician of commemorative stamps has to account for Elvis Presley, Buddy Holly, Marilyn Monroe, and James Dean as well as for Robert E. Lee. Perhaps the American predilection for "celebrity" is enough to explain all of these examples. I still doubt, though, that Hugh Hefner, easily as important as Buddy Holly (and probably as well known to most Americans), will grace one of our stamps after his death. In any event, it seems to be entirely untenable to pretend that the United States Postal Service must be "neutral" in regard to deciding who is fit to be commemorated, any more than we can realistically expect city councils to adopt politically neutral theories of street naming and the like. And we should admit that our hope, at least when we support specific state speech in the circumstances I have described, is that contrary voices will indeed fall silent and that the consciousness of the next generation will be "regulated" in the proper direction.[60]

Notes

I am grateful for the responses of my fellow conferees during the initial presentation of this paper at the Getty Research Institute on 15 December 1995 and for comments received during later presentations to the Ohio Legal History Seminar at the Ohio State University, the Seminar on the Letter of the Law at Stanford University on 22 April 1996, and faculty colloquia at Chicago Kent Law School, the University of Chicago Law School, and the University of Wisconsin. I am particularly grateful to Robert Post for inviting me to participate in the Getty Research Institute program and, even more important, for his luminously intelligent responses and suggestions. I also appreciate the careful reading and comments given me by Jack Balkin and Betty Sue Flowers. This essay also reflects the impact of conversations over many years with Richard Rabinowitz.

1. See, for example, the chapters by Leslie Green and David Wasserman. In "Pornographizing, Subordinating, and Silencing" (pages 285–311 of this volume), Green explicitly focuses on "*coercive public action*" and "the coercive policies that we ordinarily think of as censorship" (286; emphasis in original). Similarly, in "Public Funding for Science and Art: Censorship, Social Harm, and the Case of Genetic Research into Crime and Violence" (pages 169–93 in this volume), Wasserman presents censorship as restrictions that "violate an individual right to free expression" (175).

2. Owen M. Fiss, "State Activism and State Censorship," *Yale Law Journal* 100 (1991): 1087, 1101, reprinted in Owen M. Fiss, *Liberalism Divided: Freedom of Speech and the Many Uses of State Power* (Boulder: Westview Press, 1996), 101. See also Owen M. Fiss, *The Irony of Free Speech* (Cambridge, Mass.: Harvard University Press, 1996).

3. See Steven H. Schiffrin, "Government Speech," *UCLA Law Review* 27 (1980): 565; and Mark G. Yudof, *When Government Speaks: Politics, Law, and Government Expression in America* (Berkeley: Univ. of California Press, 1983).

4. Fiss, *Liberalism Divided* (see note 2), 102.

5. Illocutionary speech acts have been defined as "acts done *in* saying something." See J. Horn, "Linguistic Acts," in Ted Honderich, ed., *The Oxford Companion to Philosophy* (Oxford: Oxford Univ. Press, 1995), 489 (emphasis in original). The most powerful examples of such speech acts by the state surely arise within the context of criminal law, beginning with the declaration by the state that behavior hitherto acceptable will now be deemed "illegal" and ranging from a jury's pronouncement of "guilty" to a judge's sentence of death. But, obviously, this does not exhaust the state's speech act repertoire and its advantages over ordinary private parties. See, generally, J. L. Austin, *How to Do Things with Words* (Oxford: Oxford Univ. Press, 1961); and John Searle, *Speech Acts: An Essay in the Philosophy of Language* (Cambridge: Cambridge Univ. Press, 1969). I am grateful to Dr. Glenn Butterton, of the University of Chicago, for his comments directed at my use of speech act theory.

6. As one reader suggested, though, it is necessary to note that the "dominance" of the state is at bottom an empirical question rather than a conceptual given. A pervasive theme of our time, after all, is the *de facto* dissolution of the state as a hegemonic entity that can in fact exercise control over anything very important, whether it be economic development or general cultural developments. There is a certain desperation in the attempts of states to control the tidal wave of information available on the internet. King Canute, after all, apparently knew his own limitations and called on the tides only to demonstrate to his supporters how limited his actual power was. It is not clear that states share his wisdom. The state does, of course, continue to enjoy the ability to inflict death and destruction on large numbers of people, although even here we saw that the possession of nuclear weapons did not enable the Soviet Union to survive or Israel successfully to suppress the Palestinian *intifada*. Although it is undoubtedly premature to speak of the "withering away of the state," it seems clear that one must recognize an institutional pluralization in which the state is only one of many competitors for whatever goods—power, legitimacy, economic resources—are being sought. It is not clear how the waning power of the state, as an empirical matter, affects the conceptual critique of the "unneutral" state.

7. "Treaty of Peace," 26 October 1994, art. 11, *International Legal Materials* 34 (January 1995): 50.

8. See, for example, *Allegheny County v. A.C.L.U., Greater Pittsburgh Chapter*, 492 U.S. 573 (1989); *Capital Square Review and Advisory Board v. Pinette*, 115 S. Ct. 2440, 2451 (1995) (Justice O'Connor concurring).

9. I put to one side the placement of "In God We Trust" on our currency. Although it may be paradoxical, I strongly suspect that if the coinage did *not* include the

phrase, it would be deemed unconstitutional if legislation were passed to add it. For better or worse, we have gotten used as a culture to its placement on currency, and courts are not inclined to use their power to strike it down, regardless of whether there is a cogent rationale for failing to do so. I also note that not all scholars would necessarily find "In Christ Is Our Redemption" unconstitutional. See, for example, Jesse Choper, *Securing Religious Liberty: Principles for Judicial Interpretation of the Religion Clauses* (Chicago: Univ. Chicago Press, 1995), 32, who argues that this neither deprives those who do not believe in Jesus of any of their own religious liberty nor calls upon them for the kind of material support that is prohibited by the Establishment Clause of the First Amendment.

10. See, for example, Akhil Reed Amar, "Comment: The Case of the Missing Amendments: *R.A.V. v. City of St. Paul*," *Harvard Law Review* 106 (1992): 124, 151–60.

11. See Robert Post, *Constitutional Domains: Democracy, Community, Management* (Cambridge, Mass.: Harvard Univ. Press, 1995), which emphasizes the complete untenability of expecting content or viewpoint neutrality from the state in regard to its role as *manager* of public institutions with instrumental goals. See also Robert Post, "Subsidized Speech," *Yale Law Journal* 106 (1996): 151; and the distinction, borrowed from Meir Dan-Cohen, between "conduct" rules directed at the citizenry in general and "decision" rules directed at the state's own employees concerning managerial tasks. Thus, for example, the state can, through the National Endowment of Arts, order its employees to fund only "excellent" art even though it obviously could not criminalize or otherwise sanction the production of "inferior" art. It seems equally unproblematic for the state to prefer "patriotic" art, when picking out or commissioning art for public buildings, even if it just as obviously could not criminalize the production of "unpatriotic" art.

12. See Benedict Anderson, *The Imagined Community* (New York: Verso, 1991).

13. See Yael Tamir, *Liberal Nationalism* (Princeton: Princeton Univ. Press, 1995), xviii–xxi.

14. Quoted in ibid., at xxi.

15. Quoted in Wilson Smith, "Benjamin Rush on Republican Education," in idem, *Theories of Education in Early America 1655–1819* (Indianapolis: Bobbs-Merril, 1973), 251.

> NEXT to the duty which young men owe to their Creator, I wish to see a SUPREME REGARD TO THEIR COUNTRY, inculcated upon them.... Our country includes family, friends and property, and should be preferred to them all. Let our pupil learn that he does not belong to himself, but that he is public property. Let him be taught to love his family, but let him be taught, at the same time, that he must forsake and even forget them, when the welfare of his country requires it. (Ibid., 247)

16. Ibid., xx–xxi.

17. For an eloquent critique of the excesses of multiculturalism in Oakland, California, see Todd Gitlin, *The Twilight of Common Dreams: Why America is Wracked by Culture Wars* (New York: Metropolitan Books, 1995), chap. 1.

18. Sanford Levinson, "They Whisper: Reflections on Flags, Monuments and State Holidays, and the Construction of Social Meaning in a Multicultural Society," *Chicago-Kent Law Review* 70 (1995): 1079. See also Sanford Levinson, "Allocating Honor and Acting Honorably: Some Reflections Provoked by the Cardozo Conference on Slavery," *Cardozo Law Review* 70 (1996): 1969.

19. Will Kymlicka, *Multicultural Citizenship* (Oxford: Clarendon Press, 1995), 108.

20. Fiss, *Liberalism Divided* (see note 2), 107.

21. Kirk Savage, "The Politics of Memory: Black Emancipation and the Civil War Monument," in John R. Gillis, ed., *Commemorations: The Politics of National Identity* (Princeton: Princeton Univ. Press, 1994), 135–36.

22. 160 U.S. 668 (1896). I owe my familiarity with this case to Lawrence Lessig, "Translating Federalism: *United States v. Lopez*," *Supreme Court Review* 125 (1995): 199 n. 207.

23. United States Constitution, Amendment 5.

24. *United States v. Gettysburg Electric Co.* (see note 22), 682.

25. Ibid.

26. Ibid. (emphasis added).

27. Ibid.

28. Quoted in Nathan Glazer, "Monuments in an Age without Heroes," *The Public Interest*, spring 1996, 33.

29. Yet it is not at all unusual for private individuals or groups to finance monuments while seeking, through their display in a particular setting, the state's special imprimatur for the message contained within the monument. Michele H. Bogart notes, for example, that New York's Central Park quickly became a target of various groups: "Citizens groups, especially those representing European immigrants, saw gifts of statues for Central Park as an appropriate way to beautify their city *and to legitimate their heritage as well as their newfound status as Americans*" (emphasis added). Thus two early donations included statues of Alexander von Humboldt in 1869 and Giuseppe Mazzini in 1878. See Michele H. Bogart, *Public Sculpture and the Civic Ideal in New York City: 1890–1930* (Chicago: Univ. of Chicago Press, 1989), 18–19. See also Edward Linenthal, *Preserving Memory: The Struggle to Create America's Holocaust Museum* (New York: Viking, 1995), where placement on the edge of the National Mall in Washington, and the legitimation such placement was thought to give, was an important objective of the museum's private sponsors.

30. On "sacred space," see the important "Introduction" by David Chidester and Edward T. Linenthal, in David Chidester and Edward T. Linenthal, eds., *American Sacred Space* (Bloomington: Univ. of Indiana Press, 1995), 1–42.

31. Ibid., 17.

32. Ibid., 15 (emphasis added). They go on to quote Foucault's insistence that "space is fundamental in any exercise of power." Michel Foucault, "Space, Knowledge, and Power," in idem, *The Foucault Reader*, ed. Paul Rabinow (New York: Pantheon, 1984), 252.

33. The photograph on p. 202, taken during the 1956 Hungarian Revolution, appeared in *The New York Times* with the caption "Hungarians gaze at a toppled

statue of Stalin during the 1956 uprising." See Jane Perlez, "Thawing Out Cold War History," *The New York Times*, 6 Oct. 1996, E4. No photograph could better capture the exhilaration of the moment and, therefore, the hopes that were dashed by the entry of Soviet tanks that suppressed the revolution.

34. Bill Keller, "After the Coup; Gorbachev Says Coup Will Hasten Reform: Yeltsin Leads the Celebration in Moscow," *The New York Times*, 23 Aug. 1991, A1.

35. Lawrence Wechsler, "Slight Modifications," *The New Yorker*, 12 July 1993, 59.

36. Ibid.

37. See "Tirana Journal: Dictator Liked Bunkers. My, They Mushroomed!" *The New York Times*, 13 April 1996, A4.

38. See Ken Stephens, "Berlin," *Dallas Morning News*, 25 Aug. 1996, G5. Stephen's story is the lead story of Section G, the travel section. The first page features a photo of the statue of Marx and Engels, with the caption "Symbols of a failed system still have a place on the Alexanderplatz—for now." We are also told that "one photograph of former East German leader Erich Honecker has been all but scratched away by vandals" (G5). One might wonder, incidentally, if "vandals" is quite the *mot juste* to describe those who might resist the celebration of Honecker on one of Berlin's main public venues.

39. Stuart Omer Landry, *The Battle of Liberty Place: The Overthrow of Carpet-Bag Rule in New Orleans—September 14, 1874* (New Orleans: Pelican Publishing, 1954).

40. See Joe Gray Taylor, *Louisiana Reconstructed 1863–1877* (Baton Rouge: LSU Press, 1974), 291–96. See, generally, Judith Kelleher Schafer, "The Battle of Liberty Place," *Louisiana Cultural Vistas* 5 (1994): 8–17.

41. Quoted in ibid., 16.

42. Ibid., 17.

43. New Orleans had seven years earlier erected a giant monument to Robert E. Lee that continues to preside over Lee Circle.

44. Shafer (see note 40), 17.

45. These facts are taken from an extremely helpful UPI posting of 20 October 1989 by Royal Brightbill, "Reconstruction Era Battle Still Being Fought in New Orleans." In fact, the 1872 elections of Jonathan McEnery and Davidson B. Penn were nullified by a federal court. See also Christina Cheskalos, "Monument Debate Divides New Orleans," *Atlanta Constitution*, 15 Dec. 1992, A3.

46. Robin W. Winks, "A Place for Liberty Monument," *New Orleans Times Picayne*, 17 Aug. 1992, B7.

47. Ibid.

48. Ibid.

49. Catharine A. MacKinnon, *Only Words* (Cambridge, Mass.: Harvard Univ. Press, 1993), 31.

50. Betty Sue Flowers offered in a personal communication the following comment in regard to this sentence:

> Surely the "desire"—insofar as we can claim to know—was to honor those who fought for the right to a representative government. It's easy to get a mob to ignite against a "multi-racial government"—but to get a sustained fundraising effort going, you have to have a principle at work rather than simply a prejudice. The principle in this case was connected (in the [white] Southerner's minds at least) to the reason they came to America in the first place. In the carpetbagger governments set up, they had no vote; their property was often confiscated, etc., etc. I think you have to take seriously the stated reason for the "honor" bestowed on the fallen—they fought for "liberty and home rule." Were they also anti-black racists? Yes. But the *meaning* of the statue must surely take into account the point of view of these Southerners as well as our more enlightened one.

Professor Flower's comment surely exemplifies the problem of "polysemousness" in regard to assigning meaning (or signification) to any given object-signifier. This is one reason for the fudge words "for many" in the disputed sentence. To the extent that any society is genuinely multicultural, the meaning of public edifices like the Liberty Monument will be "essentially contested." I consider this issue at greater length in Levinson, "They Whisper" (see note 18).

51. Winks (see note 46), B7 (emphasis added). Recall that it had been taken down during the riverfront construction.

52. Ibid.

53. See "New Orleans Tries to Erase a Symbol," *The New York Times*, 16 Oct. 1989, A18.

54. I owe this suggestion to Robert Post.

55. Winks (see note 46), B7.

56. Ian Buruma, *The Wages of Guilt: Memories of the War in Germany and Japan* (New York: Farrar, Straus & Giroux, 1994).

57. Once one becomes sensitive to the issue of public monuments, examples become legion. I cannot resist mention of an article by Michael J. Ybarra, "San Francisco Journal: Century-Old Monument Feels the Clash of History," *The New York Times*, 7 May 1996, A8, which details a current controversy in that city concerning the Pioneer Monument, a "huge granite pedestal topped by a bronze statue [that] has four life-sized groups of sculpture around the base, including one that shows an Indian on the ground, with a friar standing over him who is pointing to heaven and a Spanish vaquero raising a hand in triumph." The monument was moved from what had become a somewhat seedy area of the city to a place "between the old and new libraries and across a park from the new City Hall." As Ybarra points out, "preservationists objected to moving the statue at all; Indians wanted it junked." One member of the American Indian Movement Confederation described the monument as symbolizing "the humiliation, degradation, genocide and sorrow inflicted upon this country's indigenous people by a foreign invader, through religious persecution and ethnic prejudice." The solution to such objections was a decision by the city's art commission to "install a brass plaque to explain the misfortunes suffered by the indigenous population." The original draft of the plaque was to read: "With their efforts over in 1834, the missionaries left behind about 56,000 converts—and 150,000 dead. Half the orig-

inal Native American population had perished during this time from disease, armed attacks and mistreatment." This provoked a response from a Catholic Archbishop of the Archdiocese of San Francisco, complaining that it insulted the church, a complaint echoed by the consul general of Spain. Kevin Starr, a distinguished historian of California's past, complained that the wording was "a horrible and hateful distortion of the truth"; others suggested that it was in fact too light on the church. Following an extended debate, the art commission voted to delete "and 150,000 dead" and to add a phrase that, in Ybarra's words, "attribut[es] the decline of the Indian population to European contact, taking the onus off the church. The commission also discussed soliciting an additional monument giving the Indian point of view." I note without additional comment the bland assumption that there is a single "Indian point of view."

58. *Lochner v. New York,* 198 U.S. 45, 76 (1905).

59. Or perhaps the person in question has taken advantage of the opportunity offered by contemporary computer technology to have the ex-spouse removed from family photos. See "High-Tech Service Zaps Ex-Spouses Out of Family Photos," *San Antonio Express-News,* 7 Jan. 1996, J1.

60. One must recognize as well the most common (and poignant) reality in regard to almost all public monuments, which is their irrelevance to the future generations who are supposed to be tutored. Thus the great Austrian novelist Robert Musil wrote that "The most important [quality of monuments] is somewhat contradictory: what strikes one most about monuments is that one doesn't notice them. There is nothing in the world as invisible as monuments." Robert Musil, "Monuments," in idem, *Robert Musil: Selected Writings,* Burton Pike, ed., (New York: Continuum, 1986), 320. I am tempted to write an essay entitled "Remember the *Maine*?" about the Soldiers and Sailors Monument at the southeast corner of Central Park in New York, whose purpose was to encourage the citizenry indeed never to forget those who lost their lives on the battleship *Maine,* the attack on which served as the excuse for the Spanish-American War. Despite the slogan, "Remember the *Maine*," one doubts that more than a handful of New Yorkers remember the *Maine* today, and the monument could serve as Exhibit A for Musil's mordant commentary about the pathos of the monumental enterprise. Although the futility of such instances of consciousness management are clear, the implications for a "theory" of public monuments in the liberal state are not.

Censorship in the Heart of Difference: Cultural Property, Indigenous Peoples' Movements, and Challenges to Western Liberal Thought

George E. Marcus

Valorized and functional practices of censorship among contemporary non-Western peoples have acquired new meaning as these groups struggle for identity and recognition within the context of their present existence as specifically "indigenous" or "Fourth World" peoples.[1] All such peoples have had checkered and uniformly dismal histories under colonial and subsequent liberal nation-state regimes, but they now have new opportunities for recognition and repositioning both in the larger state-governed societies of which they are a part and within the framework of new transnational global formations. The official terms in which such peoples were or might have been recognized by the dominant society are in disarray, a situation that offers these groups strategies for developing a politics of identity that operates simultaneously on global and local scales. Direct calls for sovereignty and nationhood do not seem as important in contemporary indigenous peoples movements as claims to cultural property, which is precisely the framework in which complex arguments about censorship arise. At issue is censorship's status as a past practice in indigenous communities and its significance and necessity as a political tactic and a cultural norm as these groups make claims to the encompassing liberal orders, claims that collapse and entwine arguments about possession, rights, and cultural authenticity.

Valorized censorship operating in the context of indigenous peoples' movements places particular constraints on critical discussions on this topic for those in Western democracies, whose framing values (such as the priority given to free expression at the level of the individual) are not otherwise open to question. For example, are indigenous practices of censorship, traditionally internal to relationships within particular societies, identical or even related to censorship that is attempted as part of a political strategy concerning claims to cultural property? Indeed, in Western value terms, what difference does it make if censorship that is wielded politically by indigenous peoples is not completely consistent, or only ambiguously so, with the cultural authenticity of internal censoring practices for such people? And, stipulating the principle of tolerance in Western liberal doctrine, how much suspicion or grudging acceptance remains in the encompassing culture for the valorized censorship that is practiced by the encompassed indigenous peoples? What does such ambivalence, apparent in Western responses to and management of claims to cultural property by its radical "Others within," indicate about the consistency and limits of Western society's recently renewed critical discussions concerning the operations of censorship? Those engaged in these discussions have often been oblivious to indigenous peoples' renewed claims for more powerful positions within the terrain of liberal society.

My concern here focuses on the principled discourse of the tutelary state. In his chapter on the tutelary function of public monuments, Sanford Levinson nicely states the implications for discussions about censorship in relation to questions about cultural property:

> "Cultural regulation" occurs not only—indeed, increasingly rarely, at least in the United States—through the negative acts of overtly silencing by threat of punishment those with given views, but, perhaps more significantly, through the *affirmative* acts of the state when it speaks on behalf of the people, or "community," in whose name the state commonly claims to rule.[2]

For my purposes, it is the *singularity* with which Levinson expresses the state's interest in cultural regulation that is important, since the liberal state faces unprecedented challenges to accommodate diverse demands for legal recognition that undermine the idea of a transcendent, integrated single "people," "community," or "nation" that the state ultimately represents. These challenges rise in the morally weighted discussions about so-called multiculturalism and the struggles for rights, recognition, and identity among diverse groups.

The unquestioned emergence of new rhetorics of participation and citizenship in society demands new discourses of law and policy that admit of distinct, enduring identities. Certain privileges and rights are required to establish these discourses, yet they must still operate within the bounds of a coherent doctrine of citizenship. It is at just such intersections of contradictory interests—those of the liberal tradition and those of the claims of aboriginal peoples to unconventional but powerfully effective forms of cultural property—where censorship is key. Liberal law and policy must mediate between these interests pragmatically and doctrinally.

The kinds of cultural property that are being claimed by aboriginal peoples—sometimes purely as a tactic, sometimes as an extension of long-standing authentic internal practices—are different from those that have been considered in legal scholarship thus far, and they carry very different implications.[3] It has usually been the recovery and protection of material culture—archaeological artifacts and sites, physical remains, and items held in museum collections—that has been at issue in cultural property cases.

Further, as Joseph Sax demonstrates, the development of concepts of cultural property in Western law is tied very closely to nationalism and the historic evolution of the nation-state.[4] In those few situations, relatively unusual in the past, where the law has restricted the disposition of cultural heritage property, it has done so in the name of "our" heritage; here the state speaks for "us" as a collective national identity. In sympathetically taking up indigenous peoples' claims to cultural property, however, the law begins to speak for the Other not only as part of the body politic but also as recognized as a distinctively and specifically different member of it. Existing legal notions of cultural property are quite unprepared to manage either, on the one hand, the less material claims by contemporary indigenous peoples' movements to images and representations as a form of mixed intellectual and cultural property or, on the other, the irreducible, nonaggregative claims to cultural property at the level of encompassed groups within the nation-state.

Perhaps less priority and legitimacy could legally be given to the cultural property claims of encompassed groups relative to those of the nation-state if it were not for the fact that the cultural property of specifically *aboriginal* or *originary* groups is in question. The indigenous peoples of the United States, Canada, and Australia all have come to occupy a special moral and symbolic status within their respective societies, a status that has been marked by a willingness to define for these groups special legal entitlements and privileges. In a sense, the liberal nation-state, perhaps in atonement for a painfully self-conscious past of abusing indigenous peoples, needs to enhance the legitimacy and standing of its original inhabitants in order to sustain its own. Thus, the special legitimacy of indigenous peoples within these societies actually gives their claims to cultural property a certain priority over those of the nation, although it is to the nation as imagined community that the notion of cultural property has historically been most strongly linked. It is precisely this originary legitimacy that sets the scene for and gives a particular edge to the element of censorship that is involved in fulfilling these claims.

The heart of this chapter will present three "exhibits" that illustrate the nature of contemporary claims to radical forms of cultural property by aboriginal peoples. First, however I will briefly explain the stake and participation of anthropology in discussions about censorship and explore the Western response to censorship.

The Contemporary Stake of Anthropology in Debates About Censorship

Anthropology as a discipline has been directly and indirectly an important historical actor in the tutelary function of cultural regulation. It has, for example, constructed the expert, authoritative representations of Native Americans in the official discourses of law and policy and in public discussion, which were in the past largely deaf to Native American voices. It seems appropriate to address reflexively the changing participation of anthropology in debate about censorship, which itself is an integral part of the active tutelary process in liberal states and societies.

Furthermore, the internal rhetorical critique of anthropology's authoritative ethnographic discourse on its traditional Others as objects of study that occurred during the 1980s and the debates since evocatively mirror the more general problem now confronting liberal law and policy making. Policy makers must determine how they will confront difference within the framework of the state's explicitly recognized tutelary function. Anthropological rhetoric and analytic tools were relatively secure as long as cultures could be conceived as easily bounded external forms of Otherness. The practices by which subjects were constituted as objects of knowledge and by which doctrines of research and a sense of disciplinary progress could be sustained have been effaced by an intimate understanding of the ongoing construction of anthropological knowledge at the level of its practices and language as well as the worldwide transformation of conditions of marginality and of the relative isolation of anthropology's traditional subjects. The critique still offers little hope for new unifying paradigms of the older sort; instead it encourages incremental and nuanced changes in modes of conceptualization and practices of research. Large effects grow from contemporary struggles with new materials, and no less can be said for contemporary transformations in liberal law and policy making.

The distinctive cultural Other, by the radicality of its own voiced claims operating within the procedures of liberal law and politics, is for law and the state, as for anthropology, no longer elsewhere — beyond a border — but is in a sense everywhere. Thus indigenous peoples can no longer be accommodated as a special case or subject of law; they are instead subjects whose status and treatment in law have direct consequences for the norms of applied liberal ideas. The implication of the cases considered here, where the traditional interests of anthropology and law happen to converge, is that the stakes are greater for the disciplinary interests together than for either set alone; questioned is liberalism's capacity to accommodate the most radical claims of democracy.

The marked trend in recent humanities scholarship on censorship, especially as it relates to literature in Western societies, has been to nuance and complicate the common and rather stark, black-and-white dichotomy of authoritarian censor versus heroic free-expressing author.[5] A general skepticism powering cultural critique has sustained the basic moral position implicated in this dichotomy while undermining its innocence. The work of the censor can sometimes be recognized in such routine practices as editing, where the relationship between the censor and author has been shown to be often more complicit than conflicting, thus making the process of silencing a much more integral factor in the actual creative process than formerly supposed. Moreover, writers are often engaged in policing themselves by the silencing entailed in mere practices of scholarly etiquette, taste, and so on. Since censorship is always somewhat self-defeating and can never totally obliterate its object (indeed, merely mentioning what is proscribed gives it some life), the censor himself is always involved in some degree of self-subversion with interesting psychological consequences that have been examined in recent scholarship.[6]

This challenge to and blurring of the stereotypic view of censorship is within the basic valorized categories and discourse of Western liberalism (including, of course, its former major opponent—authoritarian regimes of communism and socialism). The classical contribution of anthropology to this discussion would have been to provide a relativizing "outside" perspective, drawn from the cumulative ethnographic archive of what were once unapologetically designated as "exotic" or "primitive" societies. Anthropology would have revealed something about the equivalence or nonequivalence of the practice of censorship among the distant and distinctly "other" peoples recorded in classic ethnographies, such as the Nuer, the Trobriand islanders, or the Tikopians, and it would have been up to liberal scholars to make what they wished of such comparative data from the general realm of "radical difference" (the "Rest" in relation to the "West") in the framework of their own arguments. The powerful critiques of anthropological representation that appeared in the 1980s, which should be seen as an element of a broader critical trend examining colonial and postcolonial discourse in the West, undermined the discipline's traditional view of the Other, and it would be tricky at best and questionable at least for anthropologists to continue to participate in this traditional way in liberal debates such as the one on censorship.[7] Certainly the "outside" perspective, which challenges the basic categories of liberalism (for example, autonomous individualism) while cogently addressing issues such as censorship, is necessary. What then is the alternative for anthropology, a discourse historically developed fully within the frameworks of liberalism, on one hand, and colonialism, on the other?

Contemporary anthropologists must overcome in thought and practice the denial of coevality to our ethnographic subjects. In 1983, Johannes Fabian revealed that anthropologists had constructed other peoples as objects of study by denying that these peoples shared the contemporaneous lifeworlds of anthropologists themselves.[8] Recognition of coevality in ethnography has a transformative implication: it means admitting the presence of radical difference that ethnography has habitually described, freed from its construction in distant time and space, into the heart of Western discourses and their deep assumptions. For anthropology, such a possibility has stimulated complex discussions of reflexivity, giving voice to others, the nature of dialogue, and ethics generally in the conduct of ethnography. For U.S. society, and others, it has meant resonant public debates about cultural diversity, multiculturalism, and, ultimately, about the political nature of culture itself. Overcoming the powerful past denial of coevality in the construction of anthropological subjects means dealing with the question of censorship among peoples who are outside Western liberal discourse and culture but who are also deeply engaged with Western culture at its borders or within its processes and institutional operations. Traditional examples, then, of distinctive Otherness or radical difference that were provided by anthropology to fulfill liberalism's demand to complete itself by reflecting on what lay beyond its own borders (an ideological feature that has been historically and often subtly linked with colonialism) are now reconfigured as engaged and incorporated Others—peoples, that is, who are not just objects in a comparative exercise but function in themselves as decisive challenges and critical probes *within* liberal debates.

The particular anthropological complement that I want to apply to current rethinkings of censorship is a consideration of coevality in relation to particular indigenous peoples' movements, especially in contemporary nation-states that descend from British colonialization—movements such as those of Native Americans in the United States and in Canada and of aborigines in Australia. These are "Others *within*" whose practices in relation to censorship are not mere ethnographic data of comparative interest, but are an integral part of their embracing societies, and as such offer different sorts of challenges both to and within these societies.

Among many non-Western peoples organized in small-scale societies that anthropologists have traditionally studied, the possession, articulation, and circulation of knowledge are key to the definition of social distinctions relating to age, gender, and leadership and to the existence of hierarchies and the distribution of power. Censorship, the control of behavior and speech, is thus an integral feature of these societies, as are remarkable independence and freedom of choice in different measure. Past ethnographic studies of these societies sought to understand the cultural logic by which exacting censorship and openness could coexist in the same lifeworld. In the broader Western reception of such "primitive" societies, the fascinating empirical combinations of freedoms and disciplines have most often been sorted out, for particular philosophical and ideological ends, as stereotypes of what the West either desires (freedom from censorship—the Margaret Mead "Coming of Age in Samoa" syndrome) or abhors (deep and dark repression—the Derek Freeman counter-representation of Samoa).[9] The critiques of anthropological representation developed in the 1980s have liberated a large number of contemporary ethnographers from further complicity in these kinds of appropriations. Taking up the claims of indigenous peoples to cultural property, I argue, now stands in effect for the simple distanced comparison of the "outside perspective within" that anthropology would have at one time provided to Western liberal discourse's efforts to come to terms with the complexities of censorship.

A Brief Foray into the Satanic Verses *Affair*

Western liberalism's response to censorship is implicated in the workings of an unprecedentedly fluid transcultural flow of information, issues, and debates. Certain aspects of this predicament are apparent in certain aspects in the early development of the dramatic, still ongoing, and much discussed controversy over Salman Rushdie's *Satanic Verses.* On the face of it, this case differs distinctively from that of censorship practices in indigenous peoples' movements, since rather than originating from others that are within and are controlled by Western states, the *fatwa* against Salman Rushdie appears on and beyond the borders of the West, in the domain of Islam, and especially fundamentalist Islam—a massive cultural Other that is not controlled by Western states. It is all too easy to construct the Rushdie affair in the monolithic and threatening terms of the post–Cold War era as a "clash of civilizations," as ominous as the late Cold War struggle itself.[10] Western liberals quickly and easily played into this mode by rallying to the defense of artistic freedom in the face of such a "barbaric" attempt to censor. The question is whether they could have been expected to do otherwise in the Rushdie case, and how their response to that case might differ from their contemporaries.

My treatment of the Rushdie affair might be thought of as functioning as an intermediate case that examines liberal *confrontation* with censorship when the cultural Other is conceptually beyond the West's literal borders and can thus be condemned as being conventionally "alien" and "other." This should be distinguished from liberal *accommodation* to censorship that originates from the space of an Other, but that is completely within the West's literal and imaginary borders. The Rushdie affair poses an ironic frame to my primary focus on the law's consideration of the power to censor in indigenous peoples' claims to cultural property.

Satanic Verses was published in late September 1988 and was given a dismissive review in Tehran without any special concern. As Michael Fischer and Mehdi Abedi have noted:

> Rushdie was well-known: both *Midnight's Children* and *Shame* had been translated into Persian, the latter winning the state prize, awarded by President Ali Khamenei, for the best translation of a novel. Both these previous novels contain considerable satire about (mis)uses of Islam. It was only four and a half months later on 14 February 1989, that Khomeini issued the fatwa. This fatwa was disputed in its legal validity by various Muslim jurists. It is significant that the agitations against the novel began not in Iran, but in two quite different political arenas: India and Britain.[11]

Indeed, the most memorable event that ignited the controversy in the West was the protest in Bradford, England, by Pakistani migrants, which culminated in the public burning of Rushdie's book on 14 January 1989. As Fischer and Abedi and others have shown, the local dynamics of the migrant Muslim communities in Britain leading to the book burning were far from the political machinations that led to Khomeini's *fatwa:*

> In terms of political drama and skill, Khomeini, of course, by issuing a fatwa calling for Rushdie's death, out-trumped and out-classed the notice achieved by the Bradford book burning. Technically, Khomeini's fatwa is but an opinion issued in response to questions submitted to him by Muslims in Britain, and is not enforceable unless there is a trial under Islamic due process. In fact, however, Khomeini has transgressed normal Islamic law here . . . by directly using the mass media to

> incite people to kill Rushdie, and by asserting that no repentance by Rushdie could be accepted.... The timing of Khomeini's call was not arbitrary: it was a way to seize international leadership for a cause célèbre that others had created in other arenas, and it blocked a series of moves by internal factions to normalize relations with the West.[12]

Western anthropological commentary on the early Western responses to the controversy took its normal course—to demonstrate misunderstandings and ignorance of cultural subtleties and the complexities of local situations in defense or in qualification of the Other, who was so one-sidedly constructed as the villain:

> In the West, ignorance of the internal cultural politics of the Muslim world caused many people to accept the definitions of Islam, and who is a proper Muslim, proposed by the fundamentalists. Within the Muslim world, the voices of progressives and liberals, and even traditional conservatives, were muted, intimidated by the extraordinary clout fundamentalism had achieved in the preceding two decades. Western intellectuals eventually defined the issue as one of illegitimate censorship and the right of expression. They did not know enough about Islam to pick up the few timid calls by moderates among Muslim traditionalists that Rushdie be at least tried before being sentenced,... that his book be refuted, and that the bounties on Rushdie's head besmirched Islam. That is, these Muslims were trying to remind the world that Islam was being violated by Khomeini.... Admission was being made that perhaps the book could not be refuted because, with one partial exception, all the stories about Islam in it... are drawn from the hadith, and thus any effort by Muslims to write a refutation would require a self-examination of precisely the sort that the novel itself engages. Moreover, Western intellectuals seemed not to be aware of the long tradition of satire in the Islamic world, including what various gate-keepers regard as blasphemy, nor of the moral parables within Islam promoting tolerance in dealing with blasphemers and doubters.[13]

Who were those in the West—those engaged in righteous protests against the lethal censorship of Khomeini and the totalitarianism he represented—silencing? Far from being a product of the feared "Other without" on the borders of the West, which Western responses had helped construct, the Muslim world's reaction to *Satanic Verses* sprang from complex local situations, including those involving migrant Muslims.

While the liberal response in defense of free expression was not inappropriate or unjustified, it was naive in its attempt to cross cultural boundaries, and it thus inadvertently helped to Orientalize Islam. In the West, Rushdie is considered a Western writer (or at least a writer in a universal normative sense), but his actual transcultural identifications are considerably more complex than those implied by the heroic image of the writer as a victim of censorship. More nuanced arguments about Rushdie's relation to Islam, which do not necessarily exonerate him as innocent, need to be incorporated into the responses of a thoroughly transcultural West, for which traditional liberal notions of cultural difference are inadequate.

Finally, as an act of censorship, the Bradford book burning, although violent and dramatic, was not at all equivalent to Khomeini's act of censorship. The book burning is symbolic of a sort of politics and struggle that is quite different from the *fatwa*. In terms of Western liberal values, the book burning deserves to be criticized, but it needs even more to be understood in a context that moves us on to the practices of censorship in the life and politics of Fourth World peoples.[14]

Censorship among Indigenous Peoples and Its Uses in Making Claims to Cultural Property

The issues in the Rushie case were not unrelated to those of indigenous peoples encapsulated within Western liberal political orders, whose difference is only partially accommodated through limited reigning concepts of tolerance and pluralism. The following three fragments, drawn from different sources, document attempts made by indigenous peoples in North America and Canada to restrict the circulation of sacred knowledge.

Exhibit 1

The first exhibit is a passage from a paper presented at a scholarly meeting.

> The new repatriation laws—the Native American Graves Protection and Repatriation Act (NAGPRA) 1990, and the National Museum of the American Indian Act, 1989—are historic acts. Their stated aim of giving back the wrongful possessions of museums and other scientific institutions appears to prepare the way for the process of decolonization in relation to the officially recognized Indian tribes of the United States. In the various meetings I've attended between Indian peoples and museum representatives over the implementation of these laws, there is one concern on the part of Native Americans that keeps resurfacing: namely, how can sacred knowledge be given more protection. For example, NAGPRA has nothing to say about what happens to tribal secrets that may be revealed to museum staff as proof of an object's sacred nature. What legal recourse do Indians have to ensure that sacred knowledge is not caught up in the boundlessly public pathways of academic exchange? Will these secrets need to be protected as intellectual property in the same way that the sacred object itself is protected by NAGPRA as cultural property?[15]

Exhibit 2

The second exhibit is a passage from an article in an academic journal.

> The University of Nebraska Press is planning to publish the book, *The Hopi Salt Journey*, by Ekkehart A. Malotki, a professor of modern language at Northern Arizona University, early next year. Some Hopi cooperated in the current research, and in Mr. Malotki's other projects, but tribal leaders say that publishing data from the research that spurred the controversy steps over the line of acceptability,

> widely revealing what should remain closely guarded knowledge transmitted only to a few privileged religious initiates. Lori Minkler, an assistant to the Hopi tribal leader, said such revelations would strike at the roots of Hopi religion, which is based on distinctions about who has access to sacred rituals and ceremonies.[16]

Exhibit 3

The third exhibit is comprised of notes from a conversation with Fred Myers, author of an ethnography of the Pintupi, an Australian aboriginal people.[17]

Myers related to me and commented on the well-known events surrounding the publication of *Yiwara,* written by anthropologist Richard Gould in 1969. The book included photographs of sacred places and objects of the Yiwara, and a copy was eventually taken back to the Yiwara community by a girl who had worked with Gould. She was speared (a traditional penalty), and members of the community said that they would kill Gould if he ever returned. Gould apologized and never returned. This incident is still discussed among Australian anthropologists and within aboriginal communities. From 1973 through 1975, when Myers was doing fieldwork in Australia, there was extreme sensitivity about the Gould incident among other aboriginal peoples. The Pintupi were concerned about the circulation of their acrylic paintings in the Western art world, and although Myers was allowed by the Pintupi to go to every initiation, he was not allowed to make any notes or take any photographs. On his return to Australia in 1980, Myers was not even allowed to attend the same initiation rituals he had witnessed earlier because the Pintupi had begun to initiate whites. Myers could attend only if he agreed to be initiated, and he declined.

The point of these three exhibitions is that there are constantly changing boundaries in aboriginal societies about what knowledge and practices must be censored in relation to whom. Myers notes that this censoring on the borders of aboriginal society is completely consistent with the prevalence of internal controls on the rights to display, or otherwise make known, objects, forms, and images (including those that secure rights to land, which of course has had a major impact on the legal adjudication of aboriginal land claims, a protracted project of the Australian government).[18] It is not always clear who has rights to the display of particular objects or forms, and it is very difficult for people to get full authorization to do so. Merely declaring that you have the right does not mean that the statement will be generally accepted: there is no Lockean concept of the autonomous individual in aboriginal society. Yet, notions of property are intimately bound up with the self, making the complete alienation of sacred property from one individual to another, or one group to another, always incomplete. Even if a vision or display is your own, it might also be someone else's. This matter is always on the edge of contestation, and there is a real threat of violence on the part of persons who have not been consulted about displays in which they also claim to have rights.

The commodification of aboriginal images as works of tourist and fine art, as ethnographic data, and as museum specimens has made the control of sacred knowledge all the more complicated. The works of Myers and of Howard Morphy have demonstrated the subtle and successful accommodations that aboriginal artists have made in the production of images and objects, but the danger of violating the censorship that is so vital to the production of cultural meaning in aboriginal society is always present when the cultural images are circulated beyond the confines of aboriginal society.[19] Myers notes that there is now a white man who runs a copyright service to pay aboriginal people for reproducing their images in Western settings.

Myers reminded me, however, that the cover of *Rereading Cultural Anthropology*, which I edited for Duke University Press, reproduces aboriginal designs that were merely appropriated by the art director of the press without any consultation with or payment to aboriginal peoples. In response to Myers's complaint, the editor at Duke, known for its list in cultural studies and cultural critique, showed indifference.[20] Little wonder then that aboriginal societies have a heightened interest in controlling and censoring the circulation of their knowledge beyond their borders. The integrity of life within the aboriginal community comes in part from the control and censorship of sacred knowledge among its members. The continuance of this integrity demands no less an effort at exterior control and censorship as this knowledge begins to circulate far beyond the borders and reach of the community. Anthropologists themselves, as well as other scholars, are perhaps the major "victims" as indigenous peoples worldwide reclaim their cultural and intellectual property through practices of censorship.

The three exhibits are typical examples. Historically subject to policies of physical displacement and literal genocide by white settlers who came to dominate their lands, contemporary indigenous peoples have long struggled for recognition and position in the nation-states in which they have become encapsulated by claiming the lands and territories that are tied to their traditional cultures.[21] Only recently have such peoples created a politics of identity and recognition through a more generic struggle over cultural property, an initiative which is at once more radical and more complex than are claims only to traditional lands.[22] Claims to land and the status of past treaties remain important, but there is a sense in which all lands, no matter how remote or physically separated from national society, have been degraded in a traditional sense by the spread of media, markets, corporate development schemes, and consumer culture. Even though indigenous peoples may retain control of particular territories, they can still be invaded by a corrosive mass culture in which they operate with the disadvantages of poverty, unequal access to education, and so on. The land cannot perhaps be as effectively "sacred" as it once was.

To make claims to cultural property more broadly conceived is a much more radical, and in a sense, postmodern strategy for the pursuit of identity politics and for movements of cultural renewal and survival. For one thing, to

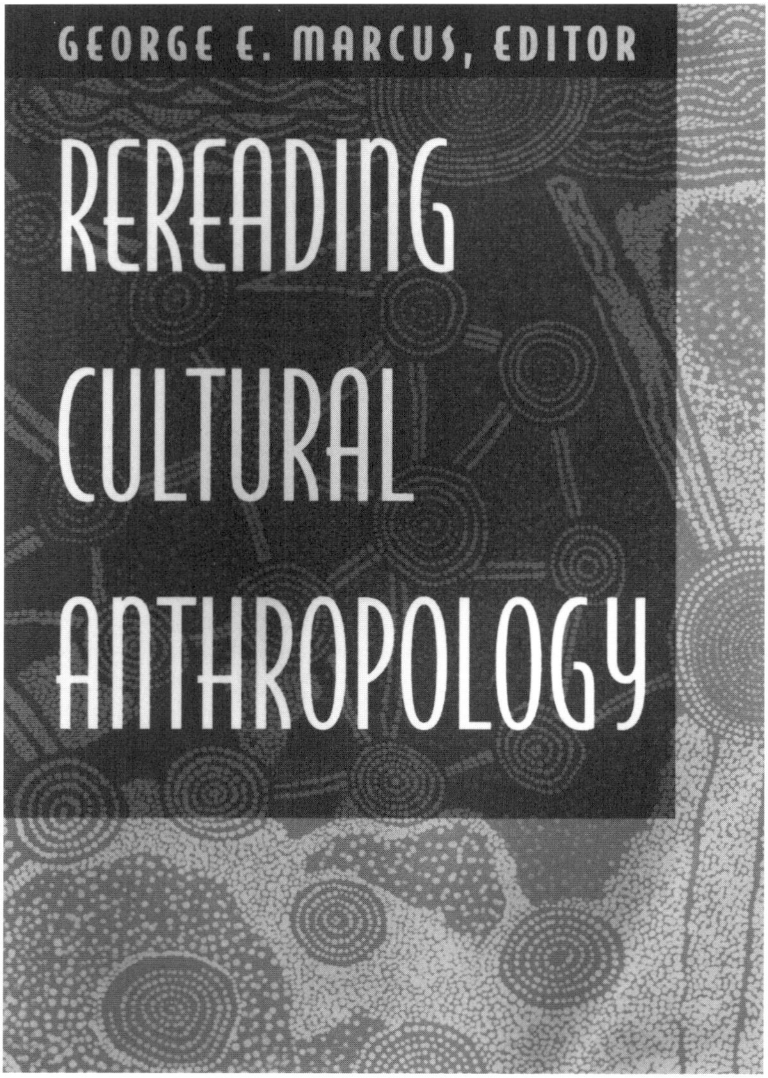

Cover of *Rereading Cultural Anthropology*
(Duke University Press, 1992).
Cover design by Jill Mahanna.
Reprinted with permission.

claim cultural property is to make the struggle of indigenous peoples within their larger social and political orders much more intimate, since claims to cultural property go to the heart of the cultural appropriations that dominant societies have made in the interest of constructing their self-identity. Certain representations of indigenous peoples in law, popular culture, and national mythology, and their circulation as objects, images, and items of specialized knowledge, have been vital to the West's own sense of itself. The capacity of indigenous peoples to control and to censor vital aspects of the West's identity give these claims a provocatively critical dimension in current discussions of the state of liberal democracies.

Claims to cultural property have been forged from pre-existing bodies of law concerning cultural property as it applies to national patrimony and to intellectual property law, particularly in relation to artistic production.[23] What makes the claims of indigenous peoples so potentially provocative to Western liberal thought is that they define a form of cultural property that does not respect the nation-state but instead stands for the exclusive Other that operates within and across the boundaries of nation-states. These claims violate the law's assumption of autonomous individualism.

The autonomous individual is the basic construct of the subject—the liberal person—in intellectual property law. Legal discourse takes this construct virtually for granted, and the cultural assumptions that are deeply embedded in this construct create the conditions for liberal legal discourse itself. More important, the autonomous individual bears the norms of what Jürgen Habermas identified as communicational competence, one kind of rational discourse that enables the routine assimilation of society's conflicts into case law.[24] When faced with challenges from collectivities and groups, liberal law has successfully preserved the construct of the autonomous individual, which is essential to its entire normative framework of practice, through the fictive corporate individual, which treats powerful collectives as if they were persons.

Merely by accepting to operate within the legal system, claimants to cultural property accept identification as corporate individuals and the consequent embedded norms of communicational competence; however, the nature and substance of the claims themselves—which, in their most legitimate expression among aboriginal peoples, reflect long-standing customs and internal practices—push against and cannot but challenge the identification as a corporate individual which claimants must accept in order to act within the law. It is in this rather subversive sense (sometimes in spite of the intention of claimants) that the corporate individual device is "double-voiced," especially given that in the legal tradition contemporary judicial authority is inclined to accept, encourage, or at least entertain claims to cultural property of the sort discussed here.

The demand for the recognition of cultural property would not have been so readily entertained by English-based legal systems were it not for the special standing of indigenous peoples. Cultural property has been defined and claimed on the basis of such instances of cultural violence as

> the seizure of land, government suppression of Indian religious practice, the prohibition on the speaking of Indian languages in residential schools, the expropriation of ceremonial objects for museum collections, the unauthorized excavation of indigenous graves and collection of material culture by archaeologists, the definition and description of Native culture by non-Native anthropologists, the loss of Indian status to children of mothers who married non-Natives, the apprehension of aboriginal children from reserves, the separation of families, the withholding from a generation of children of their very identity as First Nations people, and a related legacy of sexual abuse.[25]

Central to these practices is the experience of having cultural identity extinguished, denied, or suppressed, and classified, named, or designated by others. The strongest immediate power that would be conferred by the recognition of cultural property would be the capacity to censor representations and constrict the circulation of indigenous knowledge. For example, Metis video maker Loretta Todd defines the inability to speak on one's own behalf as constitutive of the experience of cultural appropriation:

> For me, the definition of appropriation originates in its inversion, cultural autonomy. Cultural autonomy signifies a right to one's origins and histories as told from within the culture and not as mediated from without. Appropriation occurs when someone else speaks for, tells, defines, represents, uses or recruits the images, stories, experiences, dreams of others for their own. Appropriation also occurs when someone else becomes the expert on your experience.[26]

Apparently in the present era there has been an increasing willingness on the part of Western liberal governments to meet this demand, and this can be seen to some degree in the more general liberal opinion of scholars, intellectuals, and others not otherwise concerned with indigenous peoples. Out of a current mood of critical self-examination, notions of cultural property have been incorporated into law (for example, NAGPRA, land claim cases, the overcoming of the "*terra nullius*" doctrine in Australia on which the colony and nation were founded), even though the new laws contain radical implications for, and in some cases contradictions to, liberal practices and principles. Such willingness is not, however, without a detectable sense of regret, suspicion, inconvenience, and "grudgingness."

This general ambivalence has been registered as a questioning of the integrity or authenticity of claims at the individual and group level to Indian identity as well as a questioning of the authenticity of long-standing customs.[27] It is also registered by the tendency to ignore claims to cultural property if it is easy to do so with impunity and if it is in the interests of commerce and the flow of information (as in the instance of the cover design for *Rereading Cultural Anthropology*). Even among anthropologists and other scholars who respect the indigenous control of cultures, there is a sense of regret and inconvenience that they must observe a censorship that they would not otherwise tolerate.

This uneasiness undoubtedly arises from a fear that if groups claiming special identities are granted exclusive privileges that interrupt the free flow of information, liberal societies with rapidly changing demographic compositions and concomitant transcultural influences could begin to slide toward fragmentation. Also, particularly with regard to Native peoples, the recognition of cultural property has substantially disrupted the self-construction of white society—and this helps drive the ambivalence and suspicion that accompanies the current accommodation of the demands of indigenous peoples.

In some sense, Western liberal ambivalence in the face of valorized censorship is understandable in cases that are culturally ambiguous— where it is not clear that the tight control of knowledge functions internally and traditionally in the same way that it does when it is used as a powerful tactic to assert exclusive claims against outsiders. In other words, there may be no cultural integrity or authenticity to particular claims other than as an effective politics of identity in relation to the larger society. This is precisely the sort of issue that sensitive ethnography could vitally inform and clarify. Yet, while the identification of censorship as an authentic traditional practice might make liberals feel better about recognizing it as part of a justified claim to cultural property, the fact of its authenticity would probably make no difference at all to activists within indigenous societies, since the right to censor the appropriation of their histories, images, and knowledge does not rest on consistency with the internal moral and social practices of their cultures, but on the history of domination itself.

Furthermore, the claim to identity, albeit collective, as a form of property seems contradictory to the demand of indigenous peoples for the recognition of cultural tenets that are different in principle from the doctrine of possessive or autonomous individualism, a foundational assumption of Western liberal culture. Indeed, there has been much discussion among scholars concerned with indigenous peoples' movements and multiculturalism about the tricky play of this contradiction. As Rosemary Coombe has remarked,

> First Nations peoples may well be compelled to articulate their claims "in a language that power understands" but in the substance of their claims they contest the logic of possessive individualism, even as they give voice to its metaphors. Native peoples engage in "double voiced rhetoric" when they employ the tropes of a dominant language—simultaneously engaging and subverting these metaphors through the character of the claims they make in the voice of the Other.[28]

The perils of making claims in the language of possessive individualism, writ large, are real ones, as Native peoples in Canada have discovered. For example, when, in a presentation on Native cultural autonomy and the appropriation of aboriginal imagery at a meeting of independent film makers, Todd quoted Walter Benjamin, she was promptly accused of appropriating Western culture. She responded that she was part of Western culture—as a product of colonization, how could she be otherwise?—and that Benjamin was part of that culture. Her interlocutors informed her that white use of Native imagery was equivalent to her use of Benjamin, because Native imagery was now simply a part of contemporary Culture — with a capital "C."

Below the din caused by such intricate twists in seminar rooms and lecture halls is a "purer," more consistent, and unquestionably culturally integral case of extending a regime of internal censorship over a larger society, not primarily as a contemporary tactic in the politics of identity and recognition (although it is that too), but simply as a matter of the playing out of the complex internal cultural logics of a people — that of Australian aborigines, for example. This is the sort of case that makes Western liberals feel better, in that they value a high degree of cultural authenticity and consistency when they are used as factors in justifying the granting of "inconvenient" rights to control and censor cultural property.

Australian aborigines do not have perhaps the same crucial place in the imaginary and cultural expressions of national self-identity among white Australians as do Native Americans in the mythos of white America. In terms of the popular cultural assimilation of knowledge about indigenous peoples' lifeways, Australian aborigines are far more "exotic" and less familiar to white Australians than are Native Americans to white Americans (consider the strong presence of the Indian through the western film; there is nothing comparable in Australian popular culture). Furthermore, although Australian aborigines are just as decimated and displaced as Native Americans, they seem to have preserved a complex cosmology — the Dreaming — through the practice of a rigorous economy of knowledge, the distribution and restriction of which shape the main institutions of social control in their communities.

Operating on the level of everyday life, then, Australian aboriginal societies have an ideology of speech and action that is radically different from that of the West. For us, speech — the displaying of knowledge — should be open and free at the level of individual agency. For Australian aborigines, speech is potentially dangerous, as indicated in exhibit 3. Much of the integrity of aboriginal culture depends on the microprocesses of control by which a certain economy of knowledge is sustained. Very little of the politics of attempting to censor the flow of sacred knowledge beyond the boundaries of aboriginal societies cannot be traced to the complex principles by which aboriginal societies operate.

Aboriginal claims to cultural property are thus commensurate with their long-standing practices, down to and including the very act of speech, and as such their case starkly poses for the West a strongly justified countercase against the condemnation of censorship. This countercase is not presented through a blurring of the stereotypic binary — hard censor versus heroic author — in contrast to much of the current critical discussion of this relation, but it actually *reinforces* the stereotype from a radically different set of cultural principles: the aborigines attempt to be the hard censor of the heroic liberal (romantic?) author's appropriation of their sacred knowledge. This is definitely not a relation for blurring if it is to be an effective claim to cultural property.

Furthermore, aborigines are not Others whose coevality can any longer be denied. They are censors within liberal society as well as "Others without," and they are now directly addressing some of liberal society's sacred principles. This in turn poses special predicaments for even the most self-critical discussions among liberal intellectuals who may want to blur simplistic conceptions of the operations of censorship without necessarily dismantling the moral principles and assumptions on which the basic argument against censorship rests. The practices of the Australian aborigines, which often operate basically and consistently in the interest of censorship, present an unavoidable challenge to those who would complicate the relationship of censorship and free expression in liberal thought.

Implications

For their part, after a century or more of virtual invisibility, surviving indigenous peoples have finally found, through claims to cultural property, an unprecedentedly effective means to develop their position within and their relation to the postcolonial societies that have long ignored them as citizens or potential citizens. Much is indeed at stake for liberal social and political orders themselves in their formal recognition of such claims, since the debate that surrounds them concerns long-standing tenets of the liberal social order —namely, consistency in the rule of law, the foundational truth of the deep and often unstated assumptions that cluster around individualism, the priority given to the free flow of information, and even aspects of national self-identities that are dependent in part upon past license to appropriate the images, objects, and knowledge of indigenous peoples. Philosophical arguments against relativism will not suffice, since such peoples are not distant radical, exotic Others, but are and have long been integral parts of a liberal body politic founded in an often obscured or ignored history of colonialism.

Somehow Western liberal societies must learn to think of themselves in multi- or transcultural terms, qualitatively and to a degree that they have never done before. The problem is that there is probably no discourse of general principle, universal truth, or sure procedure—all characteristic of and dear to liberal thought—that will effect such a change. All that seems possible is an informed muddling through, characterized by endless, cumulative negotiation, compromise, and accommodation, marked by unresolved issues and trailing sentiments. Pragmatism is of course as deeply ingrained in liberal orders as is a taste for universalism, and it would seem to be the strength on which to rely in this transition.

Still, pragmatism may not be enough to satisfy the need to act morally and on principle and to justify policies across situations. This need for general truth seems essential to enable major Western institutions to have faith and confidence in themselves. Many critically edged and subtle discussions of censorship fail to lessen the condemnation of censorship, or conversely, deny the nobility of authorship, despite all the demonstrated blurrings, complicities, ironies, and ambiguities of familiar arguments.[29] It would be perverse to efface this position in complicating the understanding of censorship within classic liberal modes of thought. Forcing the boundaries of classic liberal thought requires the contemplation of a multicultural liberalism, and only the latter-day identity politics of so-called exotic Others within, such as indigenous peoples or First Nations (and not unlike non-Anglo migrant and exiled populations), can do so effectively. The specific challenge is not to liberal thought as its relates to censorship, copyright, and, ultimately, autonomous individualism, but to the necessity for liberal thought to recognize and deal with difference within its familiar arenas of constructing subjects, making judgments, and authorizing the use of force.

I find an interesting alignment of the politics of claims to cultural property with Carl Schmitt's acute critique of and challenge to liberalism, although not with the conservative, even fascistic, implication that is associated with his thought. For Schmitt, the category of "the political" itself represents the most basic demands of democracy for equality against the response of liberalism which is to substitute perpetual discussion for political action. As Tracey Strong has said of Schmitt's analysis of modern bourgeois politics,

> First, it is a system which rests on compromise; hence all of its solutions are in the end temporary, occasional, never decisive. Second, such arrangements can never resolve the claims of equality inherent in democracy.... Third, liberalism will tend to undermine the possibility of the political in that it wishes to substitute procedure for struggle. Thus, last, legitimacy and legality cannot be the same; indeed, they stand in contradiction to each other.[30]

What is then so formidable about claims to cultural property among indigenous peoples, operating within processes of liberal law and policy making, is that they undermine liberal ideology and call for different accommodations while abiding by its standard procedures and terms. The demand for the recognition and integration of absolute difference into a liberal order (partly through the capacity to censor and restrict the free flow of information in the name of identity and difference) is in effect an effort to normalize Schmitt's stark requirement of political action within a liberal regime of compromise and preference for procedural rationality. As is clear from twentieth-century European history, the confrontation of political action and the liberal law tradition is indeed precarious, but the pressing need for new models, understandings, and concepts of plural, multicultural, and still somehow liberal societies leaves little choice.

Because this implication of claims to cultural property operates within conventional legal discourse, there is often a double-voiced quality in the use of the essential concepts of legal process that are most taken for granted. The constructs of the autonomous individual and the corporate individual provide a case in point. Precisely because extraordinary powers of control are being claimed over the circulation of images and ideas, based on principles of communicational competence quite different than those implied in the construct of the autonomous individual (the regime of secrecy that values the group instead of the individual and lends degrees of power to traditional knowledge), and because these powers are being claimed to apply not only within a distinctly bounded group or culture but also within a wider and diverse society that has a vested interest in the same images and representations, the easy containment of indigenous peoples as corporate individuals, consonant with liberal norms of communication, will not hold.

The contradiction here in this key construct of the subject in liberal legal discourse is so potentially disruptive that it merits evocation in Schmitt's bold, and distasteful, position that political action, which will not be put off by liberal compromise, must be defined in terms of a stark distinction between friends and enemies. So, here, claims to cultural property, to unqualified difference as the basis for equal participation in a democracy, will not be satisfied with the status of corporate individuals—those who act with communicational competence in the perpetual discussions, compromises, and procedures of the liberal order. This is what is ultimately at stake in the sorts of claims to cultural property that indigenous peoples have been making within liberal legal systems. Moderate and compromised outcomes are no doubt possible, as long as claimants submit to the authority of liberal law, but in the process toward such outcomes, as new expressions of "the political" develop, a broad revision of liberal law theory and practice will have been defined.

Notes

1. Indigenous peoples in different national contexts of the English-speaking world are variously referred to as "Fourth World," "First Nations," or simply "Native" peoples.

2. Sanford Levinson, "The Tutelary State: 'Censorship,' 'Silencing,' and the 'Practices of Cultural Regulation,'" pages 195–219 in this volume.

3. See, for example, Patty Gerstenblith, "Identity and Cultural Property: The Protection of Cultural Property in the U.S.," *Boston University Law Review* 75 (1995): 559; John Moustakas, "Group Rights in Cultural Property," *Cornell Law Review* 74 (1989): 1179; Joseph Sax, "Heritage Preservation as a Public Duty: The Abbe Gregoire and the Origins of an Idea," *Michigan Law Review* 88 (1990): 1142; and Joseph Sax, "Is Anyone Minding Stonehenge? The Origins of Cultural Property Protection in England," *California Law Review* 78 (1990): 1543.

4. Sax, "Heritage Preservation as a Public Duty" and "Is Anyone Minding Stonehenge?" (see note 3).

5. See Pierre Bourdieu, "Censorship and the Imposition of Form," in idem, *Language and Symbolic Power,* ed. John B. Thompson, trans. Gino Raymond and Matthew Adamson (Cambridge, Mass.: Harvard Univ. Press, 1991); Richard Burt, ed., *The Administration of Aesthetics: Censorship, Political Criticism, and the Public Sphere* (Minneapolis: Univ. Minnesota Press, 1994); Robert Justin Goldstein, *Political Censorship of the Arts and the Press in Nineteenth-Century Europe* (London:

Macmillan, 1989); Michael Holquist, "Corrupt Originals: The Paradox of Censorship," PMLA 36, special issue (1994): 14–25; and Sue Curry Jansen, *Censorship: The Knot That Binds Power and Knowledge* (New York: Oxford Univ. Press, 1988).

6. For example, see Burt (see note 5).

7. See, for example, James Clifford and George E. Marcus, *Writing Culture: The Poetics and Politics of Ethnography* (Chicago: Univ. Chicago Press, 1986); George E. Marcus and Michael M. J. Fischer, *Anthropology as Cultural Critique: An Experimental Moment in the Human Sciences* (Chicago: Univ. Chicago Press, 1986); and James Clifford, *The Predicament of Culture: Twentieth-Century Ethnography, Literature, and Art* (Cambridge, Mass.: Harvard Univ. Press, 1988). Colonial and postcolonial discourse in the West began perhaps with Edward Said's *Orientalism* (New York: Pantheon, 1978).

8. Johannes Fabian, *Time and the Other* (New York: Columbia Univ. Press, 1983).

9. Derek Freeman, *Margaret Mead and Samoa: The Making and Unmaking of an Anthropological Myth* (Cambridge, Mass.: Harvard Univ. Press, 1983).

10. Salman Rushdie, *The Satanic Verses* (New York: Viking, 1989). Indeed, culture has entered prominently as a factor in current foreign policy thinking in an unambiguous Orientalist mode through, for example, Samuel Huntington's influential article on "the clash of civilizations." See Samuel P. Huntington, *The Clash of Civilizations?* (Cambridge, Mass.: Harvard Univ. Press, 1993).

11. Michael M. J. Fischer and Mehdi Abedi, *Debating Muslims: Cultural Dialogues in Postmodernity and Tradition* (Madison: Univ. Wisconsin Press, 1990), 388.

12. Ibid., 398–99. See also Talal Asad, "Multiculturalism and British Identity in the Wake of the Rushdie Affair" and "Ethnography, Literature, and Politics: Some Readings and Uses of Salman Rushdie's *Satanic Verses*," in idem, *Genealogies of Religion: Discipline and Reasons of Power in Christianity and Islam* (Baltimore: Johns Hopkins Univ. Press, 1993).

13. Fischer and Abedi (see note 11), 399.

14. As Fischer and Abedi (ibid.) note:

> The point is demonstrated nowhere more clearly than in the authoritarian anger of otherwise quite pragmatic Muslims in England to burn the book, kill the author, and unleash dormant British blasphemy laws against the hard-won gains of freedom of expression. That there are quite specific sociological reasons for Muslim defensiveness and anger in an increasingly racist Britain . . . is something that is acknowledged in the novel and portrayed at some length in scenes set in the West End of London. (405)

15. Kathryn Milun, "Entrusting Science: Intellectual Property Under NAGPRA," unpublished paper presented at the annual meeting of the American Anthropological Association, November 1995, Washington, D.C.

16. Chris Raymond, "Dispute between Scholar, Tribe Leaders over Book on Hopi Ritual Raises Concerns about Censorship of Studies of American Indians," *Chronicle of Higher Education* 68, (1990): 43.

17. Fred R. Myers, "Truth, Beauty, and Pintupi Painting," *Visual Anthropology* 2 (1989): 163–95; Fred R. Myers, *Pintupi Country, Pintupi Self: Sentiment, Place, and Politics among Western Desert Aborigines* (Washington, D.C.: Smithsonian Institution Press, 1986); and Fred R. Myers, "Representing Culture: The Production of Discourse(s) for Australian Aboriginal Paintings," in George E. Marcus and Fred R. Myers, eds., *The Traffic in Culture: Refiguring Art and Anthropology* (Berkeley: Univ. California Press, 1995).

18. Fred R. Meyers, personal communication.

19. Myers, "Truth, Beauty, and Pintupi Painting" and "Representing Culture" (see note 17); and Howard Morphy, *Ancestral Connections: Art and an Aboriginal System of Knowledge* (Chicago: Univ. Chicago Press, 1991).

20. George E. Marcus, ed., *Rereading Cultural Anthropology* (Durham: Duke Univ. Press, 1992).

21. Indigenous peoples' movements in lands colonized by the Spanish, Portuguese, Dutch, and French deserve separate treatment. The way that claims to cultural property have evolved among indigenous peoples in Anglo colonies is shaped by aspects of English colonialism that differ markedly, for example, from Spanish colonialism and its latter-day outcomes. As the historian Patricia Seed argues, indigenous peoples in Anglo colony situations were not considered beings capable of having economic interests or of engaging in commerce on the same level as the colonizers; they were essentially removed culturally as competitors to the colonizers. See Patricia Seed, *Ceremonies of Possession in Europe's Conquest of the New World, 1492–1640* (New York: Cambridge Univ. Press, 1995); and Patricia Seed, Inventing Indians: *The Rhetoric and Practice of Europe's Domination of Native Peoples* (New York: Cambridge Univ. Press, forthcoming).

This attitude was the consequence of the important doctrine of *terra nullius* ("empty land") by which English colonists took possession of land—the land was considered uninhabited even though there were Native peoples present (because they did not apparently practice settled agriculture they did not count as inhabitants). As such, indigenous peoples in lands colonized by the English were "moral outlaws"—they were expected to be separate and different from the colonizers as moral beings. By contrast, Spanish colonizers were always concerned with the moral welfare of indigenous communities and attempted to enforce morality within them. The Spanish also held indigenous people accountable in the same terms they applied to themselves in relation to their capacity for commerce and enterprise. Thus, the claims by indigenous peoples for radical and exclusive forms of cultural property would make much more sense in the contemporary liberal regimes that followed English colonialism than in those that followed Spanish colonialism because the English accorded little legitimacy to claims for cultural autonomy made by Indian groups.

22. For an excellent overview of the cultural context of struggles over cultural property, see Rosemary J. Coombe, "The Properties of Culture and the Politics of Possessing Identity: Native Claims in the Cultural Appropriation Controversy," *Canadian Journal of Law and Jurisprudence* 6, no. 2 (1993): 249–85.

23. Ibid.

24. Jürgen Habermas, *The Theory of Communicative Action,* 2 vols., trans. Thomas McCarthy (Boston: Beacon Press, 1984, 1989).

25. Coombe (see note 22), 272.

26. Ibid., 279.

27. See Jim Clifford's well-known essay on the Mashpee case, for instance, in *Predicament of Culture* (see note 7).

28. Coombe (see note 22), 281.

29. These discussions were those by Burt (see note 5), Jansen (see note 5), Goldstein (see note 5), and Holquist (see note 5).

30. Tracey B. Strong, "Foreword," in Carl Schmitt, *The Concept of the Political,* trans. George Schwab (Chicago: Univ. Chicago Press, 1996), xv.

Your comfort
is my silence

Silencing: The Egalitarian State

Barbara Kruger,
Your Comfort Is My Silence.
Courtesy Mary Boone Gallery, New York.

Ruled Out: Vocabularies of the Censor

Judith Butler

Descriptions of censorship presuppose a more general theory of the subject of power. When we claim that an individual is censored, for instance, we tend to separate analytically the one who comes under the force of the censor from the censor itself and to conceive of the censor either as an individual or as an extension of state or institutional authority. Further, this authority is presumed to *act upon* the individual in an especially efficacious way. This conventional view of censorship commits us to understanding power as that which is wielded by the one who censors on the one who is censored, where each of these "ones" is understood as external to, or accidentally related to, the power of censorship itself. The power is usually presumed to be wielded by a subject who speaks and who declares that another shall not speak or that another's speech is not to qualify as "speech" in a restricted sense. But are there restrictions on the one who delivers the censorious declaration? Is there an operation of restriction that makes speech possible? And is there, as a corollary, a covert form of censorship that, unremarked, makes possible the overt declaration of censorship?

In the schema above, power is instanced as the act of censorship, figured as an efficacious action that one subject performs upon another. Thus, power is reduced to that which is externally imposed upon a subject. Subjects are understood as outside of power, relaying the effects of power, but not considered one of those effects. If power is understood in juridical terms, it limits and constrains the object on which it operates; if power is, however, also productive, then it contributes to making the object that it also constrains. Although somewhat paradoxical, this view maintains its own kind of sense: the power that acts on an object also constructs it in and through the operation of that constraint. The relevance of this notion of making or constitution for the question of censorship becomes clear when we realize that the subject who is censored as well as the subject who censors are constituted in part by a restrictive and productive power. This paradoxical process of constitution is occluded by the conventional view of censorship which restricts the agency of its operation to an imposition performed by a pregiven subject on another pregiven subject. This view cannot broach the question of how censorship comes to form—to produce—the subjects in question.

Conventional notions of censorship presume that censorship is exercised by the state against those who are less powerful. There are, as it were, subjects making use of power, and then there are those who are deprived of power by that prior use. A stronger argument, however, is also possible: to become a civic and political subject, a citizen-subject, one must be able to make use of power, and this ability to make use of power is, as it were, the measure of the subject. To make use of power is linked to the ability to speak insofar as the citizen is defined as one with the ability to do what one says, to translate word into deed.[1] There is, of course, a grammatical "one" that wanders into these formulations, but this "one" is not to be confused with the subject in its politically normative sense. One can live in a polity without the ability to translate words into deeds, and this is a relatively (though not absolutely) powerless way to live: it is to live on the margins of the subject or, rather, *as* its margin.

Implicit in this notion of a citizen-subject is a conception of a human subject with full control over the language one speaks. Were the sovereign conception of the speaking citizen true, the implicit domain of censorship would be fully overcome. But is the implicit domain of censorship possible to overcome? Would there be meaningful speech at all were it not for the prior foreclosures and operative principles of selectivity that form the field of linguistic intelligibility?[2] If implicit censorship makes speech possible, then the sovereignty of the citizen becomes questionable: agency in speech is conditioned by the workings of implicit censorship, by that which renders unrealizable an unconstrained notion of sovereignty.

Conventional defenses of those less powerful argue that it is their freedom that is being constrained and sometimes, more particularly, their freedom of speech. Censorship is most often referred to as that which is directed against persons or against the content of their speech. Is censorship, despite its constraining and regulatory function, a way of *producing* speech, constraining in advance what will and will not become acceptable speech? In what I have referred to as the "conventional" view, censorship appears to come after speech has been uttered: the speech has already become offensive, and some recourse to a regulatory agency has been made. But in the view that suggests that censorship *produces* speech, that temporal relation is inverted. Censorship precedes the text (by which I include "speech" and other cultural expressions), and is in some sense responsible for its production.

Two views emerged in the course of the Getty seminar on censorship and silencing that seem, interestingly, the inverse of each other; they seem together to register the tension suggested above.[3] One view maintained that uncensoring a text is necessarily incomplete.[4] This claim appears to suggest that no text can remain a text—that is, remain readable—without first being subjected to some kind of censorship. In some way that is not yet clear, this view presupposes that censorship precedes the text in question, and that a text, to become readable, is produced through a process of selection that rules out certain possibilities, and realizes others. The process of selection appears to presuppose a decision, one made by the author of the text. Yet the author does not create the rules according to which selection is made, and in some very important ways the rules that govern the intelligibility of a text are "decided" prior to any authorial decision. A more radical view would be that those rules, "decided" prior to any authorial decision, are precisely the constraining conditions that make possible any given decision. Thus, there is an ambiguity of agency at the site of selection, one to which we will return when we reconsider the relation between agency and censorship.

The other view voiced at the meeting was that "censoring a text is necessarily incomplete."[5] This view maintains that a text always escapes the acts by which it is censored and that censorship is always and only an attempted or partial action. Here, it seems, something about the text being censored exceeds the reach of the censor, suggesting that some account needs to be given of this "excessive" dimension of speech. One might appeal to a generalized theory of textuality to suggest why the effort to constrain speech cannot fully target or capture the polysemy of language. Similarly, one might argue that the communicative sphere of language necessarily posits a realm of obscenity that it seeks, with always partial success, to keep rigorously excluded from its own operation.[6] One might also argue that language is compelled to repeat what it seeks to constrain, and so invariably reproduces and restages the very text that it seeks to silence.

The generalizable character of these explanations are useful but limited: they cannot tell us when and why certain kinds of censorship are, in fact, more complete than others, why some seem to capture the offensive text, and why others seem quite helpless to effect any capture at all. What accounts for the efficacy or the failure that characterize different operations of censorship? If the censor is never fully separable from that which it seeks to censor, perhaps censorship is implicated in the material it seeks to censor in ways that produce paradoxical consequences. If censoring a text is always in some sense incomplete, it may be partly because the text in question takes on new life as part of the very discourse produced by the mechanism of censorship.[7]

To explain this last phenomenon, it is crucial to understand that censorship, as a productive form of power, may work in implicit and inadvertent ways. As a productive form of power, censorship loses its usual meaning, and it becomes unclear whether "censorship" still works to describe this operation of power. It is possible to distinguish between explicit and implicit censorship. The latter refers to implicit operations of power that rule out in unspoken ways what will remain unspeakable. In such cases, no explicit regulation is needed in which to articulate this constraint, and the operation of implicit censorship suggests that there are powerful operations of censorship that are not based in explicit state policy or regulation. Here one might wish for another term to describe this more implicit operation of censorship, and I will suggest later in this essay how the notion of "foreclosure" might be appropriated for such use. But a cautionary word on vocabulary seems important here. We might think that by distinguishing analytically between explicit and implicit forms of censorship that we more closely approximate the dual workings of censorship as a form of power. Yet it may well be that explicit and implicit forms exist on a continuum in which the middle region consists of forms of censorship that are not rigorously distinguishable in this way. Indeed, the masquerading or fugitive forms of censorship that have both explicit and implicit dimensions are perhaps the most conceptually confusing, and, by virtue of that confusion, may be the most politically effective. When we cannot tell whether or not speech is censorious, whether it is the vehicle for censorship, that is precisely the occasion in which it works its way unwittingly.

I suggest that such implicit or ambiguous forms of censorship may be more efficacious than explicit forms in rendering certain kinds of speech unspeakable. Censorship is exposed to a certain vulnerability precisely through becoming explicit, and escapes it most shrewdly when it operates without being clearly identifiable. On the other hand, explicit forms of censorship display their fault lines in various ways, but perhaps most obviously by rehearsing and proliferating the very terms that they seek to bar from discourse.

Consider the congressional statute passed in October of 1994 that put into law the "don't ask, don't tell" policy on homosexual self-declaration in the military. The statute not only constrained reference to homosexuality in the military, but proliferated such references not only in its own supporting documentation but also in the public debates fostered on the issue. The intent of the statute is not only to limit the "coming out" of military personnel, but to establish that such self-ascriptive speech constitutes either a form of homosexual conduct or a sign that a propensity to engage in homosexual conduct is likely.[8] The military thus engaged in a rather protracted discussion on the matter of what is to be considered "homosexual" and how speech and conduct are to be distinguished, whether it can or should be, and whether, finally, one might enjoy (or not enjoy) homosexual status without engaging in homosexual "conduct" (a Clinton proviso that is effectively undone by the "propensity" definition that suggests that a status is, by its very nature, always on the verge of expressing itself as a form of conduct). Regulation of the term *homosexual* is thus no simple act of censorship or silencing; on the contrary, the statute redoubles the term it seeks to constrain and can only effect this constraint through this paradoxical redoubling. The term is not itself unspeakable, but only becomes unspeakable in those contexts in which one uses it to describe oneself and fails to make an adequate or convincing distinction between that ascription of a status and the intention to engage in homosexual conduct. The regulation that *states what it does not want stated* thwarts its own desire by conducting a performative contradiction, saying precisely what it does not want said. The regulation's sovereign pretension—that is, its capacity to mean and do (only and exclusively) what it says—is put into question.[9]

Thus, the effort to constrain the term culminates in its proliferation. The term not only appears in the regulation as that discourse to be regulated but also reappears in the public debate over its fairness and value, specifically as the conjured or imagined act of self-ascription that is explicitly prohibited by the regulation, a prohibition that cannot take place without a conjuring of the very act. We might conclude that the state and the military are merely concerned to retain control over what the term will mean and the conditions under which it may be uttered by a speaking subject, restricting that speaking to precisely and exclusively those subjects who are not described by the term they utter.

The term is to remain a term used to describe others, but the term is not to be used by those who might use it for the purposes of self-description; to describe oneself by the term is to be prohibited from its use, except in order to deny or qualify the description. The term *homosexual* thus comes to describe a class of persons who are to remain prohibited from defining themselves; the term is to be attributed always from elsewhere. And this is, in some ways, the very definition of the homosexual that the military provides. A homosexual is one whose definition is to be left to others, one who is denied the act of self-definition with respect to his or her sexuality, one whose self-denial is a prerequisite for military service.

I elaborate upon this example because it illustrates the way in which the mechanism of censorship is engaged in the production of a figure of homosexuality, a figure that is, as it were, backed by the state. The regulations that determine whether homosexuals will be allowed to enter or remain in the military does not simply constrain the speech of those who would enter or stay; it appears to be about certain kinds of speech, but it is also concerned with establishing a norm by which military subjectification proceeds. In other words, the statute is engaged in the production of the military subject, one for whom homosexuality will remain unacted, publicly denied or recanted. In relationship to the masculinity of the military subject, this will mean that the norms that govern masculinity will be those that require the denial of homosexuality. For women, the self-denial requires either a return to an apparent heterosexuality or to an asexuality (sometimes linked within a dominant conception of female heterosexuality) that suits the military's notion of unit cohesion.

Thus, the mechanism of censorship is actively engaged in the production of subjects, but it is also engaged in circumscribing the social parameters of speakable discourse. The failure of censorship to effect a complete censoring of the speech under question has everything to do with a failure to institute a complete or total subjectification through legal means and a failure to circumscribe effectively the social domain of speakable discourse.

Clearly, the military's effort to regulate speech is not paradigmatic of all kinds of censorship. It does, however, introduce at least two "productive" modalities of power that contrast with the conventional view of censorship as an imposition of power. By "productive," I do not mean positive or beneficial, but rather, power as formative and constitutive, that is, not conceived exclusively as an external exertion of control or the deprivation of liberties.[10] According to this view, censorship is not merely restrictive and privative, active in depriving subjects of the freedom to express themselves in certain ways, but it is also formative of subjects and the legitimate boundaries of speech. This notion of a productive or formative power is not reducible to the tutelary function of the state, that is, the moral instruction of citizens, but operates to make certain kinds of citizens possible, and others impossible. Some arguments that take this point of view stress that censorship is not primarily about speech, that it is exercised in the service of other kinds of social aims, and that the restriction of speech is instrumental to the achievements of other, often unstated, social and state goals. One example of this includes a conception of censorship as a necessary part of the process of nation building, where censorship can be exercised by marginalized groups who seek to achieve cultural control over their own representation and narrativization. A similar, but distinct kind of argument, however, is also made typically on behalf of a dominant power that seeks to control any challenges posed to its own legitimacy. Another, related example is the use of censorship in an effort to build (or rebuild) consensus within an institution, such as the military, or within a nation;[11] another is the use of censorship in the codification of memory, as in state control over monument preservation and building,[12] or in the insistence that certain kinds of historical events be narrated only one way.

The view of censorship as productive, however, is not always coextensive with views that hold that censorship is always instrumental to the achievement of other social aims. Consider that in the examples I have just suggested, censorship is not primarily concerned with speech and the control or regulation of speech is incidental to the achievement of other kinds of social aims (strengthening particular views of legitimacy, consensus, cultural autonomy, national memory). In the most extreme version of this kind of instrumentalism, speech is cast as wholly incidental to the aims of censorship or, rather, it works as a cover for the real political aims of censorship, ones that have nothing or little to do with speech.

Censorship is a productive form of power: it is not merely privative, but formative as well. I want to distinguish this position from the one that would claim that speech is incidental to the aims of censorship. Censorship seeks to produce subjects according to explicit and implicit norms, and this production of the subject has everything to do with the regulation of speech. By the latter, I do not mean to imply that the subject's production is narrowly linked to the regulation of that subject's speech, but rather to the regulation of the social domain of speakable discourse. To become a subject means to be subjected to a set of implicit and explicit norms that govern the kind of speech that will be legible as the speech of a subject. This may seem like a convoluted formulation, but consider that political theorists from Aristotle to Arendt have made the claim that it is as linguistic that humans become political kinds of beings. My reflections constitute an extension of such a claim.[13] The process of selection mentioned above, by which certain kinds of speech become legible or permissible as intelligible speech is governed by norms, and these norms implicitly or explicitly (or partially both) determine who will and will not qualify as a speaking subject. Here the question is not whether certain kinds of speech uttered by a subject are censored, but how an operation of censorship determines who will be a subject, a determination that depends on whether the speech of the candidate for subjecthood obeys the norms that govern what is speakable and what is not. To move outside of the domain of speakability is to risk one's status as a subject; to embody the norms that govern speakability in one's speech is to consummate one's status as a subject of speech.

Let us return to one of the quandaries that opened this discussion, namely, the view that "uncensoring a text is necessarily incomplete." In this formulation, it seems that no text can be fully freed from the shackles of censorship because every text or expression is in part structured through a process of selection that is determined in part by the decisions of an author (or, speaker) and in part by the language in which one expresses oneself, a language that operates according to selective and differential rules that no individual speaker ever made (that may well be collectively forged, but not traceable to a single author, except in specific cases of grammatical revision and coinage). This thesis is a highly generalized one, and it appears to apply to any and all language. Although it may well be true and valid, I think that in its generalized form it does not directly translate into a political consideration of censorship or a normative view on how best to decide issues of censorship. Indeed, taken in its most generalized form, one normative implication of such a view is that because all expression is always already censored to some degree, it makes no sense to try to oppose censorship: to oppose censorship fully is to oppose the conditions of intelligibility—and, thus, to oppose the very terms by which the opposition is articulated.

The view that I propose, however, revises this more generalized thesis in the following direction: the conditions of intelligibility are themselves formulated in and by power, and this normative exercise of power is rarely acknowledged as an operation of power. We may classify this kind of censorship among the most implicit forms of power, constituting a domain of power that works precisely through its illegibility: it escapes the very terms of legibility that it occasions. This persistent escaping of power from what intelligibility formulates and promotes as legible insures its relative invulnerability. If there are rules of differentiation that make speech possible, then these same rules implicitly operate to make certain other kinds of speech impossible—and it is the political salience of impossible speech that I seek to underscore here. Moreover, if there are such rules, how do we account for the subjects who follow them? If a subject becomes a subject by entering the normativity of language, then in some important ways these rules precede and orchestrate the very formation of the subject. These are not rules encountered by a subject at an instrumental distance; on the contrary, these are rules that govern the inception of the speaking subject through its differentiation from an unspeakable Other.

The very distinction between what is normative and what is descriptive comes into provisional crisis with this formulation. We may be tempted to claim that a *descriptive* account of speech includes considerations of what makes speech possible—an inquiry into its conditions of possibility—and that a *normative* account seeks to answer the question of which speech is acceptable and which is not and attempts to supply persuasive reasons for that distinction. But the question of what qualifies as "speech" is itself already a question that attends to a pervasively normative operation of power, a fugitive substitution of "what will be the case" under the rubric of "what is the case." Thus, the very description of the field of speech is in no sense prior to the question of its normative operation.[14]

We see evidence of this kind of move in the kind of speech required to inaugurate the self-denying and repentant homosexual into military ranks; we see it when the emancipation from slavery into citizenship requires the bartering of one's labor power, the translation of one's value into a commodity form,[15] when litigating against domestic sexual abuse requires that a woman offer a version of herself that vitiates any doubt as to her sexual purity, her ability to coincide before the law with an idealized and desexualized version of feminine heterosexuality. When we ask what it means to qualify to petition before the law, we note something of the work of foreclosure that orchestrates and makes possible a speaking subject with a claim.[16]

In cultural contexts where there is no necessary link to the law, forms of "compulsory discursivity" still govern the conditions under which a political claim can be made.[17] Regimes of confessional discourse, for instance, structure the way in which policy issues are framed; in reference to drugs, for instance, a story about abuse and healing becomes central to the way the topic is addressed in policy; in reference to anti-affirmative action approaches to meritocracy (evidenced in the University of California resolution), narratives of individuals who heroically overcome adverse circumstances triumph over any analysis of systematic institutional discrimination in education. Such "forced" narratives, as Wendy Brown explains, impose a discursive form on politicization that not only determines (a) under what discursive form a claim becomes legible as political but, more importantly, (b) consolidates politics as a production of discourse, and establishes "silence" as a site of potential resistance to such discursive regimes and their normalizing effects.[18]

At this juncture one can see perhaps most strikingly how the more conventional view of censorship clashes with the one that is emerging in the positions enumerated above. The view of censorship as one in which a centralized or even sovereign power unilaterally represses speech suggests that the subject of speech is burdened by the exteriority of power. The subject is not quite as victimized in the alternate view, which asserts that citizens wield the power to deprive one another of the freedom of speech. When one subject, through its derogatory remarks or representations, works to "censor" another subject, that form of censorship is regarded as "silencing."[19] In that form, the citizen addressed by such speech is effectively deprived of the power to respond, reauthorized by the derogatory speech act, backed by institutional power, that it encounters. Silence is the performative effect of a certain kind of speech, where that speech is an address that has as its object the deauthorization of the speech of the one to whom the speech act is addressed. It is the subject who now is said to wield such power, not the state or some other centralized institution, although institutional power is presupposed and invoked by the one who delivers the words that silence. Indeed, the subject is described according to the model of state power, and although the locus of power has shifted from the state to the subject, the unilateral action of power remains the same: power is exerted by a subject on a subject, and its exertion culminates in a deprivation of speech.

Speech in this view is the instrument and effect of power, but there is no way that such a view of speech can take account of how power constrains and forces the production of speech. Further, there is no way that such a model of power can take account of how the speaking subject is produced through constraints on speech that precede the subject itself. This productive form of power is difficult to describe through the language of censorship. Another term is needed to designate something of the preemptive operation of this power.

It is one thing for certain kinds of speech to be censored and quite another for censorship to operate on a level that is prior to speech—namely, as the constituting norm by which the speakable is differentiated from the unspeakable. The psychoanalysts Jean Laplanche and J.-B. Pontalis have offered the term *foreclosure* as a way of designating a primary form of repression, one that is not performed by a subject but, rather, whose operation makes possible the formation of the subject.[20]

Apart from the use of the term in real estate matters to refer to legally barring the redemption of a mortgage for value, the term means, more generally, "to bar, exclude, shut out completely."[21] As an action, it appears to presuppose a subject, but that presupposition may well be nothing more than a seduction of grammar. Indeed, foreclosure is not a singular action, but a reiterated effect of a structure. To understand foreclosure as such an action is precisely not to understand it as the action of a subject.

Although the psychoanalytic use of this term is rich and complicated, I propose that we misappropriate the term for the purposes of rethinking more generally the way in which censorship might be thought as a "productive" form of power. It seems that we have been referring to this operation of power in those instances in which we ask: what must remain unspeakable for contemporary regimes of discourse to continue to exercise their power? How does the exclusion of certain sites of enunciation within the law produce the subject before the law?

To the extent that such a constitutive exclusion provides the condition of possibility for any act of speech, it follows that "uncensoring a text is necessarily incomplete." On the assumption that no speech is permissible without some other speech becoming impermissible, censorship is what permits speech by enforcing the very distinction between permissible and impermissible speech. Understood as foreclosure, censorship produces discursive regimes through the production of a domain of the unspeakable.

Although the one who speaks is an effect of such a foreclosure, the subject is never fully or exhaustively reduced to such an effect. A subject who speaks at the border of the speakable risks redrawing the distinction between what is speakable and what is unspeakable. The agency of the subject is not a property of the subject, an inherent will or freedom, but is precisely the effect of power, one that is not fully determined in advance. If the subject is produced in speech through a set of foreclosures, then it is this founding and formative limitation that sets the scene for the agency of the subject. Agency becomes possible on the condition of such a foreclosure. This is not the agency of the sovereign subject, one who only and always exercises power instrumentally on another; on the contrary, this is the agency of a postsovereign subject whose sphere of discursive operation is delimited in advance but is also open to a further and unexpected delimitation. The action of foreclosure does not take place once and for all, but must be repeated to reconsolidate its power and efficacy. The subject who speaks within the sphere of the speakable implicitly reinvokes the foreclosure on which it depends. This reinvocation, however, is neither mechanical nor sure. One speaks a language that is never fully one's own, but that language only persists through repeated occasions of that invocation. The speech act maintains temporal life only in and through the utterances that reinvoke and restructure the conditions of its own possibility.

The critical task is not simply to speak "against" the law, as if the law were external to speech and speech the privileged venue for individual freedom. If speech depends upon censorship, then the principle that one might seek to oppose is at once the formative principle of oppositional speech. There is no opposition to the lines drawn by foreclosure except through the redrawing of those very lines. This is not a dead end for agency, but the temporal dynamic and promise of its peculiar bind. The possibility remains to exploit the premises of speech for a future of language that is nowhere implied by them.

This view of the censorship, broadly construed, that is engaged in forming the subject of speech does not tell us how best to decide the questions that arise in discussions of censorship. It does not furnish criteria by which we might distinguish invidious from noninvidious instances of censorship. But it might make sense to find out what we mean by "censorship" and to understand the limits of its eradicability in order to know the scope within which such normative appeals might plausibly be made. Moreover, what we mean by "normative" necessarily alters when we recognize that the very field of speech is structured and framed through norms that precede the possibility of description. We are accustomed to claiming that we first offer a description of various practices of censorship and then decide among them through recourse to normative principles. If, however, our descriptions are themselves normatively structured in advance, through a foreclosure that establishes the domain of the speakable (and, within that, the domain of description), then to view censorship in this way means rethinking the scope of normativity.

Any decision on how to decide will be implicated in a process of censorship that it cannot fully oppose or eradicate. In this sense, censorship is at once the condition for agency and its necessary limit. This paradox does not refute the possibility of decision, but merely suggests that decision's implication in power is not to be overcome, and that, as political, it is prone to ambivalence. Although the postulation that speech is conditioned by implicit censorship—or foreclosure in the sense described above—suggests that any and all speech is so conditioned, and that what remains is to distinguish between forms of censorship that are constitutive and, hence, presumably inalterable, and social forms that are contingent and alterable. What is equally pressing, however, and less easy to address, is the question of how social forms of censorship come *to appear* and *to operate* as constitutive and inalterable conditions of speech, how certain kinds of speech are ruled out in order for "speech" in its provisionally proper sense to emerge.

Notes

1. See Rae Langton, "Speech Acts and Unspeakable Acts," *Philosophy and Public Affairs* 22 (1993): 293–330.

2. I take this to be one of the salient questions posed by Frederick Schauer's contribution to this volume.

3. A different version of this discussion appears in the context of chapter 4 of my *Excitable Speech: A Politics of the Performative* (New York: Routledge, 1997).

4. See Frederick Schauer, "The Ontology of Censorship," pages 147–68 in this volume.

5. See Richard Burt, "(Un)Censoring in Detail: The Fetish of Censorship in the Early Modern Past and the Postmodern Present," pages 17–41 in this volume, as well as *Licensed by Authority: Ben Jonson and the Discourses of Censorship* (Ithaca: Cornell Univ. Press, 1993), and his edited volume, *The Administration of Aesthetics: Censorship, Political Criticism, and the Public Sphere* (Minneapolis: Univ. of Minnesota Press, 1994).

6. See E. S. Burt, "'An Immoderate Taste for Truth': Censoring History in Baudelaire's 'Les bijoux,'" pages 111–43 in this volume.

7. Other examples of starkly oppositional claims made at this conference include: (a) censorship has no "place" but operates everywhere that language operates, and (b) censorship must be contextualized, understood in terms of the place of its operation; and (a) censorship is a term that is to be restricted to describe its actual, empirical usage in either law or psychology, and (b) censorship is coextensive with the workings of language and, hence, cannot rightly be restricted in the abovementioned way.

8. For a thorough and insightful discussion of the statute and the "propensity" clause, see Janet E. Halley, "The Status / Conduct Distinction in the 1993 Revisions to Military Anti-Gay Policy: A Legal Archaeology," *GLQ: A Journal of Lesbian and Gay Studies* 3 (1996): 159–252.

9. For a critique of the sovereign presumption in speech act theory used in some legal contexts, see my "Sovereign Performatives," in *Excitable Speech* (see note 3).

10. This is a distinction that Michel Foucault offers in the second volume of *The History of Sexuality*, trans. Robert Hurley (New York: Vintage, 1980), in his effort to counter disciplinary form of power with sovereign power. He distinguishes between power conceived as "repressive" and as "productive."

11. See George E. Marcus, "Censorship in the Heart of Difference: Cultural Property, Indigenous Peoples' Movements, and Challenges to Western Liberal Thought," pages 221–42 in this volume.

12. See Sanford Levinson, "The Tutelary State: 'Censorship,' 'Silencing,' and the 'Practices of Cultural Regulation,'" pages 195–219 in this volume.

13. Hannah Arendt cites Aristotle's definition of "man as a *zoon logon ekhon,*" one for whom exists the possibility of "a way of life in which speech and only speech made sense." *The Human Condition* (Chicago: Univ. Chicago Press, 1958), 27; see pages 25–27 for Arendt's interpretation of Aristotle on the political animal as a speaking being.

14. In this sense, I differ from Robert Post's use of this distinction in his introduction, "Censorship and Silencing," pages 1–12 in this volume.

15. See Saidiya Hartman, *Scenes of Subjection* (New York: Oxford Univ. Press, forthcoming).

16. Vicki Schultz, "Women 'Before the Law,'" in Judith Butler and Joan Scott, *Feminists Theorize the Political* (New York: Routledge, 1992).

17. Wendy Brown, "Freedom's Silences," pages 313–27 in this volume.

18. Ibid.

19. Langton (see note 1).

20. Lacan's word is *forclusion* and is introduced as the French translation of Freud's term, *Verwerfung*. *Verwerfung* in Freud is generally translated into English as "repudiation" or "rejection." In the *Vocabulaire de la psychanalyse* (Paris: Presses universitaires de France, 1967), Jean Laplanche and J.-B Pontalis refer to foreclosure as a primordial rejection of that which remains outside of the symbolic universe of the subject. This definition makes use of a specific sense of the "outside," however, one that is close to the notion of the "constitutive outside" as used by Jacques Derrida. This is an "outside" that is the defining limit or exteriority to a given symbolic universe, one which, were it imported into that universe, would destroy its integrity and coherence. In other words, what is set outside or repudiated from the symbolic universe in question is precisely what binds that universe together through its exclusion.

Laplanche and Pontalis argue that what is foreclosed is to be distinguished from what is repressed (*refoulement* in French, and *Verdrängung* in German). What is foreclosed is not integrated into the unconscious of the subject; it cannot be recalled or remembered and brought into consciousness. It does not belong to the realm of neurosis, but to that of psychosis; indeed, its entry into the symbolic universe threatens psychosis, which is to say that its exclusion guarantees symbolic coherence. Freud makes reference to *Verwerfung* in relation to the fear of castration in both "The Three Essays on the Theory of Sexuality," 7: 227, and "The History of an Infantile Neurosis," 12: 85, in *The Standard Edition of the Complete Psychological Works of Sigmund Freud,* trans. under the general editorship of James Strachey (London: Hogarth Press, 1953–1974). Whereas Freud occasionally attempts to define a form of repression that corresponds to psychosis, Lacan introduces "foreclosure" to specify that form of repression.

21. *Oxford English Dictionary,* 2nd ed., s.v., "foreclosure."

Subordination, Silence, and Pornography's Authority

Rae Langton

Preamble

On one picture, free speech is easy to have. It is a matter of saying what you want, when you want. Free speech gets hard to have only when the state starts breathing down your neck. When the state starts breathing down your neck with its threats and orders (Don't say this! Don't say that! *Or else* ...) then free speech is in trouble. But in a liberal society, like the one we live in, the state does not breathe down your neck. Censorship is nowhere. So free speech is easy to have.

On another picture, free speech is hard to have. Nothing you say is really free. Whatever you try to say is silenced before you even begin. Whatever you say is constrained. Culture, discourse, perhaps language itself, all breathe down your neck with their threats and orders (Don't say this! Don't say that! *Or else*...) and they never go away. You are a prisoner in an invisible cage, invisibly gagged, allowed to say one thing, prevented from saying others. To say one thing is to leave everything else unsaid. To speak about one thing is to be silent about everything else. The very idea that *you* say what you *want* to say is a joke. What is this *you?*—this self, this nothing, with its delusions of grandeur and agency? And whence comes the *want?* Censorship is everywhere. So free speech is hard to have.

These pictures are two sides of a coin which, however tossed, will yield the same result for a debate about pornography and women's silence.[1] If censorship is nowhere, women are not silenced at all. So women are not silenced by pornography. If censorship is everywhere, then women are silenced—but so is everyone, all the time, in every way. If censorship is everywhere, there is no point in making distinctions. If censorship is everywhere, there is no point in saying that some people are silenced, some are not; some are silenced at some times, not at others; some are silenced here, but not there; some are silenced in a bad way, some in an innocent way. If censorship is everywhere, it might as well be nowhere.

And the coin will yield the same result, however tossed, for a debate about pornography and women's subordination. The state is not breathing down women's necks, so women are not subordinated. Or else, women are indeed subordinated, imprisoned in an invisible cage, deprived of agency—but then agency always was a myth. Everyone is imprisoned, all the time. So there is nothing special about women, or about pornography.

Somewhere between these two pictures is one (at least) that has some hope of being true. And somewhere between these two pictures is one (at least) that allows debate about pornography which does not pre-ordain a conclusion. I do not know exactly what the alternative picture is, but, as I seek it, I explore once again the question of whether pornography subordinates and silences women.[2]

In thinking about this, one is led to think rather generally about what subordination and silence involve. In thinking about subordination, one is soon led to general questions about the nature of speech, whether speech holds up a mirror to reality, or creates it; and if it creates it, how it does so, and when. In thinking about silence, one is soon led to general questions about what speech, and hence silence, amounts to. In considering these questions I draw on a thought-provoking discussion by Leslie Green presented in this volume.[3] Green considers arguments that I have developed elsewhere, in which I conclude that pornography may well subordinate and silence women.[4] He thinks this is mistaken. I think it is not, and I hope to say why. Green is another who wants an alternative to the two cartoons I sketched above, and although he sometimes seems to slide towards the first picture, he also shows great sensitivity to the issues of power implicit in the second.

Pornography *is* the graphic sexually explicit subordination of women, in pictures or words, said Catherine MacKinnon. That claim was attacked for (among other things) philosophical confusion.[5] The claim was not, or not simply, that pornography depicts the subordination of women, or that it has, among its effects, the perpetuation of women's subordination, but that pornography *is* subordination. When we bring speech act theory to bear on the claim, it makes good sense—or so I argued. In terms of J. L. Austin's three-way distinction between the content of an utterance (locution), the effect it has (perlocution), and the act it is (illocution), MacKinnon's idea is clear.[6] Pornography is itself an illocutionary act of subordination, in addition to being a locutionary act that (perhaps) depicts subordination, and a perlocutionary act that perpetuates subordination. My understanding of MacKinnon's idea was developed before the appearance of *Only Words*, but her more recent work suggests I may be on the right track. MacKinnon explicitly cites Austin, seeks a "performative" understanding of pornography, and compares pornography with such utterances as "Ready, aim, fire," "Not guilty," and "I do," uttered in contexts where to say something is to do something—order an execution, find not guilty, marry.[7]

An example of subordinating speech is the utterance "Blacks are not permitted to vote," uttered in a context (thankfully past) where it enacts apartheid law. The illocutions of apartheid law subordinate blacks, I suggest, because they rank blacks as inferior, deprive them of rights and powers, and legitimate discrimination against them. Despite some evident dissimilarities, the speech acts of pornography may also be illocutionary acts of subordinating, for similar reasons. According to the feminist argument, pornography ranks women as inferior, deprives women of certain powers, and legitimates discrimination against them. Speech acts of ranking, legitimating, and depriving someone of rights and powers are *authoritative* illocutions. It takes authority to be able to perform them: an umpire, but not a bystander, can call a fault; a jury, but not a bystander, can acquit; a government, but not a private citizen, can disenfranchise. And I suggest that if pornography is to be subordinating speech, then pornography too must be authoritative. This is in harmony with MacKinnon:

> Together with all its material supports, authoritatively *saying* someone is inferior is largely how structures of status and differential treatment are demarcated and actualized. Words and images are how people are placed in hierarchies, how social stratification is made to seem inevitable and right, how feelings of inferiority and superiority are engendered, and how indifference to violence against those on the bottom is rationalized and normalized.[8]

What follows, if the speech act analysis of pornography succeeds? One thing that clearly follows is that there is nothing confused about MacKinnon's claim. Another is that there is an argument about pornography that differs from the traditional causal argument. Does anything more dramatic follow? Green seems to think so: "If saying simply *is* doing, there is no need to worry about the contingent causal connection and the problematic evidence for it. The evidence for the harm is the evidence for the saying."[9] We should be so lucky. I, for one, never suggested anything quite as easy as this. If the analysis succeeds we do face two different claims about pornography: a claim about its perlocutionary effects, and a claim about its illocutionary force. But Green's suggestion is that if pornography is an illocutionary act of subordination, we have a claim about what is *necessarily* the case, and one which requires no additional *evidence*. The causal claim, on the other hand, concerns a merely "contingent" connection, and requires "evidence" which is "problematic."

Causal questions are not the only questions that involve contingent connections and evidence: illocutionary questions may do so as well. Whether some particular speaker has authority is a contingent matter. While it is not a contingent matter that, for example, the umpire has authority over the tennis score, it is a contingent matter that *that man* is the umpire. In order to determine what illocution was performed one needs to know not only that *he said "Fault"* but also that *he is the umpire*. So one needs not only "evidence for the saying," as Green puts it, but also evidence for the authority of the speaker.[10] In the case of the umpire, evidence for the authority comes as easily as evidence for the saying. (There he is, sitting in his funny high chair by the net, in his uniform.) Likewise in the case of the speech acts of apartheid. But it is not always so; one can imagine cases in which the authority of an alleged umpire, an alleged legislator, is in dispute. And in the case of pornography, evidence for the authority is much more controversial than evidence for the saying. So the question about pornography's illocutionary force inevitably involves evidence and contingent connections: if pornography had no authority, then I think it would not subordinate, no more than that man could call a fault, if he were not the umpire. So it is a contingent, context-dependent matter whether pornography has authority and, hence, whether it subordinates. It cannot, I think, wholly be answered from the philosopher's armchair.[11]

Green goes on to argue against the feminist conclusion that pornography subordinates, and as a preamble to this he introduces two very useful tools for thinking about this difficult and complex issue. One is a thought experiment: a clear example of subordinating speech, and variants of that example that may or may not be subordinating speech. The other is a suggested analysis of authority, and in particular of *de facto* authority.[12]

Green asks us to consider a plausible case of a speaker "authoritatively saying someone is inferior" and thereby subordinating him: the Roman Catholic Church says that homosexuality is an "objective disorder" and an "intrinsic moral evil." What the Church says is not "only words," but an authoritative illocution. But who exactly does it subordinate? We are asked to consider two men, living in a location where Catholics are a minority and where there is a liberal constitution. Mick, a gay Catholic, is subordinated by the Church's authoritatively saying that he is inferior, since he is within the domain of the Church's authority, accepting its jurisdiction. But what of someone who does not accept its jurisdiction? Green considers Mick's neighbor Max, who is gay and Jewish, and asks two questions: "Is Max subordinated by the words of the Church? Does *he* have an objective disorder because the Church says he does?"[13] The implication here is that Mick, the Catholic, is subordinated, and has an objective disorder, because of the Church's say-so. Green's questions ask whether the same applies to Max.

Notice now that we have two important and different issues before us. One concerns the constructive power of authoritative speech: can saying so really make it so when the Church says that someone has an "objective disorder"? The second concerns the jurisdiction of authoritative speech: can the Church's words subordinate Max, even though he does not accept its jurisdiction? The first issue is about *how* and *whether* words "construct" reality; the second is about *whose* reality gets "constructed." The second issue brings us to Green's analysis of *de facto* authority and the limits of authority's jurisdiction. In what follows I address first the general issue of the constructive power of authoritative speech and then the issue of jurisdiction. These two issues concern the argument about subordination. The argument about silence is conducted by Green on rather different terms, and I address this as a third issue. A common theme running through all three sections is that Green's arguments are enlightening, helpful—and mistaken.

The Constructive Power of Authoritative Speech

Green's implication is that Mick is subordinated and has an objective disorder because of the Church's say-so. Postponing the question about Max, which concerns the jurisdiction of the Church's authority, let us think about this implication for Mick. What are we to make of Green's apparent assimilation of the claims that Mick is subordinated and that he has an objective disorder—or, rather, Green's assumption that these two claims have the same kind of status? It is plausible to suppose that Mick is subordinated because of the Church's say-so. But it is far less plausible to suppose that Mick has an objective disorder because of the Church's say-so. Just as well: for if Mick did have an objective disorder, the Church would, on the face of it, be *right* in saying he had. There is surely a limit to how far saying so can make it so, even when the sayings are authoritative. There are limits to what illocutions can do when they "construct" social reality, and it seems unlikely that anyone's say-so—even in conditions of authority—can simply bring it about that someone has an *objective* disorder. To be sure, Mick may believe he has an objective disorder, and he may count as having an objective disorder in the eyes of the Church and his peers—but that doesn't mean he really has one.

For some illocutions, authoritatively saying so *can* instantly make it so: "You're fired" uttered by the authoritative employer instantly makes it the case that you are fired. "This ship is named the Queen Elizabeth," uttered by the official as she smashes the champagne bottle against the ship, instantly makes it the case that the ship is named the *Queen Elizabeth*. These authoritative illocutions belong to a class Austin described as *exercitive*.

Contrast these examples with the words of the umpire who says "Out." His verdict alters the score of the game. But does he bring it about that the ball *is* outside the white line? No, or a photograph could not show that the umpire had made a mistake. It is the player, not the umpire, who brings it about that the ball *is* outside the white line, if indeed it is—and she brings it about, not by saying something, but by hitting something. To be sure, the umpire does bring something about. The ball does *count* as outside the line for the purposes of the score—something that would not hold if a bystander, or player, were to say "Out"—but that does not mean the umpire made it the case that the ball *was* outside the line. This authoritative illocution belongs to a class Austin described as *verdictive.*[14]

A verdictive illocution is an authoritative judgment that something *is* so (and it may be criticized for being false). An exercitive illocution is, as Austin put it, an authoritative decision "that something *is to be so*" (and it cannot be criticized for being false, though it may be ill-advised, mistaken, or wrong).[15] A finding of "Guilty" is verdictive; a sentencing is exercitive. "It is yours" is verdictive; "You shall have it" is exercitive. Both kinds of illocution require authority, but there is, so to speak, a difference in their direction of fit.[16] A verdictive aims to fit the world; an exercitive aims for the world to fit the words. A verdictive purports to map a reality. ("The ball is out.") An exercitive purports to create a reality. ("You're out, fired!") When a verdictive is performed, the words fit the world: he *says* "Out," because it *is* out. When an exercitive is performed, the world fits the words: you *are* fired, because he *says* "You're fired." Actions of ranking and grading are verdictive. So too is the action of saying that homosexuals have an objective disorder. The Church aims or purports to map some independent moral reality: "Homosexuality is an objective disorder, and an intrinsic moral evil." What it says aims to be true (and is doubtless believed by the speaker to be true), but saying so does not make it so, though it may make it count as so—just as the umpire's "Out" does not make the ball so, though it may count as so for the purpose of the game. Neither Mick nor Max has an objective disorder because the Church says they do, although one or both may be subordinated because it says they do.

Does this mean that verdictives do not after all "construct reality," are not truly "performative," and are hence irrelevant to the question of subordination? By no means. Consider these remarks from MacKinnon about word-world direction of fit, when it comes to the speech of those in power or authority.

> Having power means, among other things, that when someone says, "This is how it is" it is taken as being that way... [The] beliefs of the powerful become [proven], in part because the world actually arranges itself to affirm what the powerful want to see. If you perceive this as a process, you might call it force, or at least pressure or socialization or what money can buy. If it is imperceptible as a process, you may consider it voluntary or consensual or free will or human nature, or just the way things are. Beneath this, though, the world is not entirely the way the powerful say it is or want to believe it is.[17]

Clearly the thought here is close cousin to the thought in the passage above about "authoritatively saying someone is inferior," so for present purposes we can slide over the possible distinction between power and authority. MacKinnon is talking here of both the speech and the beliefs of those in power or authority, and for present purposes I will focus on speech.

When "This is how it is" is said by someone in authority, it is an authoritative judgment that something is so: it is verdictive. There is at least one clear sense in which verdictives do "construct" part of reality: when they bring it about that something *counts* as thus and so, it is "taken to be" thus and so. When someone in authority says, "This is how it is," it is "taken as being" that way. If the ball is called "Out" by the umpire, it is "taken as being" out: it *counts* as out for the purposes of the match. Part of the world—namely the score—does indeed adjust itself to fit the umpire's words. And in this latter respect a verdictive has an exercitive dimension. So a verdictive's direction of fit is a complex matter. The umpire's verdict has, on the one hand, a word-to-fit-world direction of fit, since it aims to conform to a truth about the physical location of the ball. That is why it is appropriate to say, of a correct call: the umpire *says* it is out because it *is* out. But what the umpire says also has, in part, a world-to-fit-word direction of fit, since it aims for part of the world—the score, and the beliefs of the crowd—to conform to the verdict. That is why it seems almost as appropriate to say: the ball *is* out (it *counts* as out) because he *says* it is out.

Apply this now to people. If you are authoritatively ranked as inferior, you count socially as inferior, and in this sense your social being is constructed as inferior, where the construction concerns how you stand in the eyes of others. It may also be that as a result of the authoritative ranking you count *in your own eyes* as inferior, and in this sense you construct yourself as inferior. The ranking, on its own, ensures that you count as inferior, and since status really is a matter of how you are viewed, the ranking does alter your status for the worse. In this way, authoritatively saying that someone exists *as* thus-and-so can indeed construct the social reality of what someone *is*[18]—though it does not make it the case that you have an objective disorder, or that you are objectively inferior, independent of what you count as being in the eyes of others.

There are certain realist assumptions behind the distinction between verdictive and exercitive speech. (That realism is implicit in MacKinnon's view when she says "the world is not entirely the way the powerful say it is or want to believe it is.") Whether the ball *is* out is a fact independent of people's sayings and believings; whether it *counts* as out is not. In the case of verdictives, but not exercitives, there is a difference between being thus-and-so and counting as thus-and-so according to authoritative judgment. There is a difference between really being out and counting as out (in the verdictive case); there is no difference between really being fired and counting as fired (in the exercitive case). And someone who rejects these realist assumptions might object.

Someone who thinks reality is exhausted by social, or mental, or textual reality may find the alleged distinction implausible. If the ball is authoritatively called out, it counts as out, is believed to be out—the ball *is* out, and there is no point wasting breath and time on drawing these apart. But the implications of abandoning the realist assumptions are grim. If the Church authoritatively says Mick has an objective disorder, he not only counts as having an objective disorder and is believed to have an objective disorder in the eyes of Church and community—he *does* have an objective disorder. But it is surely no waste of breath and time to draw *these* apart. The Church's verdictive saying so may make it seem so, make it count as so, make it believed to be so. But the Church's saying so does not make it so.

There is a second way in which verdictives, while aiming to reflect the world, may actively construct it. MacKinnon suggests that when the powerful say "This is how it is," what they say can *become true,* at least in part, "because the world actually arranges itself to affirm" what the powerful say. This suggests a different way in which saying so can make it so. This second kind of construction has to do with the causal effects of verdictive speech—the perlocutionary acts associated with verdictive illocutionary acts, the effects that depend on circumstance, contingencies of psychology, and the influence of expectation on behavior and ability. The illocutions of ranking can have perlocutionary effects that are disastrous: acts of ranking can sometimes be self-fulfilling, not just with respect to the rank a person counts as having, but with respect to certain real properties she comes to have (properties caused, but not constituted, by the way she is viewed). When a person "counts" as thus and so in the eyes of others, he or she can, at least in part, really become so.

An old example may help here—provided that we can avoid being sidetracked into contested questions about intelligence, IQ, and their probable or possible noncorrelation. The point, I hope, will be clear. When a child is authoritatively ranked as having a lower than average intelligence, and is accordingly believed by her teachers to have a lower than average intelligence, the child can, to a certain degree, really come to have a lower than average intelligence or, in any case, one that is lower than she would otherwise have. When you are ranked as worse, you are believed to be worse, and then you really become worse.[19]

Whether and to what degree this happens depends very much on contingencies of psychology and context, and this empirical self-fulfilling aspect of some verdictives is to be sharply distinguished from the constitutive self-fulfilling aspect of the exercitive illocution—the self-fulfilling "You're fired," which instantly makes it the case that you are fired. The verdictives of the Pygmalion studies—"Anna has a low IQ score"—are by no means instantly self-fulfilling, though with time and the classroom neglect of Anna which they legitimate, the verdictives may become true. In saying "Anna has a low IQ score," the experimenter ranks Anna's intelligence as inferior. He says something false, at the time of his saying. But by saying "Anna has a low IQ score," the experimenter causes Anna to have a low (or lower) IQ score. His ranking has become true (or at any rate, more accurate than it had been at the time of uttering.) His illocutionary verdictive has in a sense been made true later, causally, by his associated perlocutionary act.

When verdictives are self-fulfilling, their world-altering power can resemble the world-altering power of simple exercitives. As a verdictive, an act of ranking ("Anna has a low IQ score") purports to conform to reality, claims to hold up a mirror to the world. In its exercitive aspect, the speech act constructs some small part of the social world: it constitutively alters the social analog of the score in tennis, what Anna's intelligence *counts* as in the eyes of teachers and classmates, though not—yet—what Anna's intelligence really is. But now what Anna's intelligence *counts* as being begins to have an effect on what Anna's intelligence really *is,* and the speech act constructs a different small part of the social world—it empirically alters Anna's abilities, because people's lives and abilities are sensitive to rankings in a way that balls and lines on a court are not.

So in short there are two ways in which verdictive saying so can sometimes, at least partly, make it so, two ways in which verdictive speech can "construct" reality. The first, and constitutive, way is by making it count as so. ("When the powerful say 'This is how it is,' it is taken to be that way.") The second, and empirical, way, is by sometimes making it (in part) really so. ("When the powerful say 'This is how it is,' the world arranges itself to affirm" what the powerful say.)

One result is that verdictives *disguise* their own constructive power. When someone says "This is how it is," what he says does not seem to be constructing the world: he purports to represent the world. His words aim to fit the world. A mirror does not create, it merely reflects. But words which aim merely to mirror—which purport merely to mirror—can also create, and make the world fit the words.[20]

In what ways, then, does *subordinating* speech "construct" reality? The notion of subordination I described at the outset incorporates a mixed bag of verdictive and exercitive speech acts: the speech acts of apartheid, I suggested, *rank* a particular group as inferior, *deprive* them of powers and rights, *legitimate* discrimination against them. Illocutions of ranking are basically verdictive; illocutions of legitimating certain behavior, and depriving of powers, are basically exercitive. We can see that this mixed bag of authoritative speech acts is probably present in Green's example as well. The Church ranks homosexuals as inferior; deprives at least some of them of powers and rights (Mick cannot, for example, obtain the Church's blessing for his relationship with his partner); and legitimates discrimination against them whether in the workplace or in social life. The Church has a role that is in some ways comparable to the role I attributed to pornography, as a source of normative guidance about sex that legitimates certain patterns of sexual behavior and not others. Green thinks the Church is in fact *unlike* pornography in this respect: "It would be hopelessly naive... to think that each [pornographic] image bears the message 'Look, this is how it is to be done: this is right and proper.'"[21] Perhaps so. But it would also be hopelessly naive to think that everything that is a source of normative guidance bears the message "Look, this is how it is to be done: this is right and proper." Pornography legitimates—makes permissible—certain ways of acting in part by representing them as ordinary, as normal.

That is why MacKinnon says that "words and images are how... social stratification is made to seem inevitable and right... and how indifference to violence against those on the bottom is rationalized and normalized."[22] Empirical work suggests MacKinnon is right: whatever their intentions in consuming pornography, people's *normative beliefs are indeed altered* by exposure to it. They are more likely to view women as inferior, more likely to accept rape myths (that women enjoy rape, and that they do not mean to refuse when they say no), more likely to think rape a less serious offense, more likely to think that rape victims deserve their treatment, more likely to say that they themselves would rape if they could get away with it. These perlocutionary effects on normative beliefs are well explained by supposing that pornography has *legitimated* such beliefs. Such data are ignored and left unexplained by theorists who decide *a priori* that pornography presents its norms as impossible, as unrealizable, or as not-to-be-realized.[23] So we can allow that the say-so of the Catholic Church and pornography are alike in being illocutions that legitimate certain patterns of sexual behavior. Such speech acts, as Green says, "create a status hierarchy of desires, acts, relationships, and thus, in certain respects, people."[24]

When the Church authoritatively says that "homosexuals have an objective disorder," while its verdict does not make it true that gays have "an objective disorder," it does *subordinate* gays, in part because it makes them *count* —in the eyes of Church and community—as beings who have an objective disorder. They are, to shift MacKinnon's words out of context, "taken as being that way."[25] Just as the umpire's verdict has an exercitive dimension in the way it alters one social part of the world—the score of the game—so the Church's verdict has an exercitive dimension in the way it alters one social part of the world—the status of gays. In addition there are the empirical psychological and social harms that befall an individual who is taken to be subordinate, harms that are the effects of being made to count that way, in the eyes of Church and community.

So far we have been thinking about the first of the two issues raised by Green's questions, the issue of the constructive power of authoritative speech, the different ways in which saying so can really make it so, the different ways in which words can "construct" reality. It is time now to turn to the second of the issues he raised, the question of authority's jurisdiction—the question of *whose* reality gets "constructed."

De Facto *Authority and Its Jurisdiction*

Assuming that Mick is subordinated and has an objective disorder, Green asks whether the same is true of Max. We need to restrict the question, however, since not even Mick has an objective disorder because of the Church's say-so. We can think about whether Max is *subordinated*. Green's conclusion is that Max is *not* subordinated, despite the fact that the Church's verdicts are, as claims about natural law, addressed to him as well as Mick. Max is insulated from the Church's verdicts, not only because he himself rejects the Church's jurisdiction but also because his country has a liberal constitution, the Church is in a minority, and its speech is merely tolerated, not endorsed, by the broader society. These factors mean, according to Green, that Max is not within the jurisdiction of the Church's authority. If, on the other hand, "the Church were established and its dictates widely accepted as binding standards of behavior," then the Church *would* have effective authority—*de facto* authority—over Max, and he too, like Mick, would be subordinated, notwithstanding his own rejection of its jurisdiction.[26]

The guiding principle behind Green's argument is in harmony with my own, namely that "whether speech has the power to subordinate is not simply a function of what is said but on the whole social context in which it occurs."[27] His example convincingly shows how speakers whose authority is less than, and different from, that of the state can nonetheless subordinate. His conclusion about the jurisdiction of authority is based on a particular analysis of *de facto* authority and its conditions, however, and it is this which grounds his later conclusions about pornography. It is, I think, a mistaken analysis.

According to Green, the first necessary condition for the Church's *de facto* authority over someone like Max, who does not accept the Church's authority, is one of a perceived legitimacy: "the norms prescribed by the Church must be generally accepted as setting binding standards of behavior." Since the idea is that the norms be *generally* accepted, I'll call this a condition of *general perceived legitimacy*. The second is one of efficacy:

> The Church's norms must also be generally efficacious. There must be ... significant contact between Max and those who do endorse the Catholic view: they must, for example, have the power to hire or fire him, to control his education, to affect his civil rights, and so on, and they must sometimes actually exercise their power.[28]

Since the idea here again is that the norms be *generally* efficacious, I'll call this a condition of *general efficacy*. Is Green right about these being *necessary* conditions for the Church to have authority — *de facto* authority — over Max?

Surely not. First, suppose that the norms prescribed by the Church are not "generally accepted," but that the Church is a powerful minority, whose members accept its voice as authoritative while nonmembers are substantially in the power of the members: suppose, in other words, that general efficacy is satisfied, though general perceived legitimacy is not. The minority, being powerful, have the power to hire and fire Max and most other gays, have the power to control his civil rights, and they sometimes exercise that power. In these conditions, I suggest, Max would indeed be subordinated. What surely matters is that the ones in power over Max (and other gays) take the voice of the Church to be authoritative — not that *everyone* takes it to be authoritative. Thinking about this variation of Green's example leads us to two conclusions: first, general perceived legitimacy is not, after all, a necessary condition of the Church having the kind of authority needed to subordinate Max; and second, general efficacy appears to be a sufficient condition of *de facto* authority.[29]

Indeed we can say more. Max would surely be subordinated if there were merely *local* analogs of both of Green's two general conditions. Suppose there is a local version of Green's first general condition: call it *local perceived legitimacy*. Suppose that the norms prescribed by the Church are locally accepted as setting standards of behavior in Max's community. Suppose, moreover, that there is a local version of Green's second general condition: call it *local efficacy*. Suppose there is significant contact between Max and those in his community who endorse the Catholic view, so that they have the power to hire or fire him, control his education, and affect his civil rights, and suppose that they sometimes exercise it. Suppose that this authority is merely local, so that in some — perhaps many — places beyond Max's local community the norms prescribed by the Church are not accepted as binding, and that if he lived in any of these places he would be outside the coercive and restrictive power of those who endorse the Church's norms. Shouldn't we say that *where he is*, he is subordinated — though if he lived elsewhere, perhaps he would not be? Why should the absence of *general* perceived legitimacy and *general* efficacy of the Church's norms undermine the apparent fact that Max is subordinated, here and now? Demanding *general* perceived legitimacy and *general* efficacy comes close to demanding that no gay non-Catholics are subordinated unless all are.[30]

Perhaps the reasoning is that if legitimacy and efficacy are merely local, Max can escape the authority by moving elsewhere—so he is not subordinated where he is. But surely if he *can* escape his community (and this questionable assumption supposes he has the requisite knowledge, inclinations, and material resources), then what he escapes is the local *de facto* authority of the Church and of the local community where he *is* subordinated. I conclude that Green's analysis is mistaken: neither general perceived legitimacy nor general efficacy is a necessary condition for the church's *de facto* authority over Max and hence for its ability to subordinate Max. Instead, it seems that local perceived legitimacy and local efficacy are sufficient conditions for the Church's ability to do so.[31] This conclusion about the conditions for the jurisdiction of *de facto* authority is important, given its role in Green's argument about pornography.

In applying his analysis to pornography, Green begins by supposing that women are not directly within the domain of pornography's authority: "The first chain of command is . . . the authority of pornographers . . . over *men and boys*."[32] Women are to be compared not with Mick, but with Max, the outsider to Catholicism. This means that the conditions under which women could be subordinated by pornography are like the conditions under which Max would be subordinated according to Green's analysis—namely, when the two (alleged) necessary conditions of general perceived legitimacy and general efficacy are in force. Green says, however, that it is implausible to think that pornography subordinates women, precisely because the two conditions of general perceived legitimacy and general efficacy are not fulfilled. After all, pornography "must compete with other putative social authorities, including the state, the family, and the church." In a liberal society the state merely tolerates the speech of pornographers; it does not endorse it, and it denounces sexual violence. Pornography is "private, nonauthoritative speech."[33] The competing authoritative voices contradict the voice of pornography, and this undermines the perceived legitimacy of pornography and its efficacy.

One could remark on the swiftness with which Green casts women as the outsiders to the illocutions of pornography. (Perhaps there are women who accept pornography's jurisdiction as Mick accepts that of the Church: are they most subordinated of all?) One could remark on Green's denial of a general perceived legitimacy of pornography and his assumption that the voice of the courts unequivocally contradicts the voice of pornography, rather than all too often echoing it. ("Women who say no do not always mean no. It is not just a question of saying no," says judge to jury.[34]) One could remark on Green's sanguine belief that "the broader society condemns [rape] and regularly prosecutes it"[35]—when rape is the most underreported crime because women know that the broader society also condemns rape victims, and regularly torments them in the courts. One could remark on Green's denial of general efficacy, his assumption that there is no "significant contact" between women and men who accept pornography's authority—his assumption that most women are *never* in the power of men who consume pornography, men who have power in women's workplaces, homes, and sexual relationships and who sometimes exercise that power. I shall not argue that Green's two conditions of general perceived legitimacy and general efficacy are in fact satisfied, though I believe it can well be argued. For these conditions are not after all necessary conditions for women's being subordinated by pornography.

We saw that Max would be subordinated if there were merely *local* analogs of Green's two general conditions, and the case is likewise for women. Suppose that the norms prescribed by pornography are locally accepted as setting standards of behavior in a woman's community, although she does not accept them. Suppose, in other words, that the condition of local perceived legitimacy is satisfied. And suppose there is a local version of Green's second general condition: suppose there is significant contact between the woman and those in her community who accept the norms of pornography, so that locally they have the power to hire or fire her, control her education, affect her civil rights, and suppose that they sometimes exercise that power. Suppose, in other words, that the condition of local efficacy is satisfied. It is not true that "in these circumstances, pornography has the character ... of a private view," notwithstanding the presence of competing norms elsewhere.[36] Perhaps the woman could escape that local community by moving elsewhere, but that, again, supposes requisite knowledge, inclinations, and material resources, an especially questionable assumption given many women's poverty and material dependency on men. And again, the possibility of escape does not alter the fact that such a woman, where she is, in that context, *is subordinated*—for the reasons we thought Max would be subordinated, under conditions of local perceived legitimacy and local efficacy. To demand otherwise comes close to demanding that no women are subordinated by pornography unless all are.

Pornography does subordinate some women, even if one grants Green's very questionable assumptions about the absent conditions of general perceived legitimacy and efficacy. Then the question is not whether, but how many: How many women are subordinated? And how many women must be subordinated before it begins to matter?

Silence

In addition to his negative verdict on the claim that pornography subordinates women, Green delivers a negative verdict on the second, and distinct, claim that pornography silences women. He argues that the notion of illocutionary silencing I develop to elucidate this claim is quite irrelevant: free speech does not protect illocutionary speech acts. To determine whether his argument is just, I shall need to return to what I initially said.

In "Speech Acts and Unspeakable Acts" I argue for the coherence and plausibility of the claim that pornography silences women.[37] Speech act theory helps in two ways: first, when we focus on the speech of women, it provides a way of understanding how women can be silenced because of pornography; second, when we focus on the speech of pornographers, it provides a way of understanding how pornography, as speech, can be a kind of speech that silences. My chief task in "Speech Acts" was to show how women's speech may be silenced because of pornography. Notice that it is really this first task that matters in developing a free speech argument against pornography. Regardless of whether pornography is speech or whether speech act theory helps us to understand pornography, if pornography silences women's speech, then there is at least the beginning of a free speech argument against pornography.

I suggest in "Speech Acts" that women are silenced when they are unable to perform the illocutions they intend to perform, and I introduce a notion of illocutionary disablement, first by examples. An actor has a role in which he shouts, "Fire! I mean it! Look at the smoke!"; but then a real fire breaks out in the theater, and he shouts, "Fire! I mean it! Look at the smoke!" A man fills out a ballot slip, but he is black, in apartheid South Africa. Someone tries to divorce by *talak; "Mutallaqa, Mutallaqa, Mutallaqa,"* she says to her spouse; but she is a woman. A couple try to marry; both say "I do," but the two speakers are men. The speakers in these examples fail to warn, vote, divorce, or marry—although they intend to, and they use words appropriate to their intentions. These "misfires," as Austin would have called them, show illocutionary disablement.[38] The speakers fail to satisfy the success conditions—the felicity conditions—of the illocutions they intend to perform. And they fail to do these things because they are prevented from doing so—by law, in the last three examples. The law prevents them far more thoroughly than if it threatened such attempts with legal sanction. The law does not forbid such illocutionary acts, but makes them literally unspeakable, for those speakers. And the law is itself a special kind of speech.[39] So some speech makes other potential speech acts unspeakable.

I use these highly conventionalized examples because they are clear examples of something I want to emphasize. The silencings in these cases are clearly distinguishable from a failure to perform an intended locutionary act (saying no words at all) and from a failure to perform an intended perlocutionary act (failing merely to achieve the effect wanted—for example, the evacuation of a crowded theater). Most of the examples have an obvious political dimension, an asymmetry of power between classes, which is appropriate. They illustrate the idea that one's power to do illocutionary things with words can sometimes be constrained and circumscribed by someone else's speech—that some speech builds a space that makes other speech possible and still other speech impossible.

When MacKinnon says that pornography silences women, she is speaking not of the highly conventional illocutionary acts whose conditions involve specific ceremonial procedures, but of illocutionary acts generally. She is concerned about some of the ways that women's ordinary communicative speech acts can go wrong in sexual contexts.[40] She doubtless has a variety of problems in mind, but one may be this. When a woman says "No," her "no" sometimes fails to count as an act of refusal: it fails to achieve the necessary recognition—what Austin would call "uptake"—on the part of the hearer. She is like the actor who says "Fire," intending to warn, and using the right words, but failing to warn. She is silenced there and then. It may be that her hearer is unusual, unreasonable, idiosyncratic—though perhaps not all will share Green's optimism about the near ubiquity of reason and competence.[41] It may be that a reasonable, competent hearer would recognize what she said as what she meant to say: that "any reasonable person would take the refusal for what it is."[42] That is to say: in other circumstances she would not be silenced. That does not help her this time, however. To suppose that a woman is silenced only if *no* hearers recognize a woman's refusal—to suppose that a woman is silenced only if the reasonable and competent hearer would also fail to recognize a woman's refusal—is to suppose that no woman is ever silenced unless all women's refusals are silenced always. Here we have an echo of the all-or-none-ism of Green's story about subordination. Just as it would be a mistake to think that no woman is subordinated unless all, or most, are, so it would be a mistake to think that no woman is silenced unless all, or most, are. (That, to steal Green's nice phrase, would be much too tidy for such an unruly subject.)[43]

Pornography may contribute to this illocutionary disablement by undermining reciprocity, a background condition of receptiveness that enables the performance of ordinary communicative speech acts.[44] Illocutionary disablement, in general, is a matter of failure to satisfy the felicity conditions of illocutions, conditions that are sometimes highly conventional, as with some of the earlier examples, and sometimes utterly minimal, as with ordinary communicative illocutionary acts. With the latter, doing illocutionary things with words can be very easy—when reciprocity obtains. Saying something, intending it to be taken a certain way, and then having it taken that way by your hearer, is enough for you to succeed in doing the illocutionary thing you intend. Reciprocity is something like: mutual capacity for uptake. When reciprocity is present, a hearer is able to recognize what it is a speaker is trying to do with her words, and a speaker is able to secure uptake, and do the illocutionary thing she intends to do with her words.

Perhaps pornography undermines reciprocity in the cases of disabled sexual refusal by creating an expectation—legitimating an expectation—that when a woman says "No," she does not really intend her "no" as a refusal. If pornography legitimates "rape myths" as the evidence suggests, then it may make refusal unspeakable for some women in some contexts. And so pornography silences women.

Free speech is not a matter of mere freedom of locution, which would be satisfied if one said words in a solitary room. Free speech includes illocution.[45] Free speech is not freedom to perform any old illocution (knighting, *talak* divorcing, canonizing, making wills—or subordinating), but then that was never my claim (though Green misses this).[46] If that were the claim, then my first argument, that pornography itself is an illocutionary act of subordination, would amount to a *defense* of pornography, not an attack: pornography is an illocutionary act, all illocutionary acts are to be protected, therefore pornography is to be protected. No. The idea is simply that the ability to refuse is an important illocutionary capacity, an important communicative power. If there are conflicts between freedoms to speak—if (as MacKinnon puts it) the free speech of men silences the free speech of women—then there is a choice about which speech is to be protected.[47] If there is a conflict—for example, between freedom to perform illocutions of subordination and freedom to perform illocutions of refusal—it just might be that refusal matters more.

Against this argument Green develops a distinction between two kinds of silencing, one of which is intolerable, the other tolerable. He wants to argue that silencing of the kind I describe falls within the tolerable class. He distinguishes between what he calls *narrow* and *broad* silencing. Narrow silencing occurs when "one cannot realize one's communicative intentions because someone stops that person from speaking." Broad silencing occurs when "one cannot realize one's communicative intentions because even if that person succeeded in speaking, there is no guarantee that he or she will be heard as intended."[48] The silencing I describe—the silencing that is illocutionary disablement—amounts in his view to broad silencing. Narrow silencing is not to be tolerated, but broad silencing must be tolerated. After all, Green says, narrow silencing "requires someone's intervention or blameworthy omission," whereas broad silencing does not. Narrow silencing "is *prima facie* harmful," whereas broad silencing is not.[49]

Little wonder that it seems that way, for Green has offered the reader a false dichotomy. What is missing, in what he offers, is precisely the notion of silencing at issue. Narrow silencing, as he describes it, has these ingredients: (a) you fail to speak at all; (b) you fail because someone else stops you. (That is: locutionary silence, because of interference.) Broad silencing has these ingredients: (a) you speak, but fail to be heard as you intend; (b) you fail because there is no universal guarantee that you will be heard as you intend. (That is: illocutionary silence, but not because of interference.) Because narrow silencing seems bad and broad silencing does not, Green concludes (in effect) that locutionary silencing is bad and that illocutionary silencing is not.[50] But it is the *interference,* or lack of it, that is doing the intuitive work here.

What is missing is this alternative: (a) you speak, but fail to be heard as you intend; (b) you fail because some else stops you. (That is: illocutionary silence, because of interference). Now it is this kind of illocutionary silencing, not the broad illocutionary silencing described by Green, that most resembles the silencing that I describe. The example was this. (a) A woman speaks, but fails to be heard as she intends. (She says "No," but her "no" is not recognized as the refusal she intends.) (b) She fails because someone else stops her (pornography interferes with the reciprocity that is a condition of her successfully performing the illocution of refusal). This silencing does require "someone's intervention or blameworthy omission," and it is *prima facie* harmful. Since Green evidently thinks these are good reasons for restricting speech that silences, perhaps he will think they are good reasons for restricting pornographic speech that silences.

A Surprise Ending

At the end of his chapter, Green raises an interesting possibility. He points out that pornography is not bought and sold with the intentions typically involved in speech: pornography is intended to produce sexual arousal. It is, as MacKinnon puts it, "masturbation material."[51] The ordinary notion of pornography is, Green says, a functional notion. He expresses doubt that pornography is communicative speech at all. He wonders "whether it even makes sense to extend the speech act analogy into this realm and to theorize about the force of 'pornographic utterances' in general."[52] To raise this doubt, he thinks, is to raise a doubt about the entire enterprise of bringing speech act theory to bear on the issues of pornography, silence, and subordination.

My arguments are indeed premised on the assumption that pornography is speech, as the courts have said. It is disputable that pornography is speech, and it has been disputed.[53] Notice this, however: if pornography is *not* speech, then *free speech* does not protect pornography, if anything does.[54] Either pornography is not speech, in which case a free speech principle does not protect it; or pornography is speech, in which case speech act theory can help us understand it. And notice this, too: whether pornography is speech, or whether pornography is nonspeech, speech act theory can help us understand how women may be *silenced*. It can help understand how women may be *silenced by pornography*, since here it is, without question, women's speech that is at issue. Someone may be silenced by something that is speech or by something that is not speech. A heckler may silence a would-be speaker by shouting abusive words, or by blowing a whistle. One person may silence another by gently but ominously tapping a stick. One radio station may jam another by broadcasting not words, but a blaring cacophony. And women's potential speech acts may be restricted and thwarted by pornography, whether or not pornography is itself speech. It would not then be true to say that pornography is speech that silences—but it would still be true to say that pornography silences.

Now, consider: if pornography is not even speech, as Green suggests in his conclusion, and if pornography does sometimes silence women (and it really is women's *speech* that is silenced), then a free speech argument *against* pornography looks stronger than ever.[55]

Well—it is nice to find agreement in surprising places.

Notes

1. A sense of these two pictures emerged for me at the Getty seminar on censorship and silencing, and I am indebted to all those present for comments which helped me clarify some of the ideas in this paper, written entirely since then. I doubt any of the contributors to this volume would quite endorse either picture, but a view that seems (to me) to approach the second is in Richard Burt's chapter in this volume, "(Un)Censoring in Detail: The Fetish of Censorship in the Early Modern Past and the Postmodern Present" (see pages 17–41). I am also grateful for helpful comments from Sally Haslanger, Richard Holton, and Lloyd Humberstone—though I regret I have not been able to do justice to all their suggestions.

2. The idea that pornography subordinates and silences women is developed in Catharine MacKinnon's work: see especially "Francis Biddle's Sister," in idem, *Feminism Unmodified* (Cambridge, Mass.: Harvard Univ. Press, 1987); and *Only Words* (Cambridge, Mass.: Harvard Univ. Press, 1993). For discussions drawing on speech act theory to defend the coherence and plausibility of these claims, and arguing that free speech includes illocution, see Rae Langton, "Speech Acts and Unspeakable Acts," *Philosophy and Public Affairs* 22, no. 4 (1993): 293–330; Jennifer Hornsby, "Speech Acts and Pornography," *Women's Philosophy Review* 10 (1993): 38–45, reprinted with a postscript in Susan Dwyer, ed., *The Problem of Pornography* (Belmont, Calif.: Wadsworth, 1995), 220–32; Jennifer Hornsby, "Illocution and its Significance," in S. L. Tsohatzidis, ed., *Foundations of Speech Act Theory* (London: Routledge, 1994); Jennifer Hornsby, "Disempowered Speech," *Philosophical Topics* 23, no. 2 (1997): 127–47. See also Jennifer Hornsby and Rae Langton, "Free Speech and Illocution," *Journal of Legal Theory,* forthcoming. For some critiques of my arguments (apart from those of Green, which I discuss in this volume), see Daniel Jacobson, "Freedom of Speech Acts? A Response to Langton," *Philosophy and Public Affairs* 24, no. 1 (1995): 64–79; and Wojciech Sadurski, "On 'Seeing Speech through an Equality Lens': A Critique of Egalitarian Arguments for Suppression of Hate Speech and Pornography," *Oxford Journal of Legal Studies* 16, no. 4 (1996): 713–23.

3. Leslie Green, "Pornographizing, Subordinating, and Silencing," pages 285–311 in this volume. Perhaps I can also say at this point what should go without saying: that it is a privilege to have one's arguments taken seriously, and I am grateful for the care and thought so evident in what Green has said.

4. Langton (see note 2).

5. See, for example, W. A. Parent, "A Second Look at Pornography and the Subordination of Women," *Journal of Philosophy* 87 (1990): 205–11. The claim that pornography *silences* women is philosophically confused, according to Ronald Dworkin; see his "Two Concepts of Liberty," in Edna and Avishai Margalit, eds., *Isaiah Berlin: A Celebration* (London: Hogarth Press, 1991), 108.

6. J. L. Austin, *How to Do Things with Words* (Oxford: Oxford Univ. Press, 1962), see especially chapters 8 through 10.

7. See MacKinnon, *Only Words* (see note 2), 12–13, 21, and 31 n. 31; and Austin (see note 6). MacKinnon complains that Austin did not "generalize the performative to all speech" (31 n. 31), and since she is interested in the "doing" aspect of *all* speech, she slightly distances her approach from Austin's. Of course the "doing" aspect of all speech

is captured by Austin in the notion of the *illocution,* which is indeed an aspect of all speech. So she has more in common with him than she allows. Austin thought that a "performative" is a special kind of illocution and that the notion of a performative is not synonymous with the notion of an illocution. Performatives are, roughly, illocutions achievable by using the tag "I hereby . . . ," and so are not strictly applicable to pornography, or for that matter most illocutions—though see Green (see note 3), 304, for what I take to be a suggestion about the remote conceptual possibility of pornography being a *performative* that subordinates. The distinction between performatives and illocutions is sometimes ignored or abandoned by others, possibly for the reason that the notion of *performative* wears on its face the notion of *doing* with words, whereas *illocution* does not. See, for example, Green (see note 3); and Judith Butler, who develops an interesting and different conception of the idea in *Gender Trouble: Feminism and the Subversion of Identity* (London: Routledge, 1990), and applies it to the feminist debate about pornography in her "Burning Acts," in A. Parker and E. Sedgwick, eds., *Performativity and Performance* (New York: Routledge, 1995), 197–226. Butler and I have shared interests in the topic of speech acts and pornography, though not (it seems) shared conclusions.

8. MacKinnon, *Only Words* (see note 2), 31.

9. Green (see note 3), 291.

10. Ibid.

11. This assumes a nonstipulative usage for *pornography,* following Green's usage of an "ordinary concept" of pornography (see note 3), 32, 33 (though my discussion has an implicit content restriction on the kind of pornography for which one might make a case that it subordinates women and legitimates violence). If, however, one follows MacKinnon in saying that as a matter of definition pornography subordinates, then it will no longer be a contingent matter whether *pornography* subordinates: it then becomes part of the meaning of the word that pornography subordinates. However, the question about illocutionary force will return as an empirical question, not this time in the form "Does pornography subordinate?" but in the form "*Is* there any pornography, so defined?" (Caroline West has emphasized this point in a manuscript, "The Pragmatics of Pornography.") In saying that it is a contingent matter whether pornography subordinates, I do not speak for all who have defended a noncausal understanding of MacKinnon's claim. Melinda Vadas, for example, would disagree with me about the contingency of the question of whether pornography subordinates—and not for merely definitional reasons. She argues in a forthcoming paper, "The Manufacture-for-use of Pornography and Women's Inequality," that pornography (defined functionally in terms of its masturbatory use) *necessarily subordinates women.* Vadas's argument is discussed and compared with my own view and others in Rae Langton, "Sexual Solipsism," *Philosophical Topics* 23, no. 2 (1995): 181–219. I develop a quite different noncausal argument in "Whose Right? Ronald Dworkin, Women and Pornographers," *Philosophy and Public Affairs* 19, no. 4 (1990): 311–59, but this argument too depends on contingent premises—this time about the reasons and attitudes of those who consume pornography, which are relevant to developing a Dworkinian rights-based argument against pornography.

12. Green (see note 3), 293–94.

13. Ibid., 293.

14. Austin's discussion of verdictives and exercitives occurs, with some of these examples, in *How to Do Things with Words* (see note 6), 152–56.

15. You might think (following Austin) that exercitives are neither true nor false. Alternatively, you might think that they are true, but if they are true they could be false. I incline to neither view, but rather to the view that an exercitive (for example, "You're fired") *is true* whenever it is a successful illocution (successful in the sense of having satisfied the felicity conditions); then it *cannot be false.* This distinguishes exercitives from verdictives, which, when successful at the illocutionary level (successful in the sense of having satisfied the felicity conditions), may be *either true, or false.* This gives a sense in which exercitives are instantly self-fulfilling in a way that verdictives are not. Thanks to Richard Holton for helping me to clarify this (he favors the second of the above views).

16. The distinction between what are now known as "directions of fit" was introduced by G. E. M. Anscombe in her *Intention* (Oxford: Blackwell, 1957), and it is widely used in discussions of propositional attitudes of belief and desire. For some applications to speech acts see John R. Searle, *Expression and Meaning: Studies in the Theory of Speech Acts* (Cambridge: Cambridge Univ. Press, 1979); and Lloyd Humberstone, "Direction of Fit," *Mind* 101 (1992): 60–83. The distinction is applied to feminist arguments about power and oppression in Rae Langton, "Beyond a Pragmatic Critique of Reason," *Australasian Journal of Philosophy* 71, no. 4 (1993): 364–84. The illocutionary direction of fit implicit in MacKinnon's work seems both more complex and less mysterious than Butler suggests in "Burning Acts" (see note 7): more complex, because it is different for different kinds of illocution, and less mysterious, because there is nothing magical or "divine" about it. Perhaps Butler's equation of performatives and illocutions in her interpretation of MacKinnon has disadvantages here, if it leads her to the (to my mind) oversimple view that all illocutions are supposed to be "self-fulfilling" in the same way and that pornography is supposed (by MacKinnon) to work like a divine command.

17. MacKinnon, *Feminism Unmodified* (see note 2), 164. Following a suggestion of Sally Haslanger's, I have substituted *proven* here for MacKinnon's own word *proof,* since it seems to make better sense of MacKinnon's point. See Sally Haslanger, "On Being Objective and Being Objectified," in Louise Antony and Charlotte Witt, eds., *A Mind of One's Own: Feminist Essays on Reason and Objectivity* (Boulder: Westview Press, 1992).

18. Contrary—or so it seems—to Butler, who suggests in "Burning Acts" (see note 7) that MacKinnon makes a grammatical mistake in supposing that what pornography depicts women *as* can have implications for what a woman *is:* "But if the 'as' is read as an assertion of a likeness, it is not for that reason the assertion of a metaphorical collapse into identity. Through what means does the 'as' turn into an 'is'?" (222). What I say in what follows is, in part, an attempt to explain some of the different ways in which an "as" can turn into an "is," ways that are different for exercitive and verdictive illocutions.

19. See Robert Rosenthal and Lenore Jacobson, *Pygmalion in the Classroom: Teacher Expectation and Pupils' Intellectual Development* (New York: Holt, Rinehart & Winston, 1968).

20. These conclusions about verdictive speech have connections with epistemology when we come to the *beliefs* of those in power or authority. Verdictive speech aims to fit the world. Beliefs, too, aim to fit the world. Verdictives are the speech act analogs of beliefs, or (better) of authoritative beliefs, and all the complexities of direction of fit noted above with verdictives have their exact parallel with beliefs. I noted that MacKinnon speaks not only of what the powerful *say,* but of what they *believe.* Beliefs aim to fit the world, but in some circumstances, the world comes to fit the beliefs: "[The] *beliefs* of the powerful become [proven], in part because the world actually arranges itself to affirm what the powerful want to see"; *Feminism Unmodified* (see note 2), 164. The belief that purports merely to mirror can also create, and can make the world conform to itself. The belief that claims to map reality can construct reality, at least to some extent, by the mechanisms we considered when thinking about verdictives. But again, that constructive power is disguised, as with verdictives. If belief aims to fit the world, it aims to be objective. That disguises, for the powerful believer and others, the extent to which the belief appears to match the world for the wrong reason: the belief appears to match, not because the belief fits the world, but because the world has come to fit the belief. (Despite its aim, the belief is not really objective—or so I argue.) If the belief concerns someone's subordinate status—"Women are submissive," for example—and if it appears to be true because the women encountered are made to conform to expectations, then an apparently uncomfortable conclusion looms for epistemology. The aim for objectivity—the aim for apparent fit—can help to objectify women. That is my interpretation of MacKinnon's complaint that reason is gendered: her complaint, overstated but with a point nonetheless, is that "to look at the world objectively is to objectify it"; *Feminism Unmodified* (see note 2), 50. This critique of objectivity, and its merits and faults, is a topic of my article, "Beyond a Pragmatic Critique of Reason" (see note 16). See also Sally Haslanger's extended analysis in "On Being Objective and Being Objectified" (see note 17).

21. Green (see note 3), 296.

22. MacKinnon, *Only Words* (see note 2), 31.

23. This understanding of the social science data is based on, for example, Edward Donnerstein, Daniel Linz, and Steven Penrod, *The Question of Pornography: Research Findings and Policy Implications* (New York: Free Press, 1987). These authors do not favor MacKinnon's legal solution, but instead advocate education and tort action for particular cases of incitement to rape. For authors who seem to decide *a priori* that pornography presents its norms as not-be-realized, see, for example, Butler, "Burning Acts" (see note 7), 222–23, and for a rather different version, Green (see note 3), who argues against the idea that pornography legitimates what it presents, saying that feminists ignore "the fact that [pornography] can also evoke sexual fantasies that are widely held to be *illegitimate*" (296).

24. Ibid., 293. Green seems to interpret the norms of some norm-giver with a paradigm of orders—prescriptions and prohibitions—in mind. MacKinnon sometimes does so too, as does Butler in "Burning Acts" (see note 7), 220. Perhaps some pornography does have this character—it would be too "tidy" to assume any uniform rule. Some, however, is probably better thought of in terms of permissions, as I describe

above. This discrepancy makes it difficult for me to try to couch the above points in terms of the account of authority Green develops in more detail in his book, *The Authority of the State* (Oxford: Clarendon Press, 1988), chapter 2. What Green says there about the contrast between *having* authority and *being an* authority on a subject matter seems particularly interesting. The contrast he makes seems highly relevant to the distinction between exercitives (whose speakers *have* authority) and verdictives (whose speakers typically *are* authorities on a subject matter and *have* authority). It may well be that these two notions of authority are connected (contrary to Green). These issues deserve more thought than I give them here.

25. MacKinnon, *Feminism Unmodified* (see note 2), 164.

26. Green (see note 3), 294.

27. Ibid.

28. Ibid.

29. Perhaps general perceived legitimacy would likewise be a sufficient condition —even in the absence of efficacy—but we would need to adapt the story appropriately to test intuitions about this.

30. The same idea is present in some of Butler's work, though her philosophical perspective is very different from Green's. She implies that unless pornography constructs "unilaterally" and "exhaustively" the social reality of what a woman is, MacKinnon is wrong and pornography "fails to wield the power to construct the social reality of what a woman is"; "Burning Acts" (see note 7), 222.

31. Perhaps they are also both necessary—or perhaps only the local efficacy condition is necessary. We don't need to settle this for present purposes.

32. Green (see note 3), 295.

33. Ibid., 298.

34. Judge David Wild in 1982, as discussed by Jennifer Hornsby in "Speech Acts and Pornography" (see note 2), 226. Hornsby also discusses some more recent judicial pronouncements that are in the same vein.

35. Green (see note 3), 295.

36. Ibid., 296.

37. Langton (see note 2).

38. Austin (see note 6), 16.

39. Contrary to Green (see note 3), 301, who says that law is not speech. Green also complains that disablement is not prevention. I think it is one of many kinds of preventing. He thinks forbidding is preventing, and says gay marriages are not forbidden, hence not prevented. (He thinks I am mistaken in suggesting, like Jacobson, that there are "laws forbidding same sex-marriage." Well, Jacobson is indeed mistaken. But, unlike Jacobson, I explicitly contrasted disablement with forbidding in the remark that the gay couple does not *disobediently marry,* as they could if they were merely forbidden from marrying.) Forbidding is not, or not always, preventing: theft, for example, is forbidden but not prevented by law. Disablement is a much more effective preventing. Green's own assimilation of "forbidding" and "preventing" thus seems a mistake to me, though of course he is entitled to introduce a technical usage if he wishes.

40. MacKinnon, *Feminisim Unmodified* (see note 2), passim, but see, for exam-

ple, 156, 181, 190, 193; MacKinnon, *Only Words* (see note 2), passim, but see, for example, 67–68.

41. Green (see note 3), 298.

42. Ibid.

43. Ibid., 305.

44. The notion of reciprocity is named and described by Jennifer Hornsby in the articles cited above (see note 2) and applied by her to issues about pornography and women's silence. My notion of silence as illocutionary disablement has much in common with Hornsby's idea of a person's being deprived of illocutionary potential.

45. The idea that free speech includes illocution is implicit in the arguments of Langton (see note 2) and Hornsby (see note 2) and MacKinnon (see note 2), though I don't say MacKinnon would express it in that way; it is explicit in Hornsby and Langton, "Free Speech and Illocution," (see note 2).

46. Green (see note 3), 299–301.

47. MacKinnon, *Feminism Unmodified* (see note 2), 156.

48. In describing narrow silencing Green (see note 3) says, to quote more fully, "someone stops that person from speaking or denies that person a fair opportunity to be heard" (303). I take the latter clause to involve the positive speech liberties described on the previous page: fair opportunity "to try to reach an audience" and so on. Someone deprived of such an opportunity is presumably someone who does not speak, that is, does not perform even a locutionary act.

49. Ibid.

50. Ibid.

51. Ibid., 304; and MacKinnon, *Only Words* (see note 2), 17.

52. Green (see note 3), 304.

53. For example, by Fred Schauer and (to some degree) Jennifer Hornsby. See Frederick Schauer, *Free Speech: A Philosophical Enquiry* (Cambridge: Cambridge Univ. Press, 1982); and Hornsby (see note 2).

54. On the speech versus expression issue, see Hornsby (see note 2); and Hornsby and Langton (see note 2).

55. Green (see note 3), 303–305.

Pornographizing, Subordinating, and Silencing

Leslie Green

The strongest argument for censoring pornography rests on the claim that its production or consumption is harmful to others. This argument, invoking the "harm principle," is a liberal argument because it is committed to individual autonomy—one should not be misled by the fact that its most articulate defenders are feminists who say they reject liberalism. It is also a moral argument, notwithstanding that many of those feminists would also say, with Catharine MacKinnon, that pornography is "not a moral issue."[1] What they mean is that we should not restrict pornography on the ground that it is thought shameful, disgusting, wrong, or obscene. That would be moralism, enforcing the conventional morality of a given community, and that makes no one's life go better.

The harm principle displays its commitment to individual autonomy in a second way too: it rejects the paternalistic aim of preventing harm to the producers or consumers of pornography themselves. Save in very special circumstances, people need autonomy to form, pursue, and revise their conceptions of the good, for that provides the best hope that their lives will indeed go well. Even if pornography degrades or corrupts those in its audience, we should resist forcing self-improvement on them. Whether we agree with J. S. Mill that preventing harm to others is the *sole* valid reason for restricting the liberty of rational adults, it is in this case a reason more compelling than those offered by either moralism or paternalism.[2]

To insist that censorship is justified only by harm prevention does not conclude the argument, however—it scarcely begins it. "Harm" is a complex moral notion that is, in liberal theory, subject to at least two constraints. First, it must be distinguished from the notion of "offense." Some people suffer at the thought of pornography, and some even at the thought that it is available to others; indeed, the outrage, disgust, and shame they experience is poorly captured in the technical term *offense,* which may suggest an embarrassed blush. Yet it is not the reality of these feelings that a liberal theory denies, it is their normative standing. We cannot both promote personal autonomy and protect people from every pain that accompanies the collision between different values or ways of life.[3] Second, while harm to others may comprise harm to specific public institutions and practices, it must exclude what Mill called "constructive" harm to society as an undifferentiated mass or to abstractions like the public good.[4] If we are to impose duties on determinate people and groups then it should be for the sake of determinate people and groups that we do so.

Within these limits, however, the notion of harm is quite broad. It extends well beyond injury to one's person and property to include injury to certain important statuses, especially one's civil status. Such injuries degrade one's standing and make one a second-class citizen, with inferior powers and liberties. (We might call these "wrongs" rather than "harms," but nothing turns on this.) In some of the most interesting recent work on censorship, theorists argue that pornography harms the status of women because it *subordinates and silences* them. They reach this conclusion by developing a suggestion found in the philosophy of language, that certain words have "illocutionary" force: saying them *constitutes* an act of a certain kind; they are "performative" utterances.[5] These theorists then argue that to produce, distribute, or use pornography—or, as I shall say, to "pornographize"—is sometimes also to engage in the speech acts of subordinating or silencing. The subordination of women undermines their standing as equal citizens; silencing them prevents them from fully engaging in discourse and thus undermines free expression itself. Together these constitute a profound injury that any decent regime would wish to prevent. This is supposed to strengthen (although not necessarily conclude) the case for censorship, and this is the argument I want to explore.

The Pure Pornography Problem

To be clear about the stakes I must first focus the debate. Let me call "the pure pornography problem" the question of whether it is proper for a legislative body to coercively prohibit or substantially restrict the consensual production or consumption of pornography. The problem is concerned, first, with *coercive public action*. This need not be what some lawyers call "state action," for the relevant issues arise with any action that coercively regulates, for a given group, the production or consumption of pornography. The pure pornography problem is thus faced by any body with quasi-legislative capacity, not just one with sovereign capacity. To the extent that they are able coercively to control their members, a university deciding whether to legislate a speech code, a library deciding whether to ban certain books, or a church prohibiting its youth group from showing certain movies may all be engaged in action of the sort I have in mind. In contrast, the questions of whether one should use pornography oneself, boycott its producers or retailers, dissuade others from its use, or educate people about its effects raise different moral and political issues than do the coercive policies that we ordinarily think of as censorship.

There is, naturally, overlap between censorship and other forms of regulation, and the distinction is not sharp, but this is because our notion of coercion is itself not very sharp. For example, some who oppose the criminal regulation of pornography are willing to endorse civil remedies because they see them as less coercive. Others who assimilate civil remedies to coercive threats think that even punitive taxes would be coercive. Or again, some believe that only the state can censor because they think it enjoys a monopoly of ultimate coercive power, while others maintain that powerful corporations or foundations can equally threaten free speech. Dispute is rife. A focus on coercive power does not eliminate this dispute, but it does track it, for our political concerns follow our views about the location and nature of coercion and not the applicability of the word *censorship*. Although that word now carries a negative valence,[6] we do not proceed by first licensing its use and then drawing the inference that whatever we label as censorship is wrong. After all, that word has a wide range of proper uses, including, for instance, "self-censorship." Self-censorship may be right where censorship is wrong, however: there are things that one should not say but whose utterance should not be prevented.

It is also true that every communicative act is born of a particular history in which its author and others are deeply and jointly implicated. What matters cannot therefore be the bare fact that all expression has certain *causes* and is thus, in that way, "already censored." That is trivially true, for, as Joseph Butler put it, everything is what it is, and not another thing—except for the causal history that it had, every utterance would have been different.[7] Our moral and political concerns focus not here, but on certain *kinds* of causal histories, especially those in which people are forced or extorted to remain silent or to speak in an approved way. We care about these because such interferences put at risk both individual autonomy and the public good. Thus, what matters most is not that others *influence* our speech—this is an empty truth; neither is it the more interesting truth that we sometimes care about *who* influences our speech.[8] Our interest lies in the fact that we have standing preferences about *how* others may influence our speech, and that is the importance of regulating coercive public action.

The debate also must focus on *consensually made and consumed* pornography. I do not assert that most pornography is consensually made and consumed. Some is made using "actors" or "models" who work in conditions of near slavery or under other forms of compulsion, manipulation, or exploitation, and sometimes pornography is unwillingly consumed—for instance, when it is publicly displayed. These examples cannot provide a full justification for regulating pornography, however, because pornography may be made without models (as is the case with stories, novels, drawings, paintings, computer graphics, and so on) and because most pornography is in fact privately consumed. Some maintain that the issue of consent is irrelevant, for what the legal system counts as "consenting" is so wide as to *include* sexual slavery. I do not, however, mean the phrase "consensually made and consumed" to be continued with the words "as understood by positive law currently enforced." I mean it as a critical moral judgment and thus to be continued by the phrase "as judged by proper standards of political morality." If any legal system refuses to invalidate consent that is extorted, manipulated, and so on, then that system is itself open to criticism.

Finally, my primary interest here is in the *legislative* question of whether we should endorse and enact coercive restrictions on pornography, not in the *adjudicative* question of whether such legislation, if enacted, should be held constitutional in this country or that. (These questions would be fused only in a jurisdiction whose courts had the power to strike down any legislation that was morally wrong.) We can always distinguish the scope of a body's legislative competence from the justice and wisdom of its actions within that scope. Thus, a constitutional argument showing that a legislature is competent to make a certain law is consistent with a moral or political argument that it is wrong for it to do so. Neglect of this distinction (particularly by some lawyers) has confused the debate.[9] This is unfortunate, for most constitutions—even the U.S. Constitution, even when properly interpreted—are imperfect.[10] One might believe, for instance, that although the First Amendment largely prohibits the restriction of pornography, it should not; or that although Section 2(b) of the Canadian Charter of Rights and Freedoms permits restrictions, it should not. One might also oppose the interference of courts in these matters entirely, while insisting that legislatures should rigorously respect free expression. We need to think about general matters of principle, and the way to do that is to set aside, if temporarily, constitutional law.

So conceived, the pure pornography problem is nonetheless not an *abstract* problem. The contrast is not between the *a priori* and the empirical, the universal, and the contextual, or anything of that kind. On the contrary, it involves many empirical and (as I shall urge) contextual judgments about psychology, culture, and the working of political institutions. The point of the problem is to train our attention on certain empirical and contextual questions rather than others. By considering their bearing on the propriety of the coercive public regulation of consensual pornography, we heighten the contrast between competing principles and illuminate deep and difficult questions about liberty, about justice, and about sexuality.

We must bear in mind, of course, that an argument may strengthen the case for censorship without settling it. For example, some feminists who see a *prima facie* case for criminal prohibitions on pornography also think that these should nonetheless be avoided since the criminal justice system is dominated by men and by androcentric ideas and since the accused benefits from rigorous procedural protections in criminal proceedings. On the other side, some who endorse free expression in theory concede that in the nonideal world of practice we must often compromise. For example, many pornographic films begin with a notice to the effect that all actors are of legal age and that proof of age is on file with the producer. Where false identity papers are readily available and actors and producers vanish, it would be reckless to take that information at face value. Thus theorists might endorse a broad prohibition on films in which the actors *appear* to be under age. Allowing for such important practical considerations, however, the pure pornography problem nonetheless retains its focal importance, for that is where political principles are most sharply divided. It requires no recondite theory to explain why people must not be enslaved to make pornography or why people should not to be forced to view it. On both points, the most radical libertarian will vote with the most radical feminist. It may be that too little is done to turn this conjunction of belief into policy, but that problem is a product not of bad theory but of bad faith.

Contingent versus Constitutive Harms

Given that censorship may be justified if it prevents harm, how might pornography produce the relevant sorts of harm? The standard argument appeals to the indirect and contingent harms of pornography: by influencing the beliefs, attitudes, and values of its consumers, and ultimately the whole culture of a society, pornography leads to a variety of violent, abusive, and discriminatory acts against women. This claim faces two notorious difficulties. First, it is doubtful whether these are specific effects of pornography. MacKinnon claims that U.S. law makes it hard to notice these effects by adopting an "individuated, atomistic, linear, exclusive, isolated, narrowly tortlike—in a word, positivistic—conception of injury."[11] The word is wrong, but the point is important. The causal nexus may certainly be nonlinear, and although pornography is an integral part of a sexist social system it may nonetheless have an independent effect. To acknowledge that such an effect *may* occur does not show that it does, however, nor does acknowledgment gauge how strong an effect pornography has. On those matters there is no ground for confidence.[12]

Apart from this is a second problem with the standard argument. Even if the production or consumption of pornography is causally connected to such harms, questions of intervening moral responsibility remain. There are, it is true, cases in which we might favor vicarious liability, or liability for incitement, but they are few. Unless one supposes that pornography always deprives its users of agency, the users should normally be the ones to bear responsibility for any harm they cause. Thus Melinda Vadas, in an acute discussion, says of the standard argument (which she calls, with deliberate irony, the "reasonable view"):

> Of course, those who hold the reasonable view recognize that agents acting upon the information or recommendations provided by pornographic depictions might harm others. If this occurs, however, the agents of harm are themselves responsible for the harm, not the creators or disseminators of the depictions. One who holds the reasonable view will naturally say that the agents simply should not have acted on the information or recommendations imparted.[13]

These difficulties in the standard argument are not present, or at least not in the same form, in the different argument that I consider here. According to it, pornographic expression does not *cause* a contingently connected, independent harm to women; it *is* such a harm. MacKinnon writes:

> Pornography contains ideas, like any other social practice. But the way it works is not as a thought or through its ideas as such, at least not in the way thoughts and ideas are protected as speech. Its place in abuse requires understanding it more in active than in passive terms, as constructive and performative rather than as merely referential or connotative.[14]

Pornography is performative, says MacKinnon, and thus has something in common with, for example, "saying 'kill' to a trained attack dog" which is "not seen as expressing the viewpoint 'I want you dead'—which it usually does, in fact, express. It is seen as an act tantamount to someone's destruction, like saying 'ready, aim, fire' to a firing squad."[15] She notes,

> Along with other mere words like "not guilty" and "I do," such words are uniformly treated as the institutions and practices they constitute, rather than as expressions of the ideas they embody or further. They are not seen as saying anything (although they do) but as doing something.[16]

The distinction in play here turns on the fact that an utterance (and perhaps, by extension, a text or image) has not only a content or meaning together with certain causal effects on its audience, it also has what J. L. Austin called an "illocutionary" force: it constitutes or counts as an action of a certain kind.[17] Thus, in the right conditions, to say "I promise" is to promise; to say "Watch out!" is to warn; to say "I do" is to marry; to say "I disagree" is to object. And, perhaps in the right conditions, to make, sell, buy, or watch a pornographic video is to subordinate or silence women. The standard argument notices the *locutionary acts* in pornography (the content of what is said, the "ideas" expressed), which bring it under the scope of expressive freedom. It also notices the *perlocutionary acts* in pornography (the causal effects on its audience), which encompass contingent harms (and possibly benefits) of pornography—it can arouse, incite, alarm, offend, and so on—and this is also where the doubts about evidence and responsibility emerge. But the standard argument fails to account for the *illocutionary acts* in pornography, particularly the subordinating and silencing that it constitutes. Pornography is thus not speech as distinct from action; it is itself a *kind* of action, and as Mill himself acknowledged, "No one pretends that actions should be as free as opinions."[18]

Understood in this way, however, MacKinnon's attack dog and firing squad examples are importantly different. Saying "Kill" to a trained dog triggers a conditioned reflex rather than a communicative response: it does not depend for its success on the dog's recognizing one's intention in making the utterance. It succeeds provided only the dog does what it is told; moreover, a dog that fails to respond is poorly trained but not insubordinate. The firing squad, in contrast, responds to an order by understanding that it is given with the intention of being followed because it *is* an order. This is a communicative response, and the illocutionary act depends for its success on its intended audience securing *uptake*—the recognition of the intention with which it is performed. If the firing squad took the imperative "Fire!" not as a command to shoot but as a warning that a fire had broken out, then the intended illocutionary act would fail.

Of course, the fact that speech may in such ways constitute an act does not *automatically* make it a candidate for coercive regulation. As Robert Post argues, that would be "incompatible with any viable notion of freedom of expression, for social relations are pervasively comprised by speech," and thus central cases of free speech can also constitute, for instance, the illocutionary acts of demeaning, disrespecting, and so on:

> I can, as a literary critic, speak disrespectfully and authoritatively about a new novel; I can, as an outraged moralist, speak disrespectfully and with great effect about the actions of an acquaintance; or I can, as a political partisan, speak disrespectfully and influentially about the character of the President. In each of these examples I have acted disrespectfully, and with devastating consequences to the social standing of the object of my speech. We can argue about whether or not the law should intervene to punish me in any particular case, but it surely goes too far to claim that freedom of speech is not pertinent to any of the examples because they involve acts rather than communication.[19]

The point of speech act theory, however, is not to show that pornography (for example) is an act *rather than* speech, it is to call attention to certain important effects that speech might have in addition to its familiar perlocutionary ones. Noticing this may draw our attention to harms that we might otherwise miss, harms directly and conceptually connected to the speech in question and relevant to the pure pornography problem.

There are, then, two attractions to a direct constitutive argument. First, if saying simply *is* doing, there is no need to worry about the contingent causal connection and the problematic evidence for it. The evidence for the harm is the evidence for the saying. Second, in all but unusual cases there is little doubt about who has moral responsibility. There is no question of being held responsible for remote effects of one's utterance or for the actions of others who are incited to act by one's expression; when there is a direct and conceptual connection between speech and action, the chain of responsibility generally remains intact. As Vadas puts it,

> On the civil-rights view pornography not only provides information and recommendations, but contributes to the actual and literal creation of women as a subordinated class, a class whose members may then be additionally victimized by those acting in response to this preestablished subordination.[20]

That is the power of establishing a constitutive connection between speech and harmful acts.

Subordination and the Authority of Speech

How then might pornography contribute to the actual and literal creation of women as a subordinated class, so that it constitutes, in the words of MacKinnon and Andrea Dworkin's Model Ordinance, "the graphic sexually explicit subordination of women in pictures and/or words"?[21] How can *saying* that someone is subordinate, or depicting and representing her as subordinate, end up by actually *subordinating* her?

Andrew Altman makes a suggestion in discussing the related problem of hate speech. He says that treating people as moral subordinates means "treating them in a way that takes their interests to be intrinsically less important, and their lives inherently less valuable, than the interests and lives of those who belong to some reference group"; he states further that this may be accomplished not only by acts that are "naturally" expressive of that (his examples are slavery and genocide) but also by certain *conventional* means.[22] Racial slurs and other epithets, on this view, sometimes take the force of a fundamental put-down. But this argument is incomplete. You might think it an insult to call me a "dweeb," and in your circles it might well be, but what is that to me? It is not enough that words have a derogatory conventional force, even when the purported derogation of status is fundamental. If names really can hurt in this way, it is not simply because of their conventional associations; we also need to explain what gives the conventions their bite—how they actually do affect one's status. MacKinnon provides the missing step:

> Together with all its material supports, authoritatively *saying* someone is inferior is largely how structures of status and differential treatment are demarcated and actualized. Words and images are how people are placed in hierarchies, how social stratification is made to seem inevitable and right, how feelings of inferiority and superiority are engendered, and how indifference to violence against those on the bottom is rationalized and normalized. Social supremacy is made, inside and between people, through making meanings.[23]

It is not just that words can construct reality through their performative force; that is trivially true of all speech acts. It is that certain words *authoritatively* construct reality. If a put-down is not just someone's say-so, the expression of a private and maybe even idiosyncratic view, but an authoritative judgment, assessment, or verdict about one's status, then the stakes are much higher. Then, but only then, does someone's say-so alter another's status. These names do hurt, because of the combination of their conventional meaning and their authoritative force.

This is an important advance, but it is one that raises new questions. What counts as "authoritatively saying someone is inferior," and how does that differ from stating that they are inferior, arguing that they are inferior, or persuading others that they are inferior? Authority is a large topic in political theory, and what I say here will need to be brief.[24] To begin, people may have what is sometimes called *theoretical* authority, that is, authority over belief, or they may have *practical* authority, authority over action. One has theoretical authority only if one's say-so gives (or, in the case of *de facto* theoretical authority, is accepted as giving) another person a reason to endorse what one says. One has practical authority only if one's say-so gives (or is accepted as giving) another person a reason to act. To have practical authority *over* others is to be able to change their reasons for action and, in particular, to be able to alter by one's very word their rights, powers, liberties, or duties—their normative relations. Someone in legal authority has the capacity to alter legal relations, someone in religious authority has the capacity to alter religious relations, and so on. A fully explicated statement of someone's authority thus takes the general form X has authority over Y with respect to Z, where the relata Y and Z fix the jurisdiction and scope of authority. Authority thus differs from other forms of effective social power in that it works not through brute force or manipulation, but through the giving and accepting of reasons of a certain kind.[25]

Let us therefore consider what is, I think, a plausible case of "authoritatively saying someone is inferior" and thereby subordinating him. Roman Catholic moral theology holds homosexuality to be an "objective disorder" and an "intrinsic moral evil."[26] It expresses that view in texts that issue from authoritative sources: for devout Catholics they are not mere arguments or expressions of opinion. Along with the rest of Roman Catholic sexual morality, these sources create a status hierarchy of desires, acts, relationships, and thus, in certain respects, people.[27] We may imagine, then, two men living in a country that has a minority of Roman Catholics and a liberal constitution: there is no established church and citizens enjoy reasonable freedom of religion. Mick, a gay Catholic, is subordinated by the Church's view; his church's doctrine is, for him, not mere words. The say-so of the pope, or the Sacred Congregation for the Doctrine of the Faith, works to put him down in relevant ways, deeming his erotic constitution to be a form of disorder, condemning the natural expression of his desire as sin, and derogating his loving relationship with his partner. What then should we say of his neighbor Max, a gay Jew? Is Max subordinated by the words of the Church? Does *he* have an objective disorder because the Church says he does?

This depends on the social context in which these men live. The Church may certainly *purport* to subordinate other gay people. Indeed, to the extent that some of its homophobic utterances claim the authority of natural law (thus binding, the tradition has it, on believer and nonbeliever alike), they assert a wide jurisdiction. But the mere fact that some of these texts might be *addressed* to Max will not suffice to bring him within their jurisdiction. It is one thing to purport to do something with words; it is another to actually do it. I can purport to ennoble you, to absolve you, or to marry you, but that does not show that I have succeeded. Max is not subordinated merely by the purported authority of the Church, although of course it may have other important perlocutionary effects, such as making him anxious, ashamed, or angry.

One should not suppose, however, that a church can subordinate only its willing adherents or that one may escape its social jurisdiction through apostasy. Even if consent were a necessary condition for *justified* ecclesiastical authority, it is not necessary for *effective* authority. What insulates Max in the example is not the bare fact that he is a Jew, but that his society has a liberal constitution and that the Church has a minority following. Suppose, however, that things were otherwise. What if the Church were established and its dictates widely accepted as binding standards of behavior? If Max is subjected to those standards then he too will be subordinated even though he is not a Catholic. People will now generally regard Max as a disordered personality, and clerics, because their authority is generally accepted, will be able to worsen his normative status or prevent beneficial changes to it by refusing him protection from discrimination, denying him the power to marry, and so on. He is thus subordinated by the *de facto* authority of a church of which he is not a member. Thus, whether speech has the power to subordinate is not simply a function of what is said but of the whole social context in which it occurs.

We cannot here explore all the conditions sufficient for such authority, but the above example suggests two important necessary ones. First, the norms prescribed by the Church must be perceived to be legitimate—they must be generally accepted as setting binding standards of behavior. If the Church's sexual morality is widely thought wrong, or is ignored, or is subject to significant countervailing forces, then Max is not subordinated—no matter what the Church may say. Nor would he be subordinated by a few cranks, nor even by a large minority if they were held in check by others. Second, the Church's norms must also be generally efficacious. There must be some kind of significant contact between Max and those who do endorse the Catholic view: they must, for example, have the power to hire or fire him, to control his education, to affect his civil rights, and so on, and they must sometimes actually exercise their power.

Are analogous conditions met by pornography? In an excellent discussion, Rae Langton argues,

> If you believe that pornographic utterances are made by a powerless minority, a fringe group especially vulnerable to moralistic persecution, then you will answer negatively. Not so if you believe, with MacKinnon, that pornography's voice is the voice of the ruling power. Liberal debate about pornography has typically been based on the former belief.[28]

Liberals think, wrongly, that pornographers are irrelevant cranks on the fringe of society, whereas in fact they have significant social authority over belief and action, perhaps not like that of the Catholic Church over its willing adherents, but much like the effective authority of the Church where it is established or widely accepted. Langton's suggestion is both interesting and challenging, for if pornography really is authoritative speech, then it has greater potential for harm.

To make this argument work we need a reasonably clear fix on the identity of the pornographers and the norms they articulate or follow. Presumably, pornographers are all (or most) of those who make "pornographic utterances." Now, pornography is not normally an utterance in the literal sense and, in any case, procensorship arguments are meant to apply to both the production and the consumption of pornography. Let us say, then, that anyone "pornographizes" who makes, offers for sale, displays, sells, purchases, or uses pornography, and let us say that a pornographer is just anyone who pornographizes. It is also relevant that the vast majority of this class are men.

If that is right, then the first chain of command is not found in the authority of pornographers over women, but of pornographers over *men and boys*, or, put another way, the authority of some pornographers (producers) over other pornographers (consumers).[29] It is not exactly that pornographers are the ruling power, it is that they have power over some of those who do rule. Men rule women; pornography tells them how to go about it.

What norms do pornographers prescribe, and do they meet the conditions of legitimacy and efficacy? We know what the Roman Catholic Church thinks about homosexuality because it overtly prescribes and prohibits; it even presents us with an explicit doctrine of authority so that we know which of its words count. If pornography is also authoritative speech, it must be so in some looser sense. Langton's suggestion is that it functions as an authority about sexuality:

> What is important is whether it [the "speech of pornographers"] is authoritative in the domain that counts—the domain of speech about sex—and whether it is authoritative for the hearers that count: people, men, boys, who, in addition to wanting "entertainment," want to discover the right way to do things, want to know which moves in the sexual game are legitimate.[30]

What they find is that it "rank[s] women as things, as objects, as prey" and "tell[s] its hearers which moves are appropriate and permissible."[31]

This reasoning does not reveal, however, why the only relevant domain is speech about sex and why the only relevant people are those who take normative guidance from pornography. We are considering whether pornography can harm women by injuring their civil status, but that harm depends on much more than what is said and done in speech about sex. For example, if pornography endorses rape but the broader society condemns it and regularly prosecutes it, the fact that pornography represents women as wanting abuse does not change their status. That women are subordinated-in-pornography no more shows that they are subordinated than does the fact that gays are subordinated-in-Catholicism shows that they are subordinated. The relevant speech acts must reach beyond the realm of pornography itself. The standard argument, of course, posits a powerful but contingent effect of pornography on people in general, but that unlikely route to establishing the efficacy of pornography's norms is no more promising in the constitutive argument.

There is, moreover, serious doubt about the existence and legitimacy of the norms in the first place. While it is possible that some people do use pornography for normative guidance about sex, that is certainly not its standard use. As MacKinnon rightly says, pornography is mostly "masturbation material."[32] Most consumers want their pornography to be arousing rather than didactic or even reassuring, and there is nothing in most pornographic imagery that corresponds to the orders, recommendations, verdicts, and other types of speech that characterize examples of speech act theory. It would be hopelessly naive, for instance, to think that each image bears the message "Look, this is how it is to be done; this is right and proper." One cannot even know what action is being represented in an image until one also imputes desires and beliefs to the people it represents (is she causing pain or giving pleasure?). And once we have identified an action, there is no universal function that attaches "It is permissible that..." to the action represented. The oversimple thought that pornography typically articulates and legitimates such norms ignores the fact that it can also evoke sexual fantasies that are widely held to be *illegitimate*—for instance, fantasies of sex that is adulterous, unnatural, sleazy, perverse, painful, unsafe, and so on. As Anne Snitow rightly notes, pornography's transgressive element is a standard part of its attraction: "pornography... flouts authority, which no doubt in part explains its appeal to young boys."[33]

Even pornography that does prescribe norms must compete with other putative social authorities, including the state, the family, and the church. If, for instance, these authorities recognize not only the presence of violence and discrimination against women but also that these are wrong, and if the informal order as well as the legal system criticize such behaviors and seek to repress them, then the legitimacy and efficacy of pornographers is limited. Contrast the case of a sign in apartheid South Africa that read "Whites Only." Such signs subordinated because they were part of a whole system that, formally and informally, empowered whites to rule blacks. It did not merely purport to exclude blacks, it actually did so, because there were so few countervailing norms.

This is not to deny that most societies are patriarchal. It is to observe that patriarchy is expressed in ways that do not surrender that much to pornography because societies can be in some respects patriarchal and (imperfectly) liberal. One particularly important feature of such societies is that they generally support principles of free expression and therefore tolerate pornographic utterances without either endorsing or condoning them. If this is generally understood, then the force of pornographic utterances is limited. In these circumstances, pornography has the character not of an authoritative voice of the ruling power but of a private view. Indeed, principles of free expression need not even be rooted in the formal order of the society; they too may be a matter of social convention and political culture. I think it clear that in the societies that are now most riven by debates over censorship, commitment to free expression has both formal and informal sources. That being so, these are also societies in which pornography that appears or even purports to subordinate fails to do so.

There is therefore a certain paradox about using censorship to undermine pornographic speech. In a society that respects freedom of expression, pornography receives no imprimatur: it is simply *tolerated* speech—permitted although disapproved. Many more people now use pornography than admit to it; it is not reviewed in the Sunday papers; and it is, still, able to elicit embarrassment, disgust, and shame. These are signs that pornography is, for us, low-status speech. Censorship, however, could change some of that. No one proposes to prohibit *all* pornography (although they do not always *call* what they propose to permit "pornography"). Under censorship, some pornography would be approved and authorized, for that is exactly what a regime of censorship aims to do. Using censorship to regulate pornography would thus have unintended consequences, for without a drastic shift of priorities in policing and prosecution or in the distribution of lawsuits, unauthorized pornography would still circulate, probably widely, giving rise to doubts about exactly what is officially disapproved and what is not. In those circumstances, the fear on which the constitutive harm argument rests—that pornography is authoritative speech—would in fact become more realistic.

Silencing and Illocutionary Disablement

Subordinating is not the only illocutionary force that pornography is said to have. It is also claimed to *silence* women. This is of special interest, and some believe this claim to be polemically more powerful than the claim that pornography subordinates. The subordination argument establishes a conflict between two values, equality and liberty, but provides no guarantee as to which should prevail. (Some have even suggested that in such conflicts we ought to prefer liberty.) If pornography silences, however, the issue is not a struggle between two values but a struggle over expressive freedom itself. "The free speech of men silences the free speech of women," says MacKinnon. "It is the same social goal, just other *people*."[34] And restricting one liberty in the name of a greater overall liberty is often justifiable.

Proponents of speech act theory hold that pornography silences by "illocutionary disablement": while it does not prevent women from speaking, it does ensure that their words fail to be taken with their intended illocutionary force. Langton offers two examples in which pornography may be thought to have this power. First, in the case of date rape, women may say "No" to a sexual advance but fail to prevent further advances because their words are not even heard as a refusal. Second, the political protests of women may fail. For instance, Linda Marchiano wrote a biography, *Ordeal,* about her enslavement in the making of the pornographic film *Deep Throat*. Her book later appeared in a mail-order pornography catalog and thereby was transformed into more pornography. In such cases,

> something is robbing the speech of its intended force. Whatever the conventions governing sexual interactions may be, that can mean that intending to refuse, intending to protest, is not enough. The rules fixing possible moves in the language game of sex are such that saying "no" can fail to count as making a refusal move, and telling the story of one's own subordination can fail to count as a move of protest.[35]

The suggestion is that pornography itself, by helping fix the "possible moves" in sexual interactions, robs women's speech of its force.

I argue above that in a liberal society that endorses freedom of expression, pornography is private, nonauthoritative speech. But there are other issues in the silencing analysis, and they repay scrutiny. Begin by noticing that it is unclear in these examples that women have in fact been silenced in the specified way. It is horrific when a clear refusal fails to end a sexual advance, and that may happen under a variety of different conditions: (1) the refusal is understood and ignored entirely, or (2) the refusal is understood but not taken as final, or (3) the aggressor is reckless or indifferent as to whether the victim refuses, or (4) the refusal is not understood as a refusal at all. Only the fourth statement describes an illocutionary disablement. It is an important case, but not because it is a common one. (Indeed, it is almost certainly the least likely form of date rape, the commonest being 2 and 3.) The interest of the fourth statement results from the fact that in some jurisdictions an honest mistake as to consent would exculpate, even if that mistake were not reasonable. But the fact that a certain legal system allows the *unreasonable* belief that "No means yes" to exculpate does not show that women have been deprived of speech, for any reasonable person would take the refusal for what it is.

A related point holds in the protest case. Langton asks, "Why then is *Ordeal* in a mail-order catalog for adult reading? The answer is simple. It is there because it is pornography after all."[36] But that is hasty. First, there are competing explanations: *Ordeal* may be on the list by mistake.[37] Second, and more important, selling *Ordeal* as pornography no more works an alchemy of genre than does selling *Playboy* on the news rack. Even if a book is occasionally *sold as* pornography, its author is not silenced unless it is also *bought and used as* pornography and the reader is therefore unable to grasp the intention with which it was written. Being aroused by a text does not preclude understanding or using it in other ways, however, and there is no reason to think that women's political protests normally misfire as a result of the availability of pornography, even if some works of protest are also arousing. *Ordeal* is normally bought and sold for what it is. We must take care to distinguish possible outcomes from typical outcomes. One does suffer a status injury if one is regularly deprived of speech, for one slips into a class for whom speech is not possible or does not count. Idiosyncratic or unreasonable responses to one's words do not bring that about; if anything, they call into question the status of the particular hearer.

Clearly, before we can determine whether pornography silences, we must ask how real and common illocutionary disablement is. Another, deeper, question asks how illocutionary disablement is related to expressive freedom. Consider the case of conventional illocutions.[38] Some linguistic conventions are present whenever one performs a locutionary act, for they determine what we might loosely call the meaning of the utterance: for instance, the convention in English is that the sound "dog" means dog and not cat. Distinct from these conventions are the enabling conventions of certain performatives: I cannot make a will unless there are social or legal rules providing for such things, and those rules will set the conditions under which my will is valid, that is, has the effect that it purports to have. Thus, a will must normally be signed and witnessed. In such cases, as Austin says, "the illocutionary act is a conventional act: an act done as conforming to a convention."[39] These acts therefore *presuppose* the existence of conventions: "There must be an accepted conventional procedure having a certain conventional effect, the procedure to include the utterance of certain words by certain persons in certain circumstances."[40]

In the case of a conventional illocution, what might count as "disablement"? Suppose I draft a will but someone (perhaps an aggrieved relative) bribes everyone else to refuse to witness it for me. In this case, I have been disabled from performing the felicity conditions—those conditions necessary for a successful attempt—because I have been prevented from having my will witnessed. In view of the way my actions have been prevented, we might consider this prevention a limitation on my liberty: there is something I could otherwise do—make a will—that someone has indirectly prevented me from doing. What if, instead, a provision for wills does not exist in my society? What if testamentary freedom does not exist, and my property has to be distributed according to fixed statutory rules? In this case there would be, by definition, certain things I could not do: make a will, witness a will, amend a will, and so on. At the same time, no person or group of persons disable me in the way that the aggrieved relative did. It is not as if a provision for wills exists but someone stops me from making one. It would thus be better to say not that I have been prevented from acting, but that a background presumption for a certain action has failed.

There is, I suppose, no reason why I might not wish my words to have the force they could have under that (unfulfilled) presumption. In that case, when I write my last will and testament it is bound to fall flat. There are, however, an unlimited number of possible, although nonexistent, conventions that establish an unlimited number of illocutionary acts. Some of these conventions are rival: the requirement that wills be witnessed excludes every other possible testamentary convention that dispenses with that formality. If I intend my words to count as a *valid although unsigned* will, am I silenced by the existing convention? If in playing chess I say that I intend to move my bishop horizontally, am I silenced by the fact that this will not count as a valid move? If so, does it follow that the rules of chess limit my liberty by fixing the possible moves?

Maybe these examples are misleading, for most people are broadly indifferent about the possible formalities for wills or possible rules for chess. It is reasonable, however, to have strong preferences about other social practices. For example, the Muslim practice of *talaq* divorce, as I understand it, gives husbands an exclusive power over their wives. Consider then a predominantly Christian country in which *talaq* divorce is neither socially nor legally recognized. In those circumstances, a husband's thrice uttering to his wife the words "I divorce you" does not constitute a divorce. This is, for instance, the actual state of affairs in the United States. Men may utter these words. They may go further and say, "And, by the way, I hereby divorce you, *talaq*-style; I mean it!" The act will still fail, because the relevant conventions are not operative. Have these men been silenced? If they have, are they also silenced by those things that are causally and nontrivially related to the overwhelming dominance—hegemony if you like—of Christian culture? Are they silenced by Christmas cards? That does not seem right.

Perhaps the problem here is that being "silenced" carries a negative valence: it sounds presumptively wrong, and yet the inability to conclude a *talaq* divorce, or to manumit a slave, seems unobjectionable. We do not want *talaq* divorce to exist so that people can fulfill its felicity conditions, nor do we want slavery to exist in order that people can fulfill the felicity conditions for the manumission of slaves. We thus are inclined to deny that these people are silenced merely because we think their intended actions are wrong or that they would have to take place in a context we think unjust.

We can test this hypothesis by considering whether our view would change if we thought *talaq* divorce a good idea, or even a necessity, as is the power to refuse sex or to protest enslavement. Langton offers a relevant case: "A homosexual who says 'I do' does not *disobediently marry;* he does not marry. These actions... really have been made unspeakable." She concludes:

> This shows that it is indeed possible to silence someone, not just by ordering or threatening them into simple silence, not just by frustrating their perlocutionary goals, but by making their speech acts unspeakable. It is possible to use speech to disable speakers, and possible to prevent them from satisfying the felicity conditions for some illocutions they might want to perform.[41]

This example raises two distinct questions: Is there *anything* wrong with the invalidity of gay marriages? And, if there is something wrong, is it best understood as a violation of *freedom of speech* by illocutionary disablement? The felicity conditions for marriage are usually such that a gay couple cannot be issued a valid marriage license. There are no special "words" that must be uttered in order to marry, words that fail to be understood as intended when they come from a gay couple. Everyone *understands* the relevant intentions when gay couples ask for a marriage license or undertake a marriage ceremony; what happens is that the words fail to have legal effect.[42] The legal invalidity results not from someone's speech, but from the absence of a legal power: same-sex marriages do not need to be nullified in order to be invalid; they are void *ab initio*. The case is thus more like that of the absence of testamentary freedom than of being prevented from having one's will witnessed. It is misleading to speak of gay couples being "prevented" from fulfilling the conditions for marriage, although the conditions do exclude them.

Daniel Jacobson, while disputing Langton's general thesis, nonetheless agrees that there is an unfreedom here, but he thinks it is due to an idiosyncratic feature of marriage: there is only one way to get married, and it is closed to gay couples. Options are generally available in other cases of putative disablement, he says, even in date rape. If saying "No" fails to count as a refusal, "one can also refuse by physically resisting," and "we should not say that someone cannot refuse unless she cannot do so by any means." In contrast, "gay couples in America ... can do nothing—linguistic or otherwise—that counts as marrying."[43] On this view, silencing can be the absence of a desirable convention, provided that convention is a *unique* way of performing the speech act in question.

This, however, cannot be right either. *Every* speech act is uniquely constituted by the conventions that define it. Domestic contracts are not a mode of marriage but an alternative to it; but neither is resisting sex a form of refusing sex, even though it results in managing not to have sex.[44] We cannot say that someone remains free to act provided there exists *some* means or other by which she can achieve her end. If a road is blocked, the fact that I may reach my destination another way does not show that I am free to travel the blocked road.

What seems to persuade Jacobson that the road is blocked has, I think, nothing to do with its uniqueness; rather, like Langton, he thinks that "something is preventing" them from satisfying the conditions for marriage: "Laws forbidding same-sex marriage prevent them from performing the illocutionary act of marrying by saying these, or any other, words."[45] But in jurisdictions with which I am familiar there are no laws *forbidding* such marriages. If there were, then couples who attempt to marry would find their efforts frustrated, not just by invalidity, but by being fined, jailed, or otherwise punished, and that would be even worse than things are now. The absence of a legal power is not the same as being prevented or forbidden from doing something.

Surely the most objectionable feature of the marriage case flows from the inequality between same-sex and different-sex couples. Heterosexist family law unjustly denies some people valuable powers that it confers on others. More exactly, it creates an *unequal value* of the existing power to marry, for the validity of marriage is blind to sexual orientation: neither lesbians nor straight women can marry other women, although both lesbians and straight women can marry either gay or straight men (which highlights the absurdity). To give powers to some and unjustifiably withhold them from others clearly offends equality. But this objection is based on a *comparative* consideration: what some already have others should also have. Were we to level down and abolish heterosexual marriage this complaint would dissolve, even though that would not unblock any existing option for gay people or provide them with any new option. This is not a feature of violations of expressive liberty; there the injury is *noncomparative*. Were Marxists prohibited from publishing their views, it would not restore their freedom of speech if we were to prohibit others from publishing their views on the same terms. On the contrary, this would diminish freedom of speech further.

The idea of silencing through illocutionary disablement rests, in fact, on the very general and convention-independent thesis that one is silenced whenever one's words fail to be taken with the force one intends. Jennifer Hornsby proposes this as a general condition for linguistic communication:

> Reciprocity is the condition of linguistic communication. It obtains when people are such as to recognize one another's speech as it is meant to be taken, and thus to ensure the success of attempts to perform speech acts. When reciprocity obtains, these are things that speakers do simply by being heard as doing them.[46]

This is thought to be relevant, for

> just as reciprocity may secure communication, so the absence of conditions that ensure reciprocity may prevent communication. To the extent that reciprocity fails you, you have been deprived of illocutionary potential.... Silencing is the process of depriving of illocutionary potential.[47]

Failure to ensure reciprocity is thus counted as a deprivation or prevention of speech and is, therefore, silencing.

Important as this may be to a general philosophy of language, it cannot provide what we need here, for lapses in reciprocity may be benign. Consider these examples: Hiking in the Hebrides I greet you in Gaelic, "*Cia mar a tha thu!*"[48] Speaking only English, you hear "Come here now!" and are offended. Does your misunderstanding silence me? A professor says, "Read MacKinnon for the next seminar," intending to give an order. The students hear only advice, but think it good and do the reading anyway. His bid for authority has failed; has he also been silenced? A creationist is invited to address a conference on evolution, and he speaks with the intention that his words be taken as an argument for his conclusions. His attentive but skeptical audience hear no arguments, but only a display of faith. He persuades no one; has he also been silenced? In such cases the speaker fails to reach the intended audience, but it is surely misleading to say that he has been deprived of speech or prevented from speaking. In addition, because these failures of reciprocity seem blameless, it is clear that one may be "silenced" in this sense even though these is no reason, not even *prima facie,* that the audience should bear duties or disabilities in order to ensure reciprocity.

The question here is not whether freedom of expression is "positive" or merely "negative." A plausible account of freedom of expression probably requires the following positive liberties: each must have a fair opportunity to try to reach an audience, each must therefore have fair access to media of expression, and the authorities must not only refrain from restricting expression themselves but also actively intervene to protect it. Yet none of these singly, nor all of them jointly, even approach guaranteeing people any audience for their views, let alone a receptive audience disposed to hear them as just they intend to be heard. Were we to begin to impose all the duties and disabilities needed to guarantee *that* sort of reciprocity, we would surely sacrifice not only freedom of expression but also other important liberties as well, including freedom of movement, association, opinion, and conscience.

The issue is not one of terminology. One may certainly use *silence* to cover any state of affairs in which one is not guaranteed the ability to perform an illocutionary act that one wants to perform. Nor should we complain that such a wide usage is merely "metaphorical," as if political terms must be literal, metaphorical, or senseless.[49] The relation between this usage and the narrower sense of being prevented from trying to reach an audience is not one of metaphor, but one of analogy. In the narrower case, one cannot realize one's communicative intentions because someone stops that person from speaking or denies that person a fair opportunity to be heard; in the broader case one cannot realize one's communicative intentions because even if that person succeeds in speaking there is no guarantee that he or she will be heard as intended. There are too many normatively relevant differences between these two forms of silencing. The first requires someone's intervention or blameworthy omission, the second does not; the first is *prima facie* harmful, the second is not; preventing the first is generally consistent with other important liberties, preventing the second is not. Thus, to say that some people should be silenced in the *narrow* sense in order to ensure that others are not silenced in the *broad* sense lacks the pleasing symmetry suggested by the proposal to silence the silencers.

Conclusion

Theory cannot ride on the back of definition in political philosophy. Deciding what to do about pornography is not a matter of getting the terms right, and nothing is gained by stipulating idle distinctions between, say, *pornography* (bad) and *erotica* (good). One attraction of speech act analysis is that it does not just *define* pornography as, say, "the graphic sexually explicit subordination of women"; rather, it offers an *explanation* of how pornography might amount to the subordination of women. Langton is much more cautious than MacKinnon on this point, for she claims only that, in certain circumstances, pornography *could* be the subordination or silencing of women, that these things are not inconceivable. I have not argued the contrary: I have argued, first, that under a liberal regime pornographers lack the sort of authority that is required for it to be actual, and second, that illocutionary disablement does not in itself amount to an objectionable kind of silencing. It does remain conceivable that pornographizing could amount to subordinating or silencing in some sense. Indeed, this is proved by a very brief argument. Some performatives get their force through conventions, so if there were accepted social conventions *making* pornographic utterances the subordination or silencing of women, then they would come to have that force by convention. Since this is trivially true, it is unwise to deny it, and any philosopher foolish enough to do so deserves what he gets. By the same token, however, a working theory of pornography—a plausible and normatively relevant account of its nature and effects—cannot rest with mere conceivability. It needs to place bets on the facts. Apart from those I have already mentioned, one other important fact is that sex and its representations are not as conventionalized as some theorists suppose.

The problem is this. Pornography, as it is usually understood, includes many different things. Unlike the alexandrine sonnet, the gavotte, or *trompe l'oeil* painting, pornography is not an aesthetic kind; it is not a form or practice that is marked out by stable and agreed rules. The ordinary concept of pornography is roughly this: graphic, sexually explicit words or images whose intent or typical effect is to produce sexual arousal. One would not be far off in taking MacKinnon's view that it is "masturbation material."[50] If that is true, then pornography is neither an aesthetic genre nor a term of political art. It is a functional kind that includes anything intended to be, or standardly used as, masturbation material. In the penumbra of that central case are materials that are analogically related, such as pictures that look as if they might have been produced for that purpose, those that one could easily imagine being so used, and so on.

The imprecise, vague, and contestable character of the ordinary concept of pornography is for most purposes no defect; it properly mirrors our uncertain and sometimes conflicting responses to images. (I am unsure whether the advertising campaigns for Calvin Klein were pornographic, and I want a concept of pornography that reflects my uncertainty, not one that eliminates it.) The ordinary concept of pornography is certainly not "value neutral"; we group together under that heading a diverse family of artifacts only because of the importance and salience of the human interests they touch. At the same time, however, it is not morally fraught, and it does not bring with it automatic condemnation.[51]

Because of their functional character pornographies are as diverse as our sexualities. For instance, about 10 to 15 percent of the market in pornography is directed at gay men, and a smaller percentage is directed at women. No one thinks that this is not pornography, nor that it is pornography only because, in the words of MacKinnon and Dworkin's Ordinance, it uses men "in the place of women."[52] There are other dimensions of variation too, and they should make us wonder whether it even makes sense to extend the speech act analogy into this realm and to theorize about the force of "pornographic utterances" in general. What, if anything, does selling a pornographic novel intend to communicate? The author's views? That the vendor endorses the author's views? That the vendor endorses freedom of expression? That the vendor is open to supplying any legal product for which there is demand? Parallel questions envelop speculations about audience response. A man watches a film of a woman enjoying submissive sex with a man. Does his response communicate anything? That he thinks this act arousing and therefore permissible? That he thinks it wrong and therefore arousing? Does he generalize from "that woman" to "all women"? Does he *identify* with that woman?

Our sexualities are complex and often unpredictable. Speech acts, performatives, and their felicity conditions are most at home in the realm of the conventional and predictable. To suppose that pornography subordinates and silences by fixing the possible moves in the language game of sex is, I think, much too tidy for such an unruly subject.

Coda

Rae Langton and I agree that it makes sense to suppose that pornography might subordinate and silence women and that whether this sensible thought is true depends on the social context. We disagree about how the context bears on its truth and about what it takes to be silenced.

In her contribution to this volume, Langton makes some interesting new suggestions about the ways in which words can—and cannot—construct reality, an idea that many writers, including me, have treated far too casually.[53] She also raises another important issue: is merely "local" legitimacy and efficacy enough to render pornographic speech authoritative? I doubt that, for two reasons. First, to make sense of the notion that women are subordinated by pornography, there must be something true about the status of women in general. Second, I think that if pornography expresses any norms at all, they can be binding only in the way that other customary norms are: by their general acceptance among those whose behavior they purport to guide.[54]

Langton disagrees, but I think she also misunderstands. First, she exaggerates what general acceptance amounts to: she takes it to mean *near-universal* legitimacy and then calls this my "all-or-none-ism."[55] Second, she thinks of it in territorial terms: even if only a minority take the sexual edicts of the Catholic Church as binding, she says, one is nonetheless subordinated if that minority amounts to *one's own local* community.[56] She wonders whether I think that no one is subordinated *here* provided there is some other, freer, place that one could go.

Nothing like that ever crossed my mind, and the general thesis on which it rests is one I have elsewhere criticized.[57] Contrary to Langton, I do not argue that "the presence of competing norms elsewhere" deprives pornography of its authority here.[58] My point is not that there are competing communities with different norms, it is that there are within one community competing norms. It is not that one may evade the authority of pornography by moving, but that it lacks such authority here and now. Some pornography represents women as subordinate—but that is just what *it* says. Other pornography says other things, and other, nonpornographic, acts express different views about women altogether. Pornography's authority is determined by the *net* affect of all this. Langton suggests that "pornography legitimates—makes permissible—certain ways of acting in part by representing them as ordinary, as normal."[59] But that part is not enough. Gay and lesbian pornography, for instance, may represent homosexuality as ordinary and normal, but it has not succeeded in normalizing and legitimating homosexuality, precisely because there are too many competing norms.

Thus, what Langton needs is not the doctrine of local acceptance, but rather the denial of normative conflict and more evidence for the view that pornography really is the Established Church of (hetero?)sexuality. I think it is not that established because, among other things, pornography is generally thought to be low-status speech—it is merely tolerated—whereas rape and sexual assault are criminalized and sex discrimination is illegal. Langton doubts the truth or relevance of this, but the facts she notes in passing—that the law does not "unequivocally" contradict pornography's voice, that a judge said that "No" does not always mean no, that rape is underreported—these facts do not prove otherwise. My idea is that pornographic speech faces competition as a source of norms; her facts show that its competitors do not themselves enjoy a monopoly. Is there not here a trace of her own "all-or-none-ism"?

I am unsure whether Langton still maintains her doctrine about speech and silence. She once seemed friendly to Hornsby's idea that people are silenced whenever reciprocity is not "ensured."[60] That seemed, and still seems, far too wide. Now Langton makes an adjustment: silencing flows, not from the lack of a guarantee, but from the presence of someone else stopping or interfering.[61] Obviously that is a narrower thesis: if another stops you being heard as you intend, then reciprocity is not ensured. Reciprocity, however, may not be ensured even though no one else is stopping or interfering. Interference is an idea that warrants more examination; some of my own examples in this chapter are meant to explore its limits.

There is another important clarification. Langton now maintains that freedom of speech is not the freedom to perform any illocutionary speech act; it comprises only the freedom to perform those speech acts that involve "an important communicative power."[62] These include, on her view, the ability to use words to refuse, to protest, or to marry, but not the ability to use words to canonize, to make a will, or to divorce. I am afraid I cannot correlate this distinction with the importance of the communicative powers exercised. Why does gay marriage involve important communicative powers in a way that *talaq* divorce does not? I do see how one might think that the former examples involve good uses of speech and the latter bad uses. Could it be that Langton thinks that freedom of speech includes only the freedom of good speech? Apart from the point that one needs no special license to say what is good or true, her opponents are prepared to concede that some pornographic speech is bad or false. They think that it should be tolerated anyway, because it is not in the relevant sense sufficiently harmful.

What is and is not speech? I take it to be a kind of communicative act. Absent special conditions, when there is no act, there is no communication.[63] That is why when a particular legal system *fails to provide* for some legal act,

I do not think of that vacuum as a kind of speech. It is not, as Langton says, that I think that *law* is not speech; it is that I think the *absence* of a law is normally not speech.[64] Of course, laws exist and are communicative not only when they prohibit but also when they disable, empower, or explicitly permit. None of that is in doubt. My point was only that the impossibility—and thus the invalidity—of certain legal acts need not itself result from any legal act and, *a fortiori,* not from any legal speech act.

At the end of her chapter, Langton notices that I wonder whether pornography is normally *bought and sold* with communicative intentions and also that I say that pornography itself has only the unity of a functional kind. She likes this idea because she thinks it shows that pornography is not speech and is thus ineligible for the protections due speech.[65] That does not follow. Even if selling and buying pornography are not communicative acts, *producing* pornography often is. There is nothing unusual here: a "testimonial" is a functional kind, but making a testimonial may be protected by freedom of speech. My claim is only that such unity as we may attribute to the kind "pornography" flows, not from it having a common expressive content, but rather from it having a (roughly) shared use. That is why I think that we can generalize a bit about its use, but less about its meaning and force.

Notes

I am grateful to the Getty Research Institute for the History of Art and the Humanities, to Corby Sturges, and to Terry Heinrichs, Rae Langton, and Robert Post for their comments.

1. Catharine A. MacKinnon, "Not a Moral Issue," in idem, *Feminism Unmodified: Discourses on Life and Law* (Cambridge, Mass.: Harvard Univ. Press, 1987).

2. J. S. Mill, *On Liberty,* ed. M. Warnock (London: Fontana, 1962).

3. See Jeremy Waldron, "Mill and the Value of Moral Distress," in idem, *Liberal Rights: Collected Papers, 1981–1991* (Cambridge: Cambridge Univ. Press, 1993), 115–33.

4. Mill (see note 2), 212–13.

5. Many writers have noticed this. Recent discussions include: Kent Greenawalt, *Speech, Crime, and the Uses of Language* (New York: Oxford Univ. Press, 1989); Andrew Altman, "Liberalism and Campus Hate Speech: A Philosophical Examination," *Ethics* 103 (1993): 302–17; Rae Langton, "Speech Acts and Unspeakable Acts," *Philosophy and Public Affairs* 22 (1993): 292–330; Daniel Jacobson, "Freedom of Speech Acts? A Reply to Langton," *Philosophy and Public Affairs* 24 (1995): 64–79.

6. Although, as Debora Shuger shows, this was not always so. See her "Civility and Censorship in Early Modern England," pages 89–110 in this volume.

7. Joseph Butler, *Fifteen Sermons preached at the Rolls Chapel* (London: W. Botham, 1726), preface.

8. While Frederick Schauer is therefore right to argue that the distinction between "internal" and "external" generation of speech is a frail one, I take that as a reason

for not hoping for normatively significant results from the internal-external metaphor. Whatever, if anything, might be wrong with censorship cannot simply be that it is an *external* influence on what one says, because as Schauer rightly notes, there are all sorts of external influences. There are alternatives to this apart from the one Schauer offers—a question of jurisdiction or "turf." We might also consider the *modality* of influence: whether it is persuasive, coercive, manipulative, and so on. See his "The Ontology of Censorship," pages 146–68 in this volume.

9. When MacKinnon praises the Supreme Court of Canada for upholding, on equality grounds, the criminal prohibitions on obscenity, she confuses these points. She says that the court held that "the evidence on the harm of pornography was sufficient for a law against it." Catharine A. MacKinnon, *Only Words* (Cambridge, Mass.: Harvard Univ. Press, 1993), 101. In reality, though, the court only held that the government had enough evidence to entitle it to deference on the facts; see *Butler v. R.*, 1 S.C.R. 452 (1992).

10. On *this* point Henry Monaghan is correct; see his "Our Perfect Constitution," *New York University Law Review* 56 (1981): 353–96. Note that I am not here denying that constitutional law may be, in Ronald Dworkin's sense, a "matter of principle." The point is the obvious one that principles of legal morality may, from the ideal point of view, be imperfect. See Ronald Dworkin, *A Matter of Principle* (Cambridge, Mass.: Harvard Univ. Press, 1985).

11. Catharine A. MacKinnon, *Toward a Feminist Theory of the State* (Cambridge, Mass.: Harvard Univ. Press, 1989), 208.

12. United States Commission on Obscenity and Pornography, *The Report of the Commission on Obscenity and Pornography* (Washington, D.C.: U.S. Government Printing Office, 1970); Great Britain Committee on Obscenity and Film Censorship, *Report of the Committee on Obscenity and Film Censorship* (The Williams Report) (London: HMSO, 1979).

13. Melinda Vadas, "A First Look at the Pornography/Civil Rights Ordinance: Could Pornography Be the Subordination of Women?" *Journal of Philosophy* 84 (1987): 487–511, at 511.

14. MacKinnon, *Only Words* (see note 9), 21.

15. Ibid., 12.

16. Ibid., 12–13.

17. J. L. Austin, *How to Do Things with Words*, 2nd ed. (Cambridge, Mass.: Harvard Univ. Press, 1975), 98–132.

18. Mill (see note 2), 72.

19. Robert C. Post, "Cultural Heterogeneity and the Law: Pornography, Blasphemy, and the First Amendment," *California Law Review* 76 (1988): 328. Note that Post contends only that "the argument that pornography can be regulated because it is the practice of subordination, rather than speech, thus proves too much to be useful for first amendment purposes"(ibid.). But I think that his view of constitutional interpretation would commit him to think that it is not useful for purposes of the pure pornography problem either. For discussion of Post, see Stanley Fish, "Fraught with Death: Scepticism, Progressivism, and the First Amendment," *University of Colorado Law Review* 64 (1993): 1061, 1063–70.

20. Vadas (see note 13), 511. Vadas does not draw her conclusion from the performative force of pornography, but from a different sort of direct and conceptual connection between pornography and subordination. It is the existence of the direct connection, rather than the source of it, that avoids the responsibility question.

21. Andrea Dworkin and Catharine A. MacKinnon, *Pornography and Civil Rights: A New Day for Women's Equality* (Minneapolis: Organizing Against Pornography, 1988), 36.

22. Altman (see note 5), 310.

23. MacKinnon, *Only Words* (see note 9), 31.

24. I say more in my *The Authority of the State* (Oxford: Clarendon Press, 1988).

25. Thus, an armed robber who says "Give me the keys to your car!" may be able to make his will effective, yet have no authority to do so; the bailiff who utters the same words may have the authority to take the car and yet be powerless to enforce it. The connections between authority and social power are complex and variable. Sometimes authority gives effective power; that is so when the authority is widely recognized or easily enforced. Sometimes, having effective power is among the conditions that justify one's authority; that is why Jacobites and other proponents of lost causes ultimately also lose their claim to justified authority. But effective power does not on its own amount to authority.

26. For a discussion see Andrew Sullivan, *Virtually Normal: An Argument about Homosexuality* (New York: Knopf, 1995), 19–55.

27. Not, of course, in every respect: some may still love the sinner while hating the sin. But to be a sinner on account of one's sexuality is nonetheless to be relegated in the hierarchy of sexual beings.

28. Langton (see note 5), 311.

29. Some women do, of course, fall into the class of "people, men, boys" who use pornography, but they are a small minority of that class and, in any case, censorship is not meant to prevent women from harming themselves.

30. Langton (see note 5), 311.

31. Ibid., 312.

32. MacKinnon, *Only Words* (see note 9), 17.

33. Ann Snitow, "Retrenchment versus Transformation: The Politics of the Antipornography Movement," in Varda Burstyn, ed., *Women against Censorship* (Vancouver: Douglas & McIntyre, 1985), 116.

34. MacKinnon, "Not a Moral Issue" (see note 1), 156.

35. Langton (see note 5), 323–24.

36. Ibid., 322.

37. The fact that the video *Doing it Debby's Way* appeared on a list of tapes blacklisted in Ohio did not actually transform it into what the authorities foolishly thought it was, namely, a sequel to the pornographic film *Debby Does Dallas*. It was actually an exercise video starring Debby Reynolds. Reported in Nadine Strossen, *Defending Pornography: Free Speech, Sex, and the Fight for Women's Rights* (New York: Scribner, 1995), 97.

38. Following Peter Strawson, "Intention and Convention in Speech Acts," in idem, *Logico-Linguistic Papers* (London: Methuen, 1971), 151–53.

39. Austin (see note 17), 205.

40. Ibid., 14.

41. Langton (see note 5), 319–20.

42. "Marriage," in contrast with, say, "constitutional amendment," is not an exclusively legal concept. One may be married legally, religiously, socially, or morally. In the case of heterosexual unions the four normally go together; in the case of homosexual unions only the last two do. Consider an analogy: Some but not all promises are legally enforceable, those we call "contracts." To be a contract, a promise must meet certain conditions of validity, conditions governing the capacity of contractors (for example, they must be old enough) and the seriousness of the promises (for example, there must be "consideration"). Does that mean that other sorts of promises are not binding? Certainly not. Neither does it follow that if the two men or women in the ceremony fail to marry legally then they have failed to marry at all.

43. Jacobson (see note 5), 75.

44. It may be the case that certain resisting acts are *also* acts of refusal: if I put up my hand to stop you touching me it may be both a physical barrier and a sign that you are to go no further, but its force as a sign is liable to be upset by the same things that upset other signs one might give—for instance, saying "No."

45. Jacobson (see note 5), 74.

46. Jennifer Hornsby, "Speech Acts and Pornography," in Susan Dwyer, ed., *The Problem of Pornography* (Belmont, Calif.: Wadsworth, 1995), 224.

47. Ibid., 227.

48. Pronounced, roughly, "Kimmer a how."

49. For instance, Frank Michaelman, "Conceptions of Democracy in American Constitutional Argument: The Case of Pornography Regulation," *Tennessee Law Review* 56 (1989): 294.

50. MacKinnon, *Only Words* (see note 9), 17.

51. This contrasts with other terms in the area, and in particular with *obscene,* which is inherently critical. (That partly explains the difference in sense between the expressions "obscene violence" and "pornographic violence.")

52. Dworkin and MacKinnon (see note 21), 114.

53. Rae Langton, "Subordination, Silence, and Pornography's Authority," pages 261–83 in this volume.

54. My model for authority here was that of a set of customary norms which are binding only if they are widely accepted. This is not a necessary condition for the authority of all norms: in institutionalized systems (for example, in law and in some religions) it is sufficient that the norms are accepted and applied by officials, perhaps a very small group, who can exercise *de facto* control over others. In these circumstances, a consensus of powerful elites is enough to produce de facto authority. See Leslie Green, "The Concept of Law Revisited," *Michigan Law Review* 94 (1996): 1688, 1700–1702. Perhaps Langton and others think that pornographers are such an elite?

55. Langton, "Subordination, Silence," (see note 53), 275.

56. Ibid., 272.

57. Leslie Green, "Internal Minorities and their Rights," in Will Kymlicka, ed., *The Rights of Minority Cultures* (Oxford: Oxford Univ. Press, 1995), 257–72.

58. Langton, "Subordination, Silence" (see note 53), 273.

59. Ibid., 269.

60. Ibid., 283.

61. Ibid., 275.

62. Ibid., 276.

63. I have in mind, here, cases in which background conventions give omissions expressive force, for instance, cases in which silence may give consent.

64. Langton, "Subordination, Silence" (see note 53), 282.

65. Ibid., 277.

Freedom's Silences

Wendy Brown

Hegel rendered philosophical what the ancient Athenian elites had struggled with existentially and tragically: if freedom inheres in the capacity to choose a course of action, then it is simultaneously realized and negated in the very act of choosing. Commitment to a particular action forecloses the freedom that enabled the commitment. In this regard, freedom is not merely paradoxical in its workings but self-canceling and finally, unachievable. Hence Michel Foucault's warning that freedom lies neither in institutions nor in ideals and proclamations, but only in practices.

As freedom is both realized and negated by choice, so is silence convened, broken, and structured by speech. Silence and speech are not only constitutive of one another but modalities of each other. They are different kinds of articulation that produce as well as negate one another. Silence calls for speech, yet speech, because it is always particular, vanquishes other possible speech, thus canceling the promise of full representation heralded by silence. Silence, both constituted and broken by particular speech, is neither more nor less "truthful" than speech is, and neither more nor less regulatory. Speech harbors silences; silences harbor meaning. When silence is broken by speech, new silences are fabricated and enforced; when speech ends, the ensuing silence carries meaning that can only be metaphorized by speech, thus producing the conviction that silence speaks.

The belief that silence and speech are opposites is a conceit underlying most contemporary discourse about censorship and silencing. This conceit enables both the assumption that censorship converts the truth of speech to the lie of silence and the assumption that when an enforced silence is broken, what emerges is truth borne by the vessel of authenticity or experience. Calling these assumptions into question means not only thinking about the relation between silence and speech differently but rethinking the powers and potentials of silence. Here is the way this problem unfolds politically:

Insurrection requires breaking silence about the very existence as well as the activity or injury of the collective insurrectionary subject. Even dreams of emancipation cannot take shape unless the discursively shadowy or altogether invisible character of those subjects, wounds, events, or activities is redressed, whether through slave ballads, the flaunting of forbidden love, the labor theory of value, or the quantification of housework. Nor are the silences constituted in discourses of subordination broken forever when they are broken once. They do not shatter the moment their strategic function has been exposed, but must be assaulted repeatedly with stories, histories, theories, and discourses in alternate registers, until the silence itself is rendered routinely intelligible as an historically injurious force. It is in this way that those historically excluded from liberal personhood have proceeded against the spectrum of silences limning the universal claims of humanist discourse for the last several centuries. Jews, immigrants, women, people of color, homosexuals, the unpropertied—all have pressed themselves into civic belonging not simply through asserting their personhood but through politicizing—articulating—the silent workings of their internally excluded presence within prevailing notions of personhood.

But if the silences in discourses of domination are sites for insurrectionary noise, if they are corridors to be filled with explosive countertales, it is also possible to make a fetish of breaking silence. It is possible as well that this ostensible tool of emancipation carries its own techniques of subjugation—that it converges with unemancipatory tendencies in contemporary culture, establishes regulatory norms, coincides with the disciplinary power of ubiquitous confessional practices; in short, feeds the powers it meant to starve.

Neither a defense of silence nor an injunction to silence, rather this chapter interrogates the presumed authenticity of "voice" in the implicit equation between speech and freedom entailed in contemporary affirmations of breaking silence. Borrowing tacitly from Foucault's theorization of confessional discourse, Joan Scott's problematization of experience, and Shoshana Felman and Dori Laub's identification of our time as the age of testimony, the essay asks whether our contemporary crisis of truth has not been displaced into an endless stream of words about ourselves, words that presume to escape epistemological challenges to truth because they are personal or experiential.[1] It asks as well whether this stream of words does not perpetuate the crisis of which it is a symptom.

In the course of this inquiry, silence is considered not simply as an aesthetic but also as a political value, a means of preserving certain practices and dimensions of existence from regulatory power, from normative violence, and from the scorching rays of public exposure. A link is examined too, between, on the one hand, a contemporary tendency concerning the lives of public figures—the confession or extraction of every detail of private and personal life (sexual, familial, therapeutic, financial) and, on the other, a putatively countercultural or emancipatory practice: the compulsive putting into public discourse of heretofore hidden or private experiences—from catalogs of sexual pleasures to litanies of sexual abuses, from chronicles of eating disorders to diaries of homebirths and gay parenting. In linking these two phenomena—the privatization of public life via the mechanism of public exposure of private life on the one hand, and the compulsive and compulsory cataloging of the details of marginalized lives on the other—I want to highlight a modality of regulation and depoliticization specific to our age that is not simply confessional, but that empties private life into the public domain. The effect is both to abet the steady commercialization and homogenization of intimate attachments, experiences, and emotions already achieved by the market, and to usurp public space with often trivial matters, rendering the political personal in a fashion that leaves injurious social, political, and economic powers relatively unremarked and untouched. In short, while intended as a practice of freedom (premised on the modernist conceit that the truth makes us free), these productions of truth may not only bear the capacity to chain us to our injurious histories as well as the stations of our small lives, but also to instigate the further regulation of those lives while depoliticizing their conditions.

My concern with what might be called compulsory discursivity and the presumed evil of silences has yet another source. Notwithstanding the romance with Foucault among many intellectuals invested in contemporary progressive social movements, there is an oddly non- or pre-Foucaultian quality to much left and liberal debate about censorship and silencing. Expression is cast either as that which makes us free, tells "our" truth, and puts our truth into circulation, *or* as that which oppresses us by featuring "their" truth in the form of pornography, hate speech, harassment or the representation of the world from "the male point of view."[2] If one side in such debate argues for more expression on "our" part—for example, by making our own porn or telling our own stories—and the other argues for less on "their" part, both sides nonetheless subscribe to an *expressive* and *repressive* notion of speech, its capacity either to express the truth of an individual's desire or condition or to repress that truth. Both equate freedom with voice and visibility, both assume recognition to be unproblematic when we tell our own story, and both assume that such recognition is the material of power and pleasure.[3] Neither confronts the regulatory potential of speaking ourselves, its capacity to bind rather than emancipate us.[4]

To inaugurate an analysis of the relationship between silence, speech, and freedom that questions the conventional discursive order in which they appear, I want to reflect on several passages from Foucault's work. The first is from *The History of Sexuality:*

> Discourses are not once and for all subservient to power or raised up against it, any more than silences are.... Discourse transmits and produces power; it reinforces it, but also undermines and exposes it, renders it fragile and makes it possible to thwart it. In like manner, silence and secrecy are a shelter for power, anchoring its prohibitions; but they also loosen its hold and provide for relatively obscure areas of tolerance.[5]

Foucault here marks the ambiguity of silence in relation to power, insisting that silence functions not only as a shelter *for* power but also as a shelter *from* it. Foucault's example is the putative freedom of homosexual practice in a historical age in which there is no formal discourse for or about it: "the nearly universal reticence in talking about [sodomy] made possible a twofold operation... an extreme severity... and a [widespread] tolerance."[6] This understanding of the ambivalent "freedom" contained in the silence or secret of homosexuality is corroborated by Agnes Lugo-Ortiz's work on orality, law, and silence in the making of the Puerto Rican homosexual body and by M. Jacqui Alexander's tracing of the production of "lesbian" as a category (heretofore unmarked in law) by the Sexual Offences Bill passed in 1986 in Trinidad and Tobago.[7] Albeit quite differently, each reflects on the extent to which a silence "broken" by the production of a new public or institutional discourse may bring Otherness *violently* into being as it brings a designated subject respectively into abjection, censure, or regulation. In Lugo-Ortiz's words, "through orality, a community that aspires to a totalizing self-definition exercises its law and its violence. Silence, in this case, may then be read as a radical deconstructive proposition against any pretense to political absolutism."[8] In the debate over the Sexual Offences Bill that is the subject of Alexander's study, lesbian sexuality emerges into public discourse in Trinidad and Tobago only for purposes of stigmatizing and criminalizing it, and this for the purpose of criminalizing all extra-marital and non-reproductive sexual practices. What each case makes evident is that while to be invisible within a local discourse may adduce the injuries of social liminality, such suffering may be mild compared to that of radical denunciation, hystericization, exclusion, or criminalization.

The paradoxical capacity of silence to engage opposites with regard to power—both to shelter power and to serve as a barrier against power—is rarely accented in Foucault's thinking as a consequence of his emphasis (elsewhere) on discourse as a vehicle of power. In casting silence as a potential refuge *from* power, I do not think he is reneging on this emphasis nor suggesting a prediscursive existence to things. Critical here is the difference between what Foucault calls *unitary* discourses, which regulate and colonize, and those that do not perform these functions with the same social pervasiveness, even while they do not escape the tendency of all discourse to establish norms by which it regulates and excludes. It is through this distinction that one can make sense of Foucault's otherwise inexplicable reference to sex in the eighteenth century as being "driven out of hiding and constrained to lead a discursive existence,"[9] or his troubling example of the village simpleton whose "inconsequential" habit of molesting young girls in exchange for pennies was suddenly subjected to medical, judicial, and popular scrutiny and condemnation.[10] Neither in these cases nor in others where Foucault seems to imply a "freer," because prediscursive, existence to certain practices would he appear to mean that they really occurred "outside" discourse, but rather that they had not yet been brought into the pervasive *regulatory* discourses of the age—science, psychiatry, medicine, law, pedagogy.[11] Silence, as Foucault affirms it, then is identical neither with secrecy nor with not speaking. Rather, it signifies a particular relation to regulatory discourses, as well as a possible niche for the practice of freedom *within* those discourses.

Put differently, if discourses posit and organize silences, then silences themselves must be understood as discursively produced, as part of discourse, rather than as its opposite. Hence silences are no more free of organization by power than speech is, nor are they any more inventable or protectable by us than speech is. Yet and paradoxically, silence—even that produced within discourse—may also function as that which discourse has not penetrated, as a scene of practices that escape the regulatory functions of discourse. It is this latter function that renders silence itself as a source of protection and potentially even a source of power. The Fifth Amendment of the U.S. Constitution may be understood as mobilizing precisely this power against discourse, even as the amendment itself functions discursively and leads a distinctly discursive life.

If, as Foucault insists, freedom is a practice (rather than an achievement, condition, or institution), then the possibility of *practicing* freedom in the context of regulatory discourses occurs in the interstices of a given discourse as well as in resistance to the discourse.[12] In other words, the possibility can occur either within or against the discourse but is produced by the discourse in either case. Silence can function as speech in both kinds of practices of freedom, as becomes clear in the following anecdote offered by Foucault:

> Maybe another feature of [my] appreciation of silence is related to the obligation of speaking. I lived as a child in a petit bourgeois, provincial milieu in France and the obligation of speaking, of making conversation with visitors, was for me something both very strange and very boring. I often wondered why people had to speak.[13]

In a lecture at the Swedish Academy on the occasion of receiving the Nobel Prize for Literature, Toni Morrison also resets the conventional antinomy between silence and speech. Dwelling in the ambiguity of the power of language, she argues that certain kinds of language are themselves silencing, capable of violence and even murder, as well as themselves "susceptible to death, erasure."[14]

> A dead language is not only one no longer spoken or written, it is unyielding language content to admire its own paralysis. Like statist language, censored and censoring. Ruthless in its policing duties, it has no desire or purpose other than to maintain the free range of its own narcotic narcissism, its own exclusivity and dominance. However moribund, it is not without effect, for it actively thwarts the intellect, stalls conscience, suppresses human potential. Unreceptive to interrogation, it cannot form or tolerate new ideas, shape other thoughts, tell another story, fill baffling silences. Official language smitheried to sanction ignorance and preserve privilege is a suit of armor, polished to shocking glitter, a husk from which the knight departed long ago.[15]

While Morrison is here concerned primarily with bureaucratic and other official languages, any language of regulation, including those originally designed on behalf of emancipation, has the potential to become official in the sense she describes. Indeed, language that cannot form or tolerate new ideas, language that cannot tell another story or fill baffling silences, language that functions as a suit of armor, such language would seem to characterize a number of progressive political discourses that have retreated from emancipatory aims and have consolidated into institutional ones. Consider how both the discourses of liberalism and of Marxism came to function in this fashion, notwithstanding their original liberatory promise. Consider as well how often the language of political identity is today experienced as a policing language, even and especially by those whom the language intended to figure for emancipation. "A husk from which the knight departed long ago. . . ."

Silence can be an effect of discourse; it can also function as resistance to regulatory discourse. And, just as silenced discourses may contain elements of freedom, places unnoticed and hence unregulated by powerful interests, so their disinterring, even by the well-intentioned genealogist, can signal the end of their preserve for freedom. The latter is the subject of an extended meditation by Foucault about the problem of excavating subjugated knowledges:

> Is it not perhaps the case that these fragments of genealogies are no sooner brought to light, that the particular elements of the knowledge that one seeks to disinter are no sooner accredited and put into circulation, than they run the risk of re-codification, recolonisation? In fact, those unitary discourses, which first disqualified and then ignored them when they made their appearance, are, it seems, quite ready now to annex them, to take them back within the fold of their own discourse and to invest them with everything this implies in terms of their effects of knowledge and power.[16]

Here, Foucault's concern is less with disrupting the conventional modernist equation of power with speech on one side and of oppression with silence on the other than with the ways in which potentially subversive discourse, borne of exclusion and marginalization, can be colonized by that which produced it, much as countercultural fashion is routinely commodified by the corporate textile industry. While "disqualified" discourses are an effect of domination, they nevertheless potentially function as oppositional when they are deployed by those who inhabit them. However, when annexed by those unitary discourses to which they are in putative opposition, these discourses become a particularly potent source of regulation, carrying, as they do, intimate and detailed knowledge of their subjects. Thus, Foucault's worry would appear to adhere not simply to the study but to the overt political mobilization of oppositional discourses. Consider, for example, how the discourse of multiculturalism has been annexed by mainstream institutions to generate new modalities of essentialized racial discourse; how "premenstrual syndrome" has been rendered a debilitating disease in medical and legal discourses; how "battered women's syndrome" has been deployed in the courtroom to defend women who strike back at their assailants by casting them as subrational, egoless victims of male violence; or how some women's response to some pornography was generalized by the Meese Commission as the violence done to all women by all pornography.[17]

Consider, more generally, attempts at codifying feminist discourses of women's experience in the unitary and universal discourse of the law. What happens when legal universalism's silence about women—that is, its failure to recognize or remedy the material of women's subordination—is remedied with discourses specifying women's experience and codifying that category of women through this specification? Catharine MacKinnon, for example, expressly aims to write "women's experience into law," but as many other feminists have remarked, this begs the question of which women's experience(s), drawn from which historical moments, culture, race, and class strata, are recorded. Indeed, what does it mean to write historically and culturally circumscribed experience into an ahistorical discourse, the universalist discourse of law? Is it possible to do this without rendering "experience" as ontology, "perspective" as Truth, and without unifying this ontology and this Truth in the Subject of Woman, and without encoding them in law as the basis of women's rights? What if, for example, the identity of women as keyed to sexual violation is an expressly late twentieth-century and white middle-class construction of femininity, consequent to a radical deprivatization of sexuality on the one side and the erosion of other elements of compulsory heterosexuality—such as a severely gendered division of social labor—on the other? Moreover, does a definition of women *as* sexual subordinates, and the encoding of this definition in law, work to liberate women from sexual subordination, or does it, paradoxically, legally reinscribe femaleness as sexual violability? If the law *produces* the subjects it claims to protect or emancipate, how might installation of women's experience as "sexual violation" in the law reiterate rather than repeal this identity? And might this installation be particularly unemancipatory for women whose lived experience is not that of sexual subordination to men but, for example, that of sexual outlaw?

These questions suggest that in legally codifying a fragment of an insurrectionary discourse as a timeless truth, interpellating women as unified in their victimization, and casting the "free speech" of men as that which "silences" and thus subordinates women, MacKinnon not only opposes bourgeois liberty to substantive equality but also potentially intensifies the regulation of gender and sexuality in the law, abetting rather than contesting the production of gender identity as sexual. In short, as a regulatory fiction of a particular identity is deployed to displace the hegemonic fiction of universal personhood, the discourse of rights converges insidiously with the discourse of disciplinarity to produce a spectacularly potent mode of juridical-regulatory domination.[18]

This problem is not specific to MacKinnon's work nor even to feminist legal reform, although it emerges with particular acuteness in both. Rather, MacKinnon's and kindred efforts at bringing subjugated discourses into the law merely constitute examples of what Foucault identified as the risk of recodification and recolonization of "disinterred knowledges" by those "unitary discourses, which first disqualified and then ignored them when they made their appearance."[19] These efforts exemplify how the work of breaking silence can metamorphose into new techniques of domination, how our truths can become our rulers rather than our emancipators, how our confessions shape the norms by which we are regulated.

If this kind of regulatory function is familiar enough to students of legal and bureaucratic discourse, it is less frequently recognized and perhaps more disquieting in putatively counter-cultural discourse, when confessing injury can become the act that attaches us to the injury, paralyzes us within it, and prevents us from seeking or even desiring a status other than that of injured. In an age of social identification through attributes marked as culturally significant—gender, race, sexuality, and so forth—confessional discourse, with its truth-bearing status in a postepistemological universe, not only regulates the confessor in the name of freeing her, as Foucault described that logic, but extends beyond the confessing individual to constitute a regulatory truth about the identity group: confessed truths are assembled and deployed as "knowledge" about the group. This phenomenon would seem to undergird a range of recurring troubles in feminism, from the "real woman" rejoinder to poststructuralist deconstructions of her, to totalizing descriptions of women's experience that are the inadvertent effects of various kinds of survivor stories. Thus, for example, the porn star who feels miserably exploited, violated, and humiliated in her work invariably monopolizes the feminist truth about sex work, as the girl with math anxieties constitutes the feminist truth about women and math; eating disorders have become the feminist truth about women and food, as sexual abuse and violation occupy the feminist knowledge terrain of women and sexuality. In other words, even as feminism aims to affirm diversity among women and women's experiences, confession as the site of production of truth and its convergence with feminist suspicion and deauthorization of truth from other sources tends to reinstate a unified discourse in which the story of greatest suffering becomes the true story of woman. (This may constitute part of the rhetorical purchase of confessional discourse in a postfoundational epistemological era: confession substitutes for the largely discredited charge of false consciousness on one hand, and for generalized truth claims rooted in science, god, or nature on the other.) Thus, the adult who does not manifestly suffer from her or his childhood sexual experience, the lesbian who does not feel shame about her sexuality, and the woman of color who does not primarily or "correctly" identify with her marking as such—these figures are excluded as bona fide members of the identity categories that also claim them. Their status within these discourses is that of being "in denial," of "false consciousness," or of "race traitor." This is the norm-making process in traditions of breaking silence that ironically silence and exclude the very persons these traditions mean to empower.

If these practices, however, tacitly silence those whose experiences do not parallel those whose suffering is most marked (or whom the discourse produces as suffering markedly), they also condemn those whose sufferings they record to a permanent identification with that suffering. Here, there is a *temporal* ensnaring in "the folds of our own discourses" insofar as we identify ourselves in speech in a manner that condemns us to live in a present dominated by the past. But what if speech and silence are not really opposites? Indeed, what if to speak incessantly of one's suffering is to silence the possibilities of overcoming it, of living beyond it, of identifying as something other than it? What if this incessant speech not only overwhelms the experiences of others, but overwhelms alternative (unutterable, traumatized, fragmentary, or inassimilable) zones of one's *own* experience? Conversely, what if a certain modality of silence about one's suffering—and we might consider modalities of silence to be as varied as modalities of speech—articulates a variety of possibilities not otherwise available to the sufferer?

In *The Drowned and the Saved,* Primo Levi proffers drowning as a metaphor for the initial experience of entering the concentration camps, particularly for those who did not speak German or Polish: "filled with a dreadful sound and fury signifying nothing: a hubbub of people without names or faces drowned in a continuous, deafening background noise from which, however, the human word did not surface."[20] This is a drowning in a world of unfamiliar and terrifying words and noise, a world of no civil structure yet so crowded with humanity that one's own humanness becomes a question. Primo Levi makes drowning function as a symbol for a lost linguistic order that itself signifies a lost civil order, for being at sea in words that do not communicate and by which one cannot communicate.[21] In a radically different context, Adrienne Rich also relates drowning to speech: "your silence today is a pond where drowned things live."[22] Allowing, perhaps perversely, the Rich to rest on the Levi, Rich's line need not be read only in its most obvious meaning: as an injunction to speak or die, as a mandate to speak in order to recover the drowned things, to recover life. What if the accent marks are placed differently so that silence becomes a place where drowned things *live,* a place where Levi's drowning inmates survive despite being overwhelmed by the words that fill and consume the air necessary for life? What if the drowned things *live* in the pond, where it is silent, as they could not survive if brought back into the exposure of light and air, the cacophony of the Camp? What if silence is a reprieve from drowning in words that do not communicate or confer recognition, that only bombard or drown?[23]

This possibility, of course, is heavy with paradox insofar as drowning already signals death and a pond where drowned things live thus harbors death rather than life. But this paradox may be a productive one: perhaps there are dead or deadening (anti-life) things that must be allowed to reside in a pond of silence rather than surfaced into discourse if life is to be lived without being claimed by their weight. Certain experiences—concentration camp existence or childhood abuse—may conservatively claim their subjects when those experiences are incessantly remembered in speech, when survivors can only and always speak of what they almost did not survive and thus cannot break with that threat to live in a present not dominated by it. What if, too, this endless speaking about one's past of suffering is an attempt to excoriate guilt about what one did not do to prevent the suffering, an attempt that is doomed insofar as the speaking actually perpetuates by disavowing the guilt?[24]

If to speak repeatedly of a trauma is a mode of encoding it as identity, it may be the case that drowned things must be consigned to live in a pond of silence in order to make a world—a future—in parameters not fully given by the trauma. Put slightly differently by Primo Levi, "a memory evoked too often, and in the form of a story, tends to become fixed in a stereotype... crystallized, perfected, adorned, *installing itself in the place of the raw memory and growing at its expense.*"[25] Many contemporary narratives of suffering would seem to bear precisely this character: rather than working through the "raw memory" to a place of emancipation, discourses of survivorship become stories by which one lives, or refuses to live, in the present. There is a fine but critical distinction here between re-entering a trauma, speaking its unspeakable elements, even politicizing it in order to reconfigure the trauma and the traumatized subject, and retelling the trauma in such a way as to preserve it by resisting the pain of it and thus preserving the traumatized subject. While such a distinction is probably not always sustainable, it may be all that secures the possibility that we dwell in something other than the choice between a politics of pain or a politics of pain's disavowal.

Of course, trauma is only one potential constituent of identity and its problematic relationship to speech and emancipation. Subordination is lived in many ways that have little or nothing to do with trauma. Thus, we might ask more generally if, by putting all into discourse, those attempting to emerge from a history of subordination risk sacrificing the rewards of any fragile hold acquired on autonomy and on the capacity to *craft* their lives and experiences rather than living almost fully at the behest of others. If, as Hannah Arendt maintains, some experiences "cannot withstand the glare of public light without being extinguished," do those traveling under the sign of queer, colored or female not set at risk this recent, tenuous, and partial acquisition?[26] Consider the pleasures of writing and other artistic practices; therapeutic work intended to fortify or emancipate rather than discipline (femininity) or "cure" (homosexuality); relatively uncoerced sexual lives; some modicum of choice and creativity in reproductive and productive work. When all such experiences are put into discourse—when sexual, emotional, productive, reproductive, and artistic lives are all exhaustively chronicled and thereby subjected to normativizing discourses, might this imperil the experiences of autonomy, creativity, privacy, and bodily integrity so long denied those whose subjugation included, *inter alia,* enslaving work, sexual violation or other deprivations of privacy? Are those who are subjected through sexuality, race and gender so habituated to being without privacy and autonomy that they would compulsively evade or sabotage them? Do we presume we have nothing of value to protect from public circulation and scrutiny? Are we compelled to reiterate the experience of the historically subordinated: to be without a room of one's own, without a zone of privacy in which lives go unreported, without a domain of creativity free from surveillance—this time by our own eyes? Are we so accustomed to being watched that we cannot feel real, cannot feel our experiences to be real, unless we are watching and reporting them?

If there are disturbing ways in which the practice of compulsory discursivity would appear to recapitulate the historical, psychopolitical terms of subordinated subjects, there are also ways in which this practice coincides with a contemporary cultural tendency toward the glorification of banal personal experiences and unschooled opinions. Ours is a time of diarrhetic speech and publication—from the unfathomable amount of technical, political, commercial, and personal information that travels the Internet to the opinionated ignorance that animates much of A.M. talk radio. As many cultural critics have noted, notwithstanding or perhaps in proportion to the rise of illiteracy in the United States, today anyone's political opinion is worthy of radio dissemination, and everyone's personal story is worthy of television exposure or even a memoir. Is this phenomenon, with its ability to displace world events and learned reflection, an effect of the confessional subject run amok, along with that subject's hold on Truth in a post-foundational age? Or is it a kind of anxious filling of the void where meaning, profundity, and world history are said to have existed prior to their disenchantment? To what extent does the populist valorization of the common man, common sense, and the common experience recall the disdain for knowledge and reflection that was, historically, part of the material out of which European fascism was fashioned?

While each of these speculations may partially illuminate the explosion of banal and personal reference in the public media, the most important explanation may issue from a telling feature of this kind of expression, namely that very little of it bears the character of either social connection or reflection. Most of this speech *pronounces* or *declares,* and practically none of it is aimed at developing community with others or with working through experience or transforming understanding. In other words, this speech that is aimed at bringing us together and that glorifies the common person paradoxically eschews the tonal and idiomatic material of connection. This paradox must be read as a symptom, and in particular a symptom of the predicament of the sovereign subject in a world of historically unparalleled global complexity and contingency. This subject, who is so radically in need of external resources for understanding its context and production in the late twentieth century, is deprived of these resources through this kind of pronunciative speaking. Indeed, this heavily defended creature conveys through this noncommuning speech, this tenacious dwelling in his or her own experience and opinion, a kind of rampant individual xenophobia that must be read as a terrible fear of disintegration or dissolution through connection, as the anxiety of an already profoundly weakened or disintegrated subject. The cult of personal experience and opinion, then, warns of the shakiness of the fiction of the sovereign subject and of the subject's extreme vulnerability to domination, even as this warning is expressed as a kind of hypersovereignty and hyperindividualism.[27]

If the compulsion to put all into discourse can be read as a problematic remnant not only of particular histories of subordination but also of more generic anxieties of our time, then our capacity to be silent in certain venues might become the measure of our desire for freedom, including the desire to resist this discourse of anxiety masquerading as populism. The measure of this desire, of course, requires carefully distinguishing between the pleasures and freedoms of silence on the one hand and habituation to being silenced on the other. Also necessary is a second distinction between keeping one's counsel in order to articulate a spectrum of nonobvious possibilities and silence as the consummate gesture of passive aggression. Moreover, the desire for freedom requires the development not only of skills for silence but also of skills for speech that is neither confessional nor normative in a moralizing sense (the latter, according to Nietzsche, is always a symptom of subordination or identification with subordination). Freedom requires the capacity for a kind of public speaking that neither demands concurrence from others nor entails the establishment of new norms by which to live; rather, this kind of speech willingly proffers ideas that one could argue and modify according to other characteralogically public (as opposed to confessional) arguments.

It is tempting to end on this note. But it leans too hard toward one side of a paradox about silence and silencing without recalling the other. For if silence can be a mode of resistance to power, including to our own productions of regulatory power, it is not yet freedom precisely insofar as it constitutes resistance to domination rather than its own discursive bid for hegemony. Put another way, one challenge to the convention of equating speaking with power and silence with powerlessness pertains to the practice of "refusing to speak" as a mode of resistance. Here, even as silence is a response to domination, it is not *enforced* from above but rather *deployed* from below: refusing to speak is a method of refusing colonization, of refusing complicity in injurious interpellations or subjection through regulation.

Yet it would be a mistake to value this resistance too highly, for it is, like most rights claims, a defense in the context of domination, a strategy for negotiating domination, rather than a sign of emancipation from it. In *The Alchemy of Race and Rights,* Patricia Williams coins a provocative phrase that captures this feature of silence as discourse. Following a disturbing encounter with some obnoxious young students who jostled her off the sidewalk in a largely white college town, Williams speaks of "pursuing her way, *manumitted into silence.*"[28] In this paradoxical locution, she intimates that purchased emancipation from slavery conferred a right to silence, one to which, however, she is also condemned. "Manumitted into silence"—emancipated into silence—no longer a subject of coerced speech, no longer invaded in every domain of her being, yet also not heard, seen, recognized, or wanted as a speaking being in the public or social realm. Perhaps then, one *historical-political* place of silence for collective subjects emerging into history is this crossed one: a place of potentially pleasurable reprieve in newly acquired zones of freedom and privacy, yet a place of "freedom from" that is not yet freedom to make the world.

Notes

1. Michel Foucault, *The History of Sexuality,* vol. 1, *An Introduction,* trans. Robert Hurley (New York: Vintage, 1980); Joan Scott, "'Experience,'" in Judith Butler and Joan Scott, eds., *Feminists Theorize the Political* (New York: Routledge, 1992); and Shoshana Felman and Dori Laub, *Testimony: Crises of Witnessing in Literature, Psychoanalysis, and History* (New York: Routledge, 1992).

2. Catharine A. MacKinnon, *Toward a Feminist Theory of the State* (Cambridge, Mass.: Harvard Univ. Press, 1989).

3. On this point, and for an exceptionally thoughtful meditation on the feminist politics of voice that at times parallels my own, see Valerie Hazel, "Disjointed Articulations: The Politics of Voice and Jane Campion's *The Piano,*" *Women's Studies Journal* 10, no. 2 (1994): 27–40.

4. This potential would appear to be more visible and cautionary among African Americans and other racially marked groups in the United States than among whites. Consider, as popular examples in the media, the "we don't talk about it in public" (that is, a white public) attitude voiced by many African American women about sexual harassment and spouse abuse following the Anita Hill and O. J. Simpson spectacles. Or consider, as an example in fiction, Alice Walker's "Advancing Luna and Ida B. Wells," in which an African American woman feels consigned to silence about the alleged rape of her white co-worker by an African American acquaintance. In both cases, there is deep cognizance of the racist regulatory discourses in which the "voicing of truth" would be taken up. See Alice Walker, "Advancing Luna and Ida B. Wells," in *The Norton Anthology of American Literature.*

5. Foucault (see note 1), 100–101.

6. Ibid.

7. Agnes Luga-Ortiz, "Community at Its Limits: Orality, Law, Silence, and the Homosexual Body in Luis Rafael Sanchez's 'Jum!'" in Emilie L. Bergmann and Paul Julian Smith, eds., *Entiendes? Queer Readings, Hispanic Writings* (Durham: Duke Univ. Press, 1995); and M. Jacqui Alexander, "Redrafting Morality: The Postcolonial State and the Sexual Offences Bill of Trinidad and Tobago," in Chandra Talpade Mohanty, Ann Russo, and Lourdes Torres, eds., *Third World Women and the Politics of Feminism* (Bloomington: Indiana Univ. Press, 1991).

8. Lugo-Ortiz (see note 7), 131.

9. Foucault (see note 1), 32.

10. Ibid., 31.

11. Still, there would appear to be a strangely modernist narrative at play in Foucault's account of the innocent days prior to power, a narrative in which "the fall" takes the form of being brought into regulatory discourse. Ironically, particularly in the story of the molesting villager, feminist analysis provides an easy antidote to the notion that there was pleasure and delight all around prior to sexuality's subjection by medical and juridical discourse.

Yet we might ask whether certain feminist discourses about sexual abuse are not themselves constructive of the abuse: can we really be certain that every childhood sexual act with a sibling or an adult was a traumatic one prior to the moment of its exposure to a moral discourse? When the sex is not coerced or imposed, is not the shame about the act a great part of its injury, and is not this shame potentially imposed through discourses surrounding rather than necessarily intrinsic to the act? If feminist discourses about sexuality have rendered such questioning mute, would this not be an instance of feminist discourse silencing its own subjects?

12. On Foucault's formulation of freedom as a "practice," see Paul Rabinow's interview with Foucault, "Space, Knowledge and Power," in Michel Foucault, *The Foucault Reader,* ed. P. Rabinow (New York: Pantheon, 1984), 245.

13. Michel Foucault, "The Minimalist Self," in idem, *Politics, Philosophy, Culture: Interviews and Other Writings, 1977–1984,* ed. Lawrence D. Kritzman (New York: Routledge, 1988), 4.

14. Toni Morrison, *Lecture and Speech of Acceptance, Upon the Award of the Nobel Prize for Literature, Delivered in Stockholm on the Seventh of December, Nineteen Hundred and Ninety-Three* (New York: Knopf, 1994), 13, 16.

15. Ibid., 13–14.

16. Michel Foucault, "Two Lectures," in idem, *Power/Knowledge: Selected Interviews and Other Writings, 1972–1977,* trans. and ed. Colin Gorden (New York: Pantheon, 1980), 86.

17. For a general discussion of premenstrual syndrome and the law, see Lee Solomon, "Premenstrual Syndrome: The Debate Surrounding Criminal Defense," *Maryland Law Review* 54 (1995): 571; for battered women's syndrome, see Lenore E. Walker, *The Battered Woman Syndrome* (New York: Springer, 1984); and *State v. Kelly,* 478 A2d 364 (1984), 97 NJ 178; and for the Meese Commission's conclusions, see U.S. Attorney General's Commission on Pornography, *Attorney General's Commission on Pornography* (Washington, D.C.: U.S. Department of Justice, 1986), 322–52.

18. This analysis is more fully pursued in Wendy Brown, *States of Injury: Power and Freedom in Late Modernity* (Princeton: Princeton Univ. Press, 1995), chapter five.

19. Foucault, "Two Lectures" (see note 16), 86.

20. Primo Levi, *The Drowned and the Saved,* trans. R. Rosenthal (New York: Summit, 1988), 93–94.

21. Ibid., 94.

22. Adrienne Cecile Rich, "Twenty-One Love Poems," in idem, *Dream of a Common Language: Poems, 1974–1977* (New York: Norton, 1978).

23. Note that the verb *drown* is not only both passive and active—"she drowned in the river," "he drowned her in the bathtub"—it can also connote both a condition from which one can return and a final state, one that teminates in death. There is a life-and-death difference between *drowning* and *drowned.* There is a vanishing at work in both, but Levi, it would seem, wants to capture this vanishing without giving it final say, without allowing it to turn into vanquishing. Thus, the drowning may become the saved . . . or the drowned.

24. Levi (see note 20), 76.

25. Ibid., 24.

26. Hannah Arendt, *The Human Condition* (Chicago: Univ. of Chicago Press, 1958).

27. To go further here, it would be useful to consult Freud's little book on mass

psychology, *Group Psychology and the Analysis of the Ego* (New York: Boni and Liveright, 1922), but that is the occasion for another essay.

28. Patricia J. Williams, *The Alchemy of Race and Rights* (Cambridge, Mass: Harvard Univ. Press, 1991).

Censorship and Silencing: Practices of Cultural Regulation

Conference Series, 1994–1995

Phase I

Censorship and Silencing: The Case of Pornography
4–5 November 1994
University of California, Santa Barbara
Organizer: Simon Williams, Director, Interdisciplinary Humanities Center
Participants:
- Susie Bright, Writer, Editor, Lecturer, San Francisco
- Beatrice Farwell, History of Art and Architecture, UC Santa Barbara
- Edward Donnerstein, Communication, UC Santa Barbara
- Walter Kendrick, English, Fordham University
- Daniel Linz, Communication and Law and Society, UC Santa Barbara
- Anne McClintock, English, Columbia University
- Constance Penley, Film Studies and Women's Studies, UC Santa Barbara
- Abigail Solomon-Godeau, History of Art and Architecture, UC Santa Barbara
- Linda Williams, Film Studies and Women's Studies, UC Irvine

Constitutions and "Survivor Stories": Censorship, Silencing, and the Repetition of History
13–14 January 1995
University of California, Santa Cruz
Organizer: Robert Meister, Board of Studies in Politics
Participants:
- Judith Butler, Rhetoric and Comparative Literature, UC Berkeley
- Eugene Volokh, UCLA Law School
- Jeremy Elkings, Legal Studies, UC Santa Cruz
- Richard Wasserstrom, Philosophy, UC Santa Cruz
- Wendy Brown, Women's Studies and Legal Studies, UC Santa Cruz
- Andrei Markovits, Politics, UC Santa Cruz
- Sanford Levinson, University of Texas Law School
- Akhil Reed Amar, Yale Law School
- James Forman, Jr., Author
- Hayden White, Rhetoric and Comparative Literature, UC Santa Cruz and Stanford University
- Guyora Binder, University of Buffalo Law School

Helene Moglen, Literature and Women's Studies, UC Santa Cruz
Frances Olsen, UCLA Law School
Robert Meister, Politics and Legal Studies, UC Santa Cruz
Craig Reinarman, Sociology, UC Santa Cruz
Daniel Ortiz, University of Virginia Law School
Susan Harding, Anthropology, UC Santa Cruz

The Debate Over "Genetics and Violence": The Silencing of Socially Charged Science
26 January 1995
The California Institute of Technology
Organizer: Morgan Kousser, Humanities and Social Science
Participants:
Troy Duster, Director, Institute for the Study of Social Change, UC Berkeley
David Wasserman, Institute for Philosophy and Public Policy, University of Maryland
James Q. Wilson, Collins Professor of Management and Public Policy, UCLA

Security, Secrecy, and Silencing: A Transnational Perspective
28 January 1995
University of California, Irvine
Organizer: Margot Norris, Department of English
Participants:
Julie Bangs, Comparative Literature (Graduate Student), UC Irvine
Anne Callard, English (Graduate Student), UC Irvine
Chungmoo Choi, East Asian Languages and Literatures, UC Irvine
Daniel Ellsberg, Director, Manhattan Project II, Physicians for Social Responsibility
Kenneth W. Grundy, Political Science, Case Western Reserve University
Louisa Haefele, English (Graduate Student), UC Irvine
Jane Henning, Comparative Literature (Graduate Student), UC Irvine
Shin Jyu Kang, English and Comparative Literature (Research Associate), UC Irvine
Liisa Malkki, Anthropology, UC Irvine
Steven David Richmond, Political Science, University of Chicago
Daniel Tsang, Social Sciences, UC Irvine

Liberty, License, and Authority
4 February 1995
The Huntington Library, San Marino
Organizer: Robert Ritchie, Director of Research
Participants:
Richard Burt, English, University of Massachusetts, Amherst

Cyndia Susan Clegg, Humanities, Pepperdine University
Mark Rose, English, UC Santa Barbara
Blair Worden, St. Edmund Hall, Oxford University

Now You See It, Now You Don't: Procedural Justice and Substantive Meaning in the First Amendment
9 February 1995
University of Southern California
Organizer: Ronald Gottesman, Department of English
Participants:
Stanley Fish, Arts and Sciences Professor of English, Duke University
Ronald Gottesman, English, University of Southern California
Judith Grant, Political Science, University of Southern California
Peggy Kamuf, Comparative Literature and French and Italian, University of Southern California
Judith Resnik, Law Center, University of Southern California

Witnessing the War on Words: From *Howl* to Mapplethorpe
7–10 February 1995
Stanford University
Organizer: Wanda Corn, Director, Stanford Humanities Center
Participants:
Eric Cummins, Humanities Center, Stanford University
Estelle Freedman, History, Stanford University
Allen Ginsberg, Elliott and Rhoda Levinthal Distinguished Visitor, Stanford Humanities Center
Jan Krawitz, Communication, Stanford University
John L'Heureux, English, Stanford University
Marjorie Perloff, English, Stanford University
Rob Polheumus, English, Stanford University
Carl Rakosi, San Francisco, California
Leslie Scalapino, San Francisco, California
Ron Silliman, San Francisco, California
Kathleen Sullivan, Stanford University Law School

Silencing Women: Feminism(s), Censorship, and Difference
25 February 1995
University of California, Riverside
Organizer: Bernd Magnus, Director, Center for Ideas and Society
Participants:
Wendy Brown, Women's Studies, UC Santa Cruz
Judith Butler, Rhetoric, UC Berkeley
Nancy Fraser, Philosophy, Northwestern University
Coco Fusco, Highways Performance Space
Amelia Jones, Art History, UC Riverside

Connie Samaras, Studio Arts, UC Irvine
Gayatri Chakravorty Spivak, Avalon Foundation Professor in the Humanities, Columbia University
Marguerite Waller, English, UC Riverside
Georgia Warnke, Philosophy, UC Riverside

Censorship: The Case of Broadcasting
6 March 1995
University of California, San Diego
Organizer: Daniel Schiller, Department of Communication
Participants:
Michael Bernstein, History, UC San Diego
Deedee Halleck, Communication, UC San Diego
George Lipsitz, Ethnic Studies, UC San Diego
Robert W. McChesney, Journalism, University of Wisconsin

Inventing Modern Censorship
10 March 1995
University of California, Berkeley
Organizer: Thomas Laqueur, Director, The Doreen B. Townsend Center for the Humanities
Participants:
Marianne Constable, Rhetoric, UC Berkeley
Carla Hesse, History, UC Berkeley
Thomas Laqueur, History, UC Berkeley
David Lieberman, School of Law, UC Berkeley
Elizabeth J. MacArthur, French and Italian, UC Santa Barbara
Harold Mah, History, Queens University, Canada
Irina Paperno, Slavic Languages, UC Berkeley
Donald Shively, Japanese History and Literature, UC Berkeley
Rachel Weil, History, Cornell University

Between the Lines: "Persecution and the Art of Writing" Revisited
20–21 April 1995
University of California, Davis
Organizer: Georges Van Den Abbeele, Director, Critical Theory Program
Participants:
Réda Bensmaïa, French, Brown University
Marc Blanchard, French, Comparative Literature, and Critical Theory, UC Davis
E. S. Burt, French, UC Irvine
Kay Flavell, Critical Theory, UC Davis
Carla Freccero, Literature and Women's Studies, UC Santa Cruz
Hafid Gafaiti, Romance Languages, University of Michigan
Anna Kuhn, German, UC Davis

Smadar Lavie, Anthropology and Critical Theory, UC Davis
Michael Levine, German and Comparative Literature, Yale University
Mary Ann McGrail, University Professor, Boston University
Harriet Murav, Russian, UC Davis
Larry Peterman, Political Science, UC Davis
Steven Richmond, Political Science, University of Chicago
Israel Shahak, Hebrew University, Jerusalem
Victoria Shinbrot, Comparative Literature, UC Davis
David Van Leer, English, UC Davis
Clarence Walker, History and African American Studies, UC Davis

Silencing Sexualities
11 May 1995
University of California, Los Angeles
Organizer: Douglas Crimp, Chair, UCLA Arts Council
Participants:
Brian Freeman, Artistic Director, Pomo Afro Homos, San Francisco
Gayle Rubin, UC Santa Cruz
Richard Meyer, Art History, UC Berkeley
Carole Vance, School of Public Health, Columbia University
Michael Warner, English, Rutgers University

Phase II
Censorship and Silencing: Practices of Cultural Regulation
15–16 December 1995
Getty Research Institute for the History of Art and the Humanities
Organizer: Robert Post, Law, UC Berkeley
Participants:
Wendy Brown, Women's Studies, UC Santa Cruz
E. S. Burt, French and Italian, UC Irvine
Richard Burt, English, University of Massachusetts
Judith Butler, Rhetoric and Comparative Literature, UC Berkeley
Lawrence Douglas, Law, Amherst College
Hafid Gafaiti, Romance Languages, University of Michigan
Ruth Gavison, Law, Hebrew University
Leslie Green, Philosophy and Law, York University
Rae Langton, Philosophy, Monash University
Sanford Levinson, Law, University of Texas
George Lipsitz, Ethnic Studies, UC San Diego
George E. Marcus, Anthropology, Rice University
Frederick Schauer, John F. Kennedy School of Government, Harvard University
Debora Shuger, English, UC Los Angeles
David Wasserman, Institute for Philosophy and Public Policy, University of Maryland

Biographical Notes on the Authors

Wendy Brown is a professor of women's studies and legal studies at the University of California, Santa Cruz. She is the author of *Manhood and Politics: A Feminist Reading in Political Theory* (1988) and *States of Injury: Power and Freedom in Late Modernity* (1995). She is currently completing a book titled *Liberalism Out of History*.

E. S. Burt is a professor of French and Italian at the University of California, Irvine. She specializes in nineteenth-century poetry and autobiography, with an emphasis on Jean-Jacques Rousseau. She is currently working on a study of nineteenth-century lyric poetry and the political space.

Richard Burt is an associate professor of English at the University of Massachusetts. His extensive list of publications includes *Licensed by Authority: Ben Jonson and the Discourses of Censorship* (1993) and two edited works, *The Administration of Aesthetics: Censorship, Political Criticism, and the Public Sphere* (1994) and *Shakespeare, the Movie* (1997). He recently completed a book titled *Unspeakable ShaXXXspeare: Kiddie Culture, Queer Theory, and Academic Fantasy*, and is now working on a book about the academic unconscious.

Judith Butler is Chancellor's Professor in the departments of rhetoric and comparative literature at the University of California, Berkeley. She is the author of *Gender Trouble: Feminism and the Subversion of Identity* (1990) and *Bodies that Matter: On the Discursive Limits of "Sex"* (1993). She is coeditor of *Feminist Contentions: A Philosophical Exchange* (1993). Most recently she has published *The Psychic Life of Power: Theories in Subjection* (1997) and *Excitable Speech: A Politics of the Performative* (1997).

Lawrence Douglas is a professor of law at Amherst College. His research interests focus on law and literature, legal rhetoric, and law and the Holocaust. He has published in numerous legal journals; he is currently working on a book, *A Guilt beyond Crime: The Holocaust and the Legal Imagination*.

Ruth Gavison is Haim H. Cohn Professor of Human Rights at the Hebrew University in Jerusalem. Her research interests include legal philosophy and human rights. She is the editor of *Essays in Contemporary Legal Philosophy: The Contribution of H.L.A. Hart* (1987) and is working on a book on Israeli law and politics.

Leslie Green concentrates on legal and political theory. He has contributed articles to many journals. Recent publications include *Authority of the State* (1988, 1990) and *Law and the Community* (1989). He is a professor of philosophy and of law at York University in Toronto.

Rae Langton is a member of the philosophy program in the Research School of Social Sciences at the Australian National University. She works in moral, political, and legal philosophy, feminist philosophy, history of philosophy, epistemology, and metaphysics. She has published articles in these areas and has a book about Kant forthcoming in 1998.

Sanford Levinson is a professor of law at the University of Texas, Austin, School of Law. He has written and edited many articles and books, among them *Constitutional Faith* (1988), which received the Scribes Award for the best book on law in 1988.

George E. Marcus is a professor of anthropology and chairman of the department of anthropology at Rice University. His research interests have focused on social structures and cultural change in Tonga. He is currently editing a fin-de-siècle annual, *Late Editions.* Titles of published volumes in this series include *Technoscientific Imaginaries: Conversations, Profiles, and Memoirs* (1995), *Corporate Futures: The Diffusion of the Culturally Sensitive Corporate Form at Century's End* (1997), and *Paranoia within Reason: A Casebook of Conspiracy as Explanation at Century's End* (forthcoming).

Robert C. Post is Alexander F. and May T. Morrison Professor of Law at the University of California, Berkeley. He is the author of *Constitutional Domains* (1995) and *Law and the Order of Culture* (1991).

Frederick Schauer focuses his studies on constitutional law, the first amendment, philosophy of law, and political philosophy. He is Frank Stanton Professor of the First Amendment and Academic Dean at the Kennedy School of Government, Harvard University. His publications include *Free Speech: A Philosophical Enquiry* (1982) and *Playing by the Rules: A Philosophical Examination of Rule-Based Decision Making in Law and in Life* (1991).

Debora Shuger is a professor of English at the University of California, Los Angeles. Her research interests include rhetoric and early modern Christianity as well as Tudor and Stuart literature and culture. She is author of *The Renaissance Bible* (1994), *Habits of Thought* (1990), and *Sacred Rhetoric* (1988).

David Wasserman is a research scholar at the Institute for Philosophy and Public Policy, University of Maryland. He concentrates on issues in law, policy, and philosophy. He is the author of *A Sword for the Convicted: Representing Indigent Defendants on Appeal* (1990) and numerous essays and articles.

Index

Page references to illustrations are in italic.

Issues & Debates
A Series of the Getty Research Institute Publications and Exhibitions Program
Julia Bloomfield, Thomas F. Reese, Michael S. Roth, and Salvatore Settis, *Editors*

In Print
Otto Wagner: Reflections on the Raiment of Modernity
Editor: Harry Francis Mallgrave
(Hardback, $55.00 — ISBN 0-89236-258-8)
(Paperback, $29.95 — ISBN 0-89236-257-X)

American Icons: Transatlantic Perspectives on Eighteenth- and Nineteenth-Century American Art
Editors: Thomas W. Gaehtgens and Heinz Ickstadt
(Hardback, $55.00 — ISBN 0-89236-246-4)
(Paperback, $29.95 — ISBN 0-89236-247-2)

Art in History / History in Art: Studies in Seventeenth-Century Dutch Culture
Editors: David Freedberg and Jan de Vries
(Hardback, $55.00 — ISBN 0-89236-201-4)
(Paperback, $29.95 — ISBN 0-89236-200-6)

In Preparation
Dosso's Fate: Painting and Court Culture in Renaissance Italy
Editors: Luisa Ciammitti, Steven F. Ostrow, and Salvatore Settis
(Paperback — ISBN 0-89236-505-6)

Nietzsche and an "Architecture of Our Minds"
Editors: Alexandre Kostka and Irving Wohlfarth
(Paperback — ISBN 0-89236-485-8)

Designed by Bruce Mau Design Inc., Bruce Mau with Chris Rowat
Coordinated by Suzanne Watson Petralli
Type composed by Archetype in Sabon
Printed and bound by Thomson-Shore, Inc., on Cougar Opaque
Cover printed by Phoenix Color Corp.

Issues & Debates
Series designed by Bruce Mau Design Inc., Toronto, Canada